Political Violence and the Rise of Nazism

Political Violence and the Rise of Nazism

The Storm Troopers in Eastern Germany 1925–1934

Richard Bessel

YALE UNIVERSITY PRESS
NEW HAVEN & LONDON 1984

To the memory of my mother

Designed by Stephanie Hallin.

Filmset in VIP Times by Clavier Phototypesetting and printed in Great Britain by the Pitman Press, Bath.

Library of Congress Cataloging in Publication Data

Bessel, Richard.
  Political violence and the rise of nazism.

  Bibliography: p.
  Includes index.
  1. Nationalsozialistische Deutsche Arbeiter-Partei. Sturmabteilung. 2. Germany — Politics and government — 1918–1933. 3. Germany — Politics and government — 1933–1945. 4. Violence — Germany. 5. National socialism. 6. Prussia, East (Poland and R.S.F.S.R.) — Politics and government. I. Title.
  DD253.7.B47 1984   943.085   83–40477
  ISBN 0-300-03171-8

Contents

Preface

THIS book grew out of a desire to examine the Nazi capture of power and the destruction of the German labour movement in 1933. I was concerned not so much to trace the organisational history of the Nazi Party – that had been done many times already – as to investigate the means by which the Nazis gathered support, broke the left-wing opposition and consolidated their grip in early 1933. At the same time, I wanted to examine these processes not from the vantage point of the Nazi leadership in Munich or Berlin but from below – to examine the contribution of the Nazis' activist followers to the surprisingly rapid formation of Hitler's dictatorship. Specifically, I wanted to probe the role of political violence in bringing the Nazis to power. This was an aspect of the rise of the Nazi movement which, while historians invariably noted its importance, seldom was analysed in depth.

As the principal agents of Nazi violence during the movement's 'years of struggle' and in early 1933 were the storm troopers, the members of the *Sturmabteilungen* (SA), it was this organisation which provided the focus of my research. I hope I have not fallen into the trap of writing the history of an organisation where I wanted to write a history of political processes and events. However, some discussion of the development of the SA as an organisation is necessary, and I hope that the reader will bear with me. The core of this book concerns the violent campaigns of the SA before and during 1933, and other chapters are designed in large measure to make those campaigns more understandable.

It struck me early on that to investigate such a topic on a national plane – in Germany as a whole – would probably be counter-productive. To do so would have run the risk either of losing a sense of the storm troopers in their community, by reducing everything to 'national' trends, or of producing a narrative which degenerated into a series of anecdotes which may or may not have been representative. So I decided upon a regional study. As I did not want to duplicate material to be found in the regional studies of the Nazi Party which now abound, I chose to look eastward – to examine political violence and the rise of the Nazi movement in an area where relatively little work had been done: the eastern Prussian provinces. The reasons why I feel the eastern regions of Germany offer a good geographical space within which to examine this theme are outlined in the introduction. Here I want only to mention a further, important and perhaps obvious reason for the choice: source materials. A great deal of material was waiting to be used, especially in the regional Polish state archives in the former German territories. Thus I thought that my research also might fill a geographical gap in the rise of National Socialism and demonstrate the potential of collections in Poland for the study of German history.

This leads me to a necessary point about place names. Very few of the places to which I refer are now called what they were called in 1933. For the sake of consistency and clarity, I have chosen always to refer to places by their name at the time. Thus, for example, I would refer to a demonstration in *Breslau* in 1933, but to a book published in *Wrocław* in 1973.

Probably the most pleasant aspect of writing a book (other than *finally* getting the manuscript off one's desk!) is being able to thank in print the people who helped to bring it about. In a very real sense, this represents a collective effort. Without the generous help of librarians, archivists, colleagues and friends I never would have been able to attempt, let alone complete, this book. It gives me great pleasure to be able to express a measure of my gratitude here.

The major portion of the research for this book was undertaken while I was a postgraduate student at St Peter's College, Oxford. I am extremely grateful to the Master and Fellows of the College for providing a friendly and stimulating base from which to work. I am also very grateful to the Faculty of Modern History, the Trustees of the Arnold Fund and the Trustees of the Cyril Foster Fund at the University of Oxford for their generous financial help, which came at a critical time and made it possible for me to extend my researches into Poland. I also want to express my thanks to the German Academic Exchange Service for awarding a grant which enabled me to work in Germany during 1974–5, and to the Ludwig-Maximilians-Universität in Munich for providing an intellectual home during this period.

Like most historians, I owe a tremendous debt of gratitude to the staff of the many institutions where my research was undertaken. Special mention must be made of the archivists and staff of the Bundesarchiv in Koblenz, of the Geheimes Staatsarchiv in Berlin-Dahlem and, above all, of the regional state archives in Wrocław, Opole, Gliwice, Szczecin and Poznań. The helpfulness and friendliness with which I was greeted surpassed anything I had a right to expect. I should also express my deep thanks to the staff of the many libraries on which I depended. Especially valuable were the collections of the University Library in Wrocław, the Municipal Library in Szczecin, the library of the Centre of Scientific Research in Olsztyn and the Deutsche Staatsbibliothek in Berlin, as was the help of the inter-library loan desks of the Bodleian Library in Oxford, the Southampton University Library and the Open University Library, all of which cheerfully wrestled with requests that must have seemed impossible.

I am also greatly indebted to many friends and colleagues who have read my work and offered me advice over the years. My greatest debt is to Tim Mason, who supervised the thesis upon which this book is based. Without his advice and criticism, I doubt that I would have been spurred on to think through and develop my ideas; without his encouragement, I doubt that I ever would have completed this book. This book, and its author, owe him a great deal. I also want to take this opportunity to thank some of the people who took the time to read over parts or all of my manuscript in its various forms and who offered helpful and constructive suggestions: Mathilde Jamin, who time and again helped me find my way through source materials, clarify points and develop arguments; Jeremy Noakes and Peter Pulzer, who acted as my thesis examiners and gently but firmly probed my arguments and offered helpful advice; Tony Nicholls, whose friendly criticism was of great help at crucial stages as the manuscript took shape; Conan Fischer, who compelled me to tighten up my arguments in a number of places; Michael Geyer, who helped particularly with Chapter V; Geoff Eley and Jane Caplan, who read some of the material in Chapter I before it was published in a different guise in *Social History* ('Eastern Germany as a Structural Problem in the Weimar Republic', Vol. 3, no. 2); Dave Blackbourn, who read through the final draft; and Laura de Sherbinin, who saved me from more silly mistakes than I care to remember. I also want to express my special thanks to Karol Fiedor and Karol Jonca, both of the University of Wrocław, who gave me invaluable help in negotiating my way through Polish archive material and the history of eastern Germany. I profited enormously from all their help and encouragement. While I may not have taken up all the suggestions offered, I cannot claim I was not warned.

Stony Stratford
June, 1983

Abbreviations

Political Parties and other Organisations

ADGB	Allgemeiner Deutscher Gewerkschaftsbund
DDP	Deutsche Demokratische Partei
DNVP	Deutschnationale Volkspartei
DVFB	Deutschvölkische Freiheitsbewegung
DVFP	Deutschvölkische Freiheitspartei
DVP	Deutsche Volkspartei
Gestapo	Geheime Staatspolizei
HJ	Hitlerjugend
KPD	Kommunistische Partei Deutschlands
NSBO	Nationalsozialistische Betriebszellenorganisation
NSDAP	Nationalsozialistische Deutsche Arbeiterpartei
NSDFB	Nationalsozialistischer Deutscher Frontkämpferbund
NSFB	Nationalsozialistische Freiheitsbewegung
NSKD	Nationalsozialistische Kampfbewegung Deutschlands
RFB	Roter Frontkämpferbund
SA	Sturmabteilung
SD	Sicherheitsdienst
SPD	Sozialdemokratische Partei Deutschlands
SS	Schutzstaffel
USchlA	Untersuchungs- und Schlichtungsausschuß

Archives and Documents Collections

BA	Bundesarchiv (Koblenz)
BA/MA	Bundesarchiv/Militärarchiv (Freiburg i. Br.)
BDC	Berlin Document Center
GStA	Geheimes Staatsarchiv preußischer Kulturbesitz (Berlin-Dahlem)
IfZ	Institut für Zeitgeschichte (Munich)
NAM	National Archives Microfilm Collection
OT Gliwice	Wojewódzkie archiwum państwowe w Katowicach, Oddzial terenowy w Gliwicach

PAP Bytom	Powiatowe archiwum państwowe w Bytomiu
StAG	Staatliches Archivlager Göttingen
WAP Katowice	Wojewódzkie archiwum państwowe w Katowicach
WAP Olsztyn	Wojewódzkie archiwum państwowe w Olsztynie
WAP Opole	Wojewódzkie archiwum państwowe w Opolu
WAP Poznań	Archiwum państwowe miasta Poznania i województwa Poznanskiego
WAP Szczecin	Wojewódzkie archiwum państwowe w Szczecinie
WAP Wrocław	Wojewódzkie archiwum państwowe w Wrocławiu
ZStAM	Zentrales Staatsarchiv, Dienststelle Merseburg

Newspapers

AZ	*Arbeiter-Zeitung* (Breslau)
BUA	*Breslauer 8 Uhr-Abendblatt*
KV	*Königsberger Volkszeitung*
NSST	*National-Sozialistische Schlesische Tageszeitung* (Breslau) (until 31 June 1931, *Schlesische Tageszeitung*)
OVS	*Oberschlesische Volksstimme* (Gleiwitz)
OK	*Oppelner Kurier*
PT	*Pommersche Tagespost* (Stettin)
PZ	*Pommersche Zeitung* (Stettin)
SB	*Schlesische Bergwacht* (Waldenburg)
ST	*Schlesische Tagespost* (Breslau)
SZ	*Schlesische Zeitung* (Breslau)
VB	*Volkischer Beobachter*
VBS	*Volks-Bote* (Stettin)
VWB	*Volkswacht* (Breslau)
VWS	*Volkswacht* (Stettin)

Periodicals

RGBl	*Reichsgesetzblatt*
StDR	*Statistik des Deutschen Reichs*
StJDR	*Statistisches Jahrbuch für das Deutsche Reich*

Other

AOPG	Akten des Obersten Parteigerichts
GDR	German Democratic Republic
GRUSA	Grundsätzliche Anordnung der SA
OPO	Oberpräsidium Oppeln
OPS	Oberpräsidium Schneidemühl
OS	Oberschlesien
Reg. Bez.	Regierungsbezirk

RM	Reichsmark
RO	Rejencja Opolska (Regierung Oppeln)
RP	Rejencja w Pile (Regierung Schneidemühl)
RS	Regierung Stettin, Präsidial Abteilung Polizei
SABE	SA Befehl
TMWC	Trial of the Major War Criminals before the International Military Tribunal

Introduction

'THINGS have now gone so far that the citizen who is peaceful and loyal to the state is defenceless and is subject completely to the terror of elements hostile to the state.'[1] This was the conclusion reached by an Upper Silesian newspaper supporting the Catholic Centre Party (*Zentrum*), following a nighttime attack by Nazi storm troopers upon members of the *Kreuzschar*, the defence organisation of the *Zentrum*, in Ratibor in August 1931. The comment is remarkable not least because Upper Silesia was among those regions in Germany where the Nazi movement was, in relative terms, least successful in attracting support. The Centre Party continued to receive more votes than the NSDAP in the province until 1933, and in the Upper Silesian industrial cities the Nazis also faced a strong Communist Party. Yet by the summer of 1931, before the NSDAP reached its pre-1933 peak in terms of electoral support and party membership, Nazi terror tactics had made normal political activity extremely difficult for the most popular party in the province.

This is all the more noteworthy since it was not the *Zentrum* but the left-wing political representatives of the working class, the Communist and Social Democratic Parties and the socialist trade unions, which formed the main targets of the violence of the Nazi storm troopers. Even more than for the Centre Party, for the Left the violent attacks of Nazi activists presented a major challenge. For the KPD the growth of the Nazi movement and the escalation of Nazi violence became a central concern in the formation of its political tactics from 1929 onwards.[2] For the SPD the increase in Nazi violence presented a threat to its entire political activity; by early 1931 the 'Terror Defence Bureau' of the SPD in Berlin, established to monitor the mounting violence against Social Democrats, was pleading to the Reich Interior Minister for protection against the Nazis, painting a graphic picture of the 'insults, threats, injuries, in some cases fatal' and the 'provocation, challenges and assaults at rallies, on the streets, after rallies, at demonstrations or after demonstrations' reported throughout Germany.[3] The rise of the Nazi movement signalled not only a fundamental shift in party-political loyalties and voting behaviour during the final years of the Weimar

Republic; it also brought political discourse into the streets. Everyday political activity acquired a violent dimension which reached its peak in the months after Hitler was named Reich Chancellor, when the Nazis' opponents rapidly either became helpless onlookers or were driven into concentration camps or exile. Nazi politics, and the success of the movement in destroying the tattered remnants of the Weimar Republic, appear to have been shaped in no small measure by campaigns of political violence, carried out primarily by the storm troopers in the SA.

Violence in German political life was of course not a feature solely of the final years of the Weimar Republic. Politics during the early years of the Republic were punctuated repeatedly by serious violence, in particular the often brutal suppression of the Left by *Freikorps* units in the wake of the Revolution and the campaigns of political assassination which made German politics so hazardous a profession between 1919 and 1923.[4] Even the relatively quiet years between the currency stabilisation and the onset of the economic crisis saw instances of political violence.[5] However, the violent outbursts which followed the birth of the Republic were significantly different from those which marked its death: whereas the former were carried out in large measure by paramilitary organisations, often acting in the role of military units, the latter generally were carried out by members of party formations and often developed out of what might be described as 'normal' political activity – rallies, demonstrations and the like. The organisations whose members engaged in political violence during the early 1930s were connected closely with political parties working more or less within the constitutional framework; their activity formed part of political – not military or paramilitary – campaigns.[6]

Thus what separated the violence of the Nazi storm troopers during the final phase of the Weimar Republic from the violence of various *Freikorps* units a decade earlier was its relationship to the campaign of a political party, the NSDAP, to gain power legally. Despite rhetoric to the contrary, the activity of the SA did not constitute an attempt to seize state power militarily or extra-legally. Therefore, it is as part of a general party-political campaign that the violence of the storm troopers must be seen and examined. To what extent can the success of the NSDAP, the destruction of Weimar democracy and the crushing of the Left be attributed to this violence? What role did it play in the growth of the Nazi movement? What were its components, who were its perpetrators, what were its attractions, what were its effects? Contemporaries faced with the threat of Nazi violence understandably were concerned about its effects and convinced of its importance. Were they right in their assessments, or was the violence of the Nazi storm troopers essentially a distraction which deflects attention from other, more important, reasons for the movement's success? Was it a form of political activism which perhaps satisfied some of the youthful hotheads in the SA but which was basically irrelevant to the struggle for power? Or was the 'unparalleled defeat of the German proletariat'[7] which took place at the hands of the Nazis in 1933 due largely to their successful mobilisation of political violence?

Until recently, such questions as these have been approached in rather general terms, if at all, with the SA and the activism of its members forming one factor to be noted among the many which figured in the Nazi rise. Naturally enough, the early studies of the growth of the Nazi movement and the collapse of Weimar proceeded within the framework of national politics and the general failure of democratic political structures to cope with the crises which befell Germany during the last years of the Republic.[8] The 1960s, however, saw a number of new impulses in the study of the rise of Nazism: the close examination of the organisational history of the NSDAP at national level,[9] and the beginnings of what was to become a large body of literature on the Nazi rise at local and regional levels.[10] With some exceptions – the most important of which are the pioneering investigation by Rudolf Heberle of Schleswig-Holstein[11] and the brilliant account of society and politics in Northeim by William Sheridan Allen[12] – these local and regional studies have tended to centre upon the growth and, particularly, the organisation of the NSDAP. Thus we now have a fairly comprehensive picture of how the Nazi Party operated, with studies of Pomerania,[13] Lower Saxony,[14] Hesse,[15] Bavaria,[16] Danzig,[17] the Ruhr,[18] Baden,[19] Franconia,[20] and most recently the Bavarian *Landkreis* Günzberg[21] and the university town of Marburg.[22]

Alongside the proliferation of studies of the Nazi movement at local and regional levels, there has been a marked increase in interest in the social basis of the Nazis' support – in examining Nazism as a 'social movement'. The election returns of the final Weimar years have been sifted and analysed repeatedly in order to delineate the social support for the Nazis,[23] as have the statistics of the NSDAP membership compiled by the Party in 1935[24] and the records of Nazi Party members stored in the Berlin Document Center.[25] Not surprisingly, the mass of data available about voting behaviour and the occupational backgrounds of NSDAP members has attracted growing attention from quantitative historians, whose computer-powered labours promise to give us a much more complex and differentiated picture of the support for National Socialism than we have had hitherto.[26]

Despite this impressive and productive broadening of research into the Nazi movement during the past few years, the political violence in which so many of that movement's followers engaged has received relatively little close scrutiny. The one general attempt to correlate the incidence of political violence with the *Reichstag* election results of 1930 and 1932 is disappointingly uninformative.[27] And until recently the SA was not the focus of the detailed analysis to which the NSDAP or the Nazi electorate have been subjected. The earliest sketches of the history of the SA concerned not its role in building up the Nazi movement but its destruction as a politically powerful or influential organisation on 30 June 1934.[28] Interest in the SA as a factor in national politics stood at the centre of the first two lengthy studies of the storm troopers' organisation:the one by Wolfgang Sauer, in which the 'mobilisation of violence' was examined as a factor in the consolidation of the Nazi dictatorship;[29] the other a general history of the SA by Heinrich Bennecke, a former officer in the organisation.[30] Two further studies, which concentrated upon the events of 1934 and their relation to economic interests and power politics in Berlin, were the thesis of the GDR historian Kurt Gossweiler[31] and a more recent short volume by Charles Bloch.[32] The organisational history of the SA nationwide was mapped out in great detail by Andreas Werner in 1964,[33] while the structure and tasks of the SA have been sketched in a number of regional studies of the Nazi Party.[34] However, it was not until the past few years that the composition and activities of the SA became objects of closer study,[35] and with the exceptions of Eric Reiche's work on the Nürnberg SA[36] and Eve Rosenhaft's work on the KPD in Berlin[37] little has been done to examine the SA and Nazi violence at local level. In addition, what discussion there has been has centred upon the activity of the storm troopers in urban centres – although it was obvious by the early 1930s that Nazism drew its greatest popular support in small towns and the countryside in Protestant areas of Germany.

This book is about political violence and its role in the growth of the Nazi movement and the acquisition of political power in 1933. It examines these problems through a regional study of the Nazi movement which focusses upon the SA, taking an area in which the rise of the Nazi movement has, on the whole, received rather little attention from historians: eastern Germany. For the purposes of this study the eastern regions of Germany are defined as the former Prussian provinces of East Prussia, Pomerania, Upper and Lower Silesia, and the border Province of Posen and West Prussia; however, since the Nazi organisations in the Border Province formed subdivisions of those in Brandenburg, where their development was influenced greatly by the proximity of Berlin, these will be examined in rather less detail.

The choice of eastern Germany for a regional study of the SA has considerable attractions. There the Nazi movement developed late but then grew particularly swiftly, and there the acts of political violence in 1932 and 1933 were most extreme. While together they had a distinct identity vis-à-vis the rest of the country, the eastern Prussian provinces were sufficiently varied to provide the opportunity to examine Nazi violence in a number of different contexts: from the Catholic industrial cities of Upper Silesia to the Protestant rural expanses of Pomerania and East Prussia. It is hoped that this book, by examining Nazi violence in eastern Germany during the years 1925–34, can broaden an understanding of the rise of the Hitler movement, the catastrophic defeat of the German Left before the National Socialist advance, and the transition from the Weimar Republic to the 'Third Reich'.

THE EASTERN REGIONS OF GERMANY DURING THE WEIMAR REPUBLIC

CHAPTER I

Eastern Germany in the Weimar Republic

DURING the Weimar period the political atmosphere in the eastern Prussian provinces was determined very largely by the post-war border changes. Scarcely a political statement could be made in the East without reference to the territorial losses and the 'bleeding frontier'.[1] For the inhabitants of the eastern regions, even more than for the rest of the German population, the events which followed military defeat in 1918 must have seemed the worst of their nightmares come true. The collapse of the monarchy and the formation of workers' and soldiers' councils were followed by Polish uprisings, the loss of most of the provinces of Posen and West Prussia to the new Polish state, and a peace settlement which led to further transfers of territory along Germany's eastern frontiers.[2] Additional border changes were to be determined by referenda, in the southern portion of East Prussia together with the remainder of West Prussia east of the Vistula and in much of Upper Silesia including the entire industrial region. While the referendum in East Prussia produced an overwhelming victory of the Germans,[3] in Upper Silesia the sympathies of the population were much more sharply divided. After a narrow referendum decision favouring Germany, three Polish uprisings and considerable bloodshed, when the new border was finally drawn Germany lost the eastern third of Upper Silesia, including much of the region's industrial resources.[4]

The post-war chaos in the eastern regions had serious repercussions in later years. The role of the *Freikorps* in the bloodshed in the East convinced many Germans that these bands of right-wing freebooters were the true defenders of the nation, and the *Freikorps* campaigns proved an important training ground for many men who later became leading figures in the Nazi movement in the eastern provinces.[5] A further consequence of the border changes was the subsequent immigration into Germany of roughly 750,000 refugees from the newly Polish territories. These refugees settled largely in the eastern provinces,[6] and helped to provide a reservoir of right-wing and anti-Polish sentiment. The post-war changes led to a pervasive feeling of bitterness and betrayal, leaving a deep mark on political life in eastern Germany, and revanchism and animosity towards Poland developed into an almost unquestioned political axiom.

In addition, the border changes exacerbated long-standing economic problems and came to be seen as the root cause of the relative poverty of the eastern Prussian provinces vis-à-vis the rest of the country. That the eastern regions would be doomed economically until the Versailles Treaty was revised was regarded as self-evident, and it generally was believed that 'the gravest distress would end with one stroke if the injustice of the drawing of the frontiers in the East were made good'.[7] The truth of the matter was rather different, however. Eastern Germany's economic difficulties were deeply rooted in the area's peculiar economic structure. Since the industrial-isation drive in the nineteenth century, the eastern regions had fallen behind the rest of the country in terms of their economic development. Although the East contained a number of industrial concentrations, the development of industry had been hindered by a lack of abundant natural resources and by the considerable distances to the important markets in the West. The failure of the eastern provinces to attract industrial investment meant that they offered relatively fewer job opportunities outside the agricultural sector. The dependence upon agriculture, with its chronically low wage levels, meant that considerably lower wage rates prevailed in the East; in terms of per capita income, the eastern Prussian provinces lagged significantly behind the country as a whole.[8] This in turn hampered the development of large markets for industrial goods, which might have attracted industrial invest-ment, and led to large-scale emigration from the predominantly rural East to the factories of Berlin and the Ruhr. From 1870 until the First World War, internal migration absorbed virtually the entire natural population increase in the eastern provinces.[9]

During the Weimar period, as before the War, eastern Germany formed a distinctly poorer section of the Reich. The patterns of economic develop-ment which had been established as the industrial economy expanded during the nineteenth century were inherited by Weimar Germany. In addition, the new political configurations of the post-war world – the loss to Germany of her old eastern territories and the establishment of small eastern European states with high tariff barriers – pushed the eastern Prussian provinces even further toward the periphery of German economic life.

The central feature of eastern Germany's economic plight during the Weimar period was a relatively underdeveloped industrial base. The eastern Prussian provinces were much less urbanised than the rest of the country, and industry accounted for a relatively small portion of their economy. In almost every important industrial branch, eastern Germany accounted for a smaller proportion of the total German output than it did of the country's population.[10] Industrial investment in the East was limited largely to those industries which needed to be near specific natural resources, such as the Upper Silesian coal-mining and smelting complex, the Silesian paper indus-try, or food-processing industries. Industries which required high capital

investment and which had greater choice about where they could locate –
such as the chemical or motor-vehicle industries – generally chose to invest
in the central and western regions of Germany. Altogether, eastern Germany lagged significantly behind in investment in the more progressive
sectors of industry, investment which might have lifted incomes to levels
prevailing elsewhere in the Reich.

The other key element of the economic difficulties of the eastern regions
was the obverse of the failure to industrialise sufficiently, namely their
disproportionate dependence upon agriculture. This meant that eastern
Germany was particularly severely affected by the crisis which enveloped
German agriculture during the 1920s. The intensification of agricultural
production worldwide after the First World War, together with the deflation
of the German economy, led to a sharp fall in farm prices during the late
1920s and early 1930s.[11] Despite tariff supports, the prices paid to German
farmers fell by an average of 36 per cent between 1925 and 1932, and in
1932/3 farm income was only 62 per cent of what it had been in 1928/9.[12]
Many farmers faced an enormous and increasing burden of debt at high rates
of interest, while the prices they received for their produce and the value of
their property were falling rapidly. Agriculture in the eastern provinces was
particularly hard hit by this combination, especially since eastern German
farmers were much more heavily in debt than their western counterparts.[13]
Farmers in the East had to cope with often poorer soil and a shorter growing
season than farmers in the South and West, and the larger size of eastern
German agricultural holdings meant a greater need for mechanisation and a
consequently high level of indebtedness. Not only the level of debt but the
rates of interest as well were higher in the East, which was regarded as a
high-risk area by the financial community.[14]

The crisis enveloping eastern German agriculture led successive Reich
and Prussian governments to enact far-reaching aid programmes involving
subsidised credit facilities and funding for the improvement of the infrastructure of the area.[15] However, these aid programmes did not effect basic
structural changes which might fundamentally have altered the situation,
and met with failure both in economic and political terms. Eastern German
farmers tried to cope with their predicament through a reduction of an
already meagre standard of living, but many succumbed to the financial
pressures as the numbers of bankruptcies and forced auctions of farm
properties grew to alarming proportions, particularly in East Prussia.[16] Small
farmers were hit as well as large, and the result of the growing spectre of
insolvency and ruin was an increasing desperation among German farmers
during the last years of the Weimar Republic, a desperation which cut them
loose from their traditional political moorings.[17]

Although the relative economic backwardness of the eastern Prussian
provinces influenced their political development during the Weimar period,
the effect of the economic and social peculiarities of the eastern regions was

not to cause exclusively regional issues to dominate their political life, despite the controversy generated by the subsidy programmes. To be sure, regional economic difficulties, demands for special treatment, revanchist attitudes toward the post-war borders and uncompromising hostility to Poland were given greater emphasis by politicians in the East than in the West. The proximity of the 'bleeding frontier' gave eastern German politics an especially strident nationalistic tone; with the sole exception of the KPD, all the major political parties, from the SPD to the NSDAP, favoured some manner of border revision and tried to identify with the national cause.[18] Nevertheless, despite its more extreme tone the political debate in eastern Germany was dominated by national rather than regional issues. Even the regional issues which aroused the greatest concern were seen primarily in terms of national politics: *national* policy was regarded as necessary to redress the economic balance and essential if the post-war settlements were to be reversed. The key to the question of how the peculiar economic and social structures of eastern Germany affected political life during the Weimar period was not that regional concerns formed the dominant political issues, but that the regional structures largely governed how the population responded politically to issues of national concern.

Political preferences in Weimar Germany remained very much a function of the place of individuals within the economic system, as well as of religion. Thus regional economic and social structures, rather than the fears and resentments engendered by the 'bleeding frontier', were most important in determining patterns of political support in the East. The political behaviour of particular social groups does not appear to have differed significantly between eastern and western Germany: Protestant farming communities, Catholic market towns, industrial regions and administrative centres produced similar voting patterns in eastern Germany as in the rest of the country. The crucial difference was that in the East the social and economic basis of political support for Weimar democracy was especially weak. The disproportionally large number of people dependent upon agriculture, the absence of a developed and prosperous industrial base and the rather low level of urbanisation meant that, at least in the Protestant areas of eastern Germany, the potential support for the 'Weimar parties' was relatively small and that for the right-wing opponents of the Republic correspondingly large. Thus the economic backwardness of the East was reflected in greater political instability.

This instability became painfully apparent in the final years of the Weimar Republic, when the Nazi movement was suddenly able to attract mass support. With the startling success of the NSDAP in the eastern Prussian provinces from 1929 onward, Nazism became a mass movement on a truly national scale. The Nazi success was an expression not only of the propensity of certain groups to favour right-wing politics, but also of the revolt of these groups against the conservative Right which hitherto had represented them.[19] While the potential backing for the Right in the eastern regions remained largely a function of their social structures, the events at the end of the Weimar period provided the political climate necessary to translate this potential into active support for the NSDAP. The glaring failure of the subsidy programmes, with which the conservative Right had been closely identified, stirred great resentment and anger. Together with the general effects of the economic crisis, this helped fuel the reaction against the conservative political leadership in the eastern German countryside. Particularly revealing were the spectacular victories of the NSDAP in the elections of the Prussian agricultural chambers (*Landwirtschaftskammer*) in late 1931, especially in East Prussia, Pomerania and Lower Silesia.[20] The advance of the Nazi Party had meant that in many a rural community in eastern Germany the political hegemony of the large landowners appeared to be over.

The regional peculiarities of the eastern Prussian provinces, as well as the revolt of the traditional supporters of the conservative Right, were reflected in the election results during the Weimar period. With the important exception of Upper Silesia, voting followed a roughly similar pattern in all the eastern regions. In contrast to the Reich as a whole, the conservative Right was very strong. Thus the DNVP polled significantly better in all the eastern German elections districts than in the Reich as a whole until the Weimar system crumbled. During the 1920s the DNVP had been the strongest political party in East Prussia and Pomerania, and in Lower and Middle Silesia it was second only to a relatively strong Social Democratic Party. Even in Upper Silesia the DNVP found enough support to exceed the national average. On the other hand, due largely to the low level of urbanisation and the less well developed infrastructure of trades and services, the 'middle parties' – the DVP, the DDP and the special-interest parties – were rather weaker in the East than in the rest of the Reich. And, as a result of the lower level of industrialisation in the eastern regions, the KPD and the SPD, taken together, found somewhat less support in the East than in the country as a whole.

This combination proved extremely vulnerable to the Nazi onslaught. Once the NSDAP had established itself as a political party on a national level, it quickly captured an especially strong position in the East and received there in 1930 and 1932 some of its best election results in the entire country. If the typical Nazi voter was a rural or small-town Protestant, engaged in farming or a business enterprise, then he was much more in evidence in the eastern regions than elsewhere in the Reich.

A striking exception to the general pattern of political preference in the eastern regions was Upper Silesia. In a sense, Upper Silesia was the exception which proved the rule. The two crucial factors which set Upper Silesia apart from the other eastern German election districts were that its population was largely Catholic and that it was, in part, heavily industrialised. Thus

Reichstag election results (%) in the eastern German election districts, and in the Reich (December 1924–July 1932)[21]

7 December 1924 Election district	*(Völkisch)* NSDAP	DNVP	DVP	Small parties	*Zentrum*	DDP	SPD	KPD
East Prussia	6.2	39.2	9.0	4.7	8.0	4.0	20.8	8.1
Frankfurt/Oder	3.2	38.3	10.8	4.4	6.3	4.7	27.9	4.4
Pomerania	4.2	49.1	6.5	5.0	1.0	3.8	24.6	5.8
Breslau	1.4	28.8	7.7	3.6	19.0	4.6	31.9	3.0
Liegnitz	1.5	28.9	8.3	8.3	8.9	8.0	32.8	3.3
Oppeln	1.5	21.8	2.8	11.7	41.0	2.2	6.8	12.2
Reich	3.0	20.5	10.1	7.7	17.4	6.3	26.0	9.0

20 May 1928 Election district	NSDAP	DNVP	DVP	Small parties	*Zentrum*	DDP	SPD	KPD
East Prussia	0.8	31.4	9.8	10.5	7.4	3.8	26.8	9.5
Frankfurt/Oder	1.0	29.6	8.4	11.5	6.0	4.4	33.1	6.0
Pomerania	1.5	41.5	5.5	11.7	1.0	4.0	30.2	6.1
Breslau	1.0	22.9	6.0	9.1	15.8	2.9	37.8	4.5
Liegnitz	1.2	24.5	6.6	11.5	7.9	6.3	37.8	4.2
Oppeln	1.0	17.0	2.7	12.4	40.0	1.6	12.6	12.7
Reich	2.6	14.2	8.7	14.1	15.2	4.8	29.8	10.6

14 September 1930 Election district	NSDAP	DNVP	DVP	Small parties	*Zentrum*	DDP	SPD	KPD
East Prussia	22.5	19.6	5.4	9.2	7.9	2.5	21.1	11.8
Frankfurt/Oder	22.7	13.2	3.1	15.6	5.8	3.0	26.6	9.3
Pomerania	24.3	24.8	3.3	10.5	1.1	2.5	24.7	8.8
Breslau	24.2	8.9	2.7	9.2	16.0	1.9	29.3	7.8
Liegnitz	20.9	8.6	3.5	16.2	7.8	5.0	32.0	6.1
Oppeln	9.5	15.3	1.4	11	35.2	1.1	9.3	16.6
Reich	18.3	7.0	4.5	14.0	14.8	3.8	24.5	13.1

31 July 1932 Election district	NSDAP	DNVP	DVP	Small parties	*Zentrum*	Staatspartei	SPD	KPD
East Prussia	47.1	9.5	0.8	1.7	7.7	0.6	19.7	12.9
Frankfurt/Oder	48.1	9.2	1.0	1.6	6.3	0.7	23.5	9.6
Pomerania	48.0	15.8	0.9	2.3	1.5	0.8	21.0	10.7
Breslau	43.5	5.6	0.5	1.6	14.7	0.5	24.4	8.8
Liegnitz	48.0	6.9	0.8	2.2	7.2	1.0	26.3	7.6
Oppeln	29.2	6.9	0.3	3.0	34.7	0.2	8.7	17.0
Reich	37.3	5.9	1.2	3.0	15.7	1.0	21.6	14.3

the Centre Party dominated the middle ground of political life in Upper Silesia, while the KPD enjoyed considerable support in the industrial areas. Yet although voting patterns in Upper Silesia differed dramatically from those in the other eastern regions, one thing remained the same: it was not primarily regional concerns, but the economic and social peculiarities of the region which determined patterns of political support. It would seem that in Upper Silesia, as in the other eastern provinces, confessional, social and economic factors, rather than purely geographical ones, had the greatest effect in shaping political life.

The Nazis, guided by their aggressive nationalism, believed that the bitterness caused by the post-war frontiers and the specific economic difficulties of eastern Germany drove people to support Hitler.[22] The truth of the matter is more complex, however. Certainly many eastern Germans were bitter and had become convinced that the area's economic problems were insoluble within the context of the Weimar system; and certainly many of these embittered people supported the Nazi movement and saw in it a last chance for improvement. Yet the Nazis found fanatic supporters in other, less threatened and more prosperous regions of Germany as well. The eastern Prussian provinces did not differ from the rest of Weimar Germany in that the issues which dominated their political life were fundamentally different; it was the peculiar economic development of eastern Germany that had led to greater concentrations of those social groups most prone to support the Nazi movement, and left the East particularly vulnerable to Nazism.

CHAPTER II

The Development of National Socialism in Eastern Germany to 1933

(i) The Beginnings of the Nazi Movement in the Eastern Prussian Provinces

THE Nazi movement had a rather late and uncertain start in eastern Germany. With their relatively low population densities and the great distances separating them from the headquarters and early strongholds of the NSDAP in southern and western Germany, the eastern Prussian provinces were among the last areas of the Reich to be organised effectively by the Nazi Party. Before the 1923 Munich *Putsch* the development of the Nazi movement was centred mainly in Bavaria, and the northward expansion of the NSDAP was limited by the hostility of the Prussian government, which banned the party in 1922.[1] The first local groups of the NSDAP outside Bavaria were established during 1920 and 1921 in Mannheim, Hannover, Zwickau, Halle and Dortmund.[2] Thus the first Nazi cells formed in Prussia before the 1922 ban were to be found in its central and western provinces. In eastern Prussia right-wing racialist (*völkisch*) politics were dominated initially by other groups. The NSDAP, based in Munich, remained too small and too far away to force its way onto the political stage in eastern Germany.

After the First World War a large number of right-wing, anti-Semitic political organisations were formed in the eastern Prussian provinces. The growth of these groups was aided by the presence of remnants of the *Freikorps* which had been so active in the East, the strong tradition of conservative nationalism, and the resentments engendered by the effects of the peace settlement on the eastern border regions. Particularly in Silesia, veterans of the *Freikorps* and 'Selbstschutz' (self-defence) units formed the nuclei of a number of right-wing groups.[3] Many of these groups were purely local phenomena, without any organisational link to regional or national movements, and many were quite short-lived, one following the other into oblivion.[4] Often the same groups would re-surface under different names in the wake of bans imposed by the Prussian government. Thus, for example, the local group in Insterburg of the 'German *Völkisch* Defence and Offence League' (*Deutschvölkische Schutz- und Trutzbund*) founded in 1920 reacted to a ban in 1922 by re-emerging as the 'Völkisch-Sozialer Block', which by

1923 had grown to 400 members.[5] Such groups provided a field of early political activity for a number of people destined to become important figures in the Nazi movement in eastern Germany. For example, in Leobschütz (Upper Silesia) Georg Heidrich, who later figured prominently in the East Prussian NSDAP, was instrumental in establishing a number of *völkisch* groupings. In 1923 he founded a local group of the 'Deutsche Partei'; when this was banned he established a new independent group, the 'Junggermanen'; and, although his first two attempts at political organisation had met with little success, in 1924 Heidrich surfaced again to form a 'Nationalsozialistsche Kampfbund' which he affiliated with Ernst Röhm's 'Frontbann' organisation.[6] Similarly, in Ratibor, at the south-eastern tip of Upper Silesia, the future NSDAP *Untergauleiter* in the province, Josef-Joachim Adamczyck, was among the members of a 'Sturmabteilung' which formed in the spring of 1923 and christened itself 'Oberland'.[7]

The formation of a multitude of right-wing racialist groupings throughout eastern Germany after the First World War helped lay the groundwork for the subsequent spread of the Nazi movement. Although these organisations were generally short-lived and poorly organised, they indicated the potential support awaiting a well-organised and unified *völkisch* movement in the eastern Prussian provinces.

It is difficult to date precisely the very beginnings of the Nazi organisation in eastern Germany. It appears doubtful that there existed a regional Nazi Party organisation worthy of the name in the East before the Munich *Putsch* attempt. The first member of the NSDAP from the eastern Prussian provinces was most probably Waldemar Magunia, a nineteen-year-old baker from Königsberg who joined the party as an individual member in Munich in 1921.[8] Soon thereafter the first local Nazi Party groups in eastern Germany were established in Pomerania and Silesia. According to the *Völkischer Beobachter* in mid-1922, a group of the NSDAP had been formed in Stettin, and before the end of the year groups were reported in Breslau, Gleiwitz, Hindenburg, Oppeln, Beuthen (Upper Silesia), Rosenberg (Upper Silesia), Kreuzburg and Petersdorf (*Kreis* Hirschberg).[9] Early groups also were established in the university town of Greifswald and in Pasewalk in Pomerania; by 1923, despite the Prussian ban, groups which associated themselves with the Nazi movement had been founded in Stralsund, Cuntzow, Swinemünde, Greifenhagen, Kolberg and Stolp, and together with those in Stettin, Greifswald and Pasewalk their total membership was estimated at around three hundred.[10] The first SA groups in eastern Germany appear to have been formed in late 1922 or early 1923 in Upper Silesia, first in Hindenburg and then in Ratibor.[11] The nature of these early Nazi groups' activities and their relation to the other *völkisch* organisations which proliferated in eastern Germany remain uncertain, and their links with the Munich party headquarters must have been tenuous. Altogether, the distance from Munich, the lack of a firm organisational structure and the hostility of the Prussian government made coordinated political activity by the first Nazi groups in the East extremely difficult, if not impossible.

The Munich *Putsch* proved a turning point for the incipient Nazi movement in the East. Although years later it was asserted that the Ratibor 'Sturmabteilung' 'Oberland' had armed itself and was 'ready for action' on 9 November 1923, the *Putsch* attempt found no echo in eastern Germany and was followed by the break-up of many of the Nazi Party groups which had formed during the previous year.[12] The failure of the *Putsch* shattered the early efforts of the NSDAP to gain a foothold in the eastern Prussian provinces, and it was not until the re-formation of the party in 1925 that a coherent Nazi organisation began to be built up.

The party which Hitler founded in the Bavarian capital on 27 February 1925 was quite different from that which had existed before the *Putsch* attempt. In order to prevent a repetition of the disastrous confrontation of 1923, the Nazi attack on the Weimar system henceforth would be carried out within the framework of formal 'legality', and a strong emphasis was placed upon a unified and centralised organisation and unconditional allegiance to Hitler.[13] The organisational confusion of the pre-*Putsch* period was to be avoided: NSDAP members were forbidden to belong to other political or paramilitary groups, as frequently had been the case before November 1923. The re-establishment of a central leadership for the SA, however, did not come until late summer 1926, when Franz von Pfeffer was appointed its 'Supreme Leader' and began to formulate guidelines for its future development.[14]

The first Nazi Party group to be established in the eastern Prussian provinces in 1925 pre-dated the re-emergence of the NSDAP in Munich: on 25 February 1925 a local group was founded in Hindenburg. Building on the base created by a succession of *völkisch* groups in the city, it grew to 26 members by the end of the year.[15] Soon after the rebirth of the NSDAP in Munich, local Nazi Party groups were established in Pomerania and East Prussia as well. In Stettin a group was set up within a few days of the re-formation of the party in Munich;[16] and on 1 March Wilhelm Stich (the first local group leader), Waldemar Magunia (the first SA leader) and six of their comrades formed a group of the NSDAP in Königsberg.[17]

During the weeks that followed, regional party organisations were created, and by April the NSDAP *Gaue* of Silesia, Pomerania and East Prussia had been established in rudimentary form. The first to be set up was in Silesia. On 2 March the Breslau group of the NSFB, the coalition formed in August 1924 of the remnants of the NSDAP and its *völkisch* allies in the DVFP, held a meeting at which it was announced that the NSFB would be dissolved.[18] It then was decided to hold a final meeting on 15 March at which members would choose between the DVFB (the reconstitution of the DVFP) and the NSDAP. Among those who declared for Hitler's organisation were Helmuth Brückner, a Breslau city assembly deputy, and Erich

Rosikat, the leader of the '*Völkisch* farmers' (*Völkische Bauernschaften*) and the 'Deutsch-soziale Partei' in Breslau. With the break-up of the *völkisch* coalition, the Silesian NSDAP *Gau* organisation was founded on 15 March, with Brückner as *Gauleiter* and Rosikat as his deputy and leader of the local party group in Breslau; three days later Brückner travelled to Liegnitz, to found the NSDAP *Untergau* Lower Silesia.[19]

In Pomerania a *Gau* organisation was established in early April, under the leadership of Theodor Vahlen, a professor and former rector at the University of Greifswald. Thus the first NSDAP *Gau* headquarters in Pomerania was not in Stettin, the administrative centre of the province and the home of the first Pomeranian party group, but in Greifswald.[20] The East Prussian *Gau* organisation also dated from early April 1925. Here, on 5 April, after local Nazi Party groups had been established in Königsberg and Insterburg, the 'Gau Ostpreußen', held a 'foundation rally' presided over by 'Gauleiter' Wilhelm Stich.[21] Although according to one account a proper *Gau* organisation was not established in East Prussia until early 1926, when it was founded in Insterburg 'at the order of Adolf Hitler', it seems clear that there existed a Nazi organisation in Königsberg in 1925 and that it probably exercised a coordinating function for the NSDAP in the province.[22]

It is more difficult to pinpoint the beginnings of the SA in eastern Germany than those of the NSDAP. The roots of the SA in the East lay in the right-wing political and paramilitary activity before the 1923 *Putsch*, and the absence of a central SA organisation until late 1926 meant that the first groups of storm troopers were formed entirely at local initiative.[23] The newly formed Nazi Party groups needed protection squads, a fact which local NSDAP leaders recognised very quickly.

The beginnings of the SA in East Prussia date from May 1924, when, according to a Nazi history, it began life camouflaged as a 'patriotic protection association' (*vaterländischer Schutzbund*); in January 1925, it was claimed, this SA came out into the open under its own name.[24] Its leader was Waldemar Magunia. The precise character of this 'SA' is difficult to determine; most probably it served as a protection squad for the various *völkisch* groups active in Königsberg during 1924. Its first public appearance as an SA group did not take place until mid-May 1925, when it staged a Nazi propaganda march near the East Prussian capital. In Pomerania the first organisation of storm troopers grew out of a 'Frontbannabteilung' called into being in 1924 by the NSFB in Stettin.[25] The Stettin 'Frontbann' gathered together primarily members of the pre-*Putsch* Nazi movement, and with the re-establishment of the NSDAP in early 1925 became to all intents the SA of the local Nazi group. According to the leader of the Stettin 'Frontbann', Willy Behnke, the organisation placed itself at the disposal of the NSDAP to protect its meetings and distribute its propaganda, and by mid-1926 its 35 members all were enrolled in the Nazi Party and comprised 60 per cent of the total NSDAP membership in Stettin. Although the first mention of an SA *per se* in Pomerania dates from mid-1928,[26] the Stettin 'Frontbann' was an 'SA' in every respect but name.

In Silesia, where the NSDAP was better organised than in the other *Gaue* in eastern Germany, the SA was formed at the initiative of *Gauleiter* Brück-ner. Shortly before the first congress of the Silesian NSDAP, scheduled to take place in Breslau on 5 June 1925, Brückner decided that the party needed its own protection squads. On 3 June an SA group was established in the Silesian capital; its first leader was Paul-Willi Jakubaschk and it con-sisted of 65 men, roughly 85 per cent of whom were said to be war veterans.[27] A few days later a second SA formation was formed in Brieg, and in Upper Silesia the former *Freikorps* leader Hans Peter von Heydebreck gathered some of his old *Freikorps* associates to form an SA group. Although Heydebreck was to be described by Nazi historians as the first leader of the Silesian SA, the actual nature of his involvement with the organisation in its early days remains unclear, and the first SA formation in Upper Silesia closely connected with a particular NSDAP group was not founded until December 1925, when a storm section was established in Hindenburg.[28]

The distinction between the local NSDAP organisations and the SA groups attached to them during 1925 and 1926 was rather artificial. Often the two were identical, and the formal establishment of an SA group by a local party organisation probably made little practical difference to the people involved; the meetings of the party had to be protected in any case.[29] The differentiation between the two main pillars of the Nazi movement did not come until later, when the NSDAP and the SA developed into mass organisations with well-developed, separate hierarchies.

The growth of the Nazi movement in the eastern Prussian provinces between 1925 and 1928 was slow and uneven. The relative economic and political stability of Germany during these years effectively prevented the NSDAP from expanding beyond the political ghetto of the *völkisch* move-ment. Largely ignored by the leadership in Munich, faced with the competi-tion of other *völkisch* groups and a strong and well-organised DNVP, frequently lacking competent leaders and plagued by in-fighting, the eastern NSDAP *Gaue* made rather little progress until after the 1928 *Reichstag* elections. Many who had joined the party in the initial upsurge in 1925 lost interest and drifted away during the next few years; and when in 1928 the Nazi Party presented its own election list, independent of its *völkisch* rivals, for the first time in *Reichstag* elections, it conspicuously failed to gain support in the East.[30] The principal achievement of the Nazi movement in eastern Germany during the mid-1920s was not political success but survi-val. It was here that the unifying figure of Hitler and the organisational focus provided by Munich proved so important in keeping the movement together, until economic and political crisis lifted the NSDAP from relative obscurity at the turn of the decade.

Of all the eastern German *Gaue,* only Silesia had the same top leadership from 1925 through 1933: from March 1925, when he founded the Silesian NSDAP *Gau* organisation, until December 1934, when he was removed from office, Helmuth Brückner remained at the helm of the Silesian Nazi movement.[31] Born in the village of Peilau in *Kreis* Reichenbach (Eulengebirge) in 1896, the son of a primary-school teacher, Brückner was a veteran of four years at the front between 1914 and 1918 and of the post-war struggles in Upper Silesia, and subsequently spent four years as a student at the University of Breslau. By the mid-1920s Brückner had devoted himself full-time to politics and, following the initial burst of activity in 1925, the Silesian Nazi Party under Brückner's leadership began a long, slow process of developing its organisational net and expanding its base of support. Although the growth was far from spectacular, by early 1927 Brückner could report cheerfully that the rival DVFB was no longer functioning in Silesia, leaving the NSDAP with a virtual monopoly of *völkisch* politics in the region.[32] Especially in the urban centres of Upper Silesia the Nazi movement was able to develop an organisational base, despite the determined opposition of the KPD. By July 1927 the Nazis felt sufficiently confident to organise an SA march through Gleiwitz as part of a regional congress (*Bezirkstagung*). Although the rally which followed was disrupted by Communists and resulted in a brawl requiring police intervention, the march itself was a rather impressive display for the young movement, with 135 participants (122 in uniform) representing local NSDAP groups in Gleiwitz, Beuthen, Hindenburg, Ratibor, Oppeln, Kreuzburg and Malapane.[33]

The development of the Nazi movement in Silesia nevertheless was far from smooth. During 1927 and 1928 a serious rift grew between the *Gauleitung* and the local NSDAP group in Breslau.[34] The conflict came to involve the SA – it was the first instance in which the storm troopers' organisation rebelled against the party leadership in eastern Germany – and concerned issues which were to surface repeatedly during the following years. The unrest began with difficulties between Erich Rosikat, Deputy *Gauleiter* and leader of the Breslau NSDAP, and Brückner, who lived in Zobten (about thirty kilometers south-west of the Silesian capital) and was unable to maintain close contact with the Breslau group. In early 1927 there occurred an open break, when Brückner managed to force Rosikat out of the party, and this stirred up divisions among the Breslau Nazis. A further source of conflict was the behaviour of *Gau* business manager Rechenberg, and in December 1927 the Breslau group presented the *Gauleiter* with a list of complaints about Rechenberg's 'vindictive character', his overfondness for alchohol and alleged social contacts with Jews. A few weeks later, in January 1928, Brückner responded by disbanding the Breslau NSDAP.[35]

It was at this point that the SA became involved. After Brückner dissolved the Breslau group, a general members' meeting was held in the city at which competing factions tried to gain the support of the SA. Accusations were made that Rechenberg had attempted to turn the 'Handarbeiter' in the SA against the 'Kopfarbeiter' in the local party organisation and thus to force a split along crude class lines. Brückner supported his business manager and re-formed the Breslau group with Rechenberg as its provisional leader, a move which the party members in the city regarded as a 'slap in the face'. The troubles in Breslau were brought to the attention of the NSDAP's 'Investigation and Arbitration Committee' (USchlA), whose chief, Walter Buch, travelled to Silesia in April and agreed with Brückner to dissolve the local party organisation in the provincial capital once again. This precipitated a full-fledged revolt. On 2 May the Breslau party members formed their own group, the 'National Socialist Working Group of Greater Breslau' (*Nationalsozialistische Arbeitsgemeinschaft Groß-Breslau*), and then tried to enlist the support of the Nazi leadership in Munich against the Silesian *Gauleiter*. The SA rallied behind the rebels, accused Brückner of having slandered both the Breslau NSDAP and the SA, threatened to stop protecting meetings at which Brückner was to speak, and at one point came close to thrashing the *Gauleiter*.[36]

Soon after the break was made, however, the revolt collapsed. The rebels proved unwilling to press their revolt against the authority of Hitler, and the Munich leadership was unwilling to support breakaway groups against the party's regional leaders. On 11 June Brückner expelled the leaders of the 'Arbeitsgemeinschaft' from the NSDAP, and in July the rebel group dissolved itself.[37] Although the new SA leaders installed in Breslau by Brückner after the revolt initially aroused antipathy, the disbanding of the rebels' organisation effectively ended the threat to the *Gauleitung*. In order to rebuild the Breslau organisation, Brückner brought in the leader of the NSDAP in Upper Silesia, Kurt Kremser, who had supported the *Gauleiter* when repercussions of the revolt shook the party in Beuthen.[38] Soon afterwards Kremser assumed command of the Silesian SA.

The rebellion in Breslau in 1928 bore many similarities to the more serious revolts which occurred within the Nazi movement in later years: the bitter in-fighting, the jealous guarding of prerogatives, the alliance of the SA with groups rebelling against the NSDAP hierarchy, the success of the *Gauleiter* in protecting his position, the unwillingness of the rebels to turn their backs on Hitler, and the utter failure of the revolt. The importance of Hitler – for no one was rebelling against Hitler! – and the leverage this gave to those representing the Munich leadership formed a key strength of the Nazi organisation in the face of rebellion from within. Also significant is that the effect of this revolt upon the development of the Silesian NSDAP proved so marginal. The subsequent growth of the party meant that very quickly new members, who looked to Brückner and knew little of the conflict, outnumbered the veterans who had belonged to the organisation in early 1928 and may have supported the rebels. Finally, it is worth noting that, in this first major revolt within the Nazi movement in eastern Germany, the SA found itself on the losing side.

Even more than in Silesia, in East Prussia the early development of the Nazi movement was marked by dissension. The initial arrangement whereby Wilhelm Stich was *Gauleiter* of the East Prussian Nazi organisation and Waldemar Magunia SA leader lasted only until the spring of 1926, when Stich was forced out of the movement.[39] The vacant post of *Gauleiter* was offered first to Magunia, who declined, and then to Bruno Scherwitz – described as a 'front soldier and nothing but' – who accepted. In early 1927 Magunia also relinquished the leadership of the SA, handing over command to Werner Siegfried, supervisor of a landed estate in *Kreis* Insterburg. However, Magunia remained Siegfried's 'deputy, chief of staff, adjutant, all in one', as well as the financial mainstay of the fledgling Nazi organisation; according to a Nazi history of the movement in East Prussia, Magunia's bakery formed the 'financial backbone of the party' during this period.[40] In the meantime Stich attempted to form a breakaway 'Nationalsozialistische Arbeitsgemeinschaft', which, like its counterpart in Silesia, soon collapsed. The rebel group never posed a serious threat to the East Prussian NSDAP, and served mainly to provide an opportunity to purge Nazi ranks in the province.[41]

Nevertheless, Scherwitz soon ran into difficulties, and during 1927 the East Prussian Nazi Party continued to be plagued by strife.[42] In August Scherwitz was removed as *Gauleiter*; once again Magunia was offered the position and once again he refused, leaving the party without a leader in the province for more than a year. The chaotic state of the East Prussian NSDAP was reflected in its membership figures: by early 1928 the entire *Gau* consisted of barely 200 members;[43] less than two years before, in May 1926, it had numbered 544.[44]

The problems in East Prussia eventually led to the intervention of the Nazi Party's organisational chief, Gregor Straßer. In March 1928 Straßer travelled to Königsberg, together with the regional commander of the SA in eastern Germany Walther Stennes, in order to meet the East Prussian Nazis and sort out the question of the *Gau* leadership.[45] After discussions with the Königsberg group, Straßer offered two candidates for the position of *Gauleiter*: Heinrich Himmler, at that time Straßer's deputy, and Erich Koch, a former railway employee and deputy *Gauleiter* in the Ruhr. The choice fell to Koch, who on 3 September took up the post he was to hold until 1945.[46]

In contrast to events in Silesia and East Prussia, the development of the Nazi movement in Pomerania during the mid-1920s was quiet and uneventful. After the burst of activity in 1925, the Pomeranian NSDAP experienced neither rapid growth nor fierce internal wrangling. In 1927 Vahlen was replaced as *Gauleiter* by Walther von Corswandt, a landowner who moved the *Gau* headquarters from Greifswald to his estate in Cuntzow, and under von Corswandt the Pomeranian Nazi organisation continued to stagnate until the end of the decade.

From 1925 through 1928 the Nazi movement failed to extend its organisational net beyond the relatively few cities and market towns into the eastern German countryside. In the Border Province, which formed part of the NSDAP *Gau* 'Ostmark' and which contained no cities of appreciable size, the party made no progress at all during this period. The principal achievement of the Nazi movement in eastern Germany was to have survived intact, so that at the end of the decade, once the effects of the economic crisis began to be felt, it enjoyed a virtual monopoly of *völkisch* politics. In the process neither internal conflicts nor their absence, the existence of a strong and stable leadership nor a weak and rapidly changing one seems to have had much effect upon the *general* development of the Nazi movement. Indeed, the internal, organisational development of the Nazi Party, so often marked by the petty squabbling of small-minded men, had remarkably little to do with the wider world of German politics during the mid-1920s. Regardless of the character of its regional or local leadership, not until almost the turn of the decade did the NSDAP begin to attract a large measure of popular support in the eastern Prussian provinces.

(ii) **The Nazi Movement between 1929 and 1933**

Following the 1930 *Reichstag* elections, which marked the emergence of the NSDAP as a major national political party, Prussian Interior Minister Carl Severing surveyed the rising fortunes of the Nazi movement and concluded:

> The overall picture shows . . . a particular susceptibility of the eastern regions (East Prussia, Lower Silesia, Pomerania) for the National Socialist slogans and leads to the conclusion that the impetus of the NSDAP has passed from the South to the North and in the North is directed toward the East.[47]

Although success came rather later in the eastern Prussian provinces than in the rest of Germany, when the Nazi Party began to attract mass support in the East it quickly made up for lost time.

The turning point came in 1929. Between mid-1928 and the end of 1929 the NSDAP made great strides in the eastern regions and registered two important accomplishments. First, it established itself as the only serious contender for the votes of the radical Right. For example, in the 1928 *Reichstag* elections in East Prussia, the only election district in Germany where the NSDAP received less than one per cent of the vote, the competing 'Völkisch-nationaler Block' attracted roughly four per cent; in the provincial *Landtag* elections in 1929, however, virtually all the electoral support for the *völkisch* Right in East Prussia fell to the Nazi Party.[48] Second, by the end of 1929 the NSDAP had succeeded in attracting levels of support in the eastern Prussian provinces (with the exception of Upper Silesia) which were almost the same as in the rest of the country.

The Share of the Vote for the NSDAP in the Eastern Prussian Provinces, 1928–1930 (in %)[49]

Province	*Landtag* Elections 20 May 1928	Provincial *Landtag* Elections 17 Nov. 1929	*Reichstag* Elections 14 Sept. 1930
East Prussia	0.8	4.3	22.5
Border Province	0.7	4.7	17.0
Pomerania	1.5	4.1	24.2
Lower Silesia	1.0	5.2	22.9
Upper Silesia	1.0	2.3	9.5
Prussia	1.8	5.01	18.5
Reich	2.6 *(Reichstag)*	—	18.3

Once it became apparent in 1929 and 1930 that the Nazi Party could find a large measure of support in Protestant rural districts, it redoubled its efforts to spread into the eastern German countryside. In East Prussia, for example, in January 1929 the *Gauleitung* observed a rapid growth of the party organisation and boasted that 'especially among the farmers our idea is meeting with approval'.[50] As the movement gained momentum Nazi rallies and demonstrations were staged with rising frequency in the countryside, between election campaigns as well as during them.[51] Party propaganda was aimed specifically at the rural population, in an effort to win embittered farmers from the DNVP – farmers whose economic difficulties were leading them away from the traditional party-political structure and toward extra-legal protest, such as refusal to pay taxes – and simultaneously to attract agricultural labourers.[52] In addition special organisations were formed expressly for the farm population, such as the 'National Socialist Farmers' and Settlers' League' (*Nationalsozialistischer Bauern- und Siedlerbund*) established by the East Prussian NSDAP at the beginning of 1930 (well before Richard Walther Darré began to set up his 'agrarian-political' organisation nationally).[53]

From about the turn of the decade the number of Nazi Party groups and their membership grew phenomenally. In January 1930 the East Prussian *Gauleiter* Koch claimed, with characteristic modesty, that since he had arrived in the province the party membership had risen from roughly 200 to more than 8,000 and the number of local groups from 4 to 211.[54] The 1930 *Reichstag* elections provided a further boost for the NSDAP, which capitalised on the success at the polls to expand greatly.[55] In the *Gau* 'Ostmark' the NSDAP grew from 1,700 members at the beginning of 1930 to 9,500 at the year's end, and in Silesia in the autumn of 1931 *Gauleiter* Brückner reported that the party was growing at a rate of between 1,500 and 2,000 members per month.[56] According to the police, who were concerned to monitor the progress of the Nazis, in Upper Silesia the NSDAP began successfully to establish local groups in the market towns and farming villages during 1930, and at the end of the year there were 61 local groups with 3,012 members in the province.[57] By the end of March 1931 the Upper Silesian Nazi Party had grown to 115 groups with 5,298 members; by the end of June there were 151 groups with 6,973 members; and by the end of the year the party groups numbered 183 with a combined membership of 9,110.[58] The greatest part of this growth took place in the countryside.

Among the most important factors contributing to the growth of the Nazi movement was the drawing of support from other right-wing organisations. The first step in this direction was the absorption of former members of *völkisch* groups which had fallen by the wayside in the late 1920s. These recruits were followed by a growing number of erstwhile supporters of conservative political parties – particularly of the DNVP – who transferred their allegiance to the Nazis. As the Nazi movement grew, many politicians who had been elected to local assemblies as members of the DNVP or other right-wing groups chose to attach themselves to the NSDAP, and reports of such conversions provided welcome copy for Nazi Party newspapers.[59]

The drift of supporters from the conservative Right to the Nazi movement in rural eastern Germany was reflected in developments within the regional affiliates of the National Rural League (*Reichslandbund*). This umbrella organisation, which encompassed the largest and most influential agricultural associations in the eastern Prussian provinces, was the target for concerted efforts by the Nazis to gain support.[60] As an ever larger proportion of their membership became attracted to the NSDAP, a number of regional *Landbünde* – for example, in Pomerania and Upper Silesia – publicly drew close to the Nazis.[61] At the same time, the growing sympathy for the NSDAP frequently made it possible for the Nazis to challenge the *Landbünde* directly, by presenting their own lists of candidates for elections to chambers of agriculture (*Landwirtschaftskammer*). It was a telling sign of the erosion of traditional conservative politics when Arno Manthey, a farmer and regional SA leader, was elected chairman of the *Landwirtschaftskammer* in the Border Province in November 1932.[62]

While the Nazi movement was growing so explosively in eastern Germany, the top NSDAP leadership in the eastern *Gaue* remained relatively stable. Erich Koch in East Prussia, Helmuth Brückner in Silesia and Wilhelm Kube in the *Gau* 'Ostmark'[63] all remained *Gauleiter* of their respective regions without interruption from the late 1920s through 1933. Only in Pomerania was there a change, when von Corswandt proved unwilling to transfer the *Gau* headquarters from his estate to Stettin – a move made necessary by the rapid growth of the organisation – and was replaced in April 1931 by the 27-year-old lawyer Wilhelm Karpenstein.[64] The stability of the leadership of the eastern German *Gaue* was of considerable help in allowing the NSDAP to exploit the massive increase in its membership as it attracted support in the countryside. Conversely, the growth of the movement made the positions of the *Gauleiter* more stable and secure, by providing apparent

evidence of the success of their propaganda efforts and by offering greater
inducement to Nazi leaders to remain at their posts as the prospect of gaining
power seemed to be getting nearer.

The increase in the NSDAP membership was accompanied by an expansion of the party's bureaucracy and the establishment of special organisations to attend to the particular interests of the various social groups which
supported the Nazi movement.[65] By early 1931 the party *Gaue* in eastern
Germany possessed large staffs of *Gau Sachberater* – specialist advisors who
were to supervise the movement's propaganda activities in specific policy
areas.[66] By 1931 the NSDAP in the eastern Prussian provinces also had
launched a considerable array of party publications, and daily party newspapers appeared in each of the three major east German cities: the
Pommersche Zeitung in Stettin, the *Preußische Zeitung* in Königsberg, and
the *Schlesische Tageszeitung* (from June 1931 the *Nationalsozialistische
Schlesische Tageszeitung*) in Breslau. As the movement grew and the party
sought support among factory workers, regional outposts of the Nazi factory
cell organisation, the NSBO, were established in the East. Especially important in rural eastern Germany were efforts to set up the 'agrarian-political
department' (*agrarpolitsches Apparat*) on a regional basis. In each *Gau*
'agricultural advisors' (*landwirtschaftliche Fachberater*) were appointed, and
by the end of 1930 the 'Ostmark', Pomerania and Silesia numbered among
the fifteen *Gaue* where an 'agrarian-political office' was functioning at the
local as well as regional level.[67] In addition, in a number of places even more
specialised organisations were created. In East Prussia, for example, in 1932
the *Gauleitung* formed an 'Association of German Cattle-Traders, *Gau* East
Prussia' in order to combat Jewish cattle dealers;[68] and in the Upper Silesian
industrial region the Nazis formed a 'Committee of National Socialist Police
Officers'.[69]

Of the many organisations established by the Nazi Party, the most closely
connected to the SA (the SS excepted) was the Hitler Youth (*Hitlerjugend*).
When the SA was re-organised in the mid-1920s, the Nazi youth movement
first had been envisaged as the 'youth section' of the SA.[70] Although the
Hitler Youth in fact developed independently of the SA, the SA exercised
considerable influence on its activities. For most of the pre-1933 period the
Hitler Youth remained formally under the command of the Munich SA
leadership and its participation in marches and demonstrations was subject
to the supervision of the SA.[71] Most importantly, the Hitler Youth tended to
serve as an organisational home for adolescents until they passed their
eighteenth birthdays and could join the SA outright, and it was common for
the older HJ members to join the storm troopers at rallies and marches.[72]

The beginnings of the Hitler Youth in eastern Germany date from early
1927, when the Nazi youth organisation began to extend far beyond its early
strongholds in Saxony.[73] It nevertheless remained small until 1933, and thus
its potential as a greenhouse for SA men was rather limited. At the beginning

of 1931 the entire Hitler Youth numbered only about 14,000 members, and in January 1933 roughly 55,000.[74] In the eastern Prussian provinces HJ membership was correspondingly low: in January 1931 the organisation had only 500 members in the Breslau region (Middle Silesia), 202 in Lower Silesia, 103 in Upper Silesia, 528 in East Prussia and 547 in Pomerania; one year later it numbered 1,586 in the Breslau region, 954 in Lower Silesia, 712 in Upper Silesia, 1,730 in East Prussia and 1,591 in Pomerania.[75]

As in the rest of Germany, in the East the NSDAP used the eighteen months following the 1930 *Reichstag* elections to bombard the population with propaganda and to penetrate into virtually every town and village. Thus the Nazi Party in eastern Germany was well equipped to face the unprecedented series of elections in 1932. Within eight months, from March through November 1932, the Prussian population was subjected to five major campaigns: for the two Reich Presidential elections in March and April, the Prussian *Landtag* election in April, and the two *Reichstag* elections in July and November. The results demonstrated that the NSDAP unquestionably had become the largest political party in Germany, and had built up an organisation capable of staging tens of thousands of rallies and saturating the country with propaganda. At the same time, however, they showed the limits of what the Nazis could achieve through electoral politics, for the NSDAP exhausted its reserves of electoral support in 1932 without gaining power. In eastern Germany voting patterns remained similar to those of 1930: in all the eastern election districts, with the important exception of Upper Silesia, the Nazis attracted in 1932 a consistently higher level of support than in the country as a whole. Among the most striking aspects of the Nazi success in the East was the backing Hitler received against Hindenburg for the Reich Presidency; in *Kreis* Neidenburg, the site of the famous battle of Tannenberg which had established the aged President's reputation as the saviour of East Prussia, already in March Hitler outpolled Hindenburg by nearly two to one.[76] Indeed, the eastern election districts provided the Nazis with some of their best returns in all Germany, and in the July *Reichstag* elections the NSDAP received only slightly less than half the vote in all the eastern regions except Upper Silesia.

The Share of the Vote for the NSDAP in the Eastern Prussian Provinces, *Reichstag* Elections, 1932–1933 (in %)[77]

Province	31 July 1932	6 Nov. 1932	5 Mar. 1933
East Prussia	47.1	39.7	56.5
Border Province	46.2	42.5	53.6
Pomerania	47.9	43.1	55.2
Lower Silesia	45.3	41.1	51.7
Upper Silesia	29.3	26.8	43.2
Reich	37.3	33.1	43.9

The string of Nazi electoral successes came to an abrupt halt in the autumn of 1932, and support for the NSDAP fell in all the eastern Prussian provinces, most precipitously in East Prussia. The decline in the Nazi vote coincided with a severe crisis within the movement, as the financial position of the party became desperate and the membership of many local groups (and, with it, receipts of dues) fell rapidly. Typical were the sagging fortunes of the NSDAP in Lötzen, East Prussia, where the membership tumbled from 315 in October to only 185 in December.[78] The drop in Nazi fortunes threatened to break apart the impressive organisation built up during the previous years, as morale among the party faithful plummeted.[79]

The crisis which enveloped the Nazi movement during the final months of 1932 was overcome at a stroke with the appointment of Hitler as Reich Chancellor on 30 January 1933. The support which had drifted away during late 1932 swiftly returned once the Nazis achieved political power. In eastern Germany the upturn in the Nazi vote was even greater than in the country as a whole, and the sudden success brought thousands of new members into the NSDAP and its affiliated organisations. Local party groups, which only a few weeks before had been losing members at an alarming rate, found their membership figures growing by leaps and bounds.[80] By the summer of 1933, in most party groups the new, post-January members outnumbered the veterans who had joined before Hitler became Reich Chancellor.

The success in 1933 brought considerable dividends to the Nazi Party leadership in the eastern regions, as it did throughout Germany. With the exception of Karpenstein in Pomerania, each of the *Gauleiter* in the eastern Prussian provinces managed to get himself installed as provincial *Oberpräsident* in 1933: Brückner in Lower Silesia, Koch in East Prussia, and Kube in Brandenburg.[81] At the local level as well the party's leaders and functionaries scrambled for positions in government. Almost overnight the NSDAP was transformed from a disintegrating political party into a rapidly growing organisation enjoying the spoils of power.

(iii) The Growth of the SA to 1933

The growth of the SA in the eastern Prussian provinces before 1933 essentially reflected that of the Nazi movement as a whole. From its beginnings in 1925 until the breakthrough of 1929–30 the SA remained small and confined to the Nazis' early urban strongholds, but from the turn of the decade it grew swiftly and spread into the countryside to become, by mid-1931, the most powerful political army in eastern Germany.

As noted above, the beginnings of the SA in eastern Germany dated from 1925, when the newly formed Nazi Party groups began to form units to protect their meetings and distribute propaganda. Since the creation of the first SA groups antedated the establishment of a centrally structured, separate SA organisation in Munich, their first ties were to the local and regional party groups rather than to an SA hierarchy. In fact, the re-establishment of the SA on a nationwide level was among the last steps Hitler took when rebuilding the Nazi movement in the mid-1920s. He recognised that, in order to avoid a repetition of 1923, it would be necessary strictly to control the development of the SA and to limit it to political tasks determined by the party. In his pronouncement re-establishing the NSDAP in February 1925, Hitler specified that the SA was to be reconstructed 'according to the basic principles in effect until February 1923'[82] – that is, the SA was to remain a *political* formation and the propaganda troop of the party, and it would not be allowed to develop into an armed 'Wehrverband' as had happened during the months before the *Putsch*. In May 1925 the Munich party headquarters provided some further guidelines, urging local leaders to build up SA units. However, it was not until late summer 1926 – eighteen months after the NSDAP had been re-established – that a 'Supreme SA-Leader' was appointed and the framework for a nationwide organisation was created.[83]

Beginning in September 1926, the new 'Supreme SA-Leader' Franz Felix Pfeffer von Salomon (known generally as Franz von Pfeffer) – a former *Freikorps* leader, NSDAP *Gauleiter* in Westphalia during 1925 and 1926 and for a short period co-*Gauleiter* in the NSDAP *Gau* Ruhr – formulated a unified and hierarchical structure for the SA. He ordered the separation of the SA from the local Nazi Party organisations and in a long series of 'SA Orders' (SABE) and 'Basic SA Directives' (GRUSA) set forth organisational guidelines and disciplinary procedures, delineated the political duties of the SA and the relations between the SA and the party, and provided norms for SA uniforms and insignia.[84] The most important element of this new structure was the degree of independence from party officials given to SA leaders. Although party leaders could assign duties to the SA, it was left to the SA leaders to determine how these were to be carried out and, indeed, whether the SA could carry them out.[85] At the same time, a structure was developed which, in addition to being independent of the party hierarchy at all but the top level, was suited to rapid expansion – with the various SA units expected to split, amoeba-like, whenever they grew to sufficient size.[86]

At first von Pfeffer's guidelines were largely ignored; until almost the turn of the decade, the rather isolated Nazi groups in the eastern Prussian provinces were too small to apply them meaningfully. SA units rarely reached the strengths prescribed on von Pfeffer's charts and remained more closely tied to the party groups from which they had sprung than to regional SA leaders. As long as the SA in the eastern German *Gaue* numbered only a few hundred members concentrated in the larger cities, the question of a well-developed SA hierarchy was largely academic; only when the membership of the SA began to grow significantly, in 1929 and 1930, did its regional organisation assume importance. It was at this point that the structures outlined by von Pfeffer became a reality and the contradictions inherent in that structure (in the quasi-independent position of the SA vis-à-vis the party) became a source of considerable friction.

Of the eastern regions, the growth of the SA is best documented for Upper Silesia. Although the Nazi movement received a lower *level* of support in Upper Silesia than it did in the other eastern Prussian provinces, nevertheless its growth followed essentially the same *pattern* as elsewhere in eastern Germany. Thus a closer examination of the growth of the Upper Silesian SA should make clearer the main outlines of the development of the SA throughout eastern Germany.

Although the Upper Silesian industrial region had been an early centre of the Nazi movement in eastern Germany, during the mid-1920s the SA in Upper Silesia remained small. According to the first tally by regional authorities of the SA in the province, in February 1927, both the party and its protection squads were limited to rather tiny groups in the cities.[87] In Hindenburg there was an 'SA' of roughly 20 men; in Gleiwitz there was a 'Schutzstaffel' with 10 members; in Oppeln there was a Nazi Party group which later in the year was reported to have a 'Saalschutz' of 10 men;[88] and in Ratibor there was a 'Sportabteilung' with 40 members under the leadership of Kurt Kremser.[89] By January 1928 these groups had grown somewhat: in the industrial region, the Hindenburg SA group numbered 80 men and SA units had been established in Beuthen (20 members) and Gleiwitz (7 members); elsewhere in the province, the Oppeln group had increased to 45 men, the Ratibor SA maintained its membership of 40 and a new group was established in Kreuzburg with 12 members.[90] Thus altogether the Upper Silesian SA numbered just over 200 men at the beginning of 1928, hardly an impressive figure in a province with roughly 1.5 million inhabitants. But even this tiny membership was not sustained in the wake of the conflicts which plagued the Silesian *Gauleitung* in 1928: by April 1929 the Oppeln SA 'Sturm' had declined from 45 members to 19 and the Ratibor 'Sturm' from 40 to between 20 and 25.[91] The SA had, as yet, failed to gain a foothold in the Upper Silesian countryside.

The fortunes of the Upper Silesian Nazi movement began to change in mid-1929.[92] During the second half of 1929 the SA was given a boost when the NSDAP waged a joint campaign with the DNVP and the *Stahlhelm* against the Young Plan. Not only did the alliance with the conservatives give the Nazis additional exposure; it also brought members of the DNVP and the *Stahlhelm* into close contact with the NSDAP and the SA, allowing the SA to attract new recruits from the veterans' organisation.[93] The result was an increase in the number of storm troopers as the Upper Silesian Nazi movement made strenuous efforts to establish new NSDAP groups and strengthen the SA.[94] The upswing which began in 1929 accelerated during 1930, and by the time of the September *Reichstag* elections there were 1,857 members of the NSDAP in Upper Silesia and probably more than 500 of the SA.[95] Not only had the SA grown in the cities – in Hindenburg it numbered 80 members, in Ratibor 84 and in Oppeln 87 – but, even more important, it had begun to make inroads in the countryside. The 1930 elections provided a further impetus. According to police reports, at the beginning of October the Upper Silesian SA numbered 705 men in 25 separate groups,[96] and by June 1931 it had grown to 2,427 storm troopers in 60 groups.[97] At the end of 1931 it numbered 3,706 men in 116 groups – more than seven times the figure before the September 1930 elections.[98] By the winter of 1931/2 there was no longer a corner of the province which remained beyond the reach of the Nazi movement and its storm troopers. What is more, by the end of 1931 the SA far outnumbered its most determined opponent in Upper Silesia, the 'Fighting League against Fascism' (*Kampfbund gegen den Faschismus,* formed by the KPD in late September 1930), which in December counted roughly 2,200 members in the province. While both the KPD and the *Kampfbund* had grown steadily in Upper Silesia during 1931, they had not kept pace with the NSDAP and the SA.

Toward the end of 1931 the expansion of the Upper Silesian Nazi movement slackened. The immediate cause of the slowdown was a purge of 'undesired elements' which the NSDAP and SA felt compelled to undertake in late 1931.[99] Nevertheless, during the first four, election-filled months of 1932 the movement again grew significantly. The hectic election campaigning was accompanied by renewed efforts to extend the NSDAP and SA; according to police estimates, in April the Upper Silesian NSDAP had grown to 10,417 members in 228 groups and on 13 April, when it was banned by the Reich government, the SA numbered approximately 6,500 men.[100] The spring elections signalled a turning point, however. With the storm troopers disbanded between April and June, party membership stagnated, and when the SA re-appeared in the summer it too failed to grow further.[101] After the July *Reichstag* elections the task was no longer large-scale growth but to hold on to the adherents recruited during the previous three years. Following the November *Reichstag* elections (in which the Nazi Party lost 23,000 votes in Upper Silesia) things deteriorated further. Disheartened by the apparently ebbing fortunes of the movement, the membership of the Upper Silesian SA fell for the first time since it had become a mass organisation.[102] What rescued the SA, like the party, from disintegration was access to the spoils of power in 1933.

This basic growth pattern – and in particular the importance of late 1930 and 1931 for the crucial breakthrough into the countryside – was replicated in the other eastern Prussian provinces. In the East Prussian *Regierungsbezirk* Königsberg, for example, the storm troopers' organisation grew from roughly 250 men in April 1929 to 917 in September 1930 and to 4,450 in June 1931.[103] Whereas most of the SA men in the *Regierungsbezirk* came from the city of Königsberg in 1929, and nearly 30 per cent (265 of the 917) came from the provincial capital in the autumn of 1930, in June 1931 only

7.3 per cent (323) of the 4,450 SA men in the *Regierungsbezirk* came from Königsberg itself. The remainder came from the surrounding countryside. The development of the SA into a mass organisation in eastern Germany was largely the result of its success in the countryside, and this occurred at roughly the same time throughout the eastern Prussian provinces: in the wake of the 1930 *Reichstag* elections. Electoral success and the publicity it gave to the Nazi movement was vital to the rapid growth of the SA, which in turn made possible the increase in political violence during 1931 and 1932.

The one major respect in which the SA in Upper Silesia differed from that in the other eastern Prussian provinces was its total size; while its growth followed a similar pattern in Upper Silesia as elsewhere, the SA was relatively weaker in this predominantly Catholic region. Thus at the end of 1931 there were in the largely Protestant East Prussian *Regierungsbezirk* Allenstein approximately 3,000 Nazi storm troopers,[104] only marginally less than in Upper Silesia, which had a population roughly three times as great. The size of the SA before 1933, like the extent of electoral support for the NSDAP, was affected greatly by the religious affiliation of the population. It was in the Protestant regions of eastern Germany that the SA – like the Nazi movement as a whole – found its greatest strength, to become by far the largest formation involved in the rising tide of political violence. Indeed by 1932 in many such regions the members of the NSDAP and SA outnumbered those of *all* other parties and party formations respectively.[105] This obviously was to have devastating effects upon the ability of the Nazis' opponents to offer effective resistance to the Hitler movement.

The Size of the SA in the Eastern Prussian Provinces, 1931–1932[106]

	Upper and Lower Silesia	Pomerania	East Prussia	Border Province
January 1931	5,663	3,192	3,399	
April 1931	5,258	4,555	5,964	
September 1931		6,650		1,681
October 1931	13,715	7,856	9,745*	
November 1931	15,532	8,734	10,586*	
December 1931	17,525	10,005	11,809*	
January 1932	19,235	11,233	13,085*	
June 1932	32,217		17,385*	
July 1932	34,508		18,000*	
August 1932	36,106		17,835*	

* These figures are for the SA 'Gruppe Ostland', which included the SA in East Prussia and in Danzig. During the summer of 1932 the Danzig SA had roughly 3,500 members.[107]

The rapid expansion of the SA coincided with the appointment of Ernst Röhm as SA 'Chief of Staff' at the beginning of 1931.[108] An energetic organiser, Röhm quickly set about restructuring the SA.[109] In practice, however, the strengths of SA units often did not match those prescribed in the new guidelines. In September 1931, for example, in the Border Province SA-*Stürme* ranged from 50 to 280 members while some *Trupps* had as many as 70 to 90 members and others as few as ten, and in Pomerania the size of *Stürme* varied from 20 men in one case to 300 in another.[110] Röhm's structure, like that of von Pfeffer, was applied very flexibly; the primary concern was to recruit as many men into the SA as possible, not to preserve organisational symmetry.

As the SA in the eastern Prussian provinces expanded and its membership multiplied, a number of special formations was established. Among these was the 'SA-Reserve', first formed in 1929. The purpose of the Reserve was to bring into SA activities older party members 'who are not up to the continuous physical demands of the SA, but who nevertheless in special circumstances want to involve themselves like the active SA'.[111] The minimum age was forty; younger male members of the NSDAP were expected to join the SA proper. Due to the youthfulness of the Nazi Party membership as a whole, however, the Reserve never amounted to more than a fraction of the active SA, and it played only a small part in SA activities.[112] Other special SA formations had more specific roles. In order to provide suitable martial music for Nazi rallies and marches, 'SA-Kapellen' (SA bands) were formed, with due consideration given to storm troopers who had had musical experience during their military service.[113] SA men with access to motor vehicles often were organised in 'SA-Motorstürme'; storm troopers who had medical training were brought together to form an SA 'Sanitätsdienst' (medical service) in order to care for their injured comrades; special 'SA-Reiterabteilungen' were formed by members who owned horses; and in some coastal towns, for example in Stettin, SA 'Marine-stürme' were created.[114] In 1931 SA training schools were established in the eastern Prussian provinces, providing lower-ranking SA officers with military-style exercises and teaching them military skills it was believed they would need.[115] During 1932 special SA 'Propagandastürme' were formed in both Pomerania and Silesia; consisting primarily of unemployed storm troopers, these formations traversed the countryside spreading Nazi propaganda from village to village.[116] As the political violence mounted in 1932 yet more special formations were created to cope with especially dangerous tasks. Early in 1932 some SA *Stürme* in East Prussia set up select 'Schutzab-teilungen' (protection sections), whose duties involved protecting Nazi supporters against the 'red terror' and gathering information about the activities of their left-wing opponents.[117] Finally, toward the end of 1932 in Silesia, where the SA leadership was convinced that the Nazi movement would gain power only by means of an SA *Putsch*, special 'Bereitschaftsstürme' (stand-by *Stürme*) were prepared for the bloody confrontation believed imminent.[118]

The main problem posed by the rapid expansion of the SA was that it weakened the bonds between local SA and party groups and heightened the possibility of conflict between the two branches of the movement. Whereas during the 1920s the small bands of storm troopers generally had close relations with the party groups from which they had sprung, from 1930 onward SA units looked increasingly toward the regional and national SA hierarchy for instruction and backing in the case of dispute. Thus the growth of the Nazi movement led to the forming within the storm troopers' organisation of a separate identity vis-à-vis the 'civilian' NSDAP. With the expansion of the SA, conflicting loyalties developed within the movement which were to cause considerable difficulties for the Nazi leadership.

CHAPTER III

The SA in its Social Context

(i) The Social Composition of the SA in Eastern Germany

THE question of the social composition of the membership of the Nazi movement has occupied a central place in the discussion of the rise of National Socialism.[1] Of particular concern has been the extent to which the movement succeeded in fulfilling its oft-mentioned mission of winning the working classes for German Nationalism. As far as the NSDAP is concerned, there exists little doubt that it was largely a party of the middle classes and that, relative to the population as a whole, it attracted a rather low proportion of workers to its ranks. According to its own official membership statistics, 26.3 per cent of those who had joined by 14 September 1930 and 31.5 per cent of those who had joined by 30 January 1933 described themselves as workers, whereas in 1925 45.1 per cent of the employed German population were classified as workers.[2] In a table, probably compiled by the NSDAP for internal use, in which the occupations of recipients of the first 386,000 party membership cards (that is, of members who joined between 1925 and the end of 1930) were tabulated, only 8.4 per cent of the total were classified as 'workers' (presumably unskilled); on the other hand, shopkeepers and artisans were extremely well represented.[3] More recent statistical compilations of the NSDAP membership – by Michael Kater for the Nazi Party as a whole, and by Lawrence Stokes for the NSDAP in the town of Eutin in Holstein – have presented a basically similar picture,[4] although an examination of the NSDAP in Westphalia has led Detlev Mühlberger to stress that the party had a 'substantial working-class representation'.[5]

In the eastern Prussian provinces the social composition of the NSDAP appears to have been similar to that elsewhere in Germany, once allowance is made for the structural peculiarities of the East. Thus the more rural character of the region meant that the NSDAP in the eastern *Gaue* recruited relatively more farmers and fewer workers than did the party nationwide; and since the East contained fewer sizeable administrative and commercial centres, the party there had a rather smaller percentage of civil servants and white-collar employees among its members than in central and western Germany. On the whole, however, the Nazi Party in eastern Germany conformed to the general pattern: while it was able to attract support from virtually all sections of the community, its membership was drawn disproportionally from the *Mittelstand,* from among white-collar employees, shop-keepers, civil servants and farmers.[6]

The question of the social composition of the SA has been more difficult to answer with certainty. The Nazi organisation made less effort to document systematically the composition of the SA than of the NSDAP itself, and the often rather casual nature of SA membership made record-keeping problematic. Nevertheless, there have been a number of attempts to examine the backgrounds of the storm troopers, the first of which date from before the Nazis gained power. On the eve of Hitler's appointment as Reich Chancellor, the party published a statistical breakdown of the 593 SA leaders, from *Sturmführer* upward, in the 'Gruppe Nordmark' (Schleswig-Holstein).[7] These figures demonstrated that the SA leaders were primarily young men, most of whom came from groups of the *Mittelstand* and only a few of whom were workers. Statistical evidence about the general membership of the Berlin SA, compiled by the police from 1,824 record cards seized in raids of homes and offices of SA leaders in early 1931, yielded rather different results: the Berlin SA also was an organisation of young men – almost 90 per cent of the membership was under thirty – but workers, most of whom were skilled, formed roughly half the membership.[8]

Subsequent research has tended to confirm that the SA attracted a significant number of workers, particularly skilled workers, to its ranks. In his work on the Nürnberg SA, Eric Reiche has presented data which indicate that one third of the storm troopers in that city were workers, mostly skilled.[9] In a quantitative study of autobiographical sketches of early Nazis collected by Theodore Abel during the 1930s, Peter Merkl noted that 42 per cent of the SA members, as opposed to 33.1 per cent of the sample altogether, could be classified as 'blue-collar workers'.[10] Statistics published by Michael Kater also suggest that there was a fair number of workers in the SA, particularly in rural Bavaria, although his evidence about the SA membership in Munich and Frankfurt/Main indicates that there were surprisingly few working-class storm troopers in those cities.[11] And in his analysis of the Nazi movement in Eutin, Lawrence Stokes extrapolates from information about 54 members of the SA in the town in 1929 to assert that 'the "proletarian" character of the SA in Eutin seems indisputable'.[12]

Most recently our knowledge of the social composition of the SA has been broadened considerably by two heavily documented quantitative studies: by Mathilde Jamin of the SA leadership and by Conan Fischer of the organisation's rank and file. In a sophisticated, computer-powered investigation, Jamin has determined that relatively few workers rose within the SA hierarchy; according to her calculations, as many as three quarters of the SA officers were drawn from what may be described as the lower-middle classes.[13] Fischer, on the other hand, stresses that workers comprised a large proportion of the rank-and-file membership. According to Fischer, that proportion was much greater among the SA membership than among the membership of the NSDAP as a whole, with unskilled workers forming 13.4 per cent of his sample of SA men before 1933 and (semi-) skilled workers forming 43.8 per cent.[14] However, even these high percentages do not match the proportion of workers among the 18 to 30-year-old male German population at the time; according to calculations based upon the 1933 census data, roughly two thirds of the male labour force under the age of thirty were classified as workers.[15] It was from this age group that the SA recruited most of its members.

Unfortunately, relatively little is known about who these workers in the SA were and how they lived. Statistical evidence about the composition of the SA therefore must be approached with caution, since the categories used are often ill-defined, imprecise and even misleading.[16] One aspect of the difficulties involved in attempting to classify the SA membership was suggested by Heinrich Bennecke, a former SA leader in Saxony, when he described the SA in Leipzig and Dresden thus:

> In terms of occupation the SA consisted of roughly 40 per cent white-collar and corresponding occupations and 60 per cent workers. Nevertheless it must be kept in mind with such a rough estimate that the greater part of these workers came from artisan and middle-class families [*Handwerker- und Bürgerfamilien*] and because of the consequences of the inflation and the economic conditions of the time had not received the training which otherwise they would have obtained.[17]

The question of who came from a worker household and who from a *Mittelstand* household is far from clear, and involves a set of social and economic relationships which are probably impossible to reconstruct. Even more difficult is the problem of what conclusions may be drawn from such information as we have about the social backgrounds of the SA membership. This is particularly the case with regard to the proportion of workers in the NSDAP or SA. What does this explain? To attempt to account for the activities of the SA or its relationship to the Nazi Party by referring to the occupational backgrounds of its members is a reductionist exercise which, as will be seen, can be misleading. What such data may indicate, however, is where the Nazis got their support and some of the reasons why they got that support.

Since the Nazi organisation made little effort to record the composition of the SA membership before 1933, the most important source of information about the backgrounds of the storm troopers is the police. This, of course, has its drawbacks: such information is rather limited for eastern Germany, and it is not possible to check the accuracy of police judgements or their

classification criteria. In August 1930 the Prussian Ministry of the Interior
distributed to the regional authorities a confidential memorandum request-
ing a 'precise survey of the organisation of the storm sections', together with
details about their leaders, their strengths, the financing of the SA and the
NSDAP, and information about the social backgrounds and age breakdown
of the storm troopers.[18] Accompanying this request, apparently to serve as a
model for reports to follow, were an organisational chart of the Silesian SA
and tables of the social composition and age distribution of the SA 'in an
eastern district' (presumably Silesia as well):

34.6%	Farmers, young farmers and agricultural supervisors
27.8%	Artisans and artisans' apprentices
12.3%	Salaried employees and apprentices
9.6%	Industrial workers
7.6%	Agricultural workers
5.6%	Members of technical and miscellaneous professions
2.5%	Civil servants and white-collar workers in public service

11.5%	up to 20 years
58.5%	from 20 to 30 years
24.7%	from 30 to 40 years
5.3%	over 40 years

Responses to the Prussian Interior Ministry's request for information about
the SA have been located only for East Prussia, and it may be that reports on
the SA in industrial regions or Catholic areas, such as Upper Silesia, looked
quite different. The surviving statistical analyses by the police describe the
SA in the East Prussian *Regierungsbezirke* Königsberg and Allenstein during 1930 and 1931. Included in these reports are tabulations of the crude
occupational backgrounds and age distribution of more than 6,500 SA men,
in the provincial capital Königsberg as well as in some of the most rural
regions of the entire country, recorded at the time when the East Prussian
SA was experiencing its most rapid growth.

The SA in the *Regierungsbezirk* Königsberg, October 1930[19]

Total strength: 917 men

31.4%	Farmers, young farmers and agricultural supervisors
26.5%	Artisans and artisans' apprentices
18.5%	Salaried employees and apprentices
2.2%	Industrial workers
9.4%	Agricultural workers
6.0%	Members of technical and miscellaneous professions
2.0%	Retired civil servants and white-collar workers in public service
4.0%	Students

16.1%	up to 20 years
65.3%	from 20 to 30 years
15.4%	from 30 to 40 years
3.2%	over 40 years

The SA in the *Regierungsbezirk* Königsberg, June 1931[20]

Total strength: about 4,450 men

35.0%	Farmers, young farmers and agricultural supervisors
28.8%	Artisans and artisans' apprentices
17.2%	Salaried employees and apprentices
11.7%	Industrial and agricultural workers
4.3%	Retired civil servants and white-collar workers in public service
3.0%	Students

28.4%	up to 20 years
56.6%	from 20 to 30 years
11.0%	from 30 to 40 years
4.0%	over 40 years

The SA in the *Regierungsbezirk* Allenstein, June 1931[21]

Total strength: 2,144 men

44.9%	Farmers, young farmers and agricultural supervisors
33.3%	Artisans and artisans' apprentices
10.8%	Salaried employees and apprentices
7.7%	Agricultural workers
3.1%	Retired civil servants and white-collar workers in public service

28.4%	up to 20 years
56.2%	from 20 to 30 years
11.3%	from 30 to 40 years
4.1%	over 40 years

The statistics compiled by the East Prussian police indicate that the SA failed to make significant inroads into either the urban or rural proletariat in the province. In October 1930, when nearly 30 per cent (265 of 917) of the SA men in the *Regierungsbezirk* Königsberg came from the provincial capital, only slightly more than 2 per cent of the SA membership were described as industrial workers, although the city was the most important industrial centre in East Prussia and more than one quarter of its male labour force were workers in industry and crafts.[22] In the *Regierungsbezirk* Allenstein, which encompassed some of the areas in Germany most dependent upon agriculture and contained many large estates, agricultural labourers formed only about 8 per cent of the SA membership in 1931; by way of contrast, according to the 1925 census 50.8 per cent of the male labour force in the *Regierungsbezirk* were classified as workers and 20.7 per cent were agricultural workers.[23] A much greater proportion of the East Prussian SA were classified as artisans and their apprentices. Whereas in the *Regierungsbezirk* Königsberg 28.8 per cent of the storm troopers were placed by the police in the artisan category in 1931, according to the 1925 census figures 24.5 per cent of the male labour force in the region were employed in industry and crafts in all capacities together.[24] In the *Regierungsbezirk* Allenstein, while one third of the SA membership were classified as 'artisans and artisans' apprentices', only 18.4 per cent of the male labour force were employed in industry and crafts.[25] Salaried employees and their apprentices were also well represented in the SA; in both the *Regierungsbezirke* Königsberg and Allenstein the percentage of salaried employees in the SA more or less matched the proportion among the male labour force of salaried employees and civil servants combined.[26] Although many men placed in the 'artisan' category in the police statistics probably were classified as workers in the census data (and this, no doubt, accounts for some of the discrepancy between these figures and the findings of Reiche, Merkl and Fischer), the low proportion of workers among the East Prussian SA remains noteworthy. Where the SA made inroads among wage labourers, apparently this was principally among those employed in small workshops where, presumably, the influence of the employer over his employees was greater and the chance that workers may have been organised by the Left was less than in larger enterprises.

Not surprisingly for so rural a province as East Prussia, 'farmers, young farmers and agricultural supervisors' formed the largest category of storm troopers. Even in the *Regierungsbezirk* Königsberg in 1930, when the SA in the region was still concentrated in and around the provincial capital, this group comprised nearly one third of the membership. Here it should be noted that the SA was probably less popular among farmers themselves than among their sons. There were a number of reasons for this. In the first place, as one East Prussian district NSDAP leader noted after the November 1932 election setback, 'our farmer is by no means a revolutionary'.[27] Furthermore, for someone with full-time responsibility for a farm, including the need to look after crops and feed animals at regular intervals, the frequent travel and active commitment demanded of SA members may have made involvement in the organisation impossible. Thus the SA appears to have attracted first and foremost the younger members of the farming community – who probably were underemployed on their fathers' farms (at a time when the possibility of finding work in the cities had disappeared), who had sufficient time to devote to SA activities, and who saw themselves as 'revolutionary'.[28] That it was primarily the sons of farmers who joined the SA seems to be confirmed by detailed reports from *Kreis* Johannisburg, in the *Regierungsbezirk* Allenstein, describing the membership of the individual SA groups in the district during 1931.[29] According to these reports the farmers' sons clearly outnumbered the farmers, by a factor approaching four to one. In an organisation four fifths of whose members were under the age of thirty, it could hardly have been otherwise.

Another revealing aspect of the detailed data from *Kreis* Johannisburg is the extent to which they indicate what sorts of men banded together to form a small SA group. Personal contacts and friendships certainly were very important in the formation of such a group. As described in these reports, quite often sons of farmers and farm labourers were in the same group, sometimes together with a number of artisans as well. Certain categories tended to predominate in one group as opposed to another, but it nonetheless is noteworthy that a group of roughly fifteen SA men frequently would be so socially heterogeneous. This suggests that the social distances separating the artisan or his apprentice, the farmer's son and the farm labourers were not very great in many rural communities, and points to the effects of physical isolation upon the rapid growth of the Nazi movement in eastern Germany. In his study of the Nazi rise in Schleswig-Holstein, Rudolf Heberle observed that the NSDAP achieved its greatest election successes in small communities which were relatively isolated, far from urban centres and from public transport.[30] In such localities, Heberle argued, pressures against a pluralism of political opinion were greater than in communities having closer contact with the outside world. This observation has particular relevance for the eastern Prussian provinces, which contained some of the most remote communities in the entire country. It was in the outlying Protestant regions of eastern Germany, for example in the south-eastern corner of East Prussia, that the NSDAP achieved some of its best election results and that the SA proved especially successful in attracting members and in gaining a dominant position vis-à-vis its political opponents. The success of the SA in these isolated communities, and the heterogeneity of its membership, reflected the fact that in many such villages at the end of the Weimar period the Nazis enjoyed the support of virtually the entire population.

As the concept of leadership played so important a role in the Nazi movement, the composition of the SA leadership is also revealing. Information about the leadership, especially at the lower levels, can offer insight into the character of the organisation as a whole, since the lower-level leaders (*Schar-*, *Trupp-* and *Sturmführer*) rose from the ranks rather than being appointed from above. Thus, at the lower levels at least, there often would be little social distance between the SA leaders and the men they led. Data collected by the police in East Prussia indicate that the composition of the SA leadership bore many similarities to that of the general membership.[31] Of the 177 *Schar-*, *Trupp-* and *Sturmführer* in the *Regierungsbezirke* Königsberg and Allenstein for whom occupations were given in the police lists of June 1931, only eleven were listed as 'workers' and an additional one was an agricultural labourer (*Instmann*); of these, eight were *Scharführer*, leaders at the lowest level. As with the general membership, middle-class occupations predominated, with independent farmers, small businessmen and artisans forming the largest contingents. Unlike the membership as a whole, however, farmers were more numerous than their sons, and owners of small businesses were more strongly represented, particularly at the *Sturm-* and *Truppführer* levels. That the SA leaders tended to have more solid occupations reflected the fact that they often would use their businesses to support their group, to pay for members' uniforms, transportation costs, rent for group headquarters and so forth. The success of a local SA leader could depend upon his ability to subsidise his group, something requiring financial resources which wage labourers and the unemployed were unlikely to possess.

During the summer of 1931 the police in Pomerania also collected information about the organisational structure and leadership of the SA. In July a rather incomplete list, containing data about twenty *Sturmführer* and five *Standartenführer* in the province, was prepared.[32] As in East Prussia, occupations such as 'businessman', 'agent', 'bookkeeper' and 'pharmacy-owner' predominated, and the five Pomeranian *Standartenführer* had been employed as follows: one was a bank clerk (who was removed from the SA due to drunkenness), another a cavalry captain (*Rittmeister*), two were independent farmers, and the last was a building contractor (who left the SA to join Walther Stennes' breakaway organisation).[33] In September a more comprehensive list, with the occupations of 54 Pomeranian *Sturmführer*, was compiled.[34] Here too the absence of workers among the local SA leadership is striking; only two of the *Sturmführer* were described as workers, and middle-class occupations predominated. Especially significant was the number of *Sturmführer* who apparently had their own businesses (for example, 'inn-keeper', 'well-builder', 'estate-owner', 'cattle dealer'), as well as the number who occupied supervisory positions (for example, 'agricultural supervisor', the manager of an unnamed branch store, a former police major, a 'livestock-breeding inspector' and various master craftsmen). Clearly financial wherewithal played an important role in enabling an individual to become a successful local SA leader.

Evidence documenting the composition of the SA comparable to that from East Prussia or even Pomerania unfortunately is lacking for the other eastern Prussian provinces. For Upper Silesia there are only a few incomplete lists of SA leaders from 1930, and for Lower Silesia and the Border Province data are totally unavailable. Thus the important question of whether the social backgrounds of storm troopers in eastern Germany's industrial cities differed significantly from the picture outlined above cannot be answered. The only, scanty evidence from eastern Germany's major centre of heavy industry, Upper Silesia, concerns SA leaders, not the led. In early 1930 six *Sturmführer* were recorded: a painter, a saddlemaker, a tailor, a local government officer, a businessman and a fitter.[35] In September 1930 the police listed twelve local SA leaders in Upper Silesia: an engineer, a commercial traveller, a journeyman smith, a businessman, a carpenter, a freelance actor, a miner, a local government officer, a management trainee, a plumber and two fitters.[36] Although such evidence provides too meagre a basis to describe the SA in the Upper Silesian industrial region, it does suggest that, in terms of its lower-level leadership, the SA probably appealed to similar groups there as in East Prussia and Pomerania.

The SA leaders at *Gau* or provincial level also appear to have had what might be described as middle-class backgrounds; in eastern Germany none came from either the urban or the rural proletariat. In East Prussia the first leader of the SA had been the Königsberg baker Waldemar Magunia. His successor in 1927 was Werner Siegfried, who worked as a supervisor on a landed estate in *Kreis* Rastenburg. He in turn was followed as East Prussian SA leader by Karl-Siegmund Litzmann, a former army officer, son of General Karl Litzmann, and a landowner who directed the SA from his estate in *Kreis* Insterburg. The SA leadership in the Border Province presents a similar picture. The overall leader of the SA in the 'Ostmark' was Siegfried Kasche, a 'businessman' who had attended Gymnasium and then worked as a farmer, a bank clerk, in the glass industry and in the textile trade.[37] Kasche's 'Chief of Staff' from April 1931 was Alfred Lindemann, who likewise was a 'businessman'.[38] The leader of the SA in the Border Province itself was Arno Manthey, an independent farmer in *Kreis* Flatow. In Pomerania and Silesia as well the SA leadership tended to be drawn from the *Mittelstand* and owners of agricultural property. Hans Lustig, for example, who led the Pomeranian SA until the Stennes affair in 1931, had been a customs official.[39] His counterpart in Silesia, Kurt Kremser, was described by the police as a 'businessman'.[40] And Andreas von Flotow, who led the Upper Silesian SA during 1931 and early 1932 and the Pomeranian SA for a short period during 1932, was a landowner.

Another feature of the backgrounds of the SA leaders was the importance of their military careers. Military experience involving more than just the normal wartime service had been a central element in the lives of many, if not most, of the eastern German SA leadership. For example, after leaving Gymnasium Siegfried Kasche continued his education with the Cadet Corps Potsdam and Lichterfelde, and he went on to participate in the conflicts in the Baltic countries after the First World War. Arno Manthey had been active immediately after the war in the fighting against Polish insurgents in the Netze district and the region around Bromberg. Hans Peter von Heydebreck, the leader of the Pomeranian SA from mid-1933 until he was killed in 1934, was among the most widely known of the *Freikorps* leaders. Hans Hayn, Edmund Heines' 'Chief of Staff' with the Silesian SA, had belonged to several *Freikorps* units in eastern Germany, had been a member of the Schlageter sabotage group in the Ruhr and of the Black Reichswehr, and had participated in the aborted Küstrin *Putsch*.[41] Hans Ramshorn, leader of the

Upper Silesian SA from mid-1932 until his murder in 1934, had joined the Royal Prussian Cadet Corps at the age of ten, became an army officer before his seventeenth birthday, served in *Freikorps* units in the post-war struggles in Thorn and the Baltic, and participated in the suppression of the Ruhr uprising in 1920.[42] Thus many SA leaders had spent much of their lives in uniform; unwilling to integrate themselves into normal civilian life, they sought to remain 'soldiers' in a succession of right-wing paramilitary groups during the 1920s and finally found a home in the SA.

The most notorious of the 'political soldiers' in the SA was Edmund Heines, who commanded the Silesian SA from mid-1931 until he was shot in 1934. Although described in police reports as a 'businessman', Heines spent virtually his entire adult life either in military service or in right-wing paramilitary organisations.[43] Born in Munich, where he attended Gymnasium until volunteering for military service in 1915, Heines became a reserve officer in 1918 and after the war joined the *Freikorps Roßbach*. In the *Freikorps* he took part in the Baltic campaigns of 1919, the suppression of the Ruhr uprising in 1920, and the suppression of the Polish uprising in Upper Silesia in 1921. In 1922 he joined the NSDAP and became an SA leader in Munich, where he participated in the attempted Nazi *Putsch* in 1923. During the mid-1920s Heines spent most of his time in the active service of various right-wing groups – the *Roßbach Gruppe,* the *Bund Oberland,* and the Munich SA (from which he was expelled for a time in 1927) – and his career was chequered with violent incidents and repeated arrests. In 1928 he was found guilty for his part in the killing in 1920 of a fellow member of the *Freikorps Roßbach* suspected of betraying the group (the much publicised 'Feme' murder). He was sentenced to fifteen years imprisonment, later reduced to five years of which he served little more than one. Throughout his career Heines' only experience as a 'businessman' had been as the owner of a small firm, the 'Sportversand Schill', which sold uniforms and other materials to paramilitary groups and went bankrupt in 1926.

But for his widely known homosexuality, Heines was perhaps the archetypal 'political soldier' of the radical Right during the Weimar Republic.[44] His sole vocation had been violence from the time he left Gymnasium until he was murdered at Stadelheim in 1934. Rather than representing particular class interests in politics, Heines and SA leaders like him seem more accurately described as exponents of a military ethos and violence, almost for its own sake, in domestic political life. Nevertheless, it remains significant that these political desperados had decidedly middle-class backgrounds. Although the violent political culture exemplified by Heines was not a clear expression of social or class interests, its origins appear to have been located in a particular social milieu.

Although the composition of the SA leadership contributed towards shaping the character of the organisation as a whole, there were important differences between the leadership and the rank and file. First, for the regional leadership involvement in the SA was not merely a matter of political conviction: it was a career. The regional SA leaders were no longer primarily 'businessmen', 'farmers' or whatever; they were full-time political activists who earned their livings from their participation in the Nazi movement. Second, the regional SA leadership displayed a homogeneity which was not entirely representative of the membership, or even of the lower-level leadership. And third, while almost all the leadership shared experience at the front and in various military and paramilitary formations, the rank-and-file membership generally was too young to have had the opportunity to serve in the German armed forces. While for the leadership involvement in the SA may have meant a continuation of a military life by other means, for many of the rank and file it formed a substitute for action in a 'real' military uniform.

Discussion of the composition of the SA should take account of the concern of the Nazi movement to draw members from the working classes and the eagerness of its leaders to claim success. For example, in a report from January 1930 outlining the rapid growth of the East Prussian NSDAP, Erich Koch asserted that his organisation was gaining 1,000 new members per month and that 60 per cent of these were workers.[45] Although this claim appears exaggerated, it was echoed by many Nazi leaders. In a propaganda leaflet written in the early 1930s, an SA-*Sturmführer* in Podejuch, near Stettin, declared:

> We National Socialists are absolutely convinced that the honest and upright supporters of the Communist Party will come to us entirely of their own volition. We observe this daily. The worker who comes to us of his own volition has recognised that Adolf Hitler is the true leader of the workers.[46]

According to the propaganda chief of the NSDAP in Insterburg in early 1931, new members were flocking to the local Nazi organisation and among these were 'extremely valuable *Volksgenossen*, for the most part workers who have abandoned the left-wing camp'.[47] And from Upper Silesia Hans Ramshorn wrote in September 1932 that 'the SA recruits its members from among workers and the poorest strata of the population'.[48]

Although these claims appear buttressed by some evidence that the SA in eastern Germany was not unsuccessful in attracting proletarians into its ranks, they also often served to underpin the propaganda of the movement and the reputations of the Nazi leaders who made them. Certainly workers were welcomed into the SA, all the more since they offered 'proof' that National Socialism indeed appealed to all sections of society. Yet the self-conscious assertions that Hitler was 'the true leader of the workers' and attempts to draw workers into the SA seem to betray a relative failure in attracting working-class members. Here some remarks by the leader of the

NSDAP in Rosenberg, in the *Regierungsbezirk Westpreußen* in East Prussia, are suggestive. In late 1930 he complained to the *Gauleitung* about an incident in which the local SA leader had insulted a newly-recruited, working-class storm trooper, and lamented the damage caused by such behaviour: 'It is in any case difficult enough to attract workers into our SA' without episodes of that kind occurring.[49]

Despite an apparent underrepresentation of workers among the SA membership in eastern Germany, it seems clear that many storm troopers came from among the unemployed. Nazi leaders testified repeatedly to the large number of SA men without work. For example in November 1930 the local Nazi leadership in Pillkallen, East Prussia, claimed that 80 per cent of the SA in the district were unemployed;[50] in Breslau the SA leadership asserted in September 1932 that 60 per cent of the storm troopers in the city had been 'unemployed for years';[51] and according to a Nazi history of the Silesian SA the entire SA in Gleiwitz had been without work before 1933.[52] There is a considerable amount of evidence to suggest that these claims contained some truth, even if they were perhaps somewhat exaggerated.[53] In Stettin, for example, young men who loitered on the city's skid row, the 'Bollwerk' along the river near the main rail station, formed the membership of one SA group.[54] In particular, the SA hostels (SA-*Heime*), set up throughout the eastern regions in 1930 and 1931, attracted largely the unemployed and destitute.[55] That many of the storm troopers were without work is suggested further by the fact that those age groups to which the vast majority of the SA belonged (and which formed a disproportionally large part of the population)[56] suffered the worst unemployment.[57] Yet to note the high number of unemployed storm troopers is not to explain why they joined the SA.[58] Although unemployment and, especially in rural eastern Germany, underemployment was crucial in giving so many young men the time to devote to SA activities, it would be mistaken to see their decision to join the Nazis as a simple consequence of dissatisfaction caused by failure to get work. The paths to the SA involved an altogether more complicated set of social and political relationships.[59]

The main features of the composition of the SA in the eastern Prussian provinces appear to have been the youth of the membership, a relative underrepresentation of workers, and a remarkable degree of social heterogeneity which characterised the organisation. What emerges most clearly is that the SA was an organisation to which virtually all the young men involved with the Nazi movement belonged. It did not consist of any one of the various class elements which formed the movement as a whole, but rather an age cohort. The SA encompassed the young and able-bodied Nazi sympathisers who had sufficient time and motivation to become the activists of the movement. Thus it attracted a membership which differed from that of the NSDAP primarily in that it was younger and exclusively male; and it is this fact, rather than a fundamentally different social or political appeal, which best explains the apparent social differences between SA and party members.[60]

(ii) **Life in the SA**

Among the most striking characteristics of the Nazi movement was the amount of time and energy which its adherents devoted to it. Without the thousands of SA men prepared to commit themselves to the service of the NSDAP, the waves of propaganda which accompanied the Nazi rise hardly would have been possible. But what precisely did belonging to the SA mean? How did the political activism which marked the Nazi advance shape the lives of SA members? What made the SA attractive to so many young men, and how did the activities of the SA fit into the political strategy of the movement as a whole?

According to the guidelines drawn up in the mid-1920s, the SA was intended primarily as a protection squad for the Nazi Party and its member-ship was to be responsible for all those tasks which involved the threat of violence:

> As a disciplined organisation of [NSDAP] members, the SA is called upon above all to enforce the security of our mass meetings as stewards and protection squads and to block or subdue disturbances caused by Marxist terror attacks. The SA shall also, if necessary, take charge of the protection of individual party members on the street and in the factory. Its members also shall carry out those propaganda tasks which involve physical danger. These are: enlightenment in the factories, in workshops, the sale of newspapers in red districts of cities, the distribution of leaflets during elections, as well as the protection of the agitators of the move-ment who have been entrusted with these tasks.[61]

The duties of the SA were wide-ranging and essential to the smooth func-tioning of the NSDAP. They revolved around violence and the threat of violence, and this was directed primarily against the Left. The *raison d'être* of the SA was not, in the first instance, to act as anti-Semitic crusaders or to shape the policy of the Nazi movement, but to challenge the Nazis' left-wing opponents.

The ceaseless activity of the Nazi organisations, which has been documented for a number of regions,[62] also characterised the movement in the eastern Prussian provinces. In addition to the countless public rallies, there were members' meetings of the local NSDAP, 'Sprechabende' (infor-mal gatherings where party members invited acquaintances who had expre-ssed interest in the movement), and mass gatherings outside the local district such as those at which Hitler spoke – all of which required the protection of the SA. Over and above these were the meetings of the SA group itself and the steady stream of propaganda tasks – the distribution of leaflets, selling of party newspapers, disruption of opponents' meetings, staging of marches with the necessary flag-waving and musical accompaniment – which were reserved for the SA. Just protecting the meetings of the local Nazi Party group could be a full-time occupation, and during election campaigns political rallies were nightly affairs.[63] Thus involvement in the SA was quite different from the passive membership and token payment of dues associated with belonging to so many other organisations. Membership in the SA could easily dominate and structure the lives of the storm troopers.[64] Nightly rallies, frequent group meetings and training sessions, propaganda marches and the never-ending task of distributing party literature would leave relatively little opportunity for a social life outside the SA. Especially since taverns tended to become associated with the supporters of one or another political movement,[65] for many young Nazi activists participation in the SA was their social life.

Nevertheless, membership in the SA did not necessarily involve a deep commitment to the Nazi cause. Joining an SA group could be a rather ill-defined affair, and frequently the stipulation that storm troopers be members of the NSDAP was ignored. In *Kreis* Goldap in East Prussia one SA-*Sturmführer* was taken to task in mid-1931 by the local NSDAP leader for having expanded his *Sturm* to a strength of 118 men, *none* of whom had joined the party.[66] The issue at stake was the payment of party dues: the party organisation wanted dues paid, while the SA leader presumably found it easier to attract members if participation in SA actitivies did not involve the payment of initiation fees and monthly dues to the NSDAP. The finances of the Nazi Party clearly were placed in jeopardy when, as with one *Sturm* in the East Prussian *Kreis* Lyck in late 1931, only 10 per cent of the storm troopers paid their initiation fees and party dues.[67] At the same time, the question of the formal membership of SA men in the NSDAP often was complicated by delays in processing applications, and in one instance SA men were prevented from joining the party for a time because their initiation fees had been stolen by their group leader.[68] *De facto* membership in the SA and formal membership in the Nazi organisation were not necessarily synonymous, and the character of the SA militated against it becoming so. The first priority of the SA was to provide protection squads for the NSDAP, and the requirements of a smoothly functioning party bureaucracy often took second place.

Further complicating our picture of SA membership is the high turnover among the storm troopers. While the organisation attracted a stream of new recruits during the early 1930s, men were also constantly leaving SA ranks for a number of reasons: the internal conflicts which periodically shook the movement, the disciplining of SA members, dissatisfaction, disillusionment and waning interest. Morale reports collected by the SA leadership in September 1932 indicate the extent of this fluctuation. In Silesia, for example, the following changes in the membership were reported:

| July 1932: | 21.5% increase | 7.4% decrease |
| August 1932: | 13.8% increase | 6.9% decrease[69] |

By the end of August only about two thirds of the Silesian SA had belonged to the organisation for more than two months. The effects upon the SA of such fluctuation were considerable. It meant that, at any given time, a large number of the storm troopers had a rather fleeting involvement with the Nazi movement, and suggests that there was a great difference between the activist core of the SA, which stuck by the organisation, and the large number of 'sunshine soldiers' who attached themselves to the SA when it suited them. The volatility of the SA membership suggests further that to speak of a force fanatically committed to the Nazi ideology may be misguided.[70] The constant flux meant that SA leaders could face considerable difficulties in keeping their units together, and implies that the activities of the SA were designed not merely to support the campaigns of the party but also to keep idle hands busy and to implant a sense of active involvement. On the other hand, the rapid turnover among the SA membership gave the Nazi leadership a great advantage in dealing with revolts, as rebellious elements could be isolated quickly, outnumbered and forgotten as the membership changed.

Men came to the SA via two main routes. The first was their acquaintances. The speed with which the Nazi movement grew in eastern Germany during the early 1930s suggests the political conversion of large sections of communities virtually *en masse*. It seems that groups of young men who associated with one another socially, who worked or drank together, would often continue their acquaintance within the context of the SA. Indeed, the SA might be seen as a substitute for youth gangs, or perhaps more precisely their continuation within the framework of a political movement. The second route to the SA was the political rally. One of the most important functions of Nazi rallies was to recruit new members, and many young men who attended at the urging of friends, out of general interest or due to boredom, thus found their way into the SA.[71] It would appear that young men with time to attend such rallies, especially those who knew people in the Nazi movement already, proved susceptible to enticements to join the SA.

The SA in turn played an important role in attracting young men to the Nazi movement as a whole. The military-style hierarchy, marches and uniforms of the SA undoubtedly helped draw recruits to Nazism. This was of particular significance in a society where military life and values were praised highly but in which the armed forces could not offer the nation's youth the opportunity for military service. One perceptive contemporary observer of the SA described its marches as a 'substitute for Kaiser parades' in which 'instead of His Majesty there stands Adolf Hitler'.[72] Many joined in order to play soldier, and the disappointment felt by storm troopers when prohibited by the government from wearing their brown uniforms illustrates the importance of this aspect of the SA.[73] The military character of the SA appealed not only to its own members, but often also to the general population. The presence of a uniformed and relatively disciplined force created the impression of a young and dynamic movement and offered a visible contrast to the ageing defenders of Weimar democracy.[74]

Along with military-style trappings went the military-style training of storm troopers. It was common for groups to hold regular training sessions in methods of self-defence, such as jiu-jitsu,[75] and field exercises were scheduled frequently as well. In early 1931, shortly before he was removed as 'Supreme SA Leader' in eastern Germany, Walther Stennes underlined the importance of such training and directed the *Truppführer* under his command to give military instruction at their group meetings, instruction which was to include practice with grenades and machine guns.[76] Such orders were not just talk, for police searches often revealed considerable numbers of weapons in the hands of the SA.[77] The functions of the repeated military drill, field exercises and practice with weapons were twofold in the eyes of the SA leaders. On the one hand, many felt it necessary to prepare for a civil war believed imminent, particularly in late 1932.[78] On the other, military exercises and weapons training formed, as one Silesian SA leader put it, an 'especially good means for raising the morale and fighting spirit of the SA'.[79]

In addition to the military exercises mentioned above, there were also special 'courses' intended primarily for lower-level SA officers (*Sturm-* and *Truppführer*). Military-style drill occupied a key place in these courses, together with ideological instruction. In East Prussia such courses were held in Lyck beginning in early 1931, and in Pomerania the SA established a 'leadership school' for the training of SA officers in the summer of 1931.[80] In Silesia by mid-1931 the SA had set up a well-developed programme of activities involving sports exercises, running, marching, the building of temporary bridges over ditches, traversing obstacles such as gullies and swamplands, and instruction in warding off physical attack.[81] For one session in March 1932 it was even planned to include special training in the use of snowshoes. Many of those who took part in these courses were unemployed; someone with a steady job would have had difficulty in obtaining two or three free weeks to participate. On one Silesian course, for example, 64 of the 100 places available were allotted to unemployed members of the SA (at a fee of 6 RM) and the other 36 to employed members (at a fee of 8 RM). The training offered was often better suited to the campaigns of the First World War than to the street battles of Weimar Germany, but preparation for actual military action was not its function. Essentially these courses were used to boost morale and keep especially the unemployed SA members active and satisfied.

A further feature of membership in the SA was the amount of travel it could involve. Touring around the countryside, travelling in order to protect rallies in neighbouring districts and marching through various towns and villages took up much of the time of an SA group. Already during the late 1920s the SA had begun to use mobile tactics to help the movement expand beyond its early urban strongholds. In the summer of 1928 virtually the entire Pomeranian SA went by bicycle on 'propaganda trips' every Sunday 'in order to prepare new ground for rallies',[82] and the SA in Königsberg travelled regularly by road and rail into rural districts in order to protect party meetings.[83] During the following summer the Königsberg SA and SS were mobilised for Sunday 'Auto-Propaganda', into the surrounding countryside, with participation compulsory.[84] Similarly, in 1930 the SA in Elbing began to devote Sundays to 'Landpropaganda', partly to spread the movement into rural areas, partly to avoid the surveillance of the Elbing police, and partly because violence between Nazis and Communists had become so frequent in the city that no Elbing innkeeper would risk the destruction of his premises by hosting a Nazi rally.[85] Bringing SA men considerable distances allowed the Nazis to stage impressive demonstrations even in relatively small communities. For example, in July 1930 more than 600 storm troopers converged on the Pomeranian town of Cammin, having travelled from Wollin, Greifenberg, Naugard, Treptow a. Rega, Stettin and Pasewalk (100 kilometers distant by road).[86] In July 1932, when he spoke in Königsberg, Hitler was greeted with a march past of virtually the entire East Prussian SA.[87] The most striking example of SA travel came when hundreds of storm troopers from the eastern Prussian provinces journeyed across Germany to participate in the massive demonstration in Braunschweig in October 1931.[88] For many young men, membership in the SA offered not only activity, adventure, novelty and a substitute for military service; it also offered them a chance, perhaps the first in their lives, to escape the boredom and isolation of their own homes and communities.

(iii) **The Role of the 'SA-Heime'**

Particularly important for many unemployed Nazi activists were the SA-*Heime,* hostels established to shelter jobless and homeless storm troopers. Yet the first attempts to see to the material needs of the membership were not a response to poverty among SA men. The initial impetus was provided by the difficulties which the SA had faced in feeding the storm troopers massed at the 1927 Nürnberg party rally and which led von Pfeffer in 1929 to instruct SA units to provide their own kitchens at large demonstrations.[89] Nevertheless, it was the deepening of the economic crisis and the growth of the SA which made the provision of meals and beds for unfortunate SA men a necessity. As economic conditions deteriorated, offering room and board brought the local Nazi organisations young men constantly at their disposal, helped attract new recruits and provided a welcome subject for propaganda.

As elsewhere in Germany, in the eastern Prussian provinces SA-*Heime* were founded during late 1930 and 1931 in virtually all the major population centres. The first were set up in the larger cities; for example, the first SA hostel in East Prussia was founded in 1930 in the Nazi stronghold of Roßgarten in Königsberg.[90] During 1931 SA-*Heime* were also established in many district and market towns. The hostels in rural regions tended to be smaller than those in the cities and were less likely to offer overnight accommodation on a permanent basis, since the problem of homelessness was less severe in rural communities. The creation of a network of SA-*Heime* was particularly well documented in Upper Silesia, where they first appeared in the spring of 1931. The first was established in Beuthen in March, followed by hostels in Kreuzburg (described as a 'reading home') in June and in Neisse and Oppeln soon thereafter.[91] By September the Upper Silesian SA also had set up hostels in Groß Strehlitz, Ratibor, Hindenburg and Rosenberg.[92]

The hostels occupied a key place in the activities of many SA groups. SA-*Heime* and SA-*Lokale* (taverns where SA groups congregated) provided rooms for group meetings and training sessions, as well as for members to gather when they had nothing else to do. This often led to the further radicalisation of the storm troopers, as it removed them from society at large and kept them in contact primarily with other young men in similar circumstances.[93] The hostels also brought tactical advantages to the SA. According to the Prussian Interior Ministry, which noted their proliferation with alarm, the purpose of the SA-*Heime* was not only to provide 'unemployed members with communal board in the cheapest possible manner and to give them a place to live', but also 'to encourage attempts to keep SA groups . . . ready for action at any time'.[94] In Upper Silesia the police observed:

> The use of the SA-*Heime* has in practice not . . . been limited to providing room and board to party members who are homeless or passing through and to SA comrades; the premises of the SA-*Heime* also serve as a domicile for regular guard details, the purpose of which is to be on alert to be called into action for suppport in political disturbances and for the protection of party members. There is regular instruction for this purpose.[95]

The hostels fulfilled a number of security functions: they were often shelters for SA men who may have faced danger had they sought a place to stay on their own, and they provided a ready guard to protect local party and SA offices from attack. At the same time, the SA-*Heime* and SA-*Lokale* served as bases from which attacks against the Nazis' opponents were planned and carried out. For example, the Nazi historian of the movement in Roßgarten wrote that the local SA hostel 'often served as a refuge for SA comrades who were being pursued by political opponents' and asserted that 'originally the entire struggle against the red mob was organised from here'.[96] Predictably, the SA-*Heime* soon posed considerable problems for the police, who came to regard them as a 'danger for public security and order'[97] and frequently closed them down.[98]

Unemployment among the SA membership was central to the character of the hostels. Their inhabitants and the recipients of meals served in their 'emergency kitchens' consisted primarily of unemployed young men. In addition, it was the unemployed who were used to provide full-time guard duty for the hostel itself as well as the headquarters of the local and regional NSDAP, and the labour of the unemployed storm troopers was used for the renovation and furnishing of the hostels. In Ratibor, for example, the fifty-two wooden beds in the SA-*Heim* which opened in August 1931 had been built by unemployed SA men.[99] The presence of jobless 'party comrades' in the hostels was cited often in Nazi propaganda as evidence of the 'socialism' of the movement; special press coverage always was given to the closure of an SA-*Heim* by police, and much play was made of how the destitute occupants thus were made homeless.[100]

In the SA-*Heime* men were lodged as cheaply as possible, and it was common for a hostel to be a converted barn or disused factory warehouse owned by a party member.[101] In many ways the spartan life in the hostels resembled that in military barracks. The importance of the SA-*Heime* both for the Nazi movement and for their inhabitants perhaps can be best illustrated by a closer look at specific examples, such as the large hostel in Roßgarten, as described by the police in October 1931:

Former storage rooms in the rear building of Vorderroßgarten 17/19 have been fixed up for the SA-*Heim*. The *Heim* consists of one assembly room, a sitting room for the guard, a conference room, a so-called 'Standarten' room and a kitchen, from which needy SA men and other party members are fed. The provisions are procured from voluntary contributions from National Socialist shopkeepers and farmers. At all times of the day cold and warm food, coffee, tea, cocoa and milk, but no alchoholic drinks, are handed out. Six men of the so-called staff guard are lodged permanently in the sitting room. The staff guard consists of about 20 men and has to watch over the offices of the *Preußische Zeitung,* the *Gau* office . . . and the SA-*Heim* day and night. It also often happens that other party members, for example from other areas, stay overnight. The 'Standarten' room is used for small conferences of the leadership. In the large assembly room there are daily meetings and exercises for the individual SA-*Stürme*. The SA-*Heim* also serves as a gathering point for SA members for marches. Also lodged here are special squads which, if necessary, are transported by the NSKK – National Socialist Motor Vehicle Corps – to protect or reinforce meetings both in the area and beyond.[102]

In contrast to the Roßgarten hostel, the SA-*Heim* in Oppeln was rather smaller and more typical of the SA hostels in eastern Germany. The Oppeln hostel formed part of the city's 'Brown House' Nazi headquarters, which was opened in late August 1931 with great fanfare, a large demonstration, and speeches by Silesian *Gauleiter* Brückner, Upper Silesian *Untergauleiter* Adamczyk and Silesian SA leader Heines.[103] For the hostel itself the NSDAP had rented a former brewery from the firm Schultheiss-Patzenhofer, at a cost of 170 RM per month. The money for the necessary renovation came from donations by party members and sympathisers, and the *Heim* was to house in particular 'SA men who have lost their jobs or have been thrown out of their families because of their political views'.[104] The hostel provided full board and lodging for about sixteen unemployed SA members, who paid varying amounts (ranging from 1.50 to 8.00 RM per week) for their keep and were supposed to be ready for action at all times and keep the premises clean. These arrangements were short-lived, however, as the *Heim* was closed in October when the Nazis were accused of breaking the rental agreement by making structural changes to the building.[105]

The SA-*Heim* in the industrial city of Beuthen also had a short life, but for somewhat different reasons. The Beuthen hostel was set up in March 1931, and by mid-May twenty SA men were living in it.[106] Those who could pay (that is, those who received either unemployment benefit or other financial help) were expected to contribute 10 RM per month toward their upkeep; those who had no support whatsoever were lodged for free and given monthly pocket money of between 3 and 5 RM, the costs being met by the local NSDAP. In return for their keep, the SA men in the hostel were constantly at the disposal of the local leadership of both the SA and the NSDAP, and in addition spent time hawking newspapers for the local party organisation. It was the unusually high rent of 240 RM per month which proved the Beuthen hostel's undoing. The troubles began in July, when the SA member charged with managing the hostel absconded (it was rumoured to Argentina) with the rent he had collected from the men being lodged.[107] From August the Beuthen NSDAP, which had been quite generous in its support of needy SA men, was no longer able to pay the rent; and in October the hostel was forced to close.[108]

Without the SA men in the hostels at its disposal it would have been difficult for the Nazi movement either to mount so hectic a propaganda campaign or to present so powerful a challenge to the Left. Yet the role of the SA-*Heime* should be kept in perspective. Particularly in the rural regions of the eastern Prussian provinces, the hostels were thinly scattered and only a small proportion of the SA membership were lodged in them. Even in Upper Silesia, with its concentration of heavy industry and urban poverty, the SA-*Heime* housed only a tiny fraction of the total SA membership. In late 1931, when the development of the SA hostels in Upper Silesia was at its peak, the eight hostels in the province lodged at most 200 men on a permanent basis, while the Upper Silesian SA as a whole numbered 3,706.[109] Altogether, probably not more than 5 per cent of the SA membership lived in the hostels at any one time. The hostels housed part of the activist core of the SA, not the great mass of its members. It is for this reason that the importance of the SA-*Heime* remained rather greater than the proportion of storm troopers housed in them might imply. The SA-*Heime* formed the focus for the activities of many SA groups, and the men who lived in them made a large contribution to the violent street politics of the Nazi movement.

CHAPTER IV

The SA and the Nazi Movement

(i) The SA and the Financing of the Nazi Movement

BEFORE 1933 virtually all local regional Nazi organisations faced financial difficulties. While the movement's headquarters in Munich may have benefitted periodically from the contributions of wealthy and influential supporters, local and regional groups were left to rely largely upon their own resources. This meant that Nazi activities at the local level had to be funded primarily from membership dues, members' donations, profit from the sale of party newspapers and literature, and the proceeds from successful political rallies.[1] The largely middle-class composition of the NSDAP was a great advantage; members with relatively solid sources of income were more likely to pay dues regularly and contribute to the cause. At least as important a source of income, particularly for local party groups, were political rallies. Since admission charges invariably were levied, a good turnout could leave a local group with a healthy profit after the speaker's fee, rent for the hall and other expenses were met.[2] Thus at the local and regional levels the Nazi movement was dependent upon its own activities for the money necessary to keep it afloat.

This pattern of financing the Nazi movement had important implications for the SA. First and foremost, it made the activities of the storm troopers – particularly their services as protection squads at party rallies and as hawkers of party newspapers – indispensable for the local party organisations. The importance of the storm troopers for the financial health of the NSDAP gave them a certain leverage, and buttressed assertions that the SA was not merely an appendage of the party. At the same time, however, the generally precarious financial position of the party organisations meant that local and regional NSDAP leaders were often ill-disposed to provide extra funds for the activities of the SA, while they expected SA men to pay party dues regularly and promptly. Thus the financing of the Nazi movement gave rise to a peculiar combination of dependence and conflict which characterised the relations between the NSDAP and the SA before 1933.

The financial obligations connected with membership in the SA could be considerable. Since SA men were supposed to be members of the NSDAP they were expected to pay party dues, although the dues for storm troopers were somewhat lower than for party members who did not belong to the movement's uniformed formations. On the eve of Hitler's appointment as Reich Chancellor, for example, there were three rates of NSDAP dues: 80 Pfennig per month for members of the SA, SS and Hitler Youth who were unemployed and had no income; 1 RM for unemployed members of the SA, and Hitler Youth who had an income (unemployment benefit) and for other party members without any income; and 1.50 RM for all other members of the NSDAP [3] In addition, storm troopers were required to pay a monthly SA-insurance premium of 20 Pfennig (from March 1930, 30 Pfennig) to insure against the hazards of being in the SA,[4] and were expected as well to pay for their uniforms. If an SA member purchased the complete outfit – including brown shirt, cap, belt, dagger and brown trousers – the cost was substantial, and the sale of such clothing provided the Nazi organisation with an important source of revenue.[5] Many men lacked the complete uniform, however, and prosperous party members often would sponsor storm troopers, paying their dues or buying their uniforms.[6]

The funds which went to the SA did not come from its membership directly but via the NSDAP. Dues paid by party members were divided among the local party groups, the *Gaue* and the NSDAP Munich headquarters. Until the summer of 1930, 10 Pfennig of the monthly dues, together with some of the profit from the sale of Nazi literature and SA uniforms, were earmarked to cover the costs of the SA; after the 1930 SA rebellion in Berlin, a supplementary fee of 20 Pfennig for the SA was added to party dues.[7] This money was handed over to the 'Supreme SA Leadership' in Munich, which distributed monthly sums to regional SA groups. The regional SA groups also received money from the NSDAP *Gauleitungen*,[8] and then distributed funds to their subordinate units, to the *Untergruppen* and *Standarten*. The sums involved were not large. For example, in Upper Silesia the SA–*Untergruppe* received a monthly allowance of 300 RM in the summer of 1932, while the SA–*Standarte* in Breslau received between 30 and 50 RM.[9] In addition, the regional SA groups supplemented their income through the sale of party literature and a share of the profits of the '*Sturm*' cigarette factory in Dresden, an uneven but sometimes quite significant source of revenue.[10] These funds were intended to cover not the activities of the local SA groups but the administrative costs of the regional organisations: the costs of maintaining offices, legal expenses, aid for needy SA men, and monthly salaries for *Gau* SA leaders.[11] At the local level, the financing of SA activities was carried out on an *ad hoc* basis, as arrangements for paying for such things as transport were to be made with the appropriate local party group.

The SA was not permitted to seek new income at its own intiative at either the local or regional level. According to regulations laid down by the

NSDAP Reich Treasurer, Franz Xaver Schwarz, the *Gauleiter*, together with the *Gau* treasurers, determine the financial affairs of the regional Nazi organisations.[12] This meant that, at all levels, the SA had to look to the party for its funding; at no time did the SA establish financial autonomy, a point crucial in its relations with the NSDAP. Despite the separate hierarchy and ethos of the SA, when money became an issue the party (whether in the form of a local NSDAP leader or party treasurer Schwarz) asserted its control and assumed the role of a stern and suspicious paymaster.

This might not have led to conflict were the financial resources available sufficient to cover the costs of the propaganda activities and administrative expenses of the SA. However, they were not. At a meeting of SA leaders with Schwarz in November 1930, for example, the heads of the SA in eastern Germany were virtually unanimous in their condemnation of existing arrangements; according to Walther Stennes, all the groups in the East except those in Magdeburg and Anhalt were experiencing serious financial difficulties.[13] Silesian SA leader Kurt Kremser argued that the SA in his region was receiving less than it was due, and requested special compensation for the additional costs arising from a recent Hitler rally in Breslau.[14] From Pomerania, Hans Lustig complained that the funds he received from the *Gauleitung* (150 RM in September and 250 RM in October) were so inadequate that in order to provide his organisation with the necessary cash he had been forced to pawn his typewriter and duplicating machine. Election campaigning proved a particularly great financial drain, especially in 1932. Rent for offices and SA-*Heime* and the costs of transport to and from many Nazi rallies throughout the countryside drove the SA into debt even where relations with the party leadership remained reasonably good.[15] Where relations were poor, as in Pomerania, the problems were extreme. In eastern Pomerania during the summer of 1932 the *Gauleitung* stopped payments to the SA 'Untergruppe Pommern-Ost', which found itself 'without a Pfennig'; in order to keep his organisation afloat, *Untergruppenführer* Rosenhagen was compelled to contribute the salary he received as Prussian *Landtag* deputy.[16] In the neighbouring 'Untergruppe Pommern-West' things were little better. In August 1932 the *Untergruppe* had a total income of 1864 RM, much of which was used to help destitute SA men and to cover the costs of the special *Propagandastürme* roaming around the countryside.[17] At the same time, the accumulated debt of the *Untergruppe* amounted to 13,496.48 RM, while the *Propagandastürme* had incurred additional debts of 24,525.41 RM.

Although financial difficulties greatly affected the operations of the Nazi movement and gave rise to much friction within it, it must be stressed that this did not fundamentally restrict the activities of the SA or the NSDAP. The Nazi Party was able to mount impressive propaganda campaigns despite the problems of insufficient funds and heavy debt. The most revealing aspect of the indebtedness was not that it betrayed the poverty of the Nazi movement and its followers, but that the NSDAP and SA had someone to go into debt *to*. Unlike their Communist opponents, SA groups found it possible to run up considerable debts because there were people prepared to extend them credit. The SA was able, for example, to draw on the resources of supporters such as Otto Fuchs, a member of the NSDAP in Landsberg, *Kreis* Preußisch Eylau (East Prussia), who in February 1931 supplied SA uniforms to the local group at a cost of 1,000 RM. [18] The SA-*Heime* also demonstrate that the Nazis had access to financial resources; while the hostels frequently closed down due to failure to pay rent, it is nonetheless revealing that so many people were willing to allow the SA to use their property in the first place. Similarly, the degree to which the SA used motor transport for its propaganda activities shows that there were numerous party members who owned motor vehicles and were prepared to lend them to the movement. Thus the level of debt which the NSDAP and SA faced perhaps points less to a weakness of the movement than to a strength, to access to resources necessary for its propaganda campaigns.

(ii) The SA and the Party Organisation

According to the guidelines issued by von Pfeffer in 1926, the SA was to be strictly subordinated to the NSDAP. It was to form a part of the Nazi Party, not to stand alongside it, and the party leadership was to determine 'what shall happen with the SA'. [19] The SA was a 'means to an end'. It was not intended to play a substantive part in forming the policies or strategy of the movement; its proper role was envisaged as that of a loyal party formation which would carry out the tasks assigned to it by the NSDAP.

Despite their clarity, the guidelines delineating the position of the SA within the Nazi movement did not prevent conflict between the storm troopers' organisation and the party. The immediate causes of the friction tended to be personality conflicts, organisational disputes and quarrels arising from financial difficulties. These were often interrelated. When a local or regional chief of the Nazi Party could not get along with the SA leader in his area, this frequently led to disputes about who could and should give orders to whom and generally made more difficult the financing of the SA's activities. Withholding funds was a weapon commonly used by NSDAP leaders against their recalcitrant opposite numbers in the SA; organisational disputes often masked personal rivalries; and personal animosities were frequently exacerbated by disagreements which arose over finances and jurisdiction. Underlying many of these conflicts was the sense of separateness which had been generated within the SA. As the SA grew there had developed among its members – and, especially, its leaders – a sense that they bore the main burden of the struggle, that the activists in the SA were superior to the 'civilians' and 'politicians' among the NSDAP leadership, and that the storm troopers often were treated unfairly by party leaders who regarded the SA as the tool rather than the elite of the movement.[20] Such feelings certainly were exploited and fanned by SA leaders concerned to build up their positions against competitors in the NSDAP hierarchy, and they formed an undercurrent of resentment which gave petty squabbles between the SA and the party an explosive potential.

The rivalry between the SA and NSDAP and the tension arising from the SA's position, subordinate yet parallel to the NSDAP, meant that all the eastern German *Gauleiter* found themselves at odds with the SA leadership at some point. The case of the Silesian SA is revealing. Although *Gauleiter* Brückner and SA leader Kurt Kremser had been allies in 1928, [21] as the SA began to assume mass proportions relations between the Silesian NSDAP and SA leaders deteriorated. According to Brückner, the fault lay squarely with the SA and its leader, who in 1930 allegedly began to interfere in the affairs of the party organisation.[22] The conflict was essentially over who should command whom. In Brückner's opinion the SA was supposed to be a 'keen instrument in the hand of the political leadership', while the SA leadership denied party functionaries the right to order the storm troopers about. As the friction grew, Brückner withheld funds from the SA and sought to obtain an SA leadership more amenable to the wishes of the *Gauleitung.* At this point the Munich SA headquarters came to Kremser's aid. In November 1930 Chief of Staff Otto Wagener defended his Silesian commander against Brückner and staunchly asserted the independence of the storm troppers' organisation vis-à-vis the party, claiming that the *Gau* SA leader was 'neither subordinate to the *Gauleiter* nor does he have to report to him'.[23] Then, toward the end of 1930, after rumours had been circulated that Kremser had a Jewish background, Hermann Göring intervened. At the urging of the corpulent Nazi peacemaker an agreement was reached: the *Gauleiter* and the SA leader henceforth would refrain from attacking one another; Brückner would forbid further talk about Kremser's alleged Jewish ancestry; and Kremser would cooperate with the party leadership.[24] Nevertheless, the friction continued through the winter of 1930/1 and did not really disappear until the end of March 1931, when Kremser supported Stennes' rebellion and was thrown out of the Nazi movement.[25]

It is significant that Brückner had little difficulty with Kremser's successor, Edmund Heines. Despite his extreme brutality, flagrant law-breaking and homosexuality, Heines never challenged the authority of the Silesian party leader. NSDAP leaders were far less concerned about the propriety of the SA leadership than about challenges to their own authority.

It was in Pomerania that perhaps the greatest amount of friction developed between the party and the SA. As in Silesia, the relations between the SA and the NSDAP in Pomerania had shown signs of strain during 1930, but the decisive turn came in the spring of 1932 when both organisations received new leaders: in the wake of the Stennes revolt Hans Lustig was replaced as Pomeranian SA leader by Hans Friedrich, a former *Stahlhelm* leader from Demmin; and at almost the same time Walther von Corswandt was replaced as *Gauleiter* by the abrasive young lawyer Wilhelm Karpenstein.[26] Upon his appointment, Karpenstein immediately launched an offensive against Friedrich. The new *Gauleiter* was able to draw support from the party hierarchy as well as from some people in the SA who may have resented Friedrich's *Stahlhelm* background and sudden rise in the Nazi movement; Friedrich enjoyed the backing of the bulk of the SA and SS.[27] Within a few months Karpenstein had managed to isolate his rival, and in early August 1931 the SA leadership in Munich, concerned to maintain good relations with the party, relieved Friedrich temporarily of his post.

The trouble within the Pomeranian Nazi movement continued through 1932, and when Friedrich returned to lead the SA 'Untergruppe Pommern-West' in September he described the relationship between the SA and the party leadership in the province as 'the worst possible'.[28] The immediate cause of conflict was money. According to Andreas von Flotow, leader of the SA 'Gruppe Ostsee' (which encompassed all of Pomerania), the organisation faced a steadily deteriorating financial situation and Karpenstein was to blame for preventing the SA from receiving funds it was due.[29] Despite Karpenstein's promises of a settlement of financial arrangements, relations between the Pomeranian NSDAP and SA did not improve, even after the victory of the Nazi movement in 1933. Friedrich, appointed to head the entire Pomeranian SA for a second time in February 1933, remained on bad terms with the *Gauleiter* and soon was compelled to relinquish his post once again. (He was replaced in September 1933 by von Heydebreck, who managed to reach agreement with Karpenstein.) For more than two years the Pomeranian NSDAP had been at odds with the SA, and the source of the friction was not social conflict generated from below but conflicting ambitions at the top.

In East Prussia also relations between the SA and the NSDAP were influenced greatly by the personality of the *Gauleiter*, who aroused opposition not only from the SA but also within the East Prussian Nazi Party.[30] During 1931 a group opposed to Erich Koch formed in Insterburg. Its leader was Georg Usadel, a Nazi *Reichstag* deputy since since September 1930 and *Gau* expert on 'race and culture', and among the members of the Insterburg group was the East Prussian SA leader Litzmann.[31] The hope of the dissidents had been to force Koch and his business manager and deputy, Georg Heidrich, from their posts; when they failed to achieve this many of them resigned their party positions and joined the SA.[32] Thus the SA became the centre of inner-party opposition to Koch, who responded by turning to his friend and ally Gregor Straßer, the NSDAP organisational chief. During late 1931 Koch alleged a 'systematic alienation campaign on the part of the SA against the *Gauleiter*', accused the SA of staging rallies without consulting the party organisation, claimed that the SA leadership was spreading false rumours about its treatment by the *Gauleitung* and attempting to 'sow mistrust against the political leadership', and in December categorically refused to cooperate with Litzmann during the coming year.[33] Litzmann, for his part, levelled the criticism that the *Gauleitung* was not fulfilling its financial obligations to the SA.[34] In January 1932 the police noted that in many parts of East Prussia cooperation between the NSDAP and the SA had broken down, as party leaders failed to provide promised speakers and propaganda materials for functions organised by the SA.[35] Relations between the two branches of the Nazi movement remained bad in 1932, and reached their nadir when in some districts the SA refused to help with the autumn election campaign.[36] Once again the ambitions which the Nazi movement nurtured among its leaders erupted in conflict.

The difficulties between the *Gau* NSDAP and SA leadership were mirrored at the local level. Among the most important sources of friction was the issue of jurisdiction. Had a local party leader the right to order the SA to protect a rally or to demand the services of storm troopers without involving the local SA chief? Such questions were hotly debated. In Glogau, for example, the fact that the leader of the town's NSDAP had met with storm troopers without SA leaders present led in January 1932 to a vigorous protest by the area *Standartenführer*.[37] Local party leaders who were excluded from the affairs of SA units were equally distressed. In November 1930 the district leader of the NSDAP 'Bezirk Barthen' (which encompassed the East Prussian *Kreise* Rastenburg, Gerdauen and Bartenstein) complained:

> The SA, the pride of our movement, is at the present time no longer built on the basis of readiness for sacrifice and [is no longer] our elite; it is being degraded into a mercenary troop. The [NSDAP] *Kreisleiter* can no longer give instructions to the *Sturmführer,* the *Ortsgruppenleiter* can no longer give instructions to the *Truppführer*. The SA has meetings of its leaders in which the responsible political leader is not allowed to take part. Various SA leaders are proud of their new 'rights'. At the present time the situation is the same in many places in the province.[38]

In *Kreis* Ortelsburg an SA leader asserted in early 1930 that the storm troopers were required to protect meetings only when ordered to do so by their 'military' (i.e. SA) leaders, and after a dispute in 1931 the Ortelsburg SA threatened to withdraw all protection from party rallies.[39] In Lyck a disagreement was triggered by the establishment of a hostel which the local NSDAP (which paid the rent and running costs) claimed should serve all Nazi organisations but which the SA insisted was an SA-*Heim* exclusively; according to the local SA leadership, the NSDAP had no jurisdiction over the SA in this or any other regard.[40] In Görlitz in late 1930 local SA leaders refused to have anything to do with the party;[41] and in *Kreis* Sensburg problems arose when, after a march in early 1931, an SA leader told assembled storm troopers that the political leadership had no right to give them orders.[42]

The many disputes between the SA and the NSDAP indicate the powerful centrifugal forces within the Nazi movement and point to the crucial role of Hitler in keeping it together.[43] Lacking either a socially homogenous membership or a coherent ideological focus, the movement depended greatly upon the cult of the leader for the cement to keep it from splitting apart. The frequency and bitterness of conflict, both at *Gau* and local levels, suggests that without the figure of Hitler binding the various strands of the Nazi movement together, the SA might well have gone its own way. Yet, for all the concern which the friction between the SA and the party evoked, it did not seriously hamper the growth or the propaganda activities of the Nazi organisations. When the movement did face a grave threat in the autumn of 1932, the cause was not conflict between the SA and the NSDAP but a general downturn in electoral fortunes, financial position and morale which affected the storm troopers and the party functionaries alike. The effectiveness of the Hitler cult, together with the rapid growth of the Nazi organisations, ensured that conflict at the local and regional levels did not really threaten the survival of the movement.

Conflict between the SA and the NSDAP before 1933 seems on the whole to have been peculiarly devoid of overt political or ideological content. Only rarely did disputes appear explicitly to involve policy. Rather they generally revolved around organisational questions: who had the right to order whom; who owed money to whom; the determination to defend prerogatives; and the clash of headstrong personalities. It does not seem that supposed social differences between the membership of the SA and that of the NSDAP somehow led to conflict between the two organisations, as sometimes been asserted.[44] In none of the many disputes between the SA and the NSDAP in the eastern Prussian provinces were contradictory economic, social or class interests at stake. The picture of a self-consciously working-class SA confronting a largely middle-class NSDAP bureaucracy is not confirmed by detailed investigation of the Nazi movement in eastern Germany. Nor does the issue of homosexuality, which was prevalent among the Silesian SA leadership from 1931 onward, appear to have been a significant source of friction. The difficulties between the SA and the NSDAP tended to be sparked by the ambitions of Nazi leaders concerned to expand their little empires but unprepared to challenge Hitler or the general goals of the movement as a whole.

Not only were the types of people attracted to Nazism apparently prone to petty, quarrelsome behaviour, but the movement's organisational structure *itself* seems to have generated much of the conflict within it. The key concept which shaped both Nazi politics and the Nazi organisation was struggle. This not only meant struggle against the Left, the Jews and other enemies of the 'Volksgemeinschaft'; it also meant struggle *within* the movement, which was commanded by a leader and guided by a philosophy positing that such struggle was a healthy thing.[45] Despite the dismay of many Nazi supporters at the continual in-fighting, there was essentially no point in suppressing struggles within the movement in the interest of attaining some transcendent goal; struggle itself was a goal. It was in this *fundamental* sense that the conflicts within the Nazi movement might be regarded as ideological. While the friction between the SA and the NSDAP can be seen as largely organisationally generated, it was at the same time an expression of the ideological foundations of National Socialism (and not of social cleavages among the Nazis' supporters).

(iii) The Stennes Revolt in the Eastern Prussian Provinces

The most serious SA revolt against the party leadership in eastern Germany was the rebellion of the supporters of Walther Stennes in 1931. In a sense this revolt was a consequence of the rapid expansion of the SA from 1929. Faced with the need to better organise the growing SA, in February 1929 von Pfeffer had named six regional leaders to represent the 'Supreme SA Command' in areas covering a number of party *Gaue*. For eastern Germany – an area which included East Prussia, Danzig, Pomerania, Mecklenburg, Magdeburg-Anhalt, Brandenburg-Ostmark, Silesia and Berlin – von Pfeffer appointed as his 'Supreme SA-Leader – Deputy East' Walther Stennes, a former police captain whom he had known since 1919.[46] Stennes took seriously the need to defend the interests of the SA, if necessary against the NSDAP *Gauleitung*, and consequently achieved considerable popularity within the SA while arousing animosity among party leaders.

Stennes' concern to defend the SA involved him in in two rebellions of the Berlin storm troopers, the first in the summer of 1930 and the second in the spring of 1931.[47] The first revolt, at the end of August 1930, came during the campaign for the September *Reichstag* elections, in the wake of von Pfeffer's resignation. Due to mounting discontent within the Berlin SA, the SA leadership in the city called an extraordinary meeting on the 27 August. There it was decided to withdraw the services of the storm troopers from the party until certain demands were met: that a fixed proportion of party dues be allocated: that SA leaders be included on the list of *Reichstag* candidates, that a fixed proportion of party dues be allocated to the SA, that the SA be made independent of the NSDAP, and that the *Gauleiter* be prohibited from giving orders to SA leaders or approaching SA members other than through the SA leadership. After it proved impossible to reach agreement with the Berlin *Gauleiter,* Goebbels, SA men occupied the *Gau* headquarters. Goebbels rushed to Munich for aid, and on 1 September Hitler travelled to Berlin to quell the mutiny. Hitler first visited a number of district SA headquarters to speak with his troops, after which he met with Stennes; then he held a meeting before roughly 2,000 storm troopers and announced that he personally would take the place of von Pfeffer as 'Supreme SA Leader' and that the financial position of the SA would be improved. The intervention had the desired effect, and the SA resumed protecting party meetings and distributing party propaganda.

After the 1930 Berlin revolt, the SA underwent some important changes. While Hitler had assumed nominal command of the organisation, he left the actual running of the SA to Otto Wagener, who continued as its 'Chief of Staff', the post he had held under von Pfeffer. Meanwhile, Hitler offered the leadership of the SA to Ernst Röhm, who replaced Wagener on 4 January 1931 and immediately set about planning for re-organisation. Röhm's schemes aroused Stennes, whose position they threatened,[48] and in late March 1931 Röhm went to Berlin to discuss the matter with the eastern German SA leader. From that point the conflict escalated rapidly. Although the immediate cause of the confrontation in March/April 1931 remains unclear, it is apparent that far from settling differences the March meeting sharpened them. Afterwards Stennes met with his SA leaders in Berlin to denounce Röhm and the Munich Nazi leadership. Faced with an open revolt, Hitler dismissed Stennes at the beginning of April and expelled him from the party.

Once Stennes' dismissal was known, SA units in Berlin again occupied the *Gau* headquarters. as well as the offices of the Berlin NSDAP newspaper *Der Angriff,* surrendering these buildings only when the *Gauleitung* called the police. For a second time Goebbels fled to Munich, and Hitler published a notice in the *Völkischer Beobachter* announcing that anyone who supported Stennes would be expelled from the NSDAP. Together with the SA leaders who remained loyal to him, Stennes attempted to found his own 'national socialist' movement. However, he soon was isolated. Hitler convinced himself that Stennes had been working for enemies of the Nazi movement, and Göring was given the task of purging the SA of rebellious elements in eastern Germany; in Berlin itself the purge was supervised by Edmund Heines. The position of eastern German SA commander was filled provisionally by Paul Schulz, a former army officer who, together with Berlin SS chief Kurt Daluege, worked to prevent the rebels from influencing their old SA units. Soon thereafter Röhm abolished Stennes' old post entirely.

As in Berlin, in the eastern regions Stennes received support from among the SA leadership. In Silesia his cause was taken up by Kurt Kremser, who called publicly for the SA to stand up in Stennes' defence.[49] Kremser criticised 'the political leaders, who even today are of the opinion that the SA is here only in order to die', and ordered his subordinates to have no further contact with the party leadership. Claiming that 'the path along which Captain Stennes led us was the only practicable one which was leading to the liberation of the German people from servitude', the Silesian rebel alleged that Hitler had been misled by a sinister 'camarilla' intent on destroying the 'revolutionary SA'. According to Kremser, 'our struggle is not aimed against the person of Adolf Hitler, but rather against those around him', especially the NSDAP Reich Treasurer Schwarz. In Pomerania rebellious SA leaders, headed by Hans Lustig, issued a similar call.[50] Addressing 'all comrades with whom for years we have fought shoulder to shoulder in the NSDAP', they asserted that 'the NSDAP had abandoned the revolutionary path of true National Socialism for Germany's freedom, and has been steered onto the reactionary course of a coalition party'. Stennes, on the other hand, represented the 'pure idea' of Nazism. The Pomeranian rebels then called upon storm troopers to follow them into the new organisation being formed by Stennes, the 'National Socialist Fighting Movement of Germany' (NSKD).

Few answered the call. In Pomerania, for example, only one of the five *Standartenführer* opted for Stennes' new 'movement'.[51] According to the police in Stettin, Stennes' followers managed to attract only a small number of lower-level SA officers and SA men.[52] The Nazi press jubilantly reported that the SA stood firm behind the party leadership, and for once it told the truth. On 4 April the *Völkischer Beobachter* printed reports from the eastern *Gaue* proclaiming loyalty to Hitler and publicising the expulsion of Stennes' supporters.[53] Provisional replacements for the dismissed SA leaders were appointed quickly, and Stennes' successor, Schulz, travelled throughout eastern Germany speaking to thousands of storm troopers to ensure that the rebellion was crushed.[54] Within a few weeks of the revolt, Stennes' supporters in the East had been routed completely.

Nevertheless the rebels doggedly tried to build up their own organisation, hoping to attract disaffected elements from the Hitler movement. NSKD literature was printed and distributed to SA men.[55] Local groups of the NSKD were founded by former Nazi Party members and meetings were held. However, these groups remained small and their activities were often targets for Nazi violence.[56] Despite determined efforts – Kurt Kremser still was trying to organise Nazi dissidents in September 1932, when he became the Silesian representative of Otto Straßer's 'Black Front'[57] – Stennes' followers were unable to present a significant challenge to the Nazi movement.

Perhaps the most important consequence of the Stennes revolt in eastern Germany was the replacement of the SA leadership in Pomerania and Silesia in its wake. In Pomerania Lustig, the *Standartenführer* based in Swinemünde, a number of the staff of the provincial SA headquarters and local leaders in Stettin were expelled from the Nazi movement.[58] In Silesia Kremser and his lieutenant Valentin Nowak, as well as the SA leaders in Liegnitz, Neisse, Oppeln, Sprottau, Glogau, Hindenburg and Breslau, had to be replaced.[59] Particularly at top level, the replacements proved significant. In Pomerania the appointment of Hans Friedrich on 3 April 1931 began a long period of friction with the *Gau* leadership, and in Silesia the dismissal of Kremser brought Edmund Heines to Breslau in June.

When discussing the relationship between the SA and the Nazi Party, it is easy to stress those aspects which were disruptive. Yet despite the frequent conflicts and the considerable resentment against the party bosses which simmered among storm troopers, no SA revolt really threatened the Nazi movement. The great majority of SA members proved unwilling to oppose Hitler and the party leadership. The conspicuous failure of the rebellious SA leaders to carry their men with them again points to the peculiar insignificance of overt political ideology in determining the actions of the SA rank and file. It is revealing that when the Stennes rebels in the eastern regions began to talk about a 'revolutionary SA' and the 'revolutionary path of true National Socialism' they found few storm troopers prepared to give support. The allegiance of the SA rank and file was, in the first instance, to neither their own leaders nor a 'revolutionary' Nazi ideology, but to the movement led by Hitler.

(iv) The SA and the SS

The SS, which remained nominally subordinate to the SA until 1934, kept a relatively low profile before Hitler came to power. In eastern Germany the first few 'SS' units were established during the late 1920s. These early formations were not part of a nationwide organisation but rather were essentially outgrowths of local Nazi groups, differing from local SA units only in the name they had chosen for themselves.[60] It was not until 1930 that the SS began to expand in the eastern Prussian provinces,[61] that SS units came under the control of the Munich headquarters and regional SS commanders for the East were appointed by Himmler, and that friction developed between the SS and the SA.

Before 1933 a main source of difficulties between the SA and the SS was recruitment from the former by the latter – another example of how the structure of the Nazi movement generated conflict.[62] The storm troopers provided the best pool of potential recruits for the SS, but SA leaders understandably resisted the poaching of their members and what they saw as a consequent degeneration of the SA into a 'reservoir of second-class elements'.[63] Already by late 1930 Hitler had felt compelled to stress the responsibility of SA and SS leaders for preventing conflicts between the two formations, and upon taking up his post as SA Chief of Staff Röhm set out to regulate the growth and recruitment procedures of the SS.[64] Röhm wanted to see the SS expand, but in such a way that trouble between the SS and SA could be avoided. His plan envisaged that the SS would maintain a strength 10 per cent that of the SA, that the SA would supply 50 per cent of the membership of new SS units, and that neither organisation would recruit actively from the ranks of the other. Reasonable though this scheme may have seemed, disputes continued to arise, largely because the SS drew its membership primarily from within the Nazi movement.

The problems this could cause can be seen from the growth patterns of the two organisations in the *Regierungsbezirk* Königsberg.[65] The first mention of an SS unit in the *Regierungsbezirk* dates from January 1930, when police reported the existence of an SS *'Standarte'* of 11 men: a *'Standartenführer'* and his deputy (both students, aged twenty-five and twenty respectively), a *'Truppführer'*, and 8 further members. In June 1930 the entire SS in the *Regierungsbezirk* still comprised just 14 men, and by the end of the year it had grown only to 22. While the SA was growing by leaps and bounds, the SS remained quite small. In June 1931, when the SA in the region had mush-roomed to over 4,000 members, the SS numbered 42 men; in October it numbered 48. Then, as the growth of the SA began to slow, the SS started to expand rapidly: at the end of 1931 it had 70 members, in March 1932 approximately 200, in August about 250, and by December it reached an estimated 650 (although this last figure appears to have included 135 men in the *Regierungsbezirk* Allenstein). This growth pattern is significant in that it was out of phase with the development of the SA and the party: the greatest expansion of the SS occurred when the SA and the NSDAP were losing members, during the crisis months of late 1932.[66] Thus it appears that the growth of the SS was not part of the general success of the Nazi movement in attracting supporters from the population at large; rather, the SS found its recruits within Nazi ranks, which meant drawing men from the SA.

Already before the assumption of power in 1933 there began to develop in the SS a belief that it formed the elite of the Nazi movement.[67] In contrast with the SA, SS formations were better disciplined and always remained loyal to the party organisation. (There were no SS rebellions against the party leadership.) By late 1932 the difference between the two organisations was striking. Whereas the SA had engaged in uncontrolled violence during the summer and found large sections of its membership slipping away as the fortunes of the movement seemed to ebb, the SS maintained both its mem-bership and discipline.[68] While the SA tended to regard itself, in the words of one local SA leader, as a 'disguised military'[69] – as the core of a new Nazi army – the SS came to see itself not only as the loyal elite of the movement but also as the future Nazi police.[70] Already in 1932 SS members were informed that they were to become the elite police of the 'Third Reich', and that therefore only the most healthy specimens could be accepted into the organisation and instruction in police duties and the penal code was neces-sary.[71] While the vision of the future of the SA leadership was to bring it into conflict with Germany's Nazi rulers after 1933, the self-image of the SS turned out to be much more politically astute and realistic. Therein lay the seeds of a confrontation which the SA leadership was bound to lose.

CHAPTER V

The SA and the Reichswehr

THE policies of the Reichswehr in the eastern Prussian provinces, including its relations with the SA, were determined largely by Germany's vulnerable position along the frontiers. The Reichswehr regarded Poland as a serious military threat, and was convinced that the German armed forces lacked strength to deal with the new Polish state.[1] Thus a basic problem facing the Reichswehr during the Weimar period was how to mobilise the civilian population in order to reinforce its own insufficient strength should there be a Polish attack. One attempt at a solution was the creation of a border-defence organisation, the *Grenzschutz*, which consisted of formations of local volunteers in the border regions, led by former army officers, trained periodically by Reichswehr staff and equipped with weapons stored in secret hiding places. [2] In the event of military action, the *Grenzschutz* was to support the operations of the Reichswehr and to hinder the progress of invading forces. This strategy, by attaching such importance to the active support of the civilian population in the eastern regions, induced the Reichswehr to cooperate with political organisations such as the *Stahlhelm* and, eventually, the SA. [3]

The opportunity to work together with the Reichswehr through the *Grenzschutz* was advantageous to the SA in a number of ways. First, it allowed the storm troopers to exercise their military fantasies, at least to some extent.For members of an organisation which so praised military values, the chance to become involved in real war games, to make an apparent contribution to national defence and to gain access to weapons was hardly unwelcome. Second, involvement in the *Grenzschutz* lent the SA a certain social and policitical respectability, bringing it into closer contact not only with the Reichswehr but also with the conservative Right. In many a border community the *Grenzschutz* constituted in effect a local 'Harzburg Front', within which the Nazis could draw recruits from their right-wing rivals. At the same time it had to be recognised that a nationalist political movement could not expect to win a large following in the eastern border regions if it failed to support defence measures which enjoyed overwhelming popular approval. Thus the SA had a practical interest in participating in the defence formations along the eastern borders, an interest which overrode the Nazis' militant opposition to the Weimar state which the armed forces were serving.

During the 1920s the *Grenzschutz* in the eastern Prussian provinces was composed largely of members of the *Stahlhelm*, which had cultivated close relations with the Reichswehr.[4] Contacts between the army and the SA in eastern Germany did not develop until the final years of the Republic. Until that time the SA in eastern Germany had been too weak in the predomin- antly rural districts along the borders either to play an important role in the plans of the Reichswehr or to infiltrate the *Grenzschutz*. This changed in 1930 and 1931, with the vast expansion of the SA. By mid-1931 a significant proportion of the young male population in the eastern regions was organ- ised in the SA, which therefore had to be considered in calculations about the defence of the frontiers. This expansion coincided with the reorganisa- tion of the SA undertaken by Röhm when he assumed command in 1931, together with his attempts to cultivate contacts with the Reichswehr. In addition, the turn of the decade marked an important change in military planning, as the *Grenschutz* was formally recognised and put onto a more secure financial footing by the Reichswehr Ministry.[5] Thus during the early 1930s a number of factors combined which favoured the involvement of the SA in border-defence formations. Consequently, SA units paid little heed to the call, which Hitler was reported to have made in Lauenburg in April 1932, that 'we will protect the German borders only after removal of the leaders of the present system'.[6]

Relations between the SA and the Reichswehr were best in East Prussia, largely due to the vulnerable position of the 'island' province. This exposed position made the *Wehrkreis I* (East Prussia) all the more willing to work together with any group which might help defend the province against external attack, while simultaneously inducing groups and individuals with widely differing political aims to collaborate with the Reichswehr. The atmosphere in East Prussia was such that local government officials in the *Landratsämter* (district authorities), the *Landesfinanzministerium* (regional finance ministry) and the post office worked happily with the army, and even members of the largely Social Democratic *Reichsbanner* were welcomed into the border-defence formations.[7] Thus a political climate existed in which the Nazi movement could not afford to be hostile to the Reichswehr or uncooperative with regard to border defence. Another important reason why the Reichswehr in East Prussia welcomed the help of the SA was the character of the army leadership. In October 1929 Werner von Blomberg – who was to become Hitler's Reichswehr Minister in 1933 – had taken command of the *Wehrkreis I*. Blomberg was influenced by his Chief of Staff, Walther von Reichenau, and by the divisional chaplain, Ludwig Müller, both of whom were enthusiastic about the Hitler movement.[8]

The first contacts between the Reichswehr and the SA in East Prussia came during the late 1920s.These blossomed in 1930, as large numbers of storm troopers participated in the *Grenzschutz* and closer relations developed between the Reichswehr and the SA at local level.[9] A particularly important role in promoting the relations between the Reichswehr and the Nazi movement was played by Müller, who identified himself ever more closely with the Nazi cause during 1930 and 1931. Taking advantage of his Reichswehr position, Müller worked together with Röhm to develop collaboration between the SA and the *Wehrkreis I*.[10] At the same time, Röhm was pursuing the matter in Berlin, and during early 1931 he discussed SA participation in East Prussia's border defence with General Kurt von Schleicher in the Reichswehr Ministry.[11] In April the Nazi leadership went a step further and specifically permitted participation by storm troopers in military exercises, including border defence.[12] Far from refusing to defend the frontiers until 'the removal of the leaders of the present system', the NSDAP and SA eagerly grasped the opportunity to help the Reichswehr. Indeed, within the East Prussian SA military considerations assumed such an importance that by early 1932 SA leaders were discussing openly how the storm troopers were to be supplied with weapons and integrated *en masse* into the *Grenzschutz* in the event of a Polish attack.[13]

Even in East Prussia, however, relations between the Reichswehr and the Nazi movement were not entirely trouble-free. During late 1930 and early 1931 the *Gauleitung* in Königsberg raised objections to close cooperation with the army – partly in order to prevent the SA from developing contacts independently of the East Prussian Nazi Party, partly due to a hostile attitude toward the new Chief of Staff of the Army Command (*Chef der Heeresleitung*), General von Hammerstein, and partly because of fears that the Reichswehr might be used against the SA and would be prepared to help the Prussian police suppress the Nazis.[14] In early 1931 a large number of Nazis left the border-defence organisations in response to orders from the *Gauleitung*; according to the East Prussian party leadership, participation by SA members in the *Grenzschutz* was allowed 'only in order to create the possibility for military training and to ascertain stores of weapons'. However, Müller intervened to repair relations between the army and the East Prussian NSDAP and, with the Reich party leadership's explicit approval of SA participation in border-defence formations in April 1931, Koch's objections were overruled. As General Halder later noted, the East Prussian SA remained the 'enthusiastic and willing helper of the numerically weak army in the question of the defence of the country'.[15]

The other region along Germany's eastern frontiers in which cooperation between the SA and the Reichswehr developed on a significant scale was the Border Province. The basis for this cooperation was similar to that in East Prussia, since the exposed position of the Border Province – stretching along the Polish border, which in *Kreis* Meseritz was only 150 kilometers from Berlin – made the Reichswehr especially concerned to enlist the help of the local population. As in East Prussia, the precarious military position led to broad popular support for working with the military and a willingness among local politicians and government officials of almost all persuasions to back measures designed to protect the frontiers. And, as in East Prussia, once the Nazi movement grew to mass proportions, cultivating the support of the population meant that the Reichswehr had to accept the collaboration of Nazi sympathisers.

The first mention of Nazi participation in the *Grenzschutz* in the Border Province dates from April 1930, when the SPD police director in Schneidemühl, Erich Thiemann, noted his concern that Nazi supporters, together with local *Stahlhelm* leaders and members of the *Tannenbergbund*, were taking part in Reichswehr briefings on border defence.[16] Among those attending were the leader of the NSDAP in Schneidemühl and his deputy, a teacher who was the local Nazi spokesman on border defence. Thiemann's criticism of Reichswehr cooperation with groups outspokenly hostile to the Republic provoked a revealing response. In reply, the Chief of Staff of the *Wehrkreiskommando II* (Stettin), Kurt Liese, explained that the Reichswehr did not cooperate with political associations (*Vereine*) as such, but

> regards itself duty-bound to point out that the Germans of the Border Province, insofar as they are fit for military service, are organised almost without exception in *Vereine*. Therefore it cannot be avoided completely that the solidarity of these *Vereine* members will make its appearance in the briefings.[17]

Liese did rule that leading Nazi Party members no longer would be invited to Reichswehr briefings; however, even this concession was qualified by Liese's deputy and *Wehrkreis* expert on border defence, Major von Gablenz, who pointed out that other supporters of the Nazi movement would not be excluded from the briefings 'because hereby the NSDAP would become even more radicalised'.[18]

By late 1931 the rapid growth of the Nazi movement meant that *Grenzschutz* formations in the Border Province were composed very largely of Hitler supporters. This development was observed with alarm by Thiemann, who was worried that the Republic's opponents were gaining access to weapons, and in November 1931 he presented to *Oberpräsident* von Bülow a detailed report on right-wing penetration of the border defence formations.[19] Thiemann alleged that altogether 90 per cent of the *Grenzschutz* were members of the 'National Opposition' – the *Stahlhelm, Jungstahlhelm,* DNVP, NSDAP and SA – and that in some districts the SA had virtually taken over the border-defence organisation: The leader of the SA in the Border Province, Arno Manthey, had become the leader of the *Grenzschutz* in the northern part of the province; in *Kreis* Schlochau the *Grenzschutz* consisted largely of Nazis who participated in field exercises wearing their party pins; in *Kreis* Flatow the *Stahlhelm* took part in

Grenzschutz exercises in closed formation; in *Kreis* Deutsch Krone members of the NSDAP were building shelters for the *Grenzschutz*; in *Kreis* Jastrow the *Grenzschutz* was composed almost entirely of Nazis who trained in SA uniform and were led by the local SA-*Truppführer*; in Schneidemühl a number of Nazis were prominent in the *Grenzschutz*, together with the deputy *Gauführer* of the *Stahlhelm* and a number of lesser *Stahlhelm* leaders; and in the *Netzekreis* the *Grenzschutz* consisted almost exclusively of members of the *Stahlhelm* and the NSDAP. According to the Schneidemühl police director, the *Grenzschutz* had become an organisation composed largely of enemies of the Republic whose borders it was supposed to defend.

The Reichswehr contested Thiemann's allegations. Answering for the *Wehrkreis II*, Chief of Staff Liese claimed that the Nazis had not been so cooperative as Thiemann believed, that the *Grenzschutz* was backed by many Centre Party supporters and Social Democrats as well as people on the Right, and that, in any case, given the political composition of the Border Province it was natural that most of the support for the *Grenzschutz* should come from the Right.[20] In conclusion Liese stated that 'this report of the police director demonstrates anew that trustful, friction-free cooperation of the German army with the Prussian police is impossible in the Border Province'. Liese's response was as significant for what it omitted as for what it included. Revealingly, he did not dispute the basic allegations of Nazi involvement in the *Grenzschutz*, the leading position of SA-*Standarten-führer* Manthey, the participation of SA men in uniform, and the fact that supporters of the Nazi movement comprised a major proportion of those in the border-defence formations. Nevertheless, Thiemann's campaign against the arming of right-wing opponents of the Republic was a failure. Not only did he face the understandable hostility of the Reichswehr, he also carried on his struggle without allies in the government bureaucracy or among local population. Probably doomed from the start, Thiemann's efforts came to an abrupt end in July 1932, when he was dismissed during the purge of the police administration which followed von Papen's coup against the Prussian government.[21]

For their part, the Nazis did not display the reluctance to participate in the *Grenschutz* that Liese implied, although the involvement of SA members was not without some complications. In particular, the SA leadership was concerned that participation in the *Grenzschutz* should not cause it to lose control over its members. On 15 January 1933, Manthey spoke to the SA in Schneidemühl about its involvement in the *Grenzschutz* and explained the attitude of the SA toward cooperation with the Reichswehr:

We want to have a *Grenzschutz*. We have negotiated with the Reichswehr and were willing to stand up for the *Grenzschutz*. But first our leaders should be trained. We do not let our troops out of the hands of our leaders. . . . We have enough people who are prepared to stand up for the Fatherland.[22]

In other words, the SA was happy to cooperate with the *Grenzschutz*, provided the SA could run it. Collaboration with the Reichswehr and defence of the borders against the Poles would be welcomed, but not at the risk of dividing the allegiance of the SA membership. Yet since so many leadership positions in the *Grenzschutz* in the Border Province had been taken over by Nazis in any case, this concern proved no great stumbling block to widespread SA participation in the border-defence formations.

In Pomerania, which bordered Poland only in its easternmost districts, SA involvements in the *Grenzschutz* failed to develop as it had in the neighbouring Border Province. Here the border-defence formations remained largely in the hands of *Stahlhelm* members, not because the *Stahlhelm* was stronger in Pomerania than in the Border Province or East Prussia but most probably because of the attitudes of the provincial Nazi leadership. The Nazi leadership in Pomerania adopted a generally cool attitude toward the *Grenzschutz*.[23] Indeed, Hans Lustig denied that under his leadership the SA had either taken part in military exercises or trained with weapons at all.[24] Reluctance to serve under *Stahlhelm* officers was almost certainly one reason why, as General von Hammerstein reported in May 1932, local SA leaders in Pomerania refused to participate in the *Grenzschutz*.[25] Another may have been the rapid turnover of the Pomeranian SA leadership, which seemed insufficiently secure in its own position to develop a policy with regard to border defence. Whatever the cause, it appears that in Pomerania SA leaders did not become key figures in the *Grenzschutz* nor did storm troopers multiply its ranks – which may be why the Reichswehr found it so difficult to gather enough manpower for Pomeranian border-defence formations.[26]

Although the Pomeranian SA did not involve itself on a large scale in border defence and often was regarded with suspicion by Reichswehr officers, many soldiers had a friendly attitude toward the Nazi movement and the SA tried to cultivate contacts between soldiers and storm troopers.[27] Furthermore, despite its lack of involvement in the *Grenzschutz*, the Pomeranian SA leadership discussed defending the frontiers in the event of Polish military action. According to a report of an SA leaders' meeting in Stettin in early August 1932, instructions had been received from Munich that the SA and SS should be used as border-defence formations if there were a Polish invasion.[28] Although such a commitment was inadequate for the Reichswehr – which required a well-trained border-defence force – and despite misgivings about participating in the *Grenzschutz*, even the Pomeranian SA was prepared to defend the frontiers of the Weimar Republic.

In Silesia basically similar attitudes underpinned SA relations with the Reichswehr and the *Grenzschutz*. Although there were difficulties, neither was the SA prepared to appear unwilling to defend the Fatherland nor was the Reichswehr prepared to rule out assistance from the storm troopers. Before the Stennes revolt, the Silesian SA did not take part in military exercises.[29] However, from mid-1931 many Nazis, particularly in rural districts, involved themselves in the *Grenzschutz* even though its leadership was drawn almost exclusively from traditional conservative groups, most frequently the *Stahlhelm*.[30] During 1931 contacts with the Reichswehr grew and in December the army approached the Upper Silesian SA leadership with a proposal to bring the storm troopers together with the *Stahlhelm*, the *Landesschützenverband* and the *Selbstschutz* in order to form a 'black Reichswehr' to defend the province.[31] The army, which was limited to a strength of about 1,500 in Upper Silesia, looked to the approximately 3,500 storm troopers in the province at the time for possible reinforcements. Although nothing came of the plan, it indicates the readiness of the Reichswehr to look to the right-wing political formations – and from 1930/1 to the SA – to strengthen its precarious position along the borders.

During 1932, however, the Silesian Nazi organisation demanded that SA and NSDAP members in the *Grenzschutz* be led only by officers who were National Socialists.[32] As elsewhere, in Silesia the Nazi organisation was reluctant to share the allegiance of its supporters. SA-Reichswehr relations also were strained by political events, particularly during the tense months following the July 1932 *Reichstag* elections. From Upper Silesia the SA leadership reported that, while it had been in constant contact with the Reichswehr headquarters in Oppeln, relations deteriorated during August and September 1932: storm troopers were leaving Reichswehr 'training courses' because they felt army officers were too 'reactionary'; the SA refused to train with the *Stahlhelm*; and, in the opinion of *Untergruppenführer* Ramshorn, the Reichswehr displayed insufficient understanding that the SA wanted to take part in defence preparations only in its own formations.[33] In Breslau as well the political events of August 1932 were registered in a cooling of relations between the SA and the Reichswehr.[34] Nevertheless, in other parts of Silesia relations remained good: in Liegnitz the leader of the Lower Silesian SA went out of his way to cultivate a 'warm comradely relationship' with high-ranking Reichswehr officers;[35] and in the northern portions of Lower Silesia the SA observed the army's autumn manoeuvers and took part in 'off-duty meetings of the Reichswehr formations' while in brown uniform.[36] Specific political differences notwithstanding, both the Reichswehr and the SA in Silesia had considerable underlying interest in working together.

For the Reichswehr, relations with the SA were determined essentially by a pragmatic concern to defend the eastern borders. Despite the occasional difficulties in working with the SA, the Reichswehr leadership did not object to the presence of storm troopers in the *Grenzschutz* on political grounds. Indeed, the most striking feature in the Reichswehr attitude toward participation by the SA in the *Grenzschutz* was the lack of overt political considerations involved – except perhaps in East Prussia, where the army leadership had a particular inclination toward the Nazi movement. Seeking civilian support to defend the frontiers was essentially a matter of practical policy, not an expression of a desire to intervene in domestic politics. Thus in the eastern Prussian provinces the Reichswehr proved willing to cooperate with those groups which were willing to cooperate with it. Working together with the *Stahlhelm* probably was seen as more agreeable than working together with the SA, but from 1930 this was no longer an alternative. Once the Nazis came to dominate the right-wing politics along the eastern borders, a satisfactory *Grenzschutz* could not be constructed by relying only on the *Stahlhelm,* no matter how desirable this might have seemed to many army officers.

For the SA, relations with the Reichswehr also involved pragmatic concerns: regard for the sentiments of the eastern German population and of the SA members themselves, as well as interest in gaining military training and access to weapons. However, for the SA more explicitly political considerations played a role as well. It was due to these that the interests of the Reichswehr and the SA sometimes diverged, most clearly over whether SA men should be subordinate to *Grenzschutz* officers who were not National Socialists. Border defence was not regarded by the SA leadership as removed from party-political rivalry and competition. SA leaders continued to reveal their obsession with preserving their own prerogatives, even in their dealings with the army. Obviously this would have posed great problems were the *Grenzschutz* ever actually called upon to defend the frontiers. Fortunately for the Reichswehr, the loyalty of the Nazi supporters in the *Grenzschutz* and the military value of the border-defence formations never were put to the test.

Pragmatic considerations in the relations between the SA and the Reichswehr also were to shape the events of 1934, when the Reichswehr agreed to the purge of the SA. While the Reichswehr leadership displayed few qualms about working with the SA before 1933, it had no political commitment to do so either. Thus when the context of SA-Reichswehr relations changed – when the Nazi-led government expressed its determination to expand the armed forces and the SA appeared to pose a threat to plans for the Reichswehr – there were no reservations within the Reichswehr command about turning on the storm troopers' organisation. Significantly, in those provinces where relations between the SA and the Reichswehr had been best – in East Prussia and the Border Province – the SA escaped the purge, while in the regions in which collaboration had run into greater obstacles – in Pomerania and Silesia – the SA leadership was removed. While the relations between the Reichswehr and the SA before 1933 of course did not determine how the SA leadership fared in 1934, it is revealing that where the SA had been most keen to cooperate with the Reichswehr, there its leaders were able to survive the bloodbath of 1934.

CHAPTER VI

Nazi Violence and Terror before 1933

(i) Patterns of SA Violence

THE politics of Nazism were the politics of hatred, struggle and violence. Both the ideology of the Nazi movement and its style of politics helped make physical violence not only acceptable but also desirable in the eyes of the storm troopers. According to Goebbels:

> The SA man wants to fight, and he also has a right to be led into battle. His existence wins its justification only in battle. Without a fighting tendency the SA is absurd and pointless.[1]

This sort of posturing should be taken seriously, for it points to an important element of the Nazis' appeal. It constituted a language and described an activity which many found attractive, and the willingness of the Nazi movement – and, in particular, the SA – to engage in this kind of politics was an important drawing card. Among the strengths of the Nazi movement was the fact that, unlike its rivals either on the Left or on the Right, it appealed both to roughness *and* respectability.[2] We know, for example, that the terror campaigns of the Nazis against the Left in 1933 brought a large measure of popularity to the new regime,[3] and it is likely that SA actions against the Left before 1933 also met with approval. The same people who were concerned to restore 'law and order' also often held aggressive antipathy toward the KPD and SPD, and the Nazis were able to profit from both sets of prejudice. Thus perhaps even more important than the contradictory policy statements which emanated from Nazi spokesmen before 1933 (and which have been noted so often by historians) was the contradictory *style* of politics pursued by the Nazi movement, a style which promised a restoration of order and conservative values and simultaneously proclaimed a readiness to challenge the Left on the streets.[4] This ambiguity in the Nazi message was not really resolved until the bloodbath of 1934, and before 1933 it was used to attract both conservative Germans distressed at the way their world apparently had fallen apart under Weimar and young toughs unconcerned with bourgeois conventions and sensibilities.

The way in which the SA was organised also made it prone to violence. Not only was the SA built on a military model, but it was organised territorially (rather than, say, occupationally). From almost the beginning of their existence, SA groups became involved in battles over territory. Attacking and conquering 'red' citadels in cities, whether these be in Berlin, Beuthen or Königsberg, formed a central element of SA activities. However, it would be a mistake to see this violence as directed indiscriminately against the working class. As we have seen, the NSDAP and particularly the SA were concerned to attract workers into their ranks and to present themselves as the true political representatives of the German worker, unfortunately led astray by the internationalist Left. Thus the SA violence was directed not so much against the working class as against the *organisations* of the working class, which formed an altogether more convenient and politically acceptable target.[5]

By the time the Weimar system crumbled, there was hardly a city or town in Germany which had been spared political violence. This violence, it should be noted, was of a rather different character than that which had ushered in the Republic. It was not a succession of military or quasi-military battles, but something at once more limited and more widespread. It was limited in that it generally remained at the level of brawls and street violence, never approaching anything like a military campaign (despite the fantasies of some SA leaders); yet at the same time it became a ubiquitous feature of the German political landscape. Political violence was no longer just a matter of events one read about in the newspapers, but something which occurred in one form or another in virtually every city neighbourhood and town, and in the countryside as well. Among the clearest measures of the rising tide of Nazi violence were the claims registered by the compulsory SA insurance scheme, which covered physical injury suffered during SA duties:

1927:	110 claims
1928:	360 claims
1929:	881 claims
1930:	2506 claims
1931:	6307 claims
1932:	14005 claims[6]

Violence which resulted in serious injury or death became an increasingly frequent feature of SA activities during the early 1930s, and was marked by the growing number of Nazi 'martyrs':

	Nazis killed	Of these, SA members
1925	4	0
1926	1	1
1927	5	4
1928	5	1

1929	9	4
1930	15	12
1931	42	27
1932 (to 29 Aug)	70	50[7]

In the eastern Prussian provines 22 adherents of the Nazis movement, most of them members of the SA, lost their lives between May 1930 and September 1932,[8] and in December 1931 Edmund Heines claimed that in Silesia alone the SA had suffered 8 dead and nearly 200 seriously injured 'as a result of the Marxist terror'.[9] The Left too had numerous casualities, which were given due publicity in the Communist and Social Democratic press. The violence reached a peak during the summer of 1932, when in the ten days preceding the July *Reichstag* elections 24 people were killed and 284 seriously injured in political confrontations in Prussia alone.[10]

The growth of the Nazi movement and particularly of the SA thus led to a mounting spiral of political violence, which transformed the relatively peaceful climate of the mid-1920s into the storms of the early 1930s. The Nazis set out to challenge the grip of the Left in what the Left saw as its own territory, in working-class districts, and the SA pushed its opponents into the arena of physical violence. Not surprisingly, the challenge posed by the SA was met by the fighting organisations of the Left: the largely Social Democratic *Reichsbanner*, the 'Iron Front' (*Eiserne Front*) – formed in December 1931 by the SPD, the Social Democratic trade unions, workers' sport organisations and the *Reichsbanner* as a response to the right-wing 'Harzburg Front'–, the Communist 'Red Front Fighters' League' (*Roter Frontkämpferbund*) banned in 1929, and the Communist-inspired 'Fighting League against Fascism' (*Kampfbund gegen den Faschismus*), which was founded and began to attract recruits in late 1930.[11] For the KPD in particular the growth of the Hitler movement marked a stepping up of its own violent street politics, as it sought to attract support through its militant and aggressive opposition to National Socialism.[12] According to materials compiled by the Prussian Interior Ministry during the second half of 1932 – when the violence was at its height – Social Democrats and, above all, Communists often were the 'aggressors' in violent incidents.[13] Although they probably reflected the anti-Communist bias of the Prussian police, these materials indicate that KPD supporters probably attacked the Nazis as often as the Nazis attacked them.

The most common occasion for violence involving the SA was the political rally. The emphasis placed by the NSDAP upon rallies made ensuring their smooth progress one of the most important duties of the SA. Attempts by the Left to disrupt Nazi rallies were frequent, and when they succeeded this spelled serious defeat for the storm troopers. For example, in the East Prussian *Kreis* Oletzko in August 1930 the NSDAP staged 23 rallies, of which the SPD and KPD tried to disrupt five; in one instance the SPD succeeded, when the SA proved too weak to prevent 60 Social Democratic sympathisers from making excessive noise.[14] In many cases, particularly in the large cities and industrial centres where the Left enjoyed considerable support, rallies and marches of the Nazis were deliberate provocations and often met with a violent response.[15] Not only the storm troopers but also their left-wing opponents had reputations to defend.

The patterns of violence generated at Nazi rallies during the final Weimar years may be illustrated by a few characteristic incidents. In these we can see how situations came about in which the only alternative to violence was an unacceptable loss of face. For example, in Gleiwitz on 30 November 1930 a Nazi protest against the 'Polish terror' was disrupted by Communists in the crowd; Nazi chants were answered with Communist insults and the rally quickly degenerated into a brawl.[16] In Deutsch Eylau (East Prussia) an NSDAP rally in the market square in February 1931 ended similarly when Communists and *Reichsbanner* members tried to shout down the Nazi speaker and threw pieces of ice at the SA men present; according to the satisfied local NSDAP leader, the storm troopers then 'cleared the streets', leaving several people injured.[17] During the same month in Binz, on the island of Rügen, *Reichsbanner* members disrupted a Nazi gathering in a hotel and the fights which ensued left the building in a shambles.[18] In nearby Tribsees, in *Kreis* Grimmen, the NSDAP staged a rally on 22 September 1931 which attracted many KPD supporters; cries of 'Heil Hitler' were answered with 'Heil Moskau', fighting broke out, shots were fired and the rally was broken up.[19] Two points emerge from these examples. The first is how easily political activity degenerated into violence once the Nazi movement had attracted mass support. Political rallies became challenges and these challenges could not be left unanswered. The second point is that rural communities were no less subject to this type of political violence than were industrial cities. The political violence which accompanied the demise of Weimar was not just an urban phenomenon; it also engulfed the countryside.

The duties of the storm troopers involved not just the protection of Nazi rallies but also the planned distruption of meetings of their opponents. The SPD proved especially vulnerable to this sort of attack by the SA. Its own emphasis on rallies, together with its defensive posture and deteriorating political fortunes during the last years of the Republic, made the SPD an easy target for Nazi violence and terror tactics. From late 1930, once the Nazis were able to count on sufficient numbers, the rallies of the Social Democrats in eastern Germany were increasingly at risk. Particularly in the countryside the SA was able to gather its forces, outnumber the local *Reichsbanner* and SPD supporters, and break up the rallies of the Social Democrats with ease.[20] In fact, although such violence tends to be associated with urban surroundings, it appears to have been most effective in isolated rural areas. Often Social Democrats were assaulted even before their rallies got under way, and attempts by the SPD to celebrate 'Constitution Day', 11 August, provided an especially welcome opportunity for storm troopers to rough-up opponents.[21] Once Weimar politics became the politics of violence, the Social Democrats no longer could compete effectively.

The KPD was altogether less vulnerable to Nazi violence than was the SPD, and successful attempts to disrupt Communist rallies were rare. This was due in part to the different tactics of the KPD, which tended to hold fewer public meetings and concentrated more on so-called 'Kleinarbeit' – the cultivation of political sympathies through person-to-person discussion and canvassing. Thus the Communists left themselves much less open to Nazi terror than did the Social Democrats. In addition, the Communists were much more willing to counter violence with violence and often were able to turn the tables on the Nazis.[22]

The parties occupying the shrinking middle ground of Weimar politics – the *Staatspartei*, the *Wirtschaftspartei* and the DVP – largely escaped SA violence in eastern Germany, primarily because they held too few meetings for the storm troopers to terrorise. On the other hand, the Catholic Centre Party and its affiliated organisations were threatened by the SA, particularly in Upper Silesia.[23] Nor were the right-wing rivals of the NSDAP spared. Meetings of Erich Ludendorff's *Tannenbergbund* were broken up by the SA,[24] as were those of Stennes' breakaway NSKD.[25] During late 1932 even the Nazis' erstwhile ally, the DNVP, faced SA violence; in Breslau, for example, a large DNVP rally on 27 September 1932 was broken up by Nazi supporters who interrupted the speaker, *Reichstag* Vice-President Walther Graef, threw stinkbombs from the corners of the hall, and afterwards assaulted *Stahlhelm* members who had attended.[26]

Perhaps even more important than the violence arising from political rallies were the tactics employed by the SA elsewhere. Bands of storm troopers frequently terrorised towns, assaulted the offices of left-wing organisations, and attacked prominent members of the KPD, SPD, the trade unions and Catholic organisations. In Liegnitz, for example, SA men were responsible for a series of such incidents in late 1931: in early September a *Reichsbanner* member was attacked on the city's streets; in late October the offices of the SPD newspaper *Liegnitzer Volkszeitung* were bombed; and in mid-November an innocent bystander was beaten on the street, dragged into the hallway of a building and beaten again.[27] In Greifswald a troop of roughly 40 Nazis tried to storm the offices of the SPD *Greifswalder Zeitung* in March 1932; they were driven back at first, but returned with a force of 100 men, succeeded in taking the building, demolished the interior and sent one of the defenders to hospital.[28] At the same time attacks were made on the offices of the SPD newspaper *Der Vorpommer* in nearby Stralsund and Barth.

Such violence was particularly widespread during the July 1932 *Reichstag* election campaign. On 3 July an outing of the Breslau Social Democratic youth organisation, the *Jungfront*, was surrounded and fired upon by a band of SA men in *Kreis* Neurode; two girls were reported wounded and one youth badly beaten by the Nazis.[29] On the same day hundreds of storm troopers staged a rally in a town near Breslau and took the opportunity to break up a celebration of the local Catholic girls' association, tore down black-red-gold flags from houses, assaulted the local *Reichsbanner* leader, and attacked the home of the SPD chairman of the parish council.[30] A few days later SA men from Hirschberg attacked a work camp of the Social Democratic 'Socialist Worker Youth' (*Sozialistische Arbeiterjugend*) in Schmiedeberg; the police, completely outnumbered, were unable to stop the fighting until reinforcements arrived from Görlitz and Liegnitz.[31] In Hindenburg a band of Nazis drove into a crowd of Communist sympathisers, shooting and wounding a number of them, and in nearby Beuthen a *Kreuzschar* unit was attacked while accompanied by police officers.[32] In Bunzlau on 22 July hundreds of SA men, returning home from a mass rally in Liegnitz at which Hitler had spoken, attacked the local ADGB offices, killing one of the defenders and wounding several others.[33] Here we can see patterns of violence which foreshadowed the events of early 1933, and it was the Social Democrats who fared worst. Their cherished organisation, in particular their press and trade-union networks, offered easy targets for the SA.

Although the lion's share of Nazi violence was aimed against the Left, Jews and Poles were not exempted. The most serious outbreak of the violence against the Jewish population in eastern Germany came in the summer of 1932, in the wake of a widespread terror campaign against the Left; in East Prussia and Silesia especially Jews and Jewish-owned shops were assaulted.[34] The violence against the Polish community was less concentrated but nevertheless posed a threat to the Polish-speaking minority in Upper Silesia and the Border Province. There occurred a number of confrontations between storm troopers and Poles, and Polish-language entertainment programmes were disrupted by the SA.[35] However, although Nazi propaganda was aggressively anti-Semitic and anti-Polish, SA violence against Jews and Poles took second place behind attacks on political adversaries. The animosity of the Nazi infantry, like the political tactics of the Nazi movement, was aimed in the first instance against the Left; the most important task facing the storm troopers was not the persecution of minorities but the campaign for political power. Furthermore, neither the Jews nor the Poles posed a physical threat to the SA. Thus, compared to the level and extent of the violence between the Nazis and their left-wing opponents, the actions of the storm troopers against the Jews and Poles before 1933 were relatively modest.

At times the SA also confronted the state authorities. On one occasion even the police were challenged, when during the July 1932 election campaign approximately 50 SA and SS men attacked a police patrol near the main railway station in Hindenburg.[36] More frequent were attempts to disrupt the auctions of farm properties after their owners had been unable to pay debts and back taxes – an occurrence all too common in the depressed, predominantly rural eastern Prussian provinces. For example, during late 1931 in Naugard, in Pomerania, the SA began a campaign to prevent the local courts from carrying through forced auctions.[37] When one property, which happened to belong to the local SA-*Sturmführer,* was scheduled to be sold off, storm troopers occupied the court chambers and interrupted the session with catcalls and Nazi songs until conducting normal business became impossible. Prior to another auction, posters appeared threatening anyone who dared bid for the property in question, and when the auction finally took place the Nazis so disrupted the proceedings that these had to be called off.

However, the SA in eastern Germany generally was careful not to stage a frontal attack on the state. Where the courts were challenged, this was largely in connection with the auctions of farm properties – an issue where the Nazis were taking a clearly popular stand against state institutions which were felt to have acted unjustly. Other organs of state power tended to be left alone. The SA did not attempt to attack the Reichswehr or to sabotage army installations; SA bombing campaigns generally were aimed at political opponents, not government offices; and assaults on the police were the exception, not the rule. While SA violence no doubt was an expression of the hatreds of the Nazi rank and file, on the whole the SA leadership seems to have been aware of the limits beyond which it could not go. The SA, for all its rhetoric, stopped short of the sort of activity which would have brought it into direct confrontation with the repressive apparatus of the state.

Nevertheless, the police often dealt with SA violence quite severely, particularly in the larger cities. This was due both to the threat which SA activities posed for the maintenance of law and order and to the fact that until July 1932 the Prussian Interior Ministry and police bureaucracy were in the hands of Social Democrats. All public Nazi rallies were monitored by the police, who frequently stopped the proceedings when speakers illegally insulted the state or the black-red-gold national colours and who were able to prevent many rallies from degenerating into brawls.[38] The police also managed to infiltrate Nazi organisations in order to gain information,[39] and police raids on SA barracks and offices in the search for illegal weapons were frequent.[40] In April 1932 the nationwide ban on the SA, which lasted until June, began with widespread police searches of SA headquarters and *Heime*.[41] The Nazi press and leadership complained constantly of police repression: newspaper headlines screamed about the 'unbelievable brutality' of the police,[42] and Nazi leaders frequently accused the police of political bias. For example, in Tilsit during 1930 one local Nazi leader described the police in the city as 'completely left-wing',[43] while in a rally in Gleiwitz in March 1931 *Gauleiter* Brückner asserted that 'there is no province in Prussia where the police take action against the NSDAP so harshly as in Upper Silesia'.[44]

In fact claims that the Prussian police brutally suppressed the Nazi movement were often exaggerated or misleading. The relationship of the police to the Nazi movement was more complex, and there is evidence that the NSDAP was not without friends in the police forces. For example, the Tilsit police, which in 1930 was dismissed by a local Nazi leader as 'left-wing', had been described in positive terms by the district NSDAP leader one year earlier.[45] In Insterburg in 1931 the district Nazi propaganda chief assessed the police in his region as 'absolutely first-rate' and went on to assert that 'with only a few exceptions [the police] are quite amicably disposed toward us'.[46] In late 1932 a 'Union of National Socialist Police Officers' (*Arbeitsgemeinschaft nationalsozialistischer Polizeibeamter*) was formed in Gleiwitz, where a number of policemen were reported to have joined the NSDAP, Nazi leaflets were printed on police duplicating equipment and pictures of Hitler were to be found decorating police offices.[47] The Social Democrats in particular made frequent complaints about the leniency of the police toward the Nazis,[48] and numerous reports that the SA had been tipped off about impending police raids in April 1932 also indicate that the Nazi movement had many sympathisers within the police.[49] Such evidence suggests that there may have been a good deal of tension between the Prussian police on the ground and their Social Democratic superiors. In any event, after von Papen's 'coup' in July 1932, when SPD officials were removed from the Prussian police bureaucracy, the police became noticeably less strict with regard to the activities of the NSDAP and SA.

An element of SA tactics which created particular difficulties for the police was the use of motor transport.[50] The advantages gained by the widespread use of motor vehicles were considerable in the eastern Prussian provinces, where distances were greater and the population more scattered than in western or central Germany. Faced with a sudden invasion of two or three hundred storm troopers, isolated groups of Social Democrats often could do little to protect their own meetings or confront the Nazis.[51] Similarly, two or three police officers in an outlying village frequently found themselves unable to prevent the SA from disturbing the peace, ignoring bans on open-air demonstrations or the wearing of political uniforms, and terrorising their opponents. The new terror tactics developed by the SA greatly worried the authorities; in western Pomerania, for example, the *Regierungspräsident* even proposed to the Prussian Interior Minister that all people be banned from coming into a community from outside in order to attend political rallies.[52]

One example of the problems created by the mobile tactics of the storm troopers was an attack in March 1931 on the village of Zawadski, *Kreis* Groß-Strehlitz (Upper Silesia), where more than 150 Nazis were gathered from the surrounding region to attend a party rally and then assaulted people on the streets before the police could get reinforcements.[53] In another incident, one year later in Ostrosnitz, *Kreis* Cosel, nearly 200 Nazis – SA *Stürme* from Cosel and Kandrzin, together with some members of the Hitler Youth – marched into the village, roughed up passers-by on the street, and attacked the headquarters of the local *Reichsbanner* group; by the time they had finished, 29 people were injured including 18 *Reichsbanner* members.[54] By mid-1932 such tactics were being applied even in large cities, where the Left and the police were far from weak. Thus on the evening of 22 June 1932 approximately 2,000 SA men were driven into Breslau to attend a rally in the massive 'Jahrhunderthalle' and used the opportunity to pick fights in working-class districts of the city before marching in uniform to the hall.[55] The mobility of the SA greatly increased its effectiveness, and it is revealing that neither the Communists nor the Social Democrats seem to have had the access to motor vehicles which the Nazis obviously enjoyed.

The significance of SA violence was in large measure a function of its being so widespread. Its impact was cumulative; the most notorious acts of SA terror were important not just in and of themselves but also in that they reinforced reactions caused by countless less well-publicised incidents throughout Germany. Yet each incident had its local causes and local ramifications as well, and these should not be lost sight of in an attempt to place political violence within a general framework. Thus in order to understand the development and impact of Nazi violence during the final Weimar years, it is also necessary to examine in more detail some specific instances of SA violence and terror.

(ii) The Schweidnitz Incident: 27 September 1929

The first major instance of SA terror in the eastern Prussian provinces occurred in Schweidnitz on 27 September 1929. The incident began with a Nazi Party rally on the 26th.[56] The Schweidnitz NSDAP used the occasion to challenge the SPD, which had been the dominant political party in the area: the theme of the Nazi speaker was 'The Republican *Schutzbund* in Austria and the *Reichsbanner* in Germany, a Jewish protection troop', and Nazi leaflets were distributed throughout the city calling the *Reichsbanner* the 'protection squad of Jewish capital' and accusing it of cowardice in failing to answer the Nazi challenge. The Social Democrats responded immediately. Together with the local *Reichsbanner*, the ADGB and the Social Democratic sport club, the SPD planned a counter-rally for the following evening in the 'Volksgarten', a large beer hall in the city, where the Breslau SPD *Reichstag* Deputy Carl Wendemuth was to speak on 'The True Face of National Socialism'. There the Nazi challenge would be met.

The Nazis in the region reacted by planning the disruption of the SPD rally, and gathered forces not only from Schweidnitz itself but also by train and motor vehicle from Waldenburg, Striegau, Freiburg and Breslau. By the time the Social Democratic rally began, approximately 150 SA men, dressed in civilian clothes and waiting for the signal to create a disturbance, were among the assembled crowd. The meeting started peacefully, but once Wendemuth began his speech the Nazi discussion speaker (who was to have the floor after Wendemuth had finished) interrupted. A few members of the *Reichsbanner*, charged with keeping order, warned the Nazi spokesman to be quiet, but noise from the crowd increased when Wendemuth tried to continue. Then the leader of the Schweidnitz NSDAP, who had been sitting at the front of the hall just beneath the podium, gave the order for his troops to begin their assault. Within moments the 'Volksgarten' was in chaos. Some of the SA men jumped onto the podium to attack the speaker, the leader of the local SPD and the *Reichsbanner* members protecting the meeting; the remainder assaulted the crowd with table and chair legs, beer glasses, truncheons and knives. The Social Democrats were completely unprepared for such an attack, having brought neither weapons nor enough *Reichsbanner* men to protect the rally adequately. Equally unprepared were the police, only four of whom were on duty in the hall. Altogether nearly 50 people had to be taken to hospital afterwards, including seven women and three waiters employed by the beer garden. Money was stolen from the handbags of women as they fled in terror, and the storm troopers even managed to take pocket watches belonging to Wendemuth and the local SPD leader and to steal Wendemuth's spectacles. After completing their work, the Nazis shouted a loud 'Heil' and marched from the blood-spattered scene, singing and in closed formation. Because so few police had been present no arrests were made at the meeting, and the Nazis had demonstrated that they could, with seeming impunity, successfully assault a mass rally of the Social Democrats in a city regarded as an SPD stronghold.

The attack was a shock to the Social Democrats in the region. Their reaction was to demand better police protection and tough police action against the Nazis. According to the Social Democratic *Schlesische Berg-wacht*, the most widely circulated newspaper in the region:

> If the Nazis had to fear the truncheons of the police, then they never would have taken the liberty of performing this shameful act. They first must really feel [police truncheons], then their bestiality will disappear quickly.[57]

Unlike the Communists, the Social Democrats put their trust in the Weimar legal and political system, which they had played so large a part in creating. It was a trust which proved to be tragically misplaced.

Because the assault obviously had been planned in advance and because SA men had been transported into Schweidnitz from the entire region, the authorities responded sternly. In December trials were held, during which Hitler was called as a witness – this was the Nazi leader's first visit to Silesia –, and fifteen SA men were sentenced to prison terms for their part in the affair.[58] More importantly, the incident led the Social Democratic *Oberpräsident* in Breslau, Hermann Lüdemann, to order the dissolution of the local Nazi party groups, together with their SA units, in Breslau, Waldenburg, Schweidnitz, Reichenbach, Freiburg, Striegau and Dittersbach.[59] Although the Silesian *Gau* headquarters remained in Schweidnitz until the end of 1931,[60] the ban on these seven local groups was not lifted until February 1932, when Lüdemann's decree was overturned by the administrative court in Breslau. Yet while the ban created administrative difficulties for the Silesian NSDAP, it had remarkably little effect upon the growth of the Nazi movement in the area and SA units were able to circumvent the restrictions by re-forming as 'clubs' under various cover names.

The brawl in the Schweidnitz 'Volksgarten' was a milestone in the history of the eastern Prussian provinces. It provided sudden and terrifying confirmation of the explosive growth of the Nazi movement in eastern Germany. With the incident in Schweidnitz, the Nazi movement signalled its emergence from the fringes of politics onto the main political stage, capable of threatening the activities of what was still the largest party in Germany. The Schweidnitz incident also indicated that, despite its organisational strength and mass support, the Social Democratic movement was unable to deal with the new menace. The instinctive reliance of the SPD upon legal sanctions was symptomatic of a fundamental misjudgement both of the durability of the Weimar system and of the Nazi threat. In the event, neither rigorous police measures nor recourse to the courts were sufficient to cause the Nazi challenge to disappear, and the SPD and the trade unions were left in an extremely weak and exposed position in 1932 and 1933 when they were robbed of their influence in government and administration.

(iii) **The Ohlau Confrontation: 10 July 1932**

The summer of 1932 saw a great escalation of the brawling between the Nazis and their opponents, and, with the lifting of the SA ban on 16 June, the campaign for the July *Reichstag* elections assumed an increasingly violent character. The worst of the violence generally occurred on Sundays, when the political parties held their largest rallies and marches. One of the most serious incidents took place on Sunday, 10 July, in Ohlau, along the Oder between Breslau and Brieg.

The confrontation in Ohlau was a consequence of separate mass rallies of the SPD and the NSDAP, both of which had taken place elsewhere.[61] Groups of supporters were returning from the two rallies – members of the *Reichsbanner* and SPD sympathisers coming from a 'red day' in the village of Laskowitz in *Kreis* Ohlau, SA and SS men coming from a Nazi demonstration in Brieg – and their paths crossed in the centre of Ohlau. Almost immediately a fight began involving hundreds of people, and in the course of the brawl many shots were fired. Both sides tried to summon reinforcements – the Nazis claimed they were able to gather 300 men who rushed in from Breslau – and the Ohlau police proved incapable of containing the violence, which spread throughout the town. Police from the surrounding countryside were brought in to aid their colleagues in Ohlau, but this too was insufficient. Finally at 11.00 p.m., roughly four hours after the fighting had started, the army was called and succeeded in clearing the streets, By the time order had been restored there were dozens of casualties. A number of functionaries of the *Reichsbanner*, the trade unions and the SPD had been attacked in their homes as storm troopers roamed through the town, and two SA men had been killed and many others seriously injured.

The affair led to a trial during the following month, and a number of *Reichsbanner* members received prison sentences, ranging from three months to four years, for their part in the violence. Although the storm troopers had been far from innocent, the sentences aroused considerable anger among the Nazis. By chance the Ohlau trial took place at the same time as the trial of the Potempa murderers in Beuthen, and the sentences passed on the *Reichsbanner* men in Ohlau were much lighter than those given to the Nazis who had committed premeditated murder in Potempa.[62] Although the two cases involved different crimes and were tried on the basis of different laws – the stern anti-terrorist measures under which the Special Court in Beuthen was set up had not been in force at the time of the Ohlau incident – the juxtaposition of the stiff sentences against the Nazis in Beuthen and the comparatively mild sentences against Social Democrats in Ohlau provided welcome propaganda material for the NSDAP.[63] Yet the violence in Ohlau, unlike that in Potempa, was completely unplanned. Rather it was a particularly bloody example of how violence begat violence, as the growth of party armies threatened to turn any chance meeting between opposing groups into a major confrontation in which neither side could back down.

(iv) The Greifswald Shootings: 17 July 1932

One week after the incident in Ohlau, on the 'Bloody Sunday' of 17 July, the street violence which had mounted during the July 1932 *Reichstag* election campaign reached its peak. In Altona, near Hamburg, Nazis marching through working-class districts were fired upon and the ensuing battle left fifteen dead, and in the university town of Greifswald there occurred the most serious instance of political violence in Pomerania before 1933. In both cases members of the SA were victims of violence which their own activities had done much to provoke. The Nazis had set out deliberately to challenge the dominance of the Left in working-class neighbourhoods and the Left fought back, and the bloodshed which resulted helped to provide Reich Chancellor von Papen with the excuse for the coup against the Prussian government a few days later.

The Greifswald incident began with a march organised by the SA-*Standarte* in the city, in which there also were strong Social Democratic and Communist groups.[64] Altogether about 800 SA men took part, including many whom arrived from the surrounding countryside. The affair remained peaceful until the afternoon, when the storm troopers split up into smaller groups and went in different directions to find something to eat. One group became involved in fighting and attacked a retail outlet of the socialist co-operative society, the *Konsumverein*, and smashed its windows. Stones were thrown at the Nazis from within the *Konsumverein* and some shots were fired, but the police arrived in time to prevent the brownshirts from breaking their way into the building. At the same time another of the groups of SA men terrorised a working-class housing estate, smashing windows and doors until the police intervened. These incidents caused great tension, particularly in residential areas which were strongholds of the KPD and SPD, and in the evening, as various SA groups from outside Greifswald headed homeward, violence broke out once again. About 40 storm troopers returning to their homes in the nearby villages of Dereskow and Pansow were shot at as they passed working-class housing on the outskirts of the city. The Nazis then tried to storm the buildings and more shots were fired. When the dust had settled, three SA were dead and a large number wounded.

The significance of the Greifswald incident is twofold. In the first place it demonstrated the inability of the state authorities to prevent serious violence from arising out of the patterns of provocation and response which accompanied the growth of the Nazi movement. The *Regierungspräsident* in Stralsund admitted as much when he wrote to the Prussian Interior Minister a few days later that he no longer could guarantee public order with the police forces at his disposal,[65] and von Papen was able to take advantage of this to overthrow the SPD-led Prussian government. Secondly, the incident was indicative of the tendency of the SA to confront the Left by terrorising working-class neighbourhoods. The attempts to 'conquer the streets' and show the swastika flag in areas which the Social Democrats and Communists regarded as theirs were opening shots in a campaign aimed at breaking the links between the political parties of the Left and their working-class constituencies.

(v) The Königsberg Uprising: 1 August 1932

On the night of 1 August 1932 the East Prussian capital experienced a wave of violence which constituted probably the most concerted terror campaign carried out by the SA before 1933. The violence which occurred in Königsberg at the beginning of August and then spread throughout the province far eclipsed the periodic brawls and isolated acts of terror which had characterised the activities of the storm troopers hitherto. In Königsberg the SA unleashed, for the first time, a campaign which terrorised an entire city.

As throughout Germany, in East Prussia the campaign for the July 1932 *Reichstag* elections had been extremely violent. The tension in the Nazi camp was heightened by the generally disappointing election results: although the NSDAP captured 230 seats and became by far the largest party in the new *Reichstag*, the elections had shown the limits of the Nazi advance. The NSDAP had exhausted its reservoirs of electoral support – its vote had not increased appreciably since the Prussian *Landtag* elections of 24 April – and the parliamentary path to power appeared to have reached a dead end. In Königsberg the atmosphere was made yet more tense by the fatal stabbing by a group of Communist sympathisers of an SA member, Otto Reincke, as he was distributing propaganda leaflets.[66] The growing conviction of many storm troopers that violence offered the only possibility for the Nazis to achieve power and the death of Reincke on 30 July combined to break down the inhibitions and discipline which had kept the Königsberg SA in check.

The explosion came immediately after the *Reichstag* elections. SA units in Königsberg received reports that storm troopers had been ambushed by the 'reds' in the early hours of 1 August, and the East Prussian SA leadership, finding it increasingly difficult to control the membership, ordered the local *Sturmführer* to respond to the situation as they saw fit.[67] The wave of terror began as SA men set fires at petrol pumps throughout the city in order to confuse and divert the police and fire-fighting forces. Store windows were smashed and a gun shop was looted. There followed a series of attacks on organisations and political figures hostile to the Nazi movement: a bomb attack was carried out on the 'Otto-Braun-Haus', the headquarters of the SPD newspaper *Königsberger Volkszeitung*; an attempt was made to set ablaze the offices of the liberal-democratic *Königsberger Hartung'sche Zeitung*; a Communist member of the city council, Gustav Sauf, was shot and killed in his bed when four Nazis broke into his home; Otto Wyrgatsch, the editor of the *Königsberger Volkszeitung*, Maz von Bahrfeldt, a leading member of the East Prussian DVP and *Regierungspräsident* in Königsberg until dismissed by von Papen on 20 July 1932, and a Communist warehouseman of Königsberg's cooperative 'Konsum' organisation were shot in their homes and seriously wounded; and unsuccessful attempts were made on the lives of Walter Schütz, a KPD *Reichstag* deputy, and Kurt Sabatzky, syndic of the Königsberg office of the 'Central Association of German Citizens of Jewish Belief'.

During the next few days the SA terror spread throughout the province. On 3 August the chairman of the parish council in Norgau (Samland) and a *Reichsbanner* leader in Tilsit were shot. On 6 August the local secretary of the agricultural workers' union in Lötzen was assaulted and the area *Reichs-*

banner leader was murdered by a mob of SA men. In Marienburg attempts were made on the lives of a police inspector, a city building inspector (a member of the Centre Party), and the chairman of the local ADGB. In Elbing attacks were made on working-class areas of the city, including one in which a Nazi sympathiser fired into a crowd with a machine gun, and the offices of the Social Democratic newspaper *Freie Presse* were bombed. Particularly in the market towns in southern East Prussia the Nazi terror was aimed against Jews and Jewish businesses. In Allenstein a bomb was thrown at the home of a Jewish Communist and hand grenades hurled at a Jewish shop; in Ortelsburg the windows of Jewish-owned shops were smashed; and stores in Osterode, Johannisburg and Lyck were bombed.[68]

Rather than counter-attack, the victims of the SA terror appear to have relied on the police. Initially the police were caught off guard, especially in Königsberg. However, they soon began to take counter-measures: gathering places of the SA were closed and number of the storm troopers responsible for the outrages were arrested. Some of the guilty SA men managed to escape. A number were smuggled across the border into Danzig, while others eventually found their way to Bozen (Bolzano) in the German-speaking Tirol, where they remained until March 1933.[69] Those caught by the police were tried before special courts during the autumn election campaign, and the resulting publicity hurt the NSDAP electorally in November.[70] For the storm troopers who were tried and sentenced, German justice proved quite mild: the imprisoned SA men were freed as a result of the presidential amnesty in December. The punishment for a campaign of looting, bombing, shooting, arson and murder had been jail terms of but a few weeks.

While the events in East Prussia in August 1932 demonstrated the tremendous potential for violence within the SA, they also indicated the political limitations of SA terror. Once the violence of the SA was no longer tied to the political campaigns of the NSDAP, it proved a disaster. After the initial surprise, the police were able quickly to master the situation and within a few days SA meeting places had been shut down and the men responsible for the terror either were in jail or had fled. Although the SA succeeded in creating a major disturbance, it had left itself open to effective police counter-measures and revealed the inadequacy of its terror tactics so long as the Nazi movement did not control the levers of state power.

(vi) **The Silesian Terror Campaign: August 1932**

The uprising in East Prussia was paralleled in Silesia, where the July *Reichstag* elections were followed by a campaign of shootings, bombings and arson. The frustrations engendered by the election results, the conviction of many storm troopers that an SA coup attempt offered the Nazi movement its

only real chance of success, and the restrictions on regular political activity –
the political 'truce' (*Burgfrieden*) decreed by the Reich government on 29
July, prohibiting political rallies until 10 August[71] – channelled the energies
of the SA into a full-fledged terror campaign. Disaffection within SA ranks
grew, as the more moderate members began to leave and the more radical
members became restive.[72] Many Silesian units eagerly awaited the order to
'march', and the disappointment which followed the elections caused SA
leaders considerable difficulties in keeping their groups together.[73] The
Silesian SA leadership, not exactly renowned for moderation, tried to prevent the organisation from disintegrating by heightened combativeness and
aggressive posturing. Heines and his lieutenants stressed that the storm
troopers were neither to tolerate 'insults' to their uniform and the Nazi
'world view' nor to shrink from confronting the 'red mob',[74] and they
supported a terror campaign which appears to have been sanctioned by
Röhm.[75] The result was a wave of violence which enveloped the whole of
Silesia.

The Silesian terror campaign began in the early hours of 2 August, when a
grenade was thrown at the Liegnitz 'Volkshaus', the headquarters of the
Lower Silesian ADGB, and an attempt was made on the life of the former
SPD *Landrat* (dismissed after 20 July) in Goldberg, about 20 kilometers to
the west of Liegnitz.[76] In the days and nights which followed similar attacks
occurred with increasing frequency throughout Silesia. On 5 and 6 August
there were firearm and grenade attacks on an SPD sympathiser in Brieg,
shopkeepers in Kreuzburg, *Reichsbanner* members in Katscher and Leob-
schütz, and the Socialist Workers' Party leader, Ernst Eckstein, in Breslau.[77]
On 7 August the offices of the pro-Centre Party newspaper in Ratibor, the
Oberschlesische Rundschau, were bombed, a *Reichsbanner* leader in *Kreis*
Leobschütz shot dead, and shots fired into the home of an SPD functionary
in Goldberg. On the following evening the violence escalated further: in
Heidersdorf, between Strehlen and Reichenbach, and in nearby Groß-
Kniegnitz grenades were thrown at the homes of the local SPD leaders; in
the village of Jannowitz, about ten kilometers east of Hirschberg, a bomb
exploded in front of the local 'Konsum' outlet; in Waldenburg shots were
fired into the offices of the SPD newspaper *Schlesische Bergwacht* and the
windows of the newly-built Schocken department store were smashed; in
Dittersbach, near Waldenburg, shots were fired at the home of the SPD
chairman of the parish council; and in Gleiwitz a grenade was thrown into
the home of a Communist city council deputy.[78] The violence continued on
the following night: in Görlitz a *Reichsbanner* man was shot by storm
troopers; in Nieder-Heidersdorf shots were fired and a grenade thrown at
the local 'Konsum'; in Hindenburg SA men threw bombs into the office of
the Communist 'International Workers' Aid'; in Wünschelburg (*Kreis*
Neurode) shots were fired into the home of the local *Reichsbanner* leader; in
Markowitz (*Kreis* Ratibor) a grenade was thrown at the home of the chair-

man of the parish council and leader of the area's Polish community; and in Reichenbach an SA man was killed when the bomb he had intended to throw at the flat of Carl Paeschke, the editor of the SPD newspaper *Der Proletarier aus dem Eulengebirge*, exploded in his hand.[79]

The Nazi terrorism reached a peak on 10 August: in Bunzlau the windows of the Dresdner Bank branch, the local 'Konsum' and the office of a grain dealer were smashed; in Reichenbach shots were fired into the home of a *Reichsbanner* leader; near Oppeln a KPD sympathiser was shot and wounded by Nazis; in Lauban the labour exchange was blown up; in Penzig, about ten kilometers north of Görlitz, a grenade was thrown into the bedroom of a local *Reichsbanner* leader, wounding him slightly; in Hertwigswaldau, near Jauer, shots were fired into the flat of the local SPD leader; in Alt-Kohlfurt and Rauscha in the *Landkreis* Görlitz and in Görlitz itself the windows of the 'Konsum' branches were smashed; and in Potempa in the *Landkreis* Tost-Gleiwitz, probably the most notorious and widely publicised act of Nazi terror before 1933 took place when an unemployed Polish casual labourer with Communist sympathies was brutally murdered by a drunken band of SA men.[80] At that point, however, the terror quickly subsided. Faced with the frightening wave of violence, on 9 August the Reich government enacted two emergency decrees to combat political terrorism.[81] These extended the ban on political rallies until the end of the month, provided considerably stiffer penalties for acts of political terror – including the death penalty for politically-motivated murders – and established special courts to hear cases falling under the new provisions. The decrees came into force on 10 August, and greatly dampened the ardour of the Nazi terrorists. Showing how tough they were by terrorising Social Democrats and Communists was one thing; confronting the power of the state was quite another.

Although there were a few isolated instances of violence aimed against Nazi targets, the terror unleashed during the first ten days of August was overwhelmingly the work of the SA. Most of the incidents were planned in advance and carried out on the orders of the regional and district SA leadership. For example, in the Görlitz area, where the terror had been particularly widespread – according to the public prosecutor more than 30 incidents had taken place in 17 different communities in the area on the night of 9-10 August – the campaign of violence had been carefully planned.[82] On the morning of 9 August the SA-*Sturmbannführer* in Görlitz had called a meeting of the *Sturmführer* in the district. Here he discussed the general political situation, dwelling particularly on the negotiations underway about forming a new Reich government, and asserted that pressure should be applied in order to speed up a change in government. According to the *Sturmbannführer*, that night there were to be a series of terrorist attacks against 'Konsum' outlets and Social Democrats. In addition, a few harmless attacks were to be made on Nazi targets to give the appearance that the KPD was behind the violence, so that the SA might have an excuse to intervene and restore law and order! The *Sturmführer* then passed on orders, local SA units formed special task forces, specific targets were selected, and the assaults were carried out according to plan.[83]

During the weeks that followed many storm troopers were arrested for their part in the terror campaign, while still more fled rather than face prosecution. According to the Silesian SA leadership, roughly 50 men were arrested as a result of the wave of terror and another 150 fled.[84] Among those on the run were the leader of the SA 'Untergruppe Mittelschlesien-Süd' and his adjutant, both of whom were implicated in the bombings. The consequences of the terror campaign presented serious problems for the Silesian Nazi Party. In addition to alienating voters, the resulting court proceedings cost the regional Nazi organisations considerable amounts of money, as did aid for the families of storm troopers who had fled.[85] Significantly, however, Hitler did not reproach the SA terrorists; indeed, he publicly expressed support for the Potempa murderers.[86] The 'irresponsible' campaigns of the SA were not really criticised by the party until after the setbacks in the November *Reichstag* elections. Apparently the party leadership felt that to censure the storm troopers in August would have involved too great a risk of losing activist support.

The terror campaigns of August 1932 were evidence that the SA was getting out of hand, and showed the dangers inherent in violent politics for a party which basically was committed to seeking power by legal means and avoiding direct confrontation with the state. In the case of the East Prussian SA, the leadership seems to have lost control of the membership and the lower-level officers; in Silesia it was the leadership itself which got so wound up in its own rhetoric that it acted independently of the party and committed the SA to a campaign of terrorism. Once the SA became involved in this kind of illegal activity, the response of the state was swift and effective. There was no question of the SA actually fighting a civil war on Germany's streets in order to put Hitler into the Reich Chancellory; local police action and a few emergency decrees were sufficient to stop the wave of Nazi terror and send guilty storm troopers scurrying across the border. Thus, in the short term, events may have seened to confirm the wisdom of the Nazis' opponents' reliance upon the existing legal system. However, the significance of these terror campaigns was not just that they resulted in short-term setbacks for the NSDAP, but also that they foreshadowed the violence of the spring of 1933. Then the Nazi Party did not have to worry about free elections or the response of the state authorities.

(vii) The Crisis of Late 1932 and the Impact of Nazi Violence

The failure of the tactics of 'legality' to bring the NSDAP to power during the summer of 1932 and the terror campaigns during August combined to produce a crisis within the Nazi movement which appeared to threaten its survival. This crisis put into sharp relief a basic dichotomy within the movement: between the young activists in the SA on the one hand and the passive supporters who had voted for the NSDAP on the other. For many in the SA violent political activism had become a way of life and virtually an end in itself, while for many Nazi voters the violence seemed increasingly to threaten order and security. In the middle stood the NSDAP, which needed both to cultivate the voting public and to retain the goodwill and cooperation of the storm troopers – tasks which began to appear mutually exclusive in late 1932. As long as the Nazi movement seemed headed for success, it had proved possible to appeal to both roughness and respectability; once the prospect of taking power had begun to recede, however, the contradictions inherent in such an appeal became apparent.

In East Prussia, where the SA terror in August and the downturn in the Nazi vote in November 1932 had been especially dramatic,[87] the *Gau* propaganda chief, the Königsberg student Joachim Paltzo, had a very clear idea of what had gone wrong:

> The cause of this decrease [in votes in East Prussia] is to be sought in the events of 1 August. The acts of terror, which were executed systematically in the entire province, have, through their lack of success and the almost childish manner in which they were carried out, repelled the population from us. Our opponents on all sides have cleverly understood how to make full use of this in their propaganda. In the last 14 days before the elections in all the larger towns in the province special courts were set up which investigated the acts of terror. The reports of the special court proceedings were supplied with venomous commentary in the press of our opponents and were the best means to frighten from us the fickle bourgeois [*Spießbürger*] who previously voted for us.[88]

Morale among the Nazis' supporters plummeted. In *Kreis* Treuburg the district NSDAP leadership complained that, were another election to be held soon, not only many Nazi voters but also numerous Nazi Party members probably would not bother to vote.[89] In *Kreis* Goldap one NSDAP leader expressed fears that, if another election came in the near future, up to 70 per cent of the farmers and workers who previously had voted for the Nazi Party would turn to the Communists.[90] The leader of the NSDAP in Allenstein attributed the reversal of the party's fortunes to the 'fickle political attitude' of government employees alarmed at the terrorist trials underway in the city, and to the unwillingness of the SA to cooperate with the local party organisation.[91] And in *Kreis* Osterode the district NSDAP leadership blamed the drop in electoral support on the recent arrest of fifteen local Nazis in connection with the August bombings, for which the conservative farm population had little sympathy.[92]

Although the fall in the Nazi vote in Silesia was less sharp than in East

Prussia, there too the party leadership attributed the downturn to the SA terror campaign during August.[93] According to the NSDAP *Untergauleitung* in Liegnitz, many voters had been 'shocked by the irresponsible behaviour of the SA'. The party leadership in Upper Silesia came to similar conclusions, and accused the SA leadership of being either unable or unwilling to control the rank and file:

> The SA often give the impression of being freebooters who help the NSDAP out of a lust for adventure or other reasons, but not out of ideological conviction. The blame for this does not rest with the ordinary SA man . . . but with the leadership material of the SA which is not equal to the demands placed upon it.[94]

In Pomerania the terrorist violence of August – which included attempts on the lives of left-wing political figures in Stolp and the bombing of the offices of the SPD newspaper *Volks-Bote* in Stettin[95] – was condemned publicly by the NSDAP. Bellicose Nazi ideology notwithstanding, when warrants were issued in January 1933 for the arrest of the Stettin SA-*Standartenführer* Wilhelm Leuschner and an SA-*Sturmführer* in connection with the *Volks-Bote* bombing, the Nazi Party in Stettin disowned the accused; it was announced in the Nazi press that the two SA leaders had been thrown out of the party, that they had acted as provocateurs, and that the bombing had been calculated to harm the image of the Nazi movement.[96]

The effects of the crisis were not limted to the downturn in the Nazi vote. Once the aura of invincibility was lost, party members began to leave the organisation because, as the official historian of one NSDAP group in Königsberg put it, 'they already saw in the party a sinking ship'.[97] The main sources of income for the NSDAP were drying up, leaving many local groups in desperate straights; people were no longer attending Nazi rallies in the numbers they had done previously, and the revenue from party dues was falling steeply.[98] In late November Wilhelm Kube, *Gauleiter* in the 'Ostmark', noted that 'the receipt of dues has decreased in recent months in a manner nothing short of catastrophic' and that since May dues receipts in his *Gau* had fallen by half.[99] In addition, the loss of contributions from many of the more prosperous and conservative members of the community, who had been frightened by the August events, was particularly damaging.[100] The SA terror campaigns had seriously undermined the financial position of the Nazi Party.

Within the SA itself the situation was little better. Almost all the SA groups in the eastern Prussian provinces faced severe shortages of funds, and SA leaders were increasingly hard pressed to maintain control over their men.[101] Many storm troopers found their own circumstances growing more desperate, and in the absence of prospects for improvement they became less inclined to accept organisational discipline. In Breslau, for example, where unemployment among the storm troopers was an especially pressing problem in the autumn of 1932, local SA leaders were finding it difficult to 'keep the spirit [among SA men] fresh'.[102] In Upper Silesia *Untergruppen-führer* Ramshorn reported that even the best elements in the SA were 'depressed' and that within the SA there had grown an 'embitterment' which threatened to erupt in 'acts of violence on a large scale'.[103] In many areas the SA leadership was struggling to keep the storm troopers' organisation from falling apart.

One measure of the desperate situation in late 1932 was the preparations made by the Silesian SA for the coming 'seizure of power'. The Silesian SA leaders had long been among those most in favour of direct action, and had learnt nothing from the outcome of the August terror campaign. After the November elections special SA units were formed in Silesia and given military training and equipment so that they would be 'equal to the police in technical ability'.[104] The purpose of these special formations was to prepare for the violent seizure of power which the Silesian SA leadership believed was not far off. According to Ramshorn at that time, 'the Third Reich cannot be achieved with the ballot paper, but can be established only through bloodshed'; and at an inspection of a special SA formation in Ratibor in late December Heines asserted that 'the SA must be kept ready to fight and fit to march, because it must be reckoned that the SA will march, if not in January then in the spring at the latest'.[105] This was a recipe for disaster, raising the possibility of the sort of confrontation which Hitler had been determined to avoid since the failure of the 1923 *Putsch* attempt, a confrontation which the Nazis could not hope to win.

The problem which the crisis in late 1932 brought to the fore was outlined neatly by Pomeranian *Gauleiter* Karpenstein, who asserted after the November elections that in many places the SA was 'no longer the fighting instrument of the movement but has become an end in itself'.[106] The SA had ceased to serve the political ends of the Nazi movement and thus became a serious liability. Careful political calculation had been notably absent in the SA terror campaigns; little thought was given as to how the terror might affect the position of the NSDAP. Rather the violence seems to have consisted of the brute reactions of the storm troopers and their leaders (the Silesian SA leadership in particular), and whether this helped or harmed the movement as a whole was largely incidental. What saved the SA and the Nazi movement from the worst consequences of this political illiteracy was the timely appointment of Hitler as Reich Chancellor in January 1933.

In attempting to assess the impact of the Nazi violence a number of points are worth stressing. The first, and most obvious, is that it greatly affected the tenor of political life during the last years of the Weimar Republic. Largely as a consequence of the growth of a movement which did not shrink from physical violence, such activity became an increasingly accepted element of German politics and the Nazis' opponents were forced to fight ever more on the Nazis' terms. Some, especially Communists, adapted more easily than others, but no political party in Weimar Germany proved so willing to exploit the violent outbursts of its supporters as did the NSDAP. The activities of the SA provided the Nazi movement with a powerful tactical weapon against its opponents and considerably reduced the effectiveness of traditional forms of political campaigning. Furthermore, the readiness of the SA to engage in violence probably helped the Nazi Party gather support, for here was evidence of a nationalist movement which really did mean to smash 'Marxism' rather than just talk.

Yet SA violence before 1933 was effective also because it was kept within limits. Those good citizens who may have felt satisfaction at seeing someone else roughing up the 'reds' were at the same time spared a real civil war. Significantly, despite all the aggressive rhetoric, the SA did not actually confront the state authorities; even at the height of the August terror campaigns the storm troopers were not throwing grenades at police stations or army barracks, and in the main the SA refrained from underground terrorism and the assassination of political figures. While the violence of the SA and its opponents certainly was widespread, the street battles which engulfed Germany during the early 1930s did not constitute a civil war. Many of the deaths and injuries were the consequences not of planned confrontations (such as battles for control of a rally) but of chance meetings and unplanned escalations of minor street violence. On the whole, considering the political philosophies and the size of the organisations involved, the number of dead and seriously injured during the political battles of the early 1930s seems evidence less of an uncontrolled civil war fought on Germany's streets than of a series of incidents in which the rules of the game generally were understood and respected. When the storm troopers began to get out of hand or when the use of firearms threatened to change the rules of the game – as occurred in the summer of 1932 – SA violence became a liability for the Nazi movement, damaging its electoral fortunes, frightening away its support and exacerbating internal divisions.

Perhaps the most important aspect of SA violence before 1933 was the extent to which it pointed the way toward the terror campaigns after Hitler was appointed Reich Chancellor. After years of fighting their political opponents on the streets, veteran storm troopers had little inclination to compromise once the agencies of state power no longer stood in their way. It is here that the political violence of the SA may be seen as characteristic of a fascist takeover. Among the elements differentiating Nazi rule from the authoritarian governments which immediately preceded it was its terrorist character. By helping to create a climate in which compromise was ruled out and violence regarded as both expected and appropriate, the SA laid the groundwork for the terror campaigns of 1933.

CHAPTER VII

The SA and the Seizure of Power

(i) The SA in 1933

THE formation of the Hitler government on 30 January 1933 changed the position of the SA fundamentally. Limitations upon the activities of the storm troopers hitherto – the need of the Nazi Party to avoid alienating public opinion, the threat of effective counter-measures by the police, and the possibility of intervention by the Reichswehr – were swept away. Nazi violence took on a new significance as the storm troopers were able, virtually unhindered, to mount a campaign of terror during the first half of 1933. While Hitler and his cabinet colleagues owed their new posts to neither a 'seizure of power' by the Nazi movement nor an upsurge in popular support but to a 'backstairs intrigue',[1] the terror campaign of the SA helped the Nazi leader to consolidate his position and to transform a right-wing coalition government into the Nazi dictatorship. The activities of the SA in 1933 in effect constituted an 'uprising of the small-time Nazis',[2] which to a considerable extent determined the pace and shape of the Nazi takeover.

Assessing the political content of this uprising is complicated by the fact that it was carried out in large measure by members of an organisation whose composition was changing rapidly. By opening the SA to all 'patriotically-minded' German men in mid-March 1933, Röhm made possible the almost unlimited expansion of the organisation; and when, on 1 May, recruitment into the NSDAP was halted temporarily, the requirement that all SA men also belong to the Party ceased to have any meaning.[3] The growth which the SA experienced as a result was remarkable. By the beginning of 1934 its nationwide strength reached 2,950,000 – approximately six times the number in January 1933 .[4] Of those, 105,000 were members of the 'Gruppe Ostland' (East Prussia), 128,000 of the 'Gruppe Pommern' (Pomerania), 92,000 of the 'Gruppe Ostmark' (of which the SA in the Border Province formed a part), and 206,000 of the 'Gruppe Schleisien' (Silesia). The massive influx of new members changed not only the size of the SA but also its character, as many men who were either indifferent or opposed to the Nazi movement joined the organisation. The explosive and chaotic growth of the

SA made undisciplined and unauthorised action by the membership both more likely and more difficult to control, and subsequently was among the main reasons why the SA failed to turn its strategic importance in early 1933 into a secure position within the new power structure of the 'Third Reich'.

(ii) The Assault on the Left

Throughout eastern Germany, as in the rest of the country, the announcement of the formation of the Hitler government was greeted with jubilation by the Nazis, militant calls for protest and strike action by the Communists, and concern by the Social Democrats not to be provoked into providing an excuse for government repression.[5] The events of the next few days clearly demonstrated the vulnerability of the Left. The Communists, who were unable to muster the mass support necessary for a successful confrontation, offered the Nazis and the police a welcome pretext for suppression, while the Social Democrats sought to preserve their organisation by avoiding trouble.

Typical of the behaviour of the Nazis' active supporters and the police, and indicative of the weakness of the Left, were the reactions in Breslau to the formation of the Hitler government. On 31 January there were demonstrations in the city similar to those elsewhere in Germany.[6] The first to take to the streets were the Communists. Early in the day the local KPD distributed leaflets announcing a protest demonstration, at which the call would be raised for a general strike. However, as the Communist rally was about to begin roughly 500 SA men marched through the square where it was to take place. Because of the SA march, the police closed the square to the 5-600 unemployed supporters of the KPD, who were made to wait while the Nazis passed. Once the Communist demonstration finally got underway the police intervened again, claiming that the participants were singing 'songs of punishable content'. Police officers pulled out their truncheons and the Communists scattered, some smashing the windows of shops selling Nazi uniforms. The police then began shooting, and a 52-year-old unemployed worker was killed. Thus the planned call for a general strike against the new government was turned into a fiasco, which gave the Breslau Police President (a member of the *Staatspartei*) an excuse to ban all Communist rallies and marches in the region as threats to public order.[7] Meanwhile the Social Democratic leadership chose to do nothing rather than give the police a pretext to move against them as well, and saw the failure of the Communist demonstration as confirmation of the wisdom of their decision. That evening the Nazis celebrated their victory with a huge demonstration at which Heines addressed a crowd estimated at 50,000 people, and the centre of Breslau was inundated with swastika flags, military music and marching columns of storm troopers.[8] The collapse of the Communist protest, the reluctance of the Social Democrats to commit their forces to a struggle, and the active sympathy of the police had allowed the SA to become masters of the city's streets overnight.

The events in Breslau were repeated elsewhere, as the celebrations were joined not only by the NSDAP, SA, SS and Hitler Youth but frequently by the *Stahlhelm* as well. In Oppeln, for example, on the evening of 31 January the Nazis marched together with members of the *Stahlhelm* and the *Landesschützenverband*, as Upper Silesian SA leader Ramshorn led a torchlight parade at the head of 1,400 SA and SS men and Hitler Youth.[9] In Schneidemühl the *Stahlhelm* joined a torchlight parade with the Nazi formations, and at the rally which took place afterward the SA leader for the Border Province, Manthey, shared the podium with the district *Stahlhelm* leader.[10] Where the KPD attempted to organise counter-demonstrations, the police seized the opportunity to forbid Communist rallies. Thus by 1 February, when the Communist rallies were outlawed altogether by the Prussian Interior Ministry, the KPD already could no longer demonstrate legally anywhere in Silesia.[11] It appears that the police, having been purged of Social Democrats the previous summer, jumped at the chance to suppress the KPD during the first days of the Hitler government – before the *Reichstag* fire or a frontal attack on the Communists by the SA. The conservative Right, whose representatives generally controlled the police at that time, had few qualms about suppressing the Communist movement, and ineffectual KPD calls for mass protest provided them with the opportunity to do just that.

Immediately after assuming office Hitler submitted to Reich President von Hindenburg a formal request to dissolve the *Reichstag* and hold fresh elections, which were scheduled for 5 March. Thus for the next few weeks the main focus of SA activity was the elections which Göring, speaking to Ruhr industrialists on 20 February, claimed 'certainly would be the last for ten years, probably for one hundred years'.[12] In some places bands of SA men attacked trade-union offices, meeting places of the left-wing parties and the homes of prominent Communists and Socialists.[13] However, with the storm troopers mainly preoccupied with election campaigning, such violence was still on a relatively small scale.

A major escalation in the campaign against the Left was signalled in mid February when Göring, acting as Prussian Interior Minister, issued a series of decrees which opened new possibilities for Nazi violence. On 15 February Göring formally ordered the Prussian police to cease any surveillance of Nazi organisations;[14] on 17 February he ordered that the police were not to interfere with the SA, SS or the *Stahlhelm* and were to avoid doing anything which might create the impression that they were persecuting the storm troopers, whom they were to support 'with all their powers';[15] and on 22 February, allegedly in response to the 'increasing disturbances from left-radical, and especially Communist, quarters', he ordered the formation of the 'auxiliary police' (*Hilfspolizei*) to be composed of members of the SA, SS and the *Stahlhelm*.[16]

These measures were followed by an increase in SA violence (much of which preceded the *Reichstag* fire), and once again the Social Democrats proved particularly vulnerable. On the evening of 21 February, for example, a band of storm troopers attacked the 'Otto-Braun-Haus' in Königsberg, smashing windows but failing to get inside.[17] On 26 February the SPD headquarters in Beuthen were occupied by the SA; the swastika flag was raised, rooms were searched and documents of the local miners' union branch were destroyed, and thereafter the building was placed under SA guard with the agreement of the police.[18] Efforts by Social Democrats and Communists to continue normal political activity became increasingly risky. On 22 February an 'Iron Front' rally in Hindenburg was broken up by SA men, who then chased the Social Democrats' supporters from the hall and down nearby streets while the police looked on; that same evening an attempt by the Hindenburg KPD to hold a meeting met with a similar fate, and a number of the participants were seriously injured.[19] In the *Landkreis* Allenstein the SPD tried to hold seven rallies during February (as compared to 64 for the NSDAP) but succeeded with only four; the KPD in the district was unable to hold any meetings at all, and Communists who tried to distribute leaflets were set upon by SA and SS men.[20] Belated attempts by the Left jointly to resist the Nazi onslaught also met with failure, as for example in Gerdauen (East Prussia), where on 26 February a march of the SPD, KPD and *Reichsbanner* was broken up by the Nazis together with the *Stahlhelm*.[21] Leading members of the SPD and KPD were arrested, and the police increasingly coordinated their activities with the storm troopers. By the time the March elections were held, the combination of mounting Nazi violence, police action and administrative repression – by the end of February the entire Communist and Social Democratic press in the eastern Prussian provinces had been silenced for ever – had effectively driven the Left from public view.

Nevertheless it was after the elections that the really decisive assault was mounted. By early March the storm troopers, together with the police, had been able to paralyse the SPD and drive the KPD underground. Yet the organisational supports of Social Democracy – most importantly the trade unions – remained largely intact. But once the elections were past, the SA, freed of the need to assist with the campaigning of the NSDAP, could turn its attention to the root-and-branch destruction of the SPD and the trade-union movement.

The first major blow in eastern Germany was struck in Königsberg, immediately after the elections. On the night of 5 March the SA attacked and occupied the 'Otto-Braun-Haus', demolishing the local SPD and *Reichsbanner* offices in the process.[22] The one-time nerve centre of East Prussian Social Democracy was transformed into an SA headquarters in which Socialists and Communists were beaten, tortured and – in the case of the KPD *Reichstag* deputy Walter Schütz – killed. Three days later the ADGB headquarters in Breslau fell to the storm troopers.[23] Early in the morning of 8 March a group of about 250 SA men passed in front of the Breslau trade-union offices. According to the Nazis, shots were fired at the storm troopers from within the building; according to the defenders, the Nazis stormed the building unprovoked in order to hoist a swastika flag. In any event, the storm troopers had tried to occupy the union headquarters, there was gunfire, and as a result four people were injured seriously and one killed. Afterwards the SA searched the building, accompanied by members of the police force including the Breslau Police President and his deputy. Eleven occupants were arrested, and as soon as the police left and the search was entrusted solely to the SA, the storm troopers, some of whom were *Hilfspolizei*, proceeded to wreck the interior.

Two days later it was the turn of the ADGB in Liegnitz. On 10 March the city's police chief, under pressure from the district Nazi Party and SA leaders, agreed that the Liegnitz 'Volkshaus' (which contained both the area trade-union headquarters and the presses of the city's SPD newspaper) should be searched.[24] Late in the afternoon a contingent of local SA men, acting as *Hilfspolizei*, carried out the search and raised the swastika flag from the building. Then the police sealed the doors, while the district NSDAP leader lectured to the crowd gathered outside about the contrast between the orderliness of 1933 and the chaos of 1918. That night, however, events took a further turn when the leader of the Lower Silesian SA, Karl-Heinz Koch, returned to Liegnitz from Breslau and ordered another search of the 'Volkshaus'. The storm troopers accompanying Koch broke into the building, smashed furniture, burned trade-union documents and literature, stole typewriters and other items, and left the 'Volkshaus' a general shambles. The next morning the NSDAP *Kreisleiter*, who the day before had boasted of the order of the Nazi revolution, found what seemed to him worse than the aftermath of the Spartacist uprising. He complained to the Party *Untergauleiter*, who gave the order that no further damage was to be done. Nevertheless, on the following night Koch returned with another band of SA men and again broke into the trade-union headquarters, leaving the Nazi Party's local guardian of the propriety of its 'revolution' to lament that these 'senseless acts of destruction' stood 'in the most glaring contrast' to the expressed wishes of Hitler and Göring – a clear expression of the dismay which many party leaders, as well as the police, must have felt as the storm troopers took the seizure of power into their own hands.

The SA offensive against the trade unions gathered momentum as March progressed. On 13 March the ADGB headquarters in Görlitz were occupied by police and SA men, trade-union officials arrested and a portion of the building taken over by the SA. On 15 March storm troopers broke into trade-union offices in Reichenbach; and on the night of 18 March the SA assaulted the headquarters of the Pomeranian SPD in Stettin, wrecked the interior of the building, destroyed the SPD archive and printing presses and converted the cellar into a torture chamber for political opponents.[25] On 20 March SA and SS men attacked the trade-union headquarters in Schneidemühl, which they had occupied for a short period the week before, threatened that any resistance would be met with armed force, destroyed furniture, stole whatever cash and useable articles could be found, and, together with the police, arrested a number of union officials.[26] On 21 and 22 March groups of SA men searched trade-union offices in Stargard, seizing the property which could be carried away.[27] On 29 March in Greifswald, where police had shut the ADGB offices more than two weeks previously, SA men occupied the building during a police search and raised the swastika flag.[28] By the end of March there remained hardly a single major town in eastern Germany where the Social Democratic trade unions could still function normally.[29] By assaulting trade-union offices one-by-one, the SA managed to destroy what only weeks before had seemed the strongest bulwark against a Nazi takeover.[30]

In one sense the violence against the Left during March and April 1933 may be seen as uncoordinated and even anarchic: there is no evidence that the attacks on Social Democratic targets were carried out on orders from Berlin or Munich; the assults often appear simply to have been the sponteneous actions of bands of young men eager to prove themselves and settle old scores. However, the attacks on SPD and trade-union offices displayed a remarkably uniform pattern; if the activities of the SA in early 1933 spelt chaos, this was a structured chaos. The storm troopers were asserting in a perhaps incoherent but nonetheless unmistakable manner that they now were on top, that the former strongholds of their enemies now were *their* turf, that the old authority of the Socialist movement was at an end. Here it is important to remember that the principal target of this campaign was not the Communists (who already had borne the brunt of police repression and many of whom already had gone underground), but the generally older and more respectable Social Democrats who had been identified with the Weimar system. Thus in the components of the violence we can see an attack upon symbols of authority: in the removal of the old black-red-gold republican flag and the raising of the Nazi colours, in the destruction of the records of the trade unions, in the wrecking of property, in the public humiliation of Social Democratic funtionaries,[31] and in the conversion of many a 'Volkshaus' into an SA den where the building's former occupants could be tortured. Yet by March 1933 this attack on 'authority' carried very little risk, for the SPD and its allies already had been robbed of their press and positions of political power and were clearly on the defensive.

Of particular importance in the campaign against the Left was the coordination between the SA and the police. In Upper Silesia, for example, hundreds of prominent figures on the Left were arrested by the police and their SA auxiliaries during March and April; according to the police, 364

Communist functionaries had been arrested and 244 searches carried out in the province during the first two weeks of March alone.[32] In Breslau a bar-room brawl on 9 April which left two SA men dead provided the excuse for a wave of arrests by storm troopers and police of Communists and Social Democrats.[33] Even in outlying rural districts the arrests were numerous. In the East Prussian *Kreis* Gerdauen, for example, on 11 March 47 Communists and Social Democrats were taken into custody, including the local trade-union secretary, the director of the district savings bank and a former mayor of the town of Gerdauen.[34]

The effects of this campaign of repression were devastating. Within roughly two months of Hitler's appointment as Reich Chancellor open opposition to the Nazis virtually had disappeared. For example, in the East Prussian *Kreis* Darknehmen Nazi Party leaders proudly boasted in mid-March that neither the SPD nor the KPD could hold meetings anywhere in the district, since these would either be prohibited or broken up; SPD supporters were prevented from canvassing from house to house; local Communist functionaries had been arrested; and KPD candidates were forced to withdraw their names from the Party lists for the *Kreistag* elections on 12 March.[35] In Allenstein the local Nazi propaganda chief reported cheerfully in early April that neither the SPD nor the KPD were still active in the region; by the end of April only 23 members of the SPD were left in Allenstein and the membership of the ADGB trade unions had dropped to 167 from approximately 400 two months before.[36] And in nearby *Kreis* Ortelsburg the district Nazi propaganda leader noted in April that the Communists and Social Democrats no longer showed any signs of activity,'since virtually all the functionaries of the SPD and KPD are in custody'.[37] Not only did such repression largely destroy the once impressive organisational networks of the working-class parties; it also isolated the working-class movement from the working class. By terrorising left-wing activists, raiding the offices of left-wing organisations, closing down left-wing newspapers, preventing Socialists and Communists from distributing printed material, driving members away from trade unions and making it clear that left-wing political activity now involved considerable physical danger, the Nazis made great strides in early 1933 toward cutting off the Left from its working-class constituency.[38]

During the weeks after the formation of the Hitler government, support by the Nazi leadership for the terror campaign of the SA was conspicuously muted. Had the offensive failed, the Nazi leadership probably would have been no less prepared to distance itself from it than had been the case in late 1932. With the important exception of Göring, government and party leaders stressed the need for discipline and expressed concern that the political process set in motion not get beyond their control.[39] If the storm troopers took the initiative on Göring's encouragement, which certainly helped to legitimise the violence of the SA, then they listened only to those messages from the Nazi leadership which they liked and ignored those which they did not. The crucial assault on the trade unions during March and April appears to have been neither planned not organised by the top party or government leadership, and in a sense this proved an advantage: the piecemeal nature of the offensive made effective resistance virtually imposs-ible. Divided and on the defensive, not knowing where or when the next blow might be struck, unsure which of the hundreds of incidents might constitute the proper occasion for all-out resistance to the Nazi regime, faced with the combined forces of the SA, SS, *Stahlhelm*, police and, poten-tially, the army, the Left was in a hopeless position.

On 10 April the Hitler government proclaimed that henceforth 1 May would be a holiday, a 'Day of National Labour'.[40] A goal for which the trade unions had striven for decades was achieved by a government whose suppor-ters had smashed the trade-union movement to pieces. The festivities planned for 1 May were to be followed by a systematic offensive against the trade unions the next morning: the SA and SS were entrusted with the tasks of occupying all offices of the Social Democratic unions and arresting leading figures of the trade-union movement.[41] After weeks of watching and waiting while their supporters attacked the citadels of 'Marxism', the Nazi leaders had decided to celebrate the removal of the Left from German political life.

On the evening of 1 May Goebbels noted in his diary: 'Tomorrow we are going to occupy the trade-union offices. Resistance is not expected any-where.'[42] Goebbels' expectations were well-founded: most trade-union headquarters were occupied already and most leading figures on the Left were either in jail or exile. The real battle had already been fought, and the campaign against the trade unions on 2 May was essentially a piece of political theatre. At the same time, however, it offered a convenient oppor-tunity for a mopping-up operation: in Stettin, for example, the *Gau* head-quarters of the *Reichsbanner* were shut, the ADGB offices again occupied, and all the property of the unions seized;[43] in Königsberg the trade-union offices were converted into headquarters of the newly created 'German Labour Front', which seized the property of the unions as well as of the 'Konsum' organisation;[44] and in Schneidemühl the union offices, already occupied for some time by the SA, were turned over to the NSBO, while the SA, together with the local police, arrested a number of former trade-union functionaries.[45] The terror campaign which SA groups had been carrying out for weeks received an official government stamp of approval.

The character of the Nazi assault on the Left underlines the extent to which the 'seizure of power' was driven from below. The initiative of the SA committed the Hitler government to the complete destruction of the trade unions; while the government in Berlin and the party leadership in Munich looked on, the storm troopers dismantled organised labour. Once this had been accomplished and it became apparent that the destruction of the SPD and the trade unions involved little risk, the Nazi leaders readily took advantage of the situation created by their most violent and active supporters. The result was a defeat for the German labour movement of incalculable proportions.

(iii) **The Assault on the Jews**

The wave of Nazi violence which struck the Jews during 1933 was different, both in timing and in political significance, from the campaign against the Left. Since the Jewish population was largely defenceless and relatively isolated, the risk that the Jews might offer resistance was virtually nil. Furthermore, the assault on the Jews clearly took a second place behind the campaign against the Left. Before the *Reichstag* elections on 5 March there were a few isolated violent attacks on Jews; for example, in the Upper Silesian town of Cosel a band of Nazis, among them a drunken local SA leader (a former tax inspector with a history of criminal convictions for violent offences), fired shots into the homes and businesses of Jews in the early morning hours of 23 February.[46] On the whole, however, the Jewish population was left relatively undisturbed during February, and even in Breslau – which contained the largest Jewish community in eastern Germany and where the worst anti-Semitic excesses were to take place in the weeks ahead – it appears that the Nazi activists remained preoccupied with the upcoming elections and the struggle against the Left.[47]

This changed in mid-March. On 10 March Göring, who controlled the Prussian police, declared in a speech in Essen: 'I am unwilling to accept the notion that the police are a protection squad for Jewish shops. No, the police . . . are not here in order to protect Jewish profiteers.'[48] Göring's speech signalled an upsurge in anti-Semitic activity, including a number of SA-enforced boycotts of Jewish businesses. On 10 March in Gollnow, *Kreis* Naugard (about 25 kilometers north-east from Stettin), SA men carrying signs admonishing the public not to buy from Jews blocked the entrance to a Jewish shop.[49] On 10 and 11 March a similar incident occurred in Pasewalk, where SA men stationed themselves in front of a Jewish shop with signs reading 'Germans, buy only from Germans', 'Germans, don't buy from Jews', and 'Fellow citizens, support the native *Mittelstand*'.[50] And on the night of 12 March SA men assaulted a Jewish cattle dealer, his wife and his daughter in their home in Arys, East Prussia.[51]

It was in Breslau, however, that the most serious incidents took place, when on 13 March armed storm troopers invaded the local and regional courts and forced Jewish lawyers and judges to leave the buildings.[52] Lawyers and judges were dragged from courtrooms while cases were being heard, and some of the unfortunate victims were beaten. At the same time, SA men broke into the Breslau stock exchange, ostensibly to search Jewish stockbrokers for weapons. The police declined to intervene; and at a meeting of the Breslau Police President, the President of the Breslau Court of Appeal, Edmund Heines and other SA and SS leaders it was cynically decided that, since further attacks against Jews could not be ruled out and since the police could protect only a fraction of the Jewish lawyers, the remainder should be advised not to attempt to enter the court buildings. The Breslau events, in which the SA brought the legal system in one of Germany's major cities virtually to a standstill, led Hitler to instruct the Breslau SA leadership to put a stop to this independent action.[53] However, the activities of the Breslau SA triggered no public censure from the Reich authorities and were repeated subsequently elsewhere.

As March progressed, anti-Semitic incidents became increasingly frequent. In East Prussia, for example, the Jewish 'Central-Verein' recorded a wave of assaults by storm troopers during the second half of the month.[54] In Königsberg a Jewish businessman was murdered by the SA; in Prostken Jews were taken into custody and their homes searched for weapons; in Treuburg SA men patrolled the streets to keep an eye on possible patrons of Jewish shops; in Arys, Lyck and Osterode Jewish businessmen were taken into custody; in Ortelsburg SA men prevented customers from entering Jewish shops and smashed the windows of a store whose owner allegedly had tried to sell SA uniforms (the shopkeeper protested that the clothing in question was simply brown trousers, which he always had stocked); and in Allenstein storm troopers pulled down black-white-red national flags displayed by Jews and enforced a boycott of Jewish shops on market day (an action which was halted when the local SA leadership, alarmed at the independence shown by the rank and file, sent in the SS and threatened the SA members involved with expulsion from the organisation). A new pogrom was underway, and its instigators were not the Nazi leaders but the activists in the SA.[55]

The response of the government and Nazi Party leadership to the upsurge of anti-Semitic violence was ambivalent. On the one hand, Germany's new rulers obviously had little sympathy for the Jewish population, and it was difficult to prevent their supporters from carrying the anti-Semitic exhortations of Nazi propaganda to logical conclusions. On the other hand, however, they were concerned that they not lose control over the SA rank and file and that retail trade not be disrupted through the fervour of their supporters. Whereas on 10 March Göring appeared to have given the Nazi activists a blank cheque, at the same time Hitler issued an appeal for the 'tightest discipline' within the Nazi movement.[56] Hitler's call was echoed by East Prussian *Gauleiter* Koch, by Nazi Reich Interior Minister Frick (who demanded an end to interference with retail trade), and by the NSDAP in Munich.[57] Nevertheless the storm troopers continued their actions, and neither the police nor the NSDAP took measures to stop them. Nazi supporters were not following the instructions of their leaders, and outside Germany the terror against the Jewish population was causing a loud outcry.

The answer to the dilemma facing the Nazi leadership of what to do about this uncontrolled violence came on 26 March, when Hitler and Goebbels decided to call a nationwide boycott of Jewish businesses.[58] The boycott was scheduled for Saturday, 1 April, and was to be a response to the 'lies' and 'atrocity propaganda' in the foreign press. Plans for the boycott were announced hurriedly in the German press and were to be coordinated by the 'Central Committee' with Julius Streicher at its head. Yet despite the official preparations, many SA groups did not wait for the signal from above and immediately stepped up a campaign already underway. For example, on the evening of 27 March Jews in Gerdauen were dragged from their beds and forced to send telegrams to the British government, declaring that the reports of atrocities in Germany were 'fairy tales'.[59] In Stargard SA men searched Jewish homes, allegedly looking for Communist literature,[60] and in Swinemünde and Wollin (Pomerania) SA and SS men prevented customers from entering Jewish-owned shops.[61] In the run-up to 1 April storm troopers enforced local boycotts in cities and towns throughout Germany, including Glogau, Liegnitz, Schweidnitz and Waldenburg in Silesia and Stettin and Stolp in Pomerania.[62]

The official boycott on 1 April proceeded generally peacefully, and resembled on a coordinated, national scale the actions taken by individual groups of storm troopers during the previous weeks. In front of Jewish shops throughout the country stood SA and SS men who 'enlightened the public' and carried posters admonishing Germans not to buy from Jews.[63] In Königsberg, for example, posters were affixed to the windows of Jewish shops and the offices of Jewish doctors and lawyers, SA men guarded the doors to Jewish businesses to prevent customers from entering, and one SA troop forced the grain exchange to close.[64] In Breslau Jewish businesses received similar treatment, as the windows of shops owned by Jews were painted over with the word 'Jew' and covered with stickers which read, 'Germans, don't buy from Jews'.[65] Not content with keeping customers from entering Jewish shops, storm troopers also blocked the doors of Breslau's giant new Wertheim department store, searched Jewish business premises, and patrolled Breslau's cafés beating and/or ejecting anyone regarded as having a Jewish appearance. In Görlitz SA men forced the department store 'Zum Strauß', the local outpost of the Karstadt chain, to shut, while in Stettin most Jewish shopkeepers simply closed their doors once the storm troopers took up their posts.[66]

According to the German press the nationwide boycott had been an unqualified success, carried out 'in peace and discipline', 'according to plan' and without incident. However, while the boycott did take a peaceful course on 1 April, support for it was less than total and in a number of places the public responded by demonstratively buying from the blacklisted businesses. On the afternoon of 31 March SA men in Breslau took up positions in front of shops to be boycotted the following day because these shops were filled with customers; in some cases stores had to close not because of the Nazis but because they had run out of merchandise due to the extraordinarily heavy demand.[67] In Allenstein the district Nazi Party leader surveyed the political landscape after the boycott and noted that, although members of the public did participate in a rally against the 'Jewish atrocity stories', the response to the boycott itself left much to be desired:

> In the future actions against the Jews must be kept secret. Here in Allenstein the announcement of the boycott achieved just the opposite. On the two days directly preceding [the planned boycott] the Jewish shops were overflowing.[68]

The nationwide boycott had been planned as a one-day affair, after which a decision would be made about whether it should be continued.[69] Subsequently it was announced in the press that there would be no further boycott measures; Goebbels publicly judged the boycott to have been a tremendous success and concluded that there was no need to take the matter further.[70] It seems that economic pressure from abroad – especially threats of boycotts of German products – made in Germany's new masters think twice about allowing Julius Streicher to set the pace for the persecution of the Jews. The boycott had failed to mobilise anti-Semitic feeling among the population, and it posed a threat to the recovery of the German economy. Nevertheless, if one purpose of the nationwide boycott had been to contain SA violence, then it was not completely unsuccessful. Although storm troopers continued to enforce some local boycotts after the official action had been called off – for example, in Swinemünde[71] – the number of such incidents quickly diminished. The nationwide anti-Jewish boycott appears to have provided the necessary safety valve and a means by which the Nazi leadership could channel the activities of followers who otherwise were threatening to get out of control.

The course of the anti-Jewish boycotts of early 1933, like that of the assaults on the Left, suggests that the violence which followed the March *Reichstag* elections constituted an uprising of Nazi activists rather than a thought-out campaign of the Nazi leadership.[72] In both cases the behaviour of the storm troopers may be seen as an uncalculated striking out at people and institutions whose apparent authority or relative prosperity had made them objects of resentment – and in this context it is important to note that the anti-Jewish activities of the storm troopers were directed primarily against *economic* targets, against Jewish businesses and their owners. Yet the attacks on the Jewish population were not essential for the securing of political power. The campaign against the Jews, unlike that against the Left, appears to have aroused widespread misgivings among the public and created difficulties for the Nazi leadership without offering compensating political dividends. In the campaign against the Left unthinking violence had served an important political purpose; in the campaign against the Jews the limits of its usefulness for the Nazi leadership appear to have been reached.

(iv) Further targets of the SA

The explosion of SA violence which marked the early months of 1933 was not restricted to the Left and the Jews but extended to the Centre Party, Germany's Polish minority, outlets of chain and department stores, local government authorities and, on occasion, even the Nazis' erstwhile conservative allies. The activists in the SA were hitting out in all directions; with a wide range of targets and in the absence of police interference, it seemed that, for a few months at least, the storm troopers could do what they pleased.

Especially in Upper Silesia the Nazis set their sights on the Centre Party as well as the Left. On 17 February in Beuthen, following a rally of the Catholic youth organisation, storm troopers attacked participants as they returned home, in particular uniformed members of the *Kreuzschar* who had come along to protect the affair.[73] A few days later in Peiskretscham, near Gleiwitz, a band of SA men tossed a grenade into the home of a local Centre Party politician, a former chairman of the town council, during a wave of violence in which they also smashed the windows of emergency housing for the unemployed as well as of Jewish homes.[74] The most serious incident came shortly after the *Reichstag* elections, when the leader of the Upper Silesian Centre Party, Karl Ulitzka, was attacked by storm troopers after attempting to address a mass rally in Gleiwitz.[75] Soon after the rally began it was broken up by SA men who forced their way into the hall. Ulitzka tried to escape but his car was spotted by the Nazis, who slashed its tyres and smashed its windows. The police, who had ceased to concern themselves with the safety of left-wing political figures, still showed a readiness to shield the Centre Party leader. However, one Nazi supporter managed to strike Ulitzka on the head, landing a blow which required medical treatment, and the Catholic leader subsequently spent time in 'custody'. The routing of this Gleiwitz rally signalled the end of the Centre Party as the dominant political force in Upper Silesia.

The Polish minority also was target for the SA, particularly in the Border Province and Upper Silesia. In the Border Province, for example, the SA threatened the leader of the Polish Community in *Kreis* Flatow, searched the homes of Poles, and marched thtough villages with large Polish populations singing songs with lyrics such as 'If Polish blood spurts from the knife, so much the better'.[76] But there were limits to the excesses against the Poles. In one instance a band of SA men sang anti-Polish songs during Easter celebrations in a mixed community of 300 Germans and 1,100 Poles; the local German population, anxious to avoid conflict with its neighbours, disapproved, and the *Regierungspräsident* in Schneidemühl appealed to the province SA leader, Arno Manthey, to prohibit such behaviour.[77] Nationally as well the authorities sought to curb SA violence against Poles, fearing incidents which might be reported in the Polish press and have international repercussions. Thus in late April the SA, SS and the *Stahlhelm* were ordered to keep away from the eastern borders altogether in order to prevent anything from occurring that might be regarded as provocative.[78]

Further targets of the SA during 1933 were department stores and outlets of retail chains, which the Nazis had attacked for years as enemies of the *Mittelstand*. Among the more important in eastern Germany was the Wertheim department store chain, which had outlets in Breslau and Stralsund. The large, modern Breslau store had been opened with great fanfare in late 1930, when it provided the Nazis with a welcome propaganda theme.[79] Predictably, the Breslau Wertheim became one of the first stores to be boycotted in 1933, when on the morning of 11 March its entrances were blocked by storm troopers and police.[80] The SA returned to Wertheim on 29 March, when the doors to a number of stores in the city were barred by brown-shirted crusaders carrying placards accusing the firms in question of 'annihilating the *Mittelstand*'.[81] A month later it was the turn of Wertheim in Stralsund, where the firm had begun in 1875. There on 28 April storm troopers took up posts before the store entrances with the appropriate placards, while one of their number photographed anyone who nonetheless entered the shop.[82] When the store manager complained, citing government proclamations against such actions, he was told that the boycott decision had come 'from above'. Despite protests by the Wertheim management to the provincial administration in Stettin and to the Prussian Interior Ministry, the SA returned to the Stralsund store every Friday and Saturday throughout May. Wertheim was, of course, not the only chain in eastern Germany to suffer SA-enforced boycotts in early 1933. On 11 March the local outlet of a small department store chain in Neisse was forced to close temporarily.[83] On 29 March in Liegnitz foreign-owned chain stores, Woolworth and the Czech shoe manufacturer and retailer Bata, found storm troopers at their entrances, and similar incidents occurred in Schweidnitz and Glatz.[84]

These 'interferences in the economy' appear to have reflected the points of the Nazi Party Programme which emphasised the importance of a 'healthy *Mittelstand*'. It is questionable, however, whether they also reflected a general rejection of capitalism by the SA membership. In the eastern regions of Germany SA interference with capitalist concerns in 1933 seems to have involved almost exclusively particular types of retail outlets; industrial plants, corporate offices and commercial banks generally were spared.[85] The targets chosen by the SA were the most visible capitalist enterprises which appeared to be inflicting economic hardship upon a significant section of the Nazi Party membership. If this was anti-capitalism, it was an anti-capitalism of a rather limited kind. The actions against the chain stores were not blows for 'socialism' but expressions of resentments against highly visible and seemingly threatening commercial interests.

One activity of the SA frequently repeated in early 1933 was to hoist the swastika banner from government buildings. Storm troopers charged into the city and town halls, post offices, courthouses and schools, tore down the republican flag and raised in its place the colours of the 'new Germany'.[86] In Breslau, for example, this took place shortly after the *Reichstag* elections, on 7 March, when the SA and the *Stahlhelm* together hoisted the swastika flag and the black-white-red flag of Imperial Germany on government buildings throughout the city.[87] In Naugard, in Pomerania, on 11 March the SA, SS and the *Stahlhelm* paraded together through the town and then raised both the Imperial and Nazi flags on the *Landrat* office, the office of the district administration, the district savings bank building, the tax office, town hall, courthouse, labour exchange, schools and, appropriately, the prison.[88] Afterwards the storm troopers and their allies gathered in the town market-place and ceremoniously burned the republican flags they had removed. In raising the swastika flag the Nazis met with no opposition; with the Left on the defensive, the police cooperating with the SA, and many civil servants no doubt sympathising with the NSDAP, there was little enthusiasm for trying to prevent the symbolic confirmation of the Nazi victory.

More problematic were instances where storm troopers interferred with the day-to-day workings of local authorities. For example, on the morning of 9 March a group of SA *Hilfspolizei* in Hindenburg entered the city tax office and forced two officials to hand over tax records.[89] On 3 April in Peters-walde, in *Kreis* Schlochau in the Border Province, the district SA leader demanded the dismissal of a post-office employee whose only crime was the distribution of Centre Party leaflets the year before and who was prevented by storm troopers from carrying out his duties.[90] SA leaders also took advantage of the new political climate to pressure officials to release storm troopers from prison – as Upper Silesian SA leader Ramshorn did in the case of three men convicted of a murder in *Kreis* Kreuzburg in 1932[91] – and purge unwelcome people from public service – as attempted by the SA leader in Schneidemühl.[92] These incursions by the SA into the operation of local and regional government were a new feature of the violence in 1933, and were quite disturbing to those whose task it was to ensure the smooth running of the state administration.[93]

The explosion of SA violence in early 1933 can be seen as a legacy of the 'years of struggle'. The terror against political and ethnic groups in the months after Hitler's appointment as Reich Chancellor obviously was an extension, in much more favourable circumstances, of SA tactics of the previous years. In a broader sense, these terror campaigns were an inevitable result of the mobilisation of hundreds of thousands of young men by a militant and bellicose political movement before 1933. Once the opportunity was available to strike out in all directions, it was taken. In addition, this upsurge of violence, particularly after the March elections, was a consequence of the end of party-political campaigning as practiced in the Weimar period – hitherto the most important field of SA activity. Time which previously might have been filled protecting rallies or distributing propaganda leaflets was now spent attacking new victims, interfering with retail trade and disrupting local government. On the one hand, this allowed the new government to suppress its political opponents with unexpected speed and thoroughness; on the other hand, however, it created problems of discipline and the reassertion of law and order which would become increasingly pressing in the months ahead.

(v) The SA and the State

The offensive against the Nazis' enemies, real and imagined, was effective not least because of its ambiguous relationship to state power.[94] As we have seen, the hand of the storm troopers was strengthened considerably once their *'Führer'* headed the Reich government, once Frick and Göring headed respectively the Reich and Prussian Interior Ministries, and once the police were no longer hostile but in fact were urged to cooperate with the brown-shirted Nazi activists. The Nazi offensive in 1933 proved especially difficult to resist because it was two-pronged, carried out both within and outside the legal framework. The Nazis' victims, particularly on the Left, were confronted with both the violence of the storm troopers and the authority of the police. The effectiveness of each was enhanced by the other: the storm troopers presented a greater threat because behind them stood the state; and the threat posed by the state apparatus was all the more potent because the Left simultaneously was placed on the defensive by extra-legal SA terror. The formal manifestations of this relationship between the SA and the state during 1933 were the employment of storm troopers as auxiliary police and the appointment of SA leaders to public office. Thus the extra-legal force of the SA was granted the cloak of state authority.

The idea of using storm troopers as auxiliary police had been proposed earlier – by the Nazi Interior Minister of Braunschweig, Dietrich Klagges, in August 1932[95] – but was first put into practice on 22 February 1933, when Göring announced the formation of the *Hilfspolizei* in Prussia. Plans for the deployment of auxiliary police already had been developed in some areas before Göring's decree,[96] but whether this was in response to secret directives from Berlin remains unclear. The auxiliary police forces which Göring called into being generally were recruited in a ratio of 50 per cent SA, 30 per cent SS and 20 per cent *Stahlhelm*. They were placed at the disposal of the regional Prussian police forces, under the command of regular police officers, and were to perform their duties in the uniform of their own organisation but with a white armband bearing the inscription 'Hilfspolizei'.[97] The auxiliary police in Prussia were paid relatively little – the costs of the *Hilfspolizei* were considerably lower in Prussia than in the other German *Länder*[98] – , although the amount seems to have varied from region to region. According to one report from *Kreis* Uekermünde in Pomerania, the *Hilfspolizist* was paid 3.00 RM per day, while in Berlin he received 1.00 RM per day as pocket money.[99] In addition to pocket money, room and board were generally provided, which meant in effect that the upkeep of otherwise homeless and unemployed storm troopers living in SA hostels was to be paid from state funds.[100]

The role of the *Hilfspolizei* had two basic aspects during the early months of 1933. First, the auxiliaries performed a number of tasks at the behest of the regular police, ranging from searching the flats of suspected Communists to standing watch over a town's gas works.[101] Second, SA and SS involvement in the auxiliary police lent spontaneous Nazi violence the authority of the state. The fact that storm troopers became members of the *Hilfspolizei* allowed them to 'arrest' their victims at will and made resistance to the SA a challenge to the forces of 'law and order'. But despite the advantages to the SA of providing auxiliary police from its ranks, not all SA leaders were eager to become involved. In the Border Province the SA played no part in the *Hilfspolizei*, which was recruited there exclusively from the SS and the *Stahlhelm*.[102] The leader of the SA 'Gruppe Ostmark', Siegfried Kasche, decided that *Hilfspolizei* duties were not suited to the storm troopers and handed the task of selecting auxiliary police over to the regional SS leader, Erich von dem Bach-Zelewski. The restraint shown by the SA leadership in the Border Province with regard to the auxiliary police made little practical difference, however, since in any case the SA cooperated closely with the regular police as they assaulted the Left.[103]

Once the Nazi regime began to consolidate its position, the need for the auxiliary police forces soon disappeared. On 2 August the Prussian Interior Ministry ordered the dissolution of the *Hilfspolizei* and cut off funds for their further deployment,[104] although at the same time secret lists were prepared by the police of the former auxiliaries so that they might be reactivated in case of internal unrest.[105] Particular stress was placed on the need to collect all the weapons, instructions, armbands and identification papers with which the former auxiliary police had been issued during the previous months. The disbandment of the *Hilfspolizei* marked the beginnings of efforts by the Nazi leadership to restrict the activities of the SA, and formed a significant first step toward the liquidation of the SA as a powerful political force.

The second major aspect of the relationship of the SA to the German state during this period was the efforts of SA leaders to get the spoils of victory: government posts. During the upheavals of 1933 numerous SA leaders succeeded in acquiring public office, either as 'Special Commissars' (*Sonderkommissare*) appointed by Röhm or as heads of regional police forces.

Concern that the progress of the Nazi 'revolution' not be interrupted by officials whose sympathies were in doubt combined with a hunger for power and positions and the anxiousness of the SA leadership – and Röhm in particular – that the SA carve a place for itself in the new state structure.

Within days of the decision to establish the *Hilfspolizei*, Röhm appointed SA *Sonderkommissare* throughout Prussia, one in each province.[106] Their basic purpose was to establish and maintain contact with the heads of the provincial and regional administrations, in order to prevent friction arising between the government and the SA.[107] The Special Commissars also were meant to control undisciplined elements within the SA and SS who might try to take advantage of the new political situation, and to guard against infiltration by left-wing sympathisers into SA and SS ranks. In addition, they were to ensure that the measures of the Reich and Prussian governments in fact were carried out by the regional authorities. However, the 'dismissal of mayors, interference in private industry, the appointment of provisional heads of associations, etc.' were strictly forbidden.

The Special Commissars appointed for eastern Germany in late February were, with one important exception, the leaders of the SA in the respective provinces.[108] The exception was the *Sonderkommissar* for Upper Silesia until January 1934, the Silesian SS leader Udo von Woyrsch. Significantly, of all the *Sonderkommissare* in eastern Germany it was von Woyrsch who was the most aggressive in pursuing his duties.[109] With the exception of the Upper Silesian case, however, rather little use seems to have been made of the position. Far from enabling SA leaders to 'rule' their regions between early 1933 and mid-1934,[110] it seems that their appointment as Special Commissars caused little change in the power relationships in the eastern Prussian provinces. The tasks which were assigned to the *Sonderkommissare* – such as coordinating relations with government officials and ensuring discipline within the SA – were essentially the things which, as regional SA leaders, they should have been doing in any case. Upper Silesian SA leader Hans Ramshorn, who was not named a Special Commissar, was no less concerned than SA chiefs who were *Sonderkommissare* to maintain discipline among the storm troopers and to intervene in disputes involving the SA and government authorities. The actual power of regional SA leaders remained a function of their positions within the SA and, in some cases, of the posts they acquired in the police hierarchy; it was not particularly enhanced by their appointment as *Sonderkommissare*. Nevertheless, the Special Commissars did represent an incursion into regional government, and objections to their interference were registered by the Gestapo.[111] Thus the real significance of the *Sonderkommissare* lies more in the suspicions and opposition they aroused than in the power they held as a result of their new posts, and it is worth noting that among the first changes made by SA Chief of Staff Viktor Lutze after the 1934 purge was to dissolve the Special Commissar positions.[112]

More important in terms of real political power were the positions which SA leaders captured in the police administration. In the eastern Prussian provinces, SA leaders were able to gain a real hold on leading police posts only in Silesia. In Pomerania the police remained out of the hands of the SA leadership altogether; in Stettin the police were commanded between September 1933 and late April 1934 by SS-*Oberführer* Fritz-Karl Engel.[113] In the Border Province the reluctance of Siegfried Kasche to grab for new posts meant that the SA leadership there did not get involved in running the police.[114] In East Prussia the SA leadership did assume formal control of the Königsberg *Polizeipräsidium* but not until November 1933, when Adolf Kob (who had replaced Litzmann as leader of the SA 'Gruppe Ostland' in September) was appointed Police President.[115] Kob was succeeded two months later by Heinrich Schoene, both as East Prussian SA leader and Königsberg police chief, but the newcomer soon found himself forced on the defensive by Erich Koch. Koch, who had been appointed *Oberpräsident* of East Prussia in June 1933, in effect ran the *Polizeipräsidium* over Schoene's head.[116]

In Silesia SA leaders were able to secure appointment as Police President in Breslau, Oppeln and Gleiwitz. At the beginning of March *Gauleiter* Brückner began a campaign to remove the leading figures from regional government and police administrations, complaining to Göring that Nazi policies were being sabotaged.[117] Similarly, Ramshorn asserted that the necessary cooperation between the SA and the police was being blocked by unsuitable police chiefs and demanded the installation of '100-per-cent National Socialists' in the *Polizeipräsidien* in Oppeln and Gleiwitz.[118] Heines amplified Ramshorn's arguments,[119] and on 26 March the efforts of the Silesian Nazi bosses were rewarded: Brückner was appointed *Oberpräsident* in Breslau, Heines became the Breslau Police President, Ramshorn took over the regional police command in Gleiwitz, and SA-*Standartenführer* Metz was named Police President in Oppeln.[120] Heines in particular took advantage of his new post, and it was not long before his running of the Breslau *Polizeipräsidium* became a public scandal.[121]

In early 1933 it may have seemed an appropriate reward for SA leaders to place them at the head of regional police forces. However, it became evident very quickly that putting men such as Heines and Ramshorn in charge of police headquarters did not facilitate the creation of an orderly and efficiently repressive police state. While SA police may have been suited to the chaotic mouths of early 1933, they were quite unsuited to the period which followed. It seems hardly coincidental that those most successful in capturing important positions in 1933, Heines and Ramshorn, were among the most prominent victims of the purge in 1934. Considering the ease with which the SA leadership was purged in 1934, the striking aspect of the accumulation of offices by regional SA leaders in 1933 was that these offices ultimately counted for so little. While the positions which SA leaders got in police administrations probably were their most important spoils in 1933, real power in the emerging police state was to be found not in the various *Polizeipräsidien* but in the offices of the Gestapo, in which the SA gained no foothold whatsoever.

(vi) SA Concentration Camps

The escalation of violence and political persecution in early 1933 led to a sudden increase in arrests. By March 1933 jails throughout Germany were overflowing with thousands of prisoners rounded up in the campaigns against the Left, and official estimates put the number of people in 'protective custody' at roughly 15,000.[122] The actual figure probably was considerably higher; one Social Democratic observer has claimed that about 10,000 political prisoners were in custody in Pomerania alone during March 1933.[123] The overcrowding which resulted in existing jails and prisons, together with the desire of storm troopers to do with their prisoners what they liked, led to the establishment of a number of SA concentration camps. These bore little resemblance to the ordered and systematically brutal SS camps of later years; they tended to be rather improvised affairs, often set up at the initiative of regional SA leaders. As Rudolf Diels, the first Gestapo chief, later remarked, 'they were not founded, one day they simply were there.'[124]

During early 1933 concentration camps were established in each of the eastern Prussian provinces: at Quednau near Königsberg; at Hammerstein in *Kreis* Schlochau in the Border Province; in Stettin; and at Dürrgoy in the southern outskirts of Breslau. The camps at Quednau and Hammerstein were among six officially recognised and funded by the Prussian Interior Ministry, and both were small and short-lived.[125] The facility at Quednau was intended as a transit camp, for which the Prussian authorities had given 3,000 RM to set up. The camp at Hammerstein, toward which the Prussian Interior Ministry had contributed 15,000 RM, was rather more substantial and housed many prisoners from neighbouring Pomerania; at its height, the Hammerstein camp had a population of roughly 350.[126] Quednau and Hammerstein were essentially minor parts of an incipient state-run system of concentration camps. Both were dissolved in the summer of 1933, when the system was rationalised leaving only three camps in Prussia: at Sonnenburg in the *Regierungsbezirk* Frankfurt/Oder, at Lichtenberg near Torgau – where the prisoners from Hammerstein were sent when it was shut – and a newly enlarged camp in the Emsland marshes near Osnabrück.

The other two camps, at Stettin and Dürrgoy, were of a rather different character, examples of the 'wild' concentration camps opened during the early months of 1933. Of these 'wild' camps, Dürrgoy was among the most notorious. On 14 April, shortly after Heines had been appointed Breslau Police President, barbed wire was put into place and work began to convert the one-time camp for French prisoners of war to the south of Breslau into an SA concentration camp. Two weeks later, on 28 April, it opened to receive its first 100 inmates.[127] Among the prisoners who filled the Dürrgoy camp were Paul Löbe, the former SPD *Reichstag* President; the former SPD *Oberpräsident* in Breslau, Hermann Lüdemann; Ernst Eckstein of the Socialist Workers Party; Ernst Zimmer, the former editor of the Breslau SPD newspaper *Volkswacht*; the leaders of the *Reichsbanner* in Breslau, Hans Alexander and Max Kukielczynski; and Karl Mache, leader of the Breslau district SPD and former mayor of the city.[128] The camp had been set up solely at the initiative of Heines, without expressed authorisation from Berlin; indeed, the *Staatspolizeiamt* in Berlin first learned that the camp had been established when the American journalist Louis Lochner discovered that Löbe, who was arrested in the capital in March, had been kidnapped by Heines' SA and transported to Dürrgoy.[129] With control of the Breslau *Polizeipräsidium* and what amounted to his private concentration camp, Edmund Heines became virtually a law unto himself.

Conditions at Dürrgoy were characterised by a make-shift sadistic anarchy.[130] From the relatively modest beginning in April 1933 the number of prisoners in the camp grew to more than 500 at its peak. These had to endure the random violence of the storm troopers, the vicious behaviour of the camp commandant, Heinze, and the brutality of Heines himself. Heinze took special pleasure in holding fire drills throughout the night, during which the half-clad prisoners were forced to leave their barracks and walk along muddy paths in the darkness, to be beaten as they returned. Heines, in a particularly vengeful act, compelled former *Oberpräsident* Lüdemann to walk through the streets of Breslau wearing the costume of a harlequin to a chorus of insults by SA men. But for all its unpleasantness, the persecution of Dürrgoy's unfortunate victims remained unsystematic and, unlike in the SS camps of later years, at least the prisoners were given adequate nourishment.[131]

The camp at Dürrgoy soon became a thorn in the side of the Berlin *Staatspolizeiamt*, and reports about what was going on in Breslau, especially those concerning the treatment of Hermann Lüdemann, led Diels to send a representative to the Silesian capital to investigate.[132] The report sent back to Berlin alarmed the Gestapo chief, who presented the findings to Göring and received authorisation to discuss 'winding up' the camp with Heines. When Diels met with Heines, however, the SA leader welcomed him with a tirade against the 'softly-softly' approach of Berlin and refused to cooperate. Diels then took the matter to Hitler and received the authority to shut Dürrgoy. On 10 August, shortly after Göring ordered that the *Hilfspolizei* be disbanded, the camp was closed and its prisoners either taken to the camp near Osnabrück or brought to the Berlin police headquarters and set free.

The other 'wild' concentration camp in eastern Germany, also set up without the authorisation of the Prussian Interior Ministry, was established by the SS in late 1933 in a disused portion of the 'Vulkan' docks in Stettin.[133]

During early 1933 the SA had used the former offices of the SPD newspaper *Volks-Bote* in the centre of Stettin as place to torture left-wing opponents. These activities soon were transferred to a barracks on a sports ground toward the outskirts of the city, where many citizens, particularly wealthy Jews, were forced to contribute to a 'fund for the fight against Marxism'. The conduct of the storm troopers aroused public disquiet, however, and the informal camp on the Jahnstraße sports ground was closed down in the early summer. The vacuum thus left was filled by the Stettin SS, which opened its own camp in the docks during the autumn. Initially intended for the interrogation of prisoners and handling additional work from the busy police headquarters in the city, with the backing of Stettin Police President and SS leader Fritz-Karl Engel the camp soon developed a life of its own. Far from the city centre, SS and SA members were able to torture their victims in greater privacy, and the corpses of the more unfortunate were weighted with stones and dumped into the Oder. But the Nazi activists went too far, and when complaints about the 'Vulkan' camp were made by Field Marshal August von Mackensen and the Pomeranian 'Trustee of Labour' Rüdiger Graf von der Goltz, the Berlin authorities decided to curb the activities of the camp's overseers.[134] Göring sent a representative to Stettin with the power to move against the SS; in March 1934 the 'Vulkan' camp was shut down; and soon afterwards the camp's commandant and other SS men involved in its operation were brought to trial.

The development of the concentration camps in 1933 paralleled the fortunes of the SA as a whole. During the early months the storm troopers clearly were on the offensive; there was little that the authorities could do about their behaviour; and the camps themselves formed an important element of the successful terror campaign against the Left. Indeed, the concentration camps were the ultimate means by which to separate the working-class movement from the working class. However, once this was accomplished, wild SA terror had outlived its usefulness. In an orderly authoritarian state there was little room for a concentration camp such as Dürrgoy. Once the new government had established itself firmly in power, the 'wild' concentration camps ceased to serve any useful function and became an embarrassment and a liability. They aroused widespread unease and posed a threat both to public order and to the power of state institutions – such as the Reich and Prussian Interior Ministries and, most importantly, the Gestapo – and soon were dissolved. The success of the SA campaigns of early 1933 did not involve careful political calculations; gut-level, violent politics were sufficient, even advantageous. But once the Left had been suppressed and the storm troopers proved unwilling or unable to keep themselves in check, then the politics of violence aroused real opposition and threatened the future of the SA itself.

CHAPTER VIII

The SA after the Seizure of Power

(i) The SA and the Stahlhelm

ONCE the Nazis had consolidated their control of the government and erected a one-party state and once SA violence thus had lost its political *raison d'être*, the fundamental problem facing the SA leadership became putting its house in order and securing a power base in the 'Third Reich'. This problem permeates the main themes of the history of the SA after the seizure of power: the phenomenal growth of the organisation, the need to control the violence of its members, and its relations with the conservative Right. These themes are closely intertwined. The difficulties of exerting control over the SA membership were exacerbated by the tremendous growth of the organisation in 1933 and 1934 – a growth which brought in many men whose commitment to National Socialism was questionable; the growth of the SA involved, to a considerable degree, the takeover of the *Stahlhelm* and the absorption of its members; and the relations with the conservative Right during this period were bound up closely with the problem of uncontrolled SA violence which was undermining popular support for the Nazi movement.

The *Stahlhelm* played a key role in the changes which affected the SA from the summer of 1933 onward. The close cooperation between the Nazi storm troopers and the conservative veterans' organisation which followed the formation of the Hitler government was short-lived. The two organisations soon were drawn apart by the pressures of the March elections, when the *Stahlhelm* supported the conservative 'Fighting Front Black-White-Red' (the successor to the DNVP). On 20 February the *Stahlhelm*'s second in command, Theodor Duesterberg, ordered a halt to joint marches with the Nazis,[1] while local Nazi groups grew increasingly reluctant to work together with their erstwhile conservative allies.[2] Following the elections, relations between the SA and the *Stahlhelm* deteriorated further, and the *Stahlhelm* was attacked openly by the SA; in Ratibor the SA threatened the district *Stahlhelm* leader with arrest in late March, and in Königsberg a *Stahlhelm* rally was broken up by storm troopers in April.[3] The friendly alliance of the conservative and radical Right at grass-roots level, between the SA and the *Stahlhelm*, lasted only a few weeks.

The tension between the SA and the *Stahlhelm* grew as the latter developed into a focus for opposition to the new regime. This opposition had two main components. The first was the conservative Right. Many of the conservatives in the *Stahlhelm* regarded the new regime with suspicion and found the violence of the storm troopers distasteful. When their organisation was subordinated to the SA in July 1933, this met with the strong disapproval of many *Stahlhelm* leaders. The head of the East Prussian *Stahlhelm*, Graf Siegfried zu Eulenburg-Wicken, left the organisation in protest when its national leader, Franz Seldte, agreed to Hitler's demands that the *Stahlhelm* give up its independence, and the former chairman of the DNVP in Pomerania, Georg Werner von Zitzewitz, publicly objected to the 'sell-out' of the *Stahlhelm*.[4] Among the most serious confrontations between the conservative *Stahlhelm* leadership and the Nazis in eastern Germany occurred in June 1933 in Meseritz, in the Border Province, where NSDAP members attempted to seize control of the local 'Agrarian Association' (*Landbund*) and remove its chairman, the area *Stahlhelm* leader Graf zu Dohna von Hillergaertingen.[5] After the Nazis in the association failed to oust Dohna in an election, they enlisted the help of the area *Staatskommissar*, von Bredow, who appointed a new, Nazi leadership for the *Landbund*. When the *Stahlhelm* leader protested, von Bredow ordered the SA to arrest him. Dohna was released following *Stahlhelm* appeals to the government in Berlin, but the affair left relations between the local SA and the *Stahlhelm* extremely tense. In rural areas such as the Border Province the reservations of the traditional conservative elites about the successful Nazi movement were reflected most clearly in the attitudes of the *Stahlhelm* toward the SA.

The second source of the opposition within the *Stahlhelm* was Communists and Social Democrats who entered the veterans' organisation once their own political parties had been suppressed. Such infiltration resulted in serious violence in Braunschweig, where many supporters of the Left had joined the *Stahlhelm* and were attacked brutally by the SA, SS and police in late March.[6] In the eastern Prussian provinces as well left-wing infiltration of the *Stahlhelm* was a major cause of concern to the police and the Nazi movement. For example, in Pomerania both the Nazi Party *Gauleitung* and the police noted with alarm that 'Marxists' were entering the *Stahlhelm* in large numbers.[7] When the police made a detailed investigation of the recent recruits on the Pomeranian *Stahlhelm* in late June 1933, they found that a high proportion of the new members were former supporters of the SPD and KPD: in Uekermünde the *Stahlhelm* group, which had numbered 60 in January 1933, grew by 28 by June, of whom three were described as 'democrats', two as DVP supporters, one from the Centre Party, twelve Social Democrats and one Communist; in Greifenhagen, to the south of Stettin, of 64 *Stahlhelm* members who joined between January and June

1933 thirteen had been SPD members, nine KPD members and one member of the DDP; in Stralsund the *Stahlhelm* group, numbering about 200 members in January, doubled in size during the next six months and the police calculated that 74 of the newcomers were 'Marxists'.

The extent of opposition to the Nazi movement within *Stahlhelm* ranks became painfully clear as the SA carried out the step-by-step absorption of the veterans' organisation. The first step was taken in late April 1933, when Seldte dismissed Duesterberg and formally placed his organisation under Hitler's political leadership.[8] In return for subordinating the *Stahlhelm* formally to Hitler, Seldte felt he had secured official recognition for the organisation and thus ensured its continued independence. This independence did not last long, however. On 21 June Hitler and Seldte reached a new agreement whereby the *Scharnhorst Bund*, the youth wing of the *Stahlhelm*, became part of the Hitler Youth and the *Jungstahlhelm*, which contained the members between the ages of 18 and 35, became the *Wehrstahlhelm* and was placed directly under the command of the SA leadership. A few weeks later it was agreed that the *Wehrstahlhelm* would be integrated into the SA. This move aroused considerable anger among *Wehrstahlhelm* members, who found themselves drafted into the SA often against their will and under threat of arrest if they refused.[9] In November 1933 came the next step; the reorganisation of the remaining *Stahlhelm* members into the 'SA Reserve I' (for those aged 36 to 45) and the 'SA Reserve II' (for those over 45). The 'SA Reserve I' was integrated completely into the SA in January 1934. The 'SA Reserve II', however, regained a measure of independence when Röhm and Seldte agreed in March that it would become the 'National Socialist German Front-Fighters' League' (NSDFB). Thus except for its older members the SA largely had swallowed the *Stahlhelm*, but in so doing it took in hundreds of thousands of men who felt little sympathy for the Nazi movement.

Not surprisingly, the forced union of the *Stahlhelm* with the SA went far from smoothly. In Pomerania many *Stahlhelm* groups openly resisted the amalgamation in June 1933.[10] To deal with this, Heines (who at the time was 'Obergruppenführer' of the SA in Pomerania as well as in Silesia) was appointed 'Special Plenipotentiary for the Reorganisation of the *Stahlhelm* in Pomerania', and he disbanded numerous *Stahlhelm* units and purged the memberships of many others.[11] In Upper Silesia as well there was a vigorous campaign against a recalcitrant *Stahlhelm*.[12]

Friction between the remnants of the *Stahlhelm* and the SA persisted in 1934. Particularly in Pomerania serious conflicts developed between storm troopers and members of the NSDFB. In May a number of NSDFB leaders were arrested for alleged 'sabotage against the SA, i.e. the direct or indirect influencing of former *Stahlhelm* members not to join the SA Reserve I'.[13] Reporting to Göring about the difficulties in Pomerania, the recently appointed Gestapo chief Reinhard Heydrich observed that 'the antagonisms

between the SA, the SA Reserve I and the NSDFB have become so aggra-
vated that the functioning of the SA Reserve I is endangered considerably';
furthermore, according to Heydrich, the conduct of the Pomeranian NSDFB
had 'brought about considerable unrest in the population over and above the
ranks of the SA'.[14] By mid-1934 brawls between the SA and former *Stahlhelm* members and arrests of NSDFB members were common.[15] Tension
between the SA and the former *Stahlhelm* membership reached a peak
shortly before the 1934 purge, when an SA-*Sturmführer* was stabbed fatally
by an NSDFB member following a summer solstice festival in Quetzin,
about fifteen kilometers east of Kolberg.[16] Such was the feeling aroused by
the killing that, to prevent further violence, the police felt it necessary to ban
the NSDFB throughout Pomerania. For its part, the SA leadership
demanded the complete dissolution of the NSDFB, since 'scarcely a day
went by which did not bring friction, fights and tension' whereby 'the
instigators were almost always to be found in the ranks of the NSDFB'.[17]
Thus by the eve of the 1934 purge the SA had been drawn into open conflict
with the remnants of the *Stahlhelm*, which it had been so eager to absorb.

The SA lost more than it gained by the takeover of the *Stahlhelm*. The
absorption of the *Stahlhelm* reduced the political reliability of the SA and
increased the threat which the storm troopers' organisation posed to the
orderly running of the country. In order to acquire an important place in the
emerging Nazi state, the SA leadership felt that the organisation had to grow
as rapidly as possible – which meant swallowing the *Stahlhelm*. Yet this sort
of growth created more problems than it solved. Not only did taking over the
Stahlhelm exacerbate the unease of many older, conservative nationalists
about the Nazi rank and file; it also made the SA even less capable of serving
a useful function in the 'Third Reich'.

(ii) The SA in 1933-1934

During late 1933 and early 1934 the problem of what was to become of the
SA grew ever more pressing.[18] Some new activity had to be found for an
organisation whose only real focus had been political struggle. Like the Nazi
movement and like the 'Third Reich' as a whole, the SA could not simply
stand still; it constantly had to find outlets for the aggression of its members.
After the Nazis' domestic political opponents had been vanquished, the SA
leadership – and Röhm in particular – hoped to solve the problem by
transforming the organisation into a new National Socialist people's army.
However, achieving such a goal (even if, from the outset, it was quite
unrealistic), or indeed any solution to the problem of finding a role for the
SA, depended upon its putting its house in order, i.e. establishing and
maintaining discipline. Unlike the SS, which remained a small elite force, the
SA was growing by leaps and bounds and becoming less manageable at a

time when it had to be brought under control.

The first call to impose discipline on the storm troopers came from the SA leadership itself. Röhm was aware of the difficulties which indiscipline would cause, and discussed the issue quite openly when he appointed the *Sonderkommissare* in late February 1933.[19] Referring to reports of excesses by SA and SS men throughout Prussia, he stated that he 'appreciated completely the long-suppressed rage and the desire for retribution' but went on to stress that uncoordinated violence constituted a harmful interference with the state authorities and the police. He therefore prohibited 'excesses and acts of indiscipline', ordered that the SA and SS be on best behaviour to dispel rumours of an impending *Putsch*, and urged that special precautions be taken against 'provocateurs' in SA ranks. During March, when the SA uprising really got under way, numerous Nazi leaders echoed Röhm's call for discipline. Hitler attempted to bring his supporters under control on 10 March with an appeal to the SA and SS in which he blamed the unwelcome violence on 'unscrupulous characters, mainly Communist spies', demanded the 'tightest discipline' and insisted that 'the molesting of individuals [and] the obstruction or disturbance of businesses must cease'.[20] On 13 March Reich Interior Minister Frick issued a circular, which was published in the press the following day, sharply criticising the uncontrolled violence and instructing the police to take action to stop it; ten days later the 'politische Zentralkommission' of the NSDAP, headed by Rudolf Heß, prohibited attacks by party members on businesses.[21]

Despite the calls by Nazi leaders for discipline, the violence of the storm troopers continued, and during April, after the anti-Jewish boycott, both Frick and the NSDAP leadership reiterated their warnings. Expanding on its decree of late March, the NSDAP 'politische Zentralkommission' ordered members of the NSBO, SA, SS and the Party not to act on their own; not only unauthorised interference with the operations of economic organisations, factories and banks but actions against the trade unions were forbidden as well.[22] For his part, Frick attempted to clarify the legal position of SA and SS members – who effectively stood outside the law – 'in order to punish offences against discipline and order in the appropriate manner'.[23]

A frequent theme in the calls for discipline was the alleged threat of left-wing subversion. Hitler was not the only one concerned about violence being incited by 'unscrupulous characters, mainly Communist spies': in mid-February the Prussian Interior Ministry expressed the fear that men who were members of neither the SA nor the SS were wearing Nazi uniforms and provoking incidents in order to discredit these organisations;[24] in early March the SA leadership in Munich warned of possible Communist infiltration;[25] and ten days later Röhm issued a directive outlining how the SA should cope with the avalanche of new members, stressing the need for 'careful measures to prevent a flooding of our splendid SA with unsuitable elements, provocateurs and spies'.[26] The fears of the Nazi leadership were not totally without foundation. Immediately after Hitler's appointment as Reich Chancellor the KPD repeated calls for its supporters to 'encourage sedition in the ranks of the Nazis', to 'show the misled SA-proletarians for whose interests they are being used', and to 'pull the misled SA members over into the front of the fighting proletariat'.[27] And in a number of places the KPD met with some success; with their party driven underground, many Communist sympathisers sought to continue their political activity in Nazi ranks.[28] For example, an account of the Nazi movement in Upalten, in the East Prussian *Kreis* Lötzen, noted that almost all the Communists in the area joined the SA in early 1933 and that they succeeded in driving many of the original Nazi members from the organisation.[29] Isolated reports from the early months of 1933 mention the expulsion or arrest of SA men for being Communists, spreading Communist propaganda or 'spying' in the SA,[30] and in the districts of Kreuzburg and Rosenberg in Upper Silesia it appears that one-time Communist sympathisers in Nazi uniform were responsible for a number of violent incidents.[31] However, the main wave of left-wing infiltration seems to have come after the SA campaigns against the Left were finished, when left-wing sympathisers entered *Stahlhelm* units in large numbers. Furthermore, blaming left-wing provocateurs for unwelcome violence offered Nazi leaders a convenient method by which to distance themselves if necessary from the actions of their supporters.

The summer of 1933 brought renewed efforts to control the SA men. On 6 July Hitler proclaimed that the 'revolution' was 'not a permanent state of affairs',[32] a warning which provided Frick and Heß with the opportunity for yet another attempt to impose discipline on the Nazi rank and file. On 10 July the Interior Minister let it be known that the 'victorious German revolution' had entered the phase of evolution, 'i.e. normal, lawful reconstruction work'; according to Frick, 'any attempt to sabotage the German revolution, as can be seen particularly in unauthorised interference in the economy and the disregard of the orders of representatives of the state, must be punished with the strictest measures'.[33] Two weeks later Heß repeated the party ban on authorised violence and declared that the NSDAP too would take action against anyone who disobeyed.[34] Röhm also reiterated his position: while he remained 'eager to secure and defend in all regards the rights of the SA as the officially recognised troop of the National Socialist revolution', he felt that he could not tolerate the reports of theft, burglary, plunder and settling of scores which were reaching his desk.[35] Those responsible were, according to Röhm, 'placing the good reputation of the SA at risk', and only once indiscipline had been curbed did the SA Chief of Staff feel he could 'advocate with the necessary weight before the state authorities that SA men might be arrested not by the police but only by SA men'. Not only Röhm but even regional SA leaders occasionally went on record to condemn the unthinking violence of the men under their command. In the Upper Silesian industrial region, for example, one SA *Sturmbannführer* threatened in July 1933 to expel members who created difficulties for the police.[36] Shortly afterwards his superior, Ramshorn, also condemned the continuing violence – which had included attacks by storm troopers on party members! – and ordered that those guilty be thrown out of the SA and arrested.[37] The problem of adapting the SA to the period of 'evolution' was proving difficult indeed.

Although the summer of 1933 saw the first practical steps to curb the excesses of the SA – some of the 'wild' SA concentration camps were closed and the *Hilfspolizei* were disbanded – the problem of the uncontrolled violence of the storm troopers remained. Frick in particular continued his efforts to establish order, and in October the exasperated Reich Interior Minister stated bluntly in a memorandum:

> Despite the repeated declarations of the Reich Chancellor and despite my numerous memoranda, in recent weeks new excesses by junior officers and members of the SA have been reported again and again. In particular, SA officers and SA men have undertaken police actions for which the authorisation was lacking or which were carried out in a manner incompatible with the existing laws and the decrees of the National Socialist Government. . . . These excesses finally must come to an end.[38]

However, this was no more effective than the previous warnings. The storm troopers were paying little heed to the leaders of the Nazi Party and the German state, and it was becoming apparent that, in order to control the SA, drastic measures would have to be taken.

It is against this background of repeated efforts to establish order that the behaviour of the storm troopers during late 1933 and early 1934 should be seen. By persisting with their unruly conduct the storm troopers were ignoring clear directives from the Nazi leadership, and local and regional SA leaders were either unable or unwilling to keep their men in line. Not surprisingly, the violence alienated the public and damaged the position of the SA in its quest for a new political role in the emerging 'Third Reich'. Although they did not realise it the members of the SA guilty of this behaviour, and the SA leaders who neither could nor would control it, were playing a very dangerous game indeed.

A major part of the problem was the lack of constructive activities to take the place of the street fighting and electioneering which hitherto had formed the focus of life in the SA. Furthermore, it appears that a substantial number of storm troopers remained unemployed despite the new government's work-creation programmes; this, together with the unrealistically high expectations among Nazi activists of the spoils which would come their way after a seizure of power, meant that the SA was a reservoir of potential trouble-makers.[39] In any case, the best jobs were meant for the veterans of the pre-1933 period, and by the summer of 1933 only a minority of the SA membership fell into this category. Nevertheless, the SA violence of late

1933 and early 1934 did not involve social protest, against unemployment for example, rather it consisted essentially of the rowdy behaviour of young men who believed that once they wore a brown uniform they could do as they pleased.

Partly to keep idle hands busy and partly to emphasise the presence of their organisation, regional SA leaders arranged a succession of mass rallies designed to impress both onlookers and the participants themselves. Thus in late May 12,000 storm troopers participated in a march on the Annaberg in Upper Silesia; in early June 16,000 took part in a march through Liegnitz; and at a monster rally in Breslau in October a reported 80,000 SA men appeared.[40] Yet the attitudes of the SA leadership toward the violence of the storm troopers were far from unequivocal. While Röhm may have criticised uncoordinated violence, Edmund Heines was hardly counselling moderation when he spoke to the assembled crowd at the Liegnitz rally in June. Addressing the question of what would become of the SA, the Silesian leader bellowed, 'the future of the SA men will be decided by the SA itself. . . . The SA demands the continuation of the German revolution; it declares that whoever is not for us is against us.'[41]

With SA leaders prepared to make such statements, it is not surprising that storm troopers continued to bully communities throughout eastern Germany. In Stralsund the local SA formed special 'action committees' and threatened to occupy the city hall in early June 1933 because the mayor 'had not displayed enough energy with regard to his actions against Communist functionaries'.[42] Serious trouble was averted only by the intervention of the regional SA leadership. More frequently the intimidation assumed a less organised and less overtly political character, as SA men became involved in countless fights and public disturbances. Drunken brawls involving storm troopers were particularly common. Often personal disputes were at the root of the violence. For example, in *Kreis* Randow in Pomerania a disagreement between the fiancée of an SA man in one village and men at a nearby 'Labour Service' camp led to a major punch-up in mid June between the village SA and the men from the camp. To some extent, this was the sort of behaviour which was bound to come from the ranks of an organisation containing hundreds of thousands of young men. Nevertheless, as a result the SA was posing a serious threat to law and order.

Few aspects of the Nazi movement proved so effective in alienating the politically neutral or uncommitted public as the unruly behaviour of the storm troopers. During July 1933 in Königsberg, the NSBO – which in the East Prussian capital had attracted support mainly from white-collar workers in what were described as 'reactionary firms' – complained that the conduct of the SA was a major cause of unrest among its members.[44] New NSBO recruits, primarily previously apolitical or conservative middle-class members, were especially upset at the indiscipline and violence of SA men who 'all run around with pistols and knives'. In rural villages the activities of the SA had equally negative effects. For example, in Penkuhl, in *Kreis* Schlochau in the Border Province, the local SA leader was accused of generating 'constant unrest among the population because of his behaviour', which included causing disturbances in the village tavern and repeatedly threatening villagers with arrest and concentration camp.[45]

For the police the conduct of the SA presented a particularly thorny problem. The legal position of SA offenders was far from clear, and the police could face difficulties if they tried to bring SA men to book. A typical incident occurred in Neustadt in Upper Silesia in late October 1933, when a police officer attempted to stop a group of storm troopers from singing loudly in the town's main square late at night.[46] The officer tried to arrest the man whom he suspected was the ringleader, but the others prevented him from doing so, surrounded him and gave him a serious beating. The storm troopers then began a rampage through the town, punching passers-by and finally becoming involved in a brawl with some Reichswehr soldiers in civilian clothes.[47] In other cases the behaviour of the brown shirts was equally worrying. In Neisse on 17 December two SA men assaulted a local Jewish businessman in a café, and when a police officer came to investigate he was told not to 'proceed so harshly against SA men' and threatened with concentration camp.[48] Rather than provoke additional trouble, the police officer decided to leave the storm troopers alone.[49] In another incident, in the Upper Silesian village of Dombrovka a.d. Oder in January 1934, an SA *Truppführer* demanded from the police the keys to the local jail since he felt that 'the SA has the right to proceed with arrests on the streets and to place people in custody'.[50] It was hardly surprising in such circumstances that the SA failed to gain the confidence of the police or the public at large.[51]

The problem of how to control the SA was complicated further by Röhm's success in removing the storm troopers from the jurisdiction of the police and the courts. In December 1933 regional SA leaders were informed that disciplinary action against SA men – even when they clearly had broken the law – could be taken only by the storm troopers' organisation itself.[52] According to the 'Supreme SA Command', 'no member of the SA may be brought to trial, taken into custody, arrested in order to obtain a confession, or questioned as a witness or as an accused person without the permission of the SA leadership'. SA members were told that, should police officers summon them for questioning, the police were not to be obeyed but instead informed that SA men could not be summoned by the police forces. Where SA members were liable for arrest this was to be handled by the legal advisor of the appropriate SA-*Standarte*, and in every community of reasonable size the SA was to have its own legal council recruited from SA ranks. Despite these elaborate provisions, however, it is doubtful whether the self-disciplining of the SA actually functioned; cases of SA men punished by their own organisation were rare, and the lack of enthusiasm shown by the SA to discipline itself must have made it seem all the more dangerous. Röhm succeeded in removing the SA from the jurisdiction of the civil judicial system. However, rather than strengthening his position Röhm probably weakened it, since now only by moving directly against the SA leadership could the police authorities – which included Göring and Himmler – effectively assert control over the SA.

The threat to internal security posed by the storm troopers led to growing concern in Berlin, where the Gestapo was taking careful note of the incidents in which SA members had been involved.[53] In early January the head of the Gestapo, Diels, met with Göring to discuss the difficulties which the storm troopers were causing. Special attention was paid to conditions in Breslau, where the behaviour of the SA and the 'excesses' of Heines in particular had aroused grave concern. According to Diels, informants who travelled to Berlin to give evidence against Heines needed to remain in the capital under assumed names since they dared not return to Breslau.

Yet despite the concern of the authorities, 1934 brought little change in the conduct of the storm troopers. Far from diminishing as a result of the warnings of Nazi leaders. the number of violent incidents in which storm troopers were involved seems to have increased; in Greifswald, for example, the legal advisor of the area SA-*Standarte* admitted to a 'constantly rising number of violent and dishonourable offences by SA men' during the first six months of 1934.[54] Especially disconcerting was the tendency for SA gatherings to degenerate into fights among the storm troopers. In one instance, in Rummelsburg in eastern Pomerania, a Nazi meeting developed into a drunken brawl in which the storm troopers thrashed their own *Standartenführer*; in another, after a dance in the village of Penkun (about 25 kilometers south-west from Stettin), a heated exchange between SA leaders from Stettin and officials of the NSDAP '*Gau* Leadership School' in nearby Wartin ended with a mêlée in which the interior of a tavern was wrecked and a number of shots fired.[55]

By mid-1934 the SA had succeeded in alienating not only a large proportion of the German population; it had managed even to arouse the hostility of many of its own members. The disaffection within the SA was due to a number of factors, including the disappointment of storm troopers who remained unemployed, the tension between veteran SA men and the new members who came into the organisation via the *Stahlhelm*, and the extreme insensitivity of some local SA leaders. Perhaps the most telling evidence of the gulf between SA leaders and the rank and file in the first half of 1934 comes from *Kreis* Bomst in the Border Province. Here, according to a report filed by the *Landrat* in early May, the local SA leadership had forced 'all sections of the population capable of bearing arms' into the SA and then staged numerous rallies, marches and night-time exercises; and this was done without regard for the fact that many of the SA men, who were either farmers or farm labourers, had to work twelve hours per day in the fields.[56] In one case a local SA leader dragged from their beds at gunpoint those SA men who failed to appear at exercises. SA leaders, whose sole employment was with the SA, would drive cars during night exercises, watching men who already had worked a full day tramp on foot. The *Landrat* concluded:

> That such a situation will produce great bitterness among the people is obvious. In this way one will neither convince a single member of the working population to support the state nor produce in him a love of National Socialism.

The *Regierungspräsident* in Schneidemühl, who noted that a number of such reports had reached his desk, dutifully informed the Gestapo.[57]

After the capture of power the SA manifestly failed to adapt itself to the new circumstances. While Röhm's unsuccessful pursuit of his military aspirations for the SA was alienating the Reichswehr and other powerful interests, the rowdy behaviour of the storm troopers was alienating the population at large. It is difficult to say precisely what proportion of the SA actually was involved in this behaviour; it may have been relatively small. What was important, however, was the atmosphere created, in which many conservative Germans, who otherwise supported the new government, felt threatened.

For the most part the violence of 1933–4 was not aimed against the Nazis' political opponents, who already had been driven from public life, nor was it directed particularly against the NSDAP. Indeed, far from the SA leadership feeling 'increasing resentment' against the party chiefs,[58] it appears that relations between the SA and the NSDAP in eastern Germany were better, on the whole, after January 1933 than before – presumably because the principal source of conflict, finance, no longer posed a problem. Furthermore, calls for a 'second revolution', to which historians examining the 1934 purge have attached much significance,[59] were conspicuously absent until the eve of the purge.[60] The continuing SA violence was a consequence of an aggressive propaganda which convinced the Nazi movement's most active supporters that after the seizure of power they would be able to do what they liked, a rapid growth which made asserting adequate control over the organisation virtually impossible, and a failure of the leadership to bring this violence to a halt. The threat which this behaviour posed to the organisation was noted prophetically by Heinrich Schoene, the leader of the East Prussian SA, in February 1934. In an attempt to impress upon the men under his command the need for discipline, he warned that the unruly conduct of its members could make the SA 'appear unworthy of its lofty duties and thereby lose the trust of the *Führer*'.[61]

CHAPTER IX

The 1934 Purge

THE purge of the SA in 1934 spelled its end as a force in German politics.[1] What had seemed one of the most powerful institutions in Germany offered virtually no resistance as its leaders were dismissed, arrested and murdered. Almost overnight the SA was transformed into a politically impotent mass organisation limited largely to ceremonial functions, and many cities, towns and villages were freed of the SA bullies who had terrorised their populations during the previous eighteen months. Of course, the threat which the SA posed to law and order, serious though it had been, was not the basic reason for the bloodbath in the summer of 1934. The key issues revolved around the future of the SA and the Reichswehr. From late 1933, when Hitler opted for the expansion of the Reichswehr and closed the door to the development of the SA into Germany's new armed force, Röhm became increasingly isolated. The SA leader's unwillingness to accept Hitler's decision, the deteriorating health of Reich President von Hindenburg and the looming problem of the succession, and the hostility of a number of Nazi leaders (including Himmler and Göring) to Röhm, paved the way for the radical and bloody solution to the problems posed by the SA.

During the first half of 1934, as tension rose within the SA[2] and the question of what should be done with the organisation grew more pressing, Röhm made a series of well-publicised 'inspection' tours. Speaking at SA marches and mass meetings, the Chief of Staff attempted to strengthen his own position and criticised the Nazi Party and Reichswehr leadership; however, far from aiding his own cause, Röhm in fact was providing his enemies with further ammunition for their campaign against him.[3] The last of these tours was a trip to Pomerania in late May, which took place with great fanfare and was given extensive press coverage spotlighting Röhm personally and emphasising 'revolutionary National Socialism'.[4] Accompanied by his 25-year-old adjutant Hans Erwin Graf Spreti – who also subsequently was murdered – Röhm spent a number of days in the province and spoke at mass rallies in Stettin and Kolberg.[5] Soon after his Pomeranian visit Röhm announced that, on doctor's advice, he would take an extended rest at Bad Wiessee, to the south of Munich. At the same time he ordered the

SA to go on leave during the month of July, but warned that the 'enemies of the SA' would be disappointed if they hoped that the organisation would not emerge again afterwards. The SA, according to Röhm, remained 'the fate of Germany'.[6]

As elsewhere in Germany, in the eastern Prussian provinces the generally tense political atmosphere permeated the SA, and numerous reports testify to the disquiet among storm troopers on the eve of the purge. Although most of these reports were written after 30 June by people with no great affection for the purge victims, nevertheless they appear consistent with previous accounts of SA behaviour from late 1933 and early 1934. According to one report filed by a former *Stahlhelm* member in the SA-Reserve, the SA-*Standartenführer* from Stolp asserted in mid-June in Rummelsburg (eastern Pomerania) that 'the new state will be an SA state; whoever wants to have a post will have to come from the SA'.[7] At that point Max Heydebreck, the SA-*Standartenführer* in Rummelsburg, allegedly announced that according to Röhm 'something will happen in the near future'. From Greifswald came a similar report, that SA-*Brigadeführer* Arwed Theuermann had confided to a group of storm troopers that within a short time they would be called upon to sacrifice their 'possessions and blood'.[8] And in Stralsund it was claimed that in late May a local *Sturmführer* had spoken to his SA unit approvingly of the 'second revolution' and an imminent 'night of long knives', and that on 27 June a secret meeting of local Stralsund SA leaders was informed by another *Sturmführer* that soon there would be 'three nights of long knives'.[9]

Especially serious was the mounting friction between the Reichswehr and the SA, particularly in Pomerania and Silesia, during the late spring of 1934. Shortly before the purge SA leaders in the western portions of the *Regierungsbezirk* Köslin reportedly discussed SA-Reichswehr relations and concluded, rightly, that 'the Reichswehr stands in opposition to the SA and is trying to influence the *Führer* so that he will reduce the SA'.[11] According to a farmers' leader in *Kreis* Kolberg, Fritz Molzahn (the SA-*Sturmführer* killed in the confrontation with NSDAP members at Quetzin on 23 June) had talked of the coming 'second revolution' and asserted that when this 'second revolution' came his task would be to occupy the Reichswehr barracks at Kolberg.[12] In Rummelsburg Max Heydebreck subsequently was accused of having told two Reichswehr soldiers in the spring of 1934 that once 'Papa Hindenburg' was dead 'the SA then will march against the Reichswehr', adding: 'What will the 100,000-man Reichswehr do then against so over-whelming a force of SA men?'[13] And three days before the purge a 'political instruction evening' was held for an SA-*Standarte* in Breslau during which the speaker allegedly discussed the possibility that the Reichswehr might be called upon to fire on storm troopers.[14] Perhaps most ominous were reports of interference by SA patrols of Reichswehr supply transport shortly before the purge.[15] On the night of 28/29 June a Reichswehr supply lorry, travelling from Gleiwitz to Oppeln and back, was stopped repeatedly by armed SA patrols, and on one occasion weapons it was carrying were confiscated and the soldier in command threatened by the leader of the SA patrol.

Talk about a coming confrontation and hostility towards the Reichswehr appear to have arisen as a consequence of the mounting tensions on the eve of the purge. Such sentiments had not been especially prevalent within the SA during the previous months, and may be seen more as the result than a cause of its political isolation in mid-1934. Nevertheless, they caused concern among the Reichswehr and Nazi leadership. The spectre of millions of storm troopers challenging the Reichswehr, although rather unrealistic, was worrying, and it seems that the rumours about the Reichswehr led many SA leaders to behave in ways which aroused suspicions all the more.

It is now apparent that the Reichswehr and the SA had been placed on a collision course, and during the week before the purge rumours of an SA *Putsch* were rampant. On 24 June the Reichswehr commander in Silesia, Ewald von Kleist, was warned by the Chief of the Army Command, General Werner von Fritsch, of an 'imminent attack of the SA on the army', and was instructed to place his forces on alert.[16] During the days which followed von Kleist received 'a flood of reports . . . which gave the picture of feverish preparations on the part of the SA', and observed that 'in some garrisons dangerous tension has developed between [the Reichswehr] and the local SA'. According to von Kleist, ' a spark would be enough to send the powder keg sky high', and in order to avoid bloodshed he decided to approach Heines. When he confronted the SA leader on 28 June with the reports he had received about preparations for a coup, Heines replied that *he* had been aware of preparations being made by the Reichswehr which he had assumed were for an assault on the SA. Thereupon Heines gave his 'word of honour as an officer and SA leader' that he had neither planned nor prepared an attack against the Reichswehr.[17] Then that evening Heines telephoned von Kleist to report that throughout Germany the Reichswehr seemed 'on the alert for an SA *Putsch*'. The next day Heines flew to Röhm in Munich, while von Kleist went to Berlin to inform Generals von Fritsch and Beck of his discussions with the Silesian SA leader. Von Kleist reported that he had 'the impression that we – the Reichswehr and the SA – are being set against each other by a third party', namely Himmler. At the request of von Fritsch and Beck he repeated his observations to General von Reichenau, who answered ominously: 'That may be true, but it is too late now.'[18]

At the same time the SS and the police were making final preparations to suppress the coup supposedly planned by the SA. On 23 June the head of the political police in Breslau was ordered to file a report on more than a dozen individuals, including Edmund Heines.[19] On 24 June, the same day on which von Kleist received his orders to take precautions against the SA, Himmler called a meeting of regional SS leaders at his office in Berlin.[20] The head of the Silesian SS, Udo von Woyrsch, arrived in Berlin too late to attend, and met privately with Himmler the following morning. Repeating his message of the previous day, Himmler informed von Woyrsch that the SA was planning a revolt and that Silesia in particular was a centre of unrest. Von Woyrsch was to be responsible for suppressing this 'revolt' and for establishing law and order in the region. Close contact was to be maintained with the Reichswehr, which would take SS men into its garrisons and provide them with arms in the event of serious trouble, and if necessary a special SS formation in Dresden could be called upon.[21]

Once back in Silesia von Woyrsch passed Himmler's orders on to his subordinates and then contacted von Kleist, and the guard was strengthened at the Breslau SS headquarters.[22] Local SS leaders were informed that Hitler was planning to move against an SS 'mutiny', that 30 June was to be the 'decisive day', and that contact had been made with the Reichswehr. Lists were to be prepared of 'politically unreliable' people, and it was emphasised that only orders emanating from the SS should be obeyed. That bloodshed was on the cards was made clear as well: in Hirschberg, for example, the head of the area SS informed local SS leaders that it would be necessary to arrest many SA members, that the SS would be called upon to kill, and that the 'slightest resistance' was to be met with the use of arms.[23] In the meantime the Reichswehr had received orders to make its garrisons ready for the SS, and in Berlin the chief of the 'Security Service', Reinhard Heydrich, set up a direct telephone link with the Silesian capital. On 29 June Ernst Müller, the head of Heydrich's 'Security Service' in Breslau, was ordered to Berlin, where he received a sealed letter containing orders to be delivered to the Silesian SS leader, and then was sent back to Breslau – in a private plane provided by Göring – to await further instructions.[24] The pieces were being put into place.

The most important eastern German SA leaders killed in 1934 met their deaths in Munich. Among the SA leaders shot at Stadelheim prison on 30 June were Edmund Heines, Hans-Peter von Heydebreck (who had replaced Hans Friedrich as Pomeranian SA leader in September 1933) and Hans Hayn (the leader of the SA in Saxony and formerly Heines' Chief of Staff). Heines, who had joined Röhm at Bad Wiessee, was arrested there by Hitler, who discovered the Silesian SA leader in bed with a male companion.[25] Heydebreck was arrested along the road from Munich as he was travelling to meet Röhm, brought to Stadelheim, and shot together with Heines.[26] Elsewhere on the same day the leader of the 'SA-Gruppe Ostmark', Siegfried Kasche, was arrested and brought to Göring in Berlin.[27] However, after energetic protestations of innocence Kasche managed to save his life. Of all the leaders of 'SA-Gruppen' in the eastern Prussian provinces only Heinrich Schoene, who had taken up his duties in East Prussia only a few months before, was spared completely.

Within a few hours of Hitler's arrival at Bad Wiessee in the early morning hours of 30 June, the suppression of the SA 'revolt' was underway throughout Germany. In Silesia the purge was set in motion when Heydrich telephoned Ernst Müller and ordered him to present the sealed letter to the SS leadership as well as to ensure that the SS took control of Breslau's police headquarters and communications centres.[28] Failure, warned Heydrich, would cost Müller his head. The letter, which was written on the stationery of the Prussian Minister President (Göring) and dated 30 June 1934, spelled out how the purge was to proceed in Silesia: Röhm, according to the document, had planned a coup, but this had been checked by Hitler; a state of emergency was in effect and Göring had been given overall executive power in Prussia to deal with the crisis; and in Silesia this executive power in the hands of von Woyrsch. Enclosed was a list of SA leaders 'to be eliminated', including Edmund Heines, his brother Oscar (an SA officer in Breslau), Hans Ramshorn, Freiherr von Wechmar (who only two months before had replaced Karl-Heinz Koch as SA-*Brigadeführer* in Liegnitz), and a number of other leading figures in the Silesian SA. The SA staff guard were to be placed under arrest, the Police *Präsidium* in Breslau was to be occupied immediately, contact was to be established with the commander of the *Landespolizei*, and a barge on the Oder carrying weapons belonging to the SA was to be 'secured'. Von Woyrsch, who had been at his estate at Schwanowitz near Brieg, hurried to Breslau, where he set up office in the Police *Präsidium* and gathered his SS staff. By 11.00 in the morning the Silesian SS leader was ready to establish order.

Once von Woyrsch had taken over the Breslau Police *Präsidium* and telex links were established with Heydrich's 'Security Service' in Berlin, orders came from the Reich capital to shoot the SA leaders on the list brought by Müller, to arrest all SA leaders from the rank of *Standartenführer* upwards, and to use arbitrary powers of arrest should public order appear threatened.[29] Men under von Woyrsch's command occupied the headquarters of the Silesian SA – although, since the SA was on leave, very few of its leaders were there. With the cooperation of *Gauleiter* Brückner, who also had been informed of the 'revolt', and officers of the 'SA Reserve I', SA leaders throughout Silesia were instructed to report to their headquarters in Breslau. Thus during the afternoon of the 30th SA leaders obediently filed in to their organisation's Breslau offices and then were not permitted to leave, Other local offices of the SA were occupied as well, and more SA leaders thus were arrested and brought to the police headquarters.

While a large portion of the Silesian SA leadership were being rounded up in Breslau, orders came from Göring naming the regional police commander (*General der Landespolizei*) Niehoff 'Special Commissar' for the provinces of Upper and Lower Silesia.[30] Niehoff was instructed to inform Brückner of his appointment, disarm and arrest Heines' staff and occupy their offices, arrest Hans Ramshorn, send police officers to take over the Police *Präsidien* in Gleiwitz and Oppeln, occupy an SA work camp in Breslau and disarm and intern its occupants, secure all airports and radio transmitters, and take control of all the weapons stores of the SA while cooperating closely with the

SS and maintaining contact with the Reichswehr. The most important arrests, however, were made by the SS.[31] The chief quarry, Hans Ramshorn, telephoned the Breslau Police *Präsidium* on the morning of 30 June, spoke with von Woyrsch's chief of staff Maak, and agreed to come to Breslau. Taking no chances, Maak then sent out an SS commando unit which intercepted the Upper Silesian SA leader in Ohlau, arrested him and brought him back to the Breslau police headquarters. The Lower Silesian SA-*Brigadeführer*, von Wechmar, was brought to Breslau by a similar deception, as was the SA leader in Schweidnitz, *Brigadeführer* von Grolmann. By late afternoon arrested SA leaders had filled the cells of the Breslau police headquarters as well as its canteen, a nearby restaurant and rooms in the SS headquarters, and Müller, who in the meantime had been appointed head of the Breslau Gestapo office by Göring, began to release some of those who were felt to pose no serious threat.[32]

During the afternoon of 30 June, while arrests were being made, Heydrich repeatedly asked from Berlin whether the executions had been carried out.[33] After some confusion about whether the killings should take place in Silesia or Berlin, the order came to shoot the victims in the vicinity of Breslau. The men to be executed were assembled in the SS headquarters, and that evening, after their insignia had been torn from their uniforms, they were handcuffed herded into a van and driven to a forest hear Deutsch Lissa where they were shot by an SS commando unit in the early morning hours of 1 July. Among those murdered were four men on the Berlin death list, including Ramshorn and von Wechmar, as well as three others who held lower-rank positions in the Silesian SA hierarchy.

On Sunday, 1 July, the arrests continued. Oscar Heines was locked up at the Breslau police headquarters after, upon hearing on the radio that his elder brother had been shot, he turned himself in. Another Silesian SA-*Obersturmbannführer* whose name was on the death list, Engels, was brought to the Breslau Police *Präsidium* from Cologne, where he had been caught while on holiday. Yet another SA leader, the head of the Silesian 'mounted SA' Gerhard von Klitzing, was arrested personally by von Woyrsch, who met him by chance at a Breslau race course where the SS leader was to receive an honorary prize. Both Oscar Heines and Engels were shot near Deutsch Lissa in the early morning of 2 July, and with these killings the work of the SS in the Silesian capital was completed. Significantly, there was no resistance. Indeed, it was indicative of the limited political understanding of the SA leaders that they failed to grasp what was happening on 30 June and meekly delivered themselves, in an expression of naive loyalty, to their murderers.

Elsewhere in Silesia there was further bloodshed, and the opportunity was taken to settle personal scores. One example was the case of Emil Sembach, the *Reichstag* deputy for Brieg and an SS officer until February 1934. Sembach, who had been expelled from the SS for alleged embezzlement, had aroused the enmity of von Woyrsch – to such an extent that during the spring of 1934 Sembach asked Reich Interior Minister Frick for special police protection because he feared the Silesian SS leader.[34] When he met with Himmler before the purge von Woyrsch had discussed Sembach's fate, and Himmler decided that Sembach should be sent to Berlin. Nevertheless, on the afternoon of 30 June Sembach was arrested in Brieg and then taken to Oels, where he remained until Sunday evening when he was driven by an SS commando unit into the mountains and shot. For Udo von Woyrsch the task of establishing order in Silesia provided the opportunity to eliminate his own enemies as well as Röhm's friends.

Not only active members of the Nazi movement but also completely innocent bystanders were murdered. In Lower Silesia, where the SS-*Abschnittsführer* had let it be known that the SS would 'clean things up', local SS leaders happily used the 'action' to terrorise the public. In Hirschberg nearly 40 people were earmarked for arrest, and four of them – a Jewish lawyer, a Jewish businessman, a Jewish doctor and the doctor's non-Jewish wife – were shot 'while trying to escape'.[35] In Bunzlau and the surrounding area the SS arrested a large number of people, particularly leading local conservatives and estate owners, and mistreated them in a manner resembling the unruly behaviour of the SA.[36] In Landeshut the local SS leader ordered two innocent workers arrested and later shot, one in his cell because he had been making noise and the other in the town forest.[37] In Glogau the local SS arrested a number of SA leaders, all of whom were released within a matter of days, as well as the leader of the Jewish veterans' league in the town, who was driven to a nearby wood and shot.[38] And in Waldenburg a local SS leader, a butcher named Deponte, used the opportunity to take revenge on a former building inspector and Centre Party member named Kamphausen, whom he blamed for blocking his appointment as a supervisor of the city abbatoir: on 30 June Deponte led an SS squad which snatched Kamphausen from his home, drove him towards Schweidnitz, shot him and dumped his body at the side of the road.[39]

In addition to the arrest and execution of SA leaders and the securing of buildings which might be important in a rebellion, special effort was made to disarm the SA.[40] With the increased emphasis on military training after January 1933, the Silesian SA had gathered a quantity of arms.[41] In Upper Silesia the following (most of which had belonged to the SA) were seized: 298 rifles, 111 carbines, 24 miscellaneous weapons, 80 hunting rifles, 70 small-calibre rifles, 381 pistols, 37 drum revolvers, over 16,000 rounds of ammunition, two kilogrammes of explosives and parts of a machine gun.[42] In some cases the police confiscated everything belonging to the SA which might conceivably be used in the event of an uprising. In Groß Strehlitz, for example, in addition to arms the police seized steel helmets, field telephones, a condensor, regular table telephones, instruction booklets for setting up field communications and containers for electrical equipment.[43]

Although such weapons stores may have provided handy *post hoc* justifications for the campaign against the SA, they seem to have been amassed essentially for training exercises and clearly were insufficient for a coup attempt; in the entire province of Upper Silesia the SA apparently did not possess a single complete machine gun.

The purge of the Silesian SA met with little opposition. In the one instance where there was a slight measure of resistance, in Leobschütz, this was due more to misunderstanding than rebellious intent.[44] There storm troopers, inside a disused factory which served both as an SA headquarters and an arms store for the Reichswehr, apparently fired on an SS unit and police who had been ordered to secure the building. The police then telephoned the SA men, who surrendered their weapons and were brought first to the local Reichswehr garrison and then to Leobschütz jail. The following day all those involved, except the two SA officers in charge at the time, were released. In the meantime, however, news of the incident had reached Berlin and Breslau, and von Woyrsch ordered that the two men be killed. After some delay – there was reluctance to execute the obviously innocent young men – an SS unit took the two from their cells, stood them against a wall and shot them.

The reaction to the purge among the surviving SA leaders was to stress their 'absolute obedience' and loyalty to Hitler and to distance themselves as far as possible from Röhm and the 'unheard-of state of affairs' which had prevailed before 30 June.[45] Within the SA public discussion of the purge was forbidden, and loyalty to the murderers of their erstwhile leaders became the watchword of the storm troopers.

In Pomerania the purge proceeded rather differently than in Silesia. The role of the SS was less prominent; there was not the same level of violence against innocent members of the public; and, although the purge of the Pomeranian SA leadership was thorough, only two leading members of the organisation – Hans Peter von Heydebreck and his adjutant Walter Schulz – were killed. On the other hand, those murdered in Pomerania included former members of the SS who had been dismissed for their involvement in running the concentration camp set up in the Stettin docks.[46] The purge was set in motion in Pomerania in the early afternoon of 30 June. At about 1.00 p.m. notification came that Röhm had been arrested, and roughly one hour later the *Regierungspräsident* in Stettin was informed that emergency police powers had been delegated to the head of the Stettin police constabulary.[47] Soon thereafter the various civil and military authorities in the province were issued guidelines for the action which was to follow.[48] News of the planned 'attempt on Hitler and the Reich' was relayed, together with the information that Röhm, Heines and other SA leaders had been arrested. Since the Pomeranian capital had not yet been notified of Heydebreck's arrest, specific orders were issued for his capture (and the police searched for him feverishly until they learned that he had been shot in Bavaria).[49] At the same time SA headquarters in Stettin were to be occupied; all SA weapons stores were to be taken over by the police together with the SS; and all airports and radio transmitters were to be secured.

During the afternoon and evening of 30 June the police arrested those *Brigadeführer* they could find, as well as many other SA leaders and a number of other people who 'might use the present situation for reactionary purposes'.[50] In addition to rounding up a large portion of the Pomeranian SA leadership, the police also took control of the government buildings in Stettin as well as the SA headquarters and, for a short time, the Stettin radio transmitter.[51] Altogether more than 50 members of the SA – most of them from the guard at the Pomeranian SA headquarters – were taken into custody in Stettin on 30 June. Those arrested were held in police cells and offices until the evening of 2 July when, on the order of the Berlin Gestapo headquarters, the 20 most important prisoners were transported to the Reich capital.[52] Of these Walter Schultz was killed, while many of the others remained in custody for most of the summer.

As in Stettin, throughout the province the purge was carried out smoothly. Public buildings were secured and suspect individuals arrested.[53] Particularly common were arrests of former *Stahlhelm* members, a consequence of the tensions in Pomerania before 30 June.[54] The only serious instance of the SS taking advantage of circumstances occurred in the Greifswald area, where a young SS leader arbitrarily suspended a number of police officers from duty and proceeded to arrest people (including the elderly mayor of Wolgast) according to his whim.[55] As in Silesia special efforts were made to confiscate weapons belonging to the SA. On 1 July it was ordered that the SA surrender its weapons to the police,[56] and considerable numbers of arms were collected, although once again the amounts hardly would have been adequate for a coup. In *Kreis* Anklam, for example, the SS confiscated 94 rifles and two pistols; in Greifswald 58 rifles, one carbine, roughly 750 rounds of ammunition and communications equipment were seized; in *Kreis* Demmin the police confiscated 30 rifles and two machine guns; in Pyritz eleven rifles, four carbines, two light machine guns and a few other small arms were collected. The ease with which the arrests and the confiscation of weapons were accomplished allowed a relatively rapid return to normal. Already on 1 July the situation was judged sufficiently peaceful that pre-arranged meetings, rallies and marches were permitted, insofar as they did not involve the participation of the SA.[57] And on 2 July the press could report (truthfully) that, according to the police, 'the overall situation in the whole of Pomerania is calm. The SA stands firm and united behind the *Führer* Adolf Hitler.'[58] For the murdered SA leaders there was not a trace of support.

On Monday, 2 July, the first steps were taken to reorganise the SA. Hitler, acting as 'Supreme SA Leader', empowered SS-*Gruppenführer* Kurt Daluege to make the necessary preparations for the reorganisation of the SA 'Gruppen' in eastern Germany.[59] In Silesia and Pomerania Daluege had a large task. Nevertheless, he could be confident of the passive acceptance of the process by the SA membership.

In Silesia the SS alert had been lifted by the morning of 3 July,[60] while in Berlin Brückner conferred with Daluege about the 'reconstruction of the Silesian SA' and met with Göring and Hitler.[61] Among the first moves was Göring's decision to replace Heines as Breslau Police President with a Nazi civil servant, and on the following day Hitler named Otto Herzog, until then leader of the storm troopers in the *Gau* Weser-Ems, to lead the Silesian SA.[62] Herzog took up his new duties immediately, and on 6 July he called a meeting of all Silesian SA leaders from *Sturmbannführer* upwards in order to introduce himself to his new subordinates and to 'thank the faithful'. In Upper Silesia Hans Ramshorn's position at the head of the SA was filled by *Standartenführer* Metz, the Police President in Oppeln, as a 'reward for loyalty'.[63]

In Pomerania too the process of reorganising the SA began as soon as the arrests ceased. On 2 July a provisional leader was appointed for the 'SA Gruppe Pommern', to supervise the filling of posts left vacant by the purge; a permanent successor to Heydebreck was named two weeks later, when Hans Friedrich was appointed.[64] Thus for a second time within little more than three years Friedrich was called upon to lead the Pomeranian SA after an unsuccessful 'revolt'. A belated casualty of the purge in Pomerania was Wilhelm Karpenstein. Friedrich's appointment seems to have signalled the fall of the Pomeranian *Gauleiter*, who had been at odds with the SA leader ever since coming to the province in 1931. Certainly the purge weakened Karpenstein's position from the outset, for he had enjoyed good relations with the murdered Heydebreck. Probably with this with this in mind, while the purge still was in progress Karpenstein made repeated and effusive declarations of loyalty to Hitler, distancing himself from the dead SA leaders.[65] These efforts proved of no avail, however, and in late July Karpenstein was dismissed because of his 'repeated refusal to follow the orders of the party leadership' and replaced by the former mayor of Koburg, Franz Schwede.[66] He was arrested, taken to Berlin and held in custody there for a period at Gestapo headquarters.[67]

The suppression of the 'revolt' offered the Nazi leadership a belated opportunity to rediscover its moral standards, Indeed, among the most important aspects of the 1934 purge was that it marked a change in the face which the Nazis presented to the German public. During the 'time of struggle' before 1933 and in the campaigns immediately after Hitler had become Reich Chancellor, the Nazi Party had looked to the SA (and the SA had prided itself) as a rough-and-ready band of fighters prepared to battle for the cause – a tough organisation of young men who cared little for bourgeois conventions and scorned acceptable bourgeois behaviour. With the purge this was brought to an abrupt end; now the SA was made to recognise that a main task of the Nazi movement was gaining and holding the support of millions of Germans to whom the rowdy behaviour of the storm troopers was, at least, distasteful. While the purge still was under way, Göring asserted piously that 'the *Führer* no longer will tolerate that at the leadership of the state and the movement there stand men who, due to unfortunate inclinations, have become asocial and amoral elements'.[68] And when he named Viktor Lutze to replace Röhm as Chief of Staff, Hitler stressed that the behaviour of SA leaders, like that of party functionaries, had to be 'exemplary': drunken leaders 'who conduct themselves in front of the public in an unworthy manner, who are rowdy or cause excesses, are to be thrown out of the SA immediately', and 'offences against § 175 [homosexuality] will be answered with immediate expulsion from the SA and the Party'.[69] In early August Lutze ordered that each SA 'Gruppe' set up its own 'investigation committee' which, like the 'SA Special Court' in Munich, was to concern itself 'not only with the events which led to 30 June', but also the general 'disorderly conduct, immorality, chasing after posts, materialism, embezzlement, drink-excesses, ostentatiousness and gluttony etc.' of SA leaders,[70] Behaviour which had been tolerated for years by the SA, NSDAP and Hitler himself was now condemned. Thus the purge marked the beginning of a process whereby, as Mathilde Jamin has put it, the appearance of the Nazi regime was reconstructed so that 'the unpolitical German could regard National Socialist institutions as a constituent part of his bourgeois normality'.[71]

In Pomerania Friedrich, with the support of *Gauleiter* Schwede, showed particular concern to keep undesirable elements far removed from the SA, and at the end of July he appealed to the *Gauleitung* to expel from the party fifteen SA leaders swept up in the action of 30 June.[72] By late August many of those arrested had been released from custody, but Friedrich tried to ensure that they nevertheless remained cut off from their former power bases. On 24 August he ruled that the suspended men were forbidden to wear their uniforms, enter their old offices, contact SA or party members about the charges against them, or to leave their homes without first reporting to the local SA leader.[73] For good measure, all members of the SA were warned not to make contact with the suspended leaders.

Further insight into the nature of the purge is offered by some cases of SA leaders who lost their positions. One was Wilhelm Leuschner, who had been an SA-*Standardartenführer* in Stettin until 30 June. Leuschner, a machine fitter born in Bremen in 1907, joined the NSDAP and SA in July 1929 and rose quickly in the Stettin SA, becoming head of the 'Standarte 2' in August 1931.[74] He remained *Standartenführer* until January 1933, when he fled Stettin to avoid prosecution for his part in the bombing of the SPD newspaper *Volks-Bote* during the previous summer. Upon his return he came into conflict with Hans Friedrich, then leader of the 'Untergruppe Pommern-West' and with whom he had been at odds during 1932. In August 1933 he managed to secure a position on Heines' staff in Breslau, but returned to

Stettin in October after Heydebreck took command of the Pomeranian SA. On 1 July Leuschner was arrested; the following evening he was sent to Berlin; and he remained in custody for two months. At the end of August he was brought before the Pomeranian SA investigation committee, where the accusations against him included having had close contact with Heines, Heydebreck, Walter Schulz and Graf Spreti, knowledge of 'Röhm's plans', having expressed a desire to kill Friedrich, involvement in the Stennes 'mutiny' of 1931, homosexuality, drunken excesses and brutal behaviour toward his SA men.[75] Although it was noted that Leuschner's awareness of the 'plans' of Röhm and Heydebreck for a 'revolt' could not be proved, the committee upheld many of the charges and Leuschner was expelled from the SA.[76]

Another such case was that of Arwed Theuermann, until the purge the leader of the SA-*Standarte* headquartered in Greifswald. Like Leuschner, Theuermann was arrested on 1 July, taken to Berlin the following evening, and held there through August; his case too was reviewed in late August, and he too was expelled from the SA.[77] Theuermann stood accused on two basic counts: his close contacts with Heydebreck and his past behaviour. Among the accusations levelled against Theuermann were that he had served in the Russian army during the War (he was a Baltic German), that he had displayed cowardly behaviour in the Greifswald shooting incident of July 1932, that he had neglected his SA duties and spent too much time in taverns, and that he had spoken out against the Reichswehr. Another key accusation was that Theuermann had lost contact with his SA men, particularly after the absorption of the *Stahlhelm* by the SA, and had failed to prevent indiscipline and acts of violence by storm troopers under his command.[78]

A third example is the case of Max Heydebreck, the leader of the SA-*Standarte* headquartered in Rummelsburg. Heydebreck (no relation of Hans Peter von Heydebreck), the owner of an oven-construction business and a member of the NSDAP since 1930, also was arrested during the purge action and held in custody in Berlin for an extended period.[79] Among the charges made against him were that he had been a member of a workers' council in Rummelsburg in 1918/19,[80] that he had been friendly with *Gruppenführer* von Heydebreck, Karpenstein and Walter Schulz, and that he had prevented the police from combatting the excesses of SA members.[81] In each of these cases the accusations levelled against the erstwhile SA leaders fell into two general categories: association with men who had been killed in the purge, and improper or immoral behaviour. The first was a charge to which there was no answer, and one necessitated by the fiction of the 'revolt'; the second points to the use made of the purge to clean up the image of the Nazi movement and to help the Nazi regime pose as the defender of bourgeois morality.

As Friedrich stipulated, none of the Pomeranian SA leaders taken into custody as a result of the purge were allowed to return to their old posts. Most were expelled from the organisation after their cases had been reviewed. A few, however, were judged innocent of the more serious charges and either placed in jobs elsewhere in the SA or given a reprimand and a demotion.[82] For example, Hans-Georg Will, the former chief of staff of the 'Gruppe Pommern', was exonerated of wrong-doing because, although he was involved in financial irregularities of the 'Gruppe', it was considered that he had acted on the orders of the murdered *Gruppenführer*, and he was given another post. On the other hand, *Sturmführer* Hans Gotthard von Arnim, an SA leader from Stolp, was dismissed because of involvement in financial irregularities, heavy drinking and an 'extra-ordinarily friendly relationship' with von Heydebreck.[83] Hans-Dietrich Harries, former leader of the *Marine*-SA in Stettin, was dismissed after having been found guilty of falsifying SA documents. Hans Viewig, the *Standartenführer* in Stolp, was expelled from the SA for squandering the organisation's funds. Altogether, by the end of 1934 fifteen cases stemming from the purge had come before the investigation committee. While purging SA ranks certainly did not solve all the problems of indiscipline and rowdy behaviour in Pomerania, it proved a convenient means of removing some of the more troublesome and disruptive individuals from the organisation.

Significantly, the SA leaders disgraced and expelled during the purge did not face criminal charges, nor were they brought before regular courts. Indeed, when setting up the SA investigation committees Lutze had stipulated that the German penal code would not be employed and that the hearings were to remain short.[84] The failure to bring disgraced SA leaders before the courts exposes the difficulties facing their accusers. Firstly, many NSDAP members still at large were equally guilty of brutal and rowdy conduct, and the authorities were conscious that popular demands for a clean-up extended to the party as well.[85] Secondly, treating the transgressions of SA leaders as an internal party affair, away from public scrutiny, may have been necessary to ensure their isolation from potential followers. And finally, since the 'revolt' was a fiction, airing the affair in the courts – which would have given the accused a chance to speak up in public – might have proved extremely embarrassing for the party and the government.

As in Pomerania, in Silesia the new SA leader took up the opportunity to clean out his organisation. However, unlike Friedrich, who had a long and chequered association with the Pomeranian SA, Otto Herzog was new to the Silesian storm troopers' organisation and had no particular axes to grind. Perhaps for this reason, when he compiled a list of former members of the Silesian SA who were under suspicion at the end of July, Herzog did not stipulate that they had to lose their posts; rather, he recommended merely that they be placed on 'leave' until their cases were heard.[86] Nevertheless, the charges brought against SA leaders in Silesia were very similar to those faced by their Pomeranian counterparts, and are consistent with the accounts of SA misconduct which had been accumulating in police files during the previous year. One SA-*Brigadeführer*, for example, was accused of being 'strongly alcoholic' and having taken part in 'many excesses'; another faced similar charges, together with accusations of financial irregularities; a *Sturmbannführer* was accused of alcoholism, 'excesses' and having 'tyrannised the population'; one *Standartenführer* faced charges not only of alchoholism and 'tyrannising the population' but also of having led a 'completely immoral private life'; another was accused of 'suspicion of § 175' and having had contact with Communists in early 1933, as well as having played an 'unclear role' during the 'revolt'. The catalogue of alcoholic excesses, financial irregularities, bullying and the alienation of the public provides a revealing picture of life in Germany between January 1933 and June 1934, and helps explain why the purge did not stop with the murder of Röhm and his lieutenants but also involved so many SA officers at local and regional levels. Particularly striking is the rarity of specifically *political* offences among the accusations levelled against these SA leaders.[87] It thus becomes clear that the extension of the purge into the middle ranks of the SA leadership had less to do with strictly political issues – such as alleged calls for a 'second revolution' – than with problems of criminal behaviour and popular opinion.

This aspect of the 1934 purge – the removal from public life of rowdy and brutal SA leaders – struck a most responsive chord among the population. Many communities which had suffered for months at the hands of local SA leaders understandably were relieved to see the storm troopers' organisation humbled. The fact that this had been accomplished outside the law, by murder, mattered little. Indeed, immediately after the purge it was reported from Stettin that 'the news of the drastic action of the *Führer* has evoked general satisfaction and relief among the population'.[88] There was even criticism that the SA leadership had not been purged earlier.[89] According to the Gestapo office in Stettin, the popular reaction to Hitler's *Reichstag* speech of 13 July, in which the Nazi leader discussed the 'Röhm revolt' and posed as the defender of order and the 'morality of our people'.[90] was particularly positive.[91] From *Kreis* Cammin, north-east of Stettin, came the report that not only did 'every sensibly-thinking citizen fully and warmly greet the liberating act of the *Führer*', but also that the population 'now expects the government and the police to continue the purge down to the districts and the villages, down to the lowest levels of the party and the Labour Front'.[92] There were isolated instances of public disapproval of the more brutal and blatantly unjust killings, as for example in Silesia where the murders of Emil Sembach and the two SA men in Leobschütz aroused indignation.[93] On the whole however, the purge seems to have been genuinely popular, which was indicative of the extent to which the SA had isolated itself politically. It was, as Ian Kershaw has remarked, 'a domestic-political propaganda coup *par excellence*'.[94]

In East Prussia and the Border Province the purge was of much more limited dimensions than in Pomerania or Silesia. The leader of the 'SA Gruppe Ostmark' was arrested and held in custody for a time, and Anton von Hoberg und Buchwald, the leader of the SS 'cavalry' in East Prussia, was taken from Königsberg to his estate near Preußisch Eylau and shot on the orders of the East Prussian SS leader Erich von dem Bach-Zelewski.[95] However, there the action stopped: neither Arno Manthey, the SA leader in the Border Province itself, nor Heinrich Schoene, the leader of the SA in East Prussia, was among the purge victims; in general the SA was spared in these two provinces; and the purge there amounted to little more than a short-lived state of emergency. In East Prussia there were unfounded rumours in mid-July that Erich Koch had been arrested by the SS – rumours made plausible by Koch's close relations with the murdered Gregor Straßer and which provoked an official denial.[96] However, this had little to do with the SA, and seems to have arisen essentially because of hostility between Koch and the East Prussian farmers' associations.[97]

In his *Reichstag* speech of 13 July, Hitler admitted that 76 people had been liquidated during the purge – a number subsequently amended to 83. The killings were legalised after the fact, when on 3 July the Reich government passed a law stipulating that 'the measures taken on 30 June and 1 and 2 July to suppress the acts of high treason were legal, being necessary for the self-defence of the state'.[98] There had been no resistance to speak of, and the purge was welcomed by Reichswehr Minister von Blomberg on behalf of the army even though two generals – von Schleicher and von Bredow – had been among its victims.[99] Within a few days of the killings the cabinet post which Röhm had held – Reich Minister without Portfolio – was abolished, as were the SA Commissar posts and both the 'Political Office' and the 'Press Office' which the SA had set up in Berlin.[100] At a stroke the SA had lost almost all political importance.

Why did the purge take the form it did, and why did it claim so many lives in Silesia and Pomerania? Some answers were provided by Viktor Lutze in a conversation with Pomeranian SA leaders in August 1935 while he was on an inspection tour of the SA in central and western Pomerania.[101] On the evening of 17 August, in Stettin, the SA Chief of Staff had a long, informal discussion with the most important Nazi leaders in the province, including *Gauleiter* Schwede, SA-*Gruppenführer* Friedrich and SS-*Standartenführer* Robert Schulz. According to Schulz, who later filed a report about the conversation with the SS leadership, after drinking heavily Lutze began to talk about the purge, describing his own role in the affair and expressing anger that so many people had lost their lives. In Lutze's opinion, many killings had been quite unnecessary. He asserted that Hitler originally had wanted only seven people killed; the figure was increased to seventeen, and although Hitler had not expressly authorised the change he subsequently approved. This, Lutze said, already had been more than enough, 'but then

82 people simply were shot arbitrarily' due to malice and personal grudges. Despite Schulz' defence of the purge, Lutze stood by his account and made it clear, without naming names, that he held Himmler and, to a lesser extent, Göring responsible for the unnecessary murders.[102]

Similar claims had been made by Silesian *Gauleiter* Brückner. In October 1934, two months before he was dismissed from the Party and government posts, Brückner levelled numerous accusations at Udo von Woyrsch, criticising the personal and professional conduct of the SS leader and blaming him for the extent of the bloodshed in Silesia.[103] Although Brückner tactfully avoided mentioning the parts played by Göring, Himmler and Heydrich, he spelled out von Woyrsch's key role in helping to turn the planned elimination of a few SA leaders into a bloodbath with scores of victims. In an atmosphere of crisis and against a background of general approval for the 'liberating act of the *Führer*', von Woyrsch had been given a golden opportunity to get rid of his enemies and essentially determine the shape of the purge in Silesia.

Clearly the purge marked a turning point in the relations between the Nazi Party and the SA, which now could be ignored. Yet from events in eastern Germany, it hardly seems justified to describe the purge as a 'bloody climax' of a conflict between the SA and the NSDAP.[104] Rather, the purge appears to have been a climax of conflicts between the SA and the SS, the Reichswehr, the civil authorities and the police, conflicts which had developed as the public was growing increasingly hostile to the storm troopers. In both Silesia and Pomerania, where the purge was most thorough, the *Gauleiter* fell from power soon afterwards and in both provinces relations between the NSDAP and SA leaderships immediately preceding 30 June had been relatively good. At the local level as well, conflicts between SA leaders and Nazi Party functionaries seem to have played no significant role; and local party leaders often had been no less guilty of intimidating the public that had their counterparts in the SA. Furthermore, the purge of the SA in the eastern Prussian provinces does not appear to have been a campaign against a 'revolutionary' or 'socialist' SA; it can be better be described as a strike against an organisation unable or unwilling to control the behaviour of its members. The threat which the SA had posed to the established order before 30 June 1934 was the threat not of revolutionary transformation but of conduct incompatible with the smooth functioning of the 'Third Reich'.

The purge of the SA exposed its poltical bankruptcy in the wake of the seizure of power. By 1934 the SA leadership, through its efforts to assert its influence, had become isolated politically, and the coalition of interests which formed against the SA was a reflection of this isolation. The SA had failed to find a satisfactory political role once street battles with the Left were a thing of the past and proved unable to attract allies in 1934. Instead it exhibited an almost total failure to grasp political realities. While the army, the police and the SS were becoming increasingly hostile, a significant

portion of the SA membership continued to act in a manner which antagon-
ised a large part of the German population. At a time when Hindenburg was
on his death-bed, when the problem of succession was plain for all to see,
when relations with the army were obviously of crucial importance to the
Nazi leadership, the failure of SA leaders to perceive that their behaviour
was extremely dangerous betrayed political illiteracy of quite staggering
proportions. Having failed to secure an important role in the development of
Germany's armed forces, and having blindly cultivated enemies at every
turn, the SA was needed by no powerful interest within the power structure
of the 'Third Reich'. Having grown rapidly and haphazardly, it had no
particular political, economic or social base. Indeed, the only reason for its
continued existence was that it was there already, a relic of the 'years of
struggle' which had become painfully out of place after the Nazi leadership
had captured power.

Epilogue: The SA after the Purge

AFTER the purge the SA never regained a position of importance in the 'Third Reich',[1] nor did the behaviour of storm troopers continue to pose a serious political problem. Once the SA no longer had real power or influence, the conduct of its members could be dealt with as basically criminal behaviour. At the local level, as at the national, the SA essentially had been brought under control. Yet, although the violence of the storm troopers seems to have diminished after the purge, it did not disappear. SA members continued to become involved in violent incidents during the mid- and late-1930s, incidents which resembled much of what had occurred before June 1934: brawls, drunken excesses and the like. The difference was that these now posed at most a serious nuisance, whereas before the purge they had constituted a political threat.

To be sure, in some cases the violence was fairly widespread. For example, in December 1934 the Oppeln Gestapo office reported that storm troopers in Upper Silesia had been involved in 'one brawl after another' and that this had caused considerable tension between the SA and the public.[2] In May 1935 the Stettin Gestapo office reported that the SA had become particularly unruly in Stralsund, sparking brawls, criticising the Party leadership and creating difficulties for the local police.[3] In Breslau SA men caused a number of violent incidents during the summer of 1935, including assaults on Jews and foreigners of allegedly Jewish appearance, and thus both aroused public antipathy and made complications for the police (especially where foreign nationals were involved).[4] And with the pogrom of 9/10 November 1938 the SA participated in its last major act of political violence (and one which, like the previous outbursts, met with the overwhelming disapproval of the public).[5] Yet the storm troopers who burned synagogues and ransacked Jewish homes and businesses in November 1938 did so on the orders of their superiors. Far from being a spontaneous manifestation of anger, the pogrom was an event orchestrated by the Nazi leadership.[6] Politically significant, spontaneous SA violence was a thing of the past.

After the purge there was a predictable decline in the enthusiasm of SA members for the activities of the organisation. The fact that the SA had lost its political weight was not lost on the membership. Thus during the spring of 1935 the Stettin Gestapo office noted 'a certain lassitude and apathy' among the storm troopers, 'uncertainty over the purposes and duties of the SA', and 'doubt about the *raison d'être*' of the organisation.[7] A few months later, after the introduction of compulsory military service in May 1935, a morale problem was described even more explicitly:

> Within the SA there is still generally a lack of interest in its activities. In the SA one is of the opinion that the tasks of the SA have become redundant through the introduction of conscription. It is in fact the case that the ordinary SA man does not know at all why he is taking part in SA activities. There is a lack of a clear perspective and a firm purpose.[8]

Conscription, together with the introduction of compulsory 'labour service' in June 1935,[9] left many young men with little desire to participate in yet another militarised organisation – especially when that organisation appeared to have no clear function save preparing its members for life in the army. At the same time, many of those who had been pressured into joining the SA during 1933 and 1934 sought excuses to leave.[10] By the late 1930s few young men leaving the Hitler Youth bothered subsequently to enroll in the SA, and former SA members frequently did not re-join the organisation after their tour of duty in the Wehrmacht was finished. The 'de-politicised and morally "cleansed" SA'[11] had become essentially superfluous.

The purge marked the beginning of a long and steady fall in SA membership.[12] The tumultuous growth which had characterised the SA during 1933 and early 1934 was reversed, due partly to the cleaning out of SA ranks, partly to the increasing importance of the army and partly to the fact that there seemed little reason to remain in an organisation which was of no political consequence. Already during the late summer of 1934 the process of contraction had begun. Between August and September more than 100,000 men left the SA throughout Germany, a drop of 3.8 per cent in a single month; the East Prussian SA lost 4,980 (4.1 per cent) of its 120,964 members during August, the Pomeranian SA 3,651 (3.3 per cent) of 111,513, and the Silesian SA 8,003 (4.3 per cent) of 184,251.[13] Three years later SA membership was less than half of what it had been before the purge, both in the Reich as a whole and in the eastern regions.[14] At the end of September 1937 the SA in East Prussia numbered only 56,680, in Pomerania 55,779 and in Silesia 74,436 members.

This trend accelerated during the Second World War, when the great majority of SA men – between 70 and 80 per cent – served in the armed forces.[15] Those who remained in the SA were frequently called upon by local authorities and the Wehrmacht to guard military buildings, repair bomb-damaged transport facilities, act as air-defence squads and evacuation teams, and assist with the pre-military training of young men. The mobilisation of the population and the preparations for civilian resistance during the final stages of the War, however, were left to other organisations. Except on an *ad hoc* basis at local level, the SA was not entrusted with important tasks during the War. Thus the SA survived until 1945, as an empty shell having lost most of its members and almost totally without power or purpose.

Conclusion

LIKE the Italian Fascists a decade previously, the Nazis owed much of their success to an ability to channel violent behaviour into domestic politics.[1] Violence and struggle lay at the heart of National Socialism, and during the 'years of struggle' the SA was the principal expression of the violent impulses which helped fuel the rapid growth of the Hitler movement. Yet in many respects this aspect of the rise of the Nazi movement remains a paradox. Nazi activists often saw themselves as radically at odds with the 'system' around them, and yet by helping to crush the Left they played an important part in preserving aspects of the existing social order. The SA appeared to play a crucial role in the growth of the Nazi movement and the seizure of power, but it proved ill-suited to fulfilling any meaningful political function in the 'Third Reich' and in 1934 was relegated easily to political impotence. As the most violent element of the Nazi movement the SA seemed most clearly to embody a political ideology which revolved around struggle, yet in many respects its members were rather indifferent to ideological concerns. The SA posed as the fanatic opponent of the Weimar system, yet it generally avoided direct confrontation with the Weimar state. It harnessed hundreds of thousands of young men to the Nazi movement, yet in many instances it proved unable to hold their allegiance. It sought to grow as rapidly as possible after 1933, but this very growth undermined its position within the emerging power structures of Nazi Germany.

But to note that the history of the SA contains many contradictions and paradoxes is not to explain its role in the momentous political changes in Germany during the early 1930s. The SA was the most violent expression of a violent political movement, the shock troops in a campaign which eventually left the German labour movement in tatters. It may be true that it was not SA violence which destroyed the Left and the trade unions, that the violence revealed essentially that neither the SPD nor the ADGB had much fight left in them. But even this was an important contribution, and the fact that the SA took the initiative in early 1933 set the new Nazi government on a course which made impossible any form of compromise with trade unionism. Furthermore, the SA served as a magnet, drawing many people to National Socialism. The Nazi movement was overwhelmingly male and attracted its activists from among the young. The SA was the formation which, more than any other, organised the young male members of the movement and, by projecting an image of rough-and-ready male cameraderie, served as a powerful advertisement for Nazism during the 'years of struggle'.

The attempt to explain the attraction and activities of the SA is complicated by the fact that it is difficult to generalise about an organisation where some members were extraordinarily active and others had only an ill-defined and tenuous involvement, where turnover among the membership was very high. By the time Hitler was given the keys to the Reich Chancellory, hundreds of thousands of Germans had joined the SA and NSDAP and left again. The composition of many SA groups changed monthly, as high proportions of the membership came and went. This was a reflection of the fundamental instability of the Nazi movement as a whole – a protest movement without a strictly defined class, interest-based or religious constituency, whose support was often short-term and conditional (as was demonstrated all too clearly by the rapid disintegration of the NSDAP and SA in late 1932). As Martin Broszat has noted, the appeal of National Socialism was 'broadly-based, not deeply-rooted'.[2]

With so volatile an organisation as the SA, an attempt to understand its growth and trajectory cannot be based simply upon an analysis of the occupational backgrounds of its members or the collection of contradictions and absurdities which paraded as Nazi ideology. While they reflected to some extent the general appeal of National Socialism to various strata of German society, the social backgrounds of its membership do not explain the activities of the SA; political violence was not the preserve of any particular group.[3] As we have seen, the social backgrounds of the storm troopers (insofar as we can draw conclusions from extremely inadequate evidence of occupations) were fairly heterogeneous – about what one would expect given that the SA organised in its ranks the overwhelming majority of male Nazi activists between the ages of 18 and 30. The ideology of National Socialism, as expressed in *Mein Kampf*, the party's Programme or its electoral propaganda, likewise offers only limited insight, especially since Nazi ideology in this sense apparently concerned so few storm troopers. Their allegiance was not to a particular set of ideas, and the 'fanaticism' about which Hitler and his lieutenants boasted cannot be taken at face value. Conditional allegiance to an image rather than fanatical allegiance to an ideology seems to have been characteristic of the SA.

Yet there is a sense in which ideology may be seen to have played an important role and in which meaning may be found in the often confused and contradictory activities of the storm troopers. For whereas it probably is mistaken to believe that the actions of the SA were guided by Nazi ideology in the narrow sense, it is possible to see the actions of the SA *themselves* as Nazi ideology. It was not in the pronouncements of SA leaders that the clearest expression of Nazi ideology may be found, but in the structured actions of their followers.

What were the main characteristics of Nazi violence in the period to 1934? For one thing, it was aggressive and offensive, not defensive, and this proved of great tactical advantage in the campaigns of the early 1930s. The Social Democrats in particular found themselves pushed onto the defensive and compelled to rely on the state for protection. Such sources of protection were objects of scorn in the Nazi vocabulary. Despite the profoundly authoritarian nature of the Nazi movement, the violence of the storm troopers had an anti-authoritarian, almost anarchic character. Striking out against symbols of authority forms one of the clearest threads running through the history of the SA to 1934. The ethos of the organisation was anti-respectable; theirs was not the world of the comfortable bourgeois, and the storm troopers prided themselves in it. The leaders and supporters of the Weimar parties, and especially the Social Democrats, thus became welcome targets. For in attacking the SPD, the trade unions and other alleged representatives of the Weimar 'system', the young men in the SA were attacking symbols of authority (and, often, attacking their elders at the same time). That these anti-authoritarian impulses were used by an authoritarian movement to set up an authoritarian political system is one of the main reasons why the SA had no future in the 'Third Reich'.

Nevertheless it must be recognised that this anti-authoritarianism, if that is what it was, was exercised on the cheap. As has been noted, the SA consistently stopped short of challenging the *real* centres of authority. Nazi storm troopers may have been regarded by some (and may have regarded themselves) as 'fanatics', but they were not so fanatical as to mount frontal attacks on police stations or army barracks. For all their violent rhetoric, the storm troopers steered well clear of challenging directly the power of the state. Nor, for that matter, did they really confront authority within the Nazi movement; despite the persistent tensions between the party organisation and the SA, Hitler himself was never challenged. Somehow, the members of the SA generally knew that there were limits beyond which they should not go. There were instances when these limits were transgressed – most notably the terrorist campaigns in the wake of the July 1932 elections. However, such actions were dealt with effectively by the police, caused political problems for the Nazi Party, were halted quickly and not repeated. Indeed, the 1932 terror campaigns are the exception which seems to prove the rule. When looking at the SA we are not looking at a terrorist organisation whose members were prepared to court a life underground, who were prepared in a fundamental sense to challenge authority. The SA did not purvey the politics of terrorism so much as the politics of hooliganism.

The activities of the SA, like those of the Nazi Party as a whole, were essentially propagandistic. The marches, rallies, distribution of leaflets, sale of newspapers and confrontations with competing political formations all revolved around spreading the propaganda of the Nazi movement. And propaganda was not only the main purpose of the Nazi movement; it also provided the cement which held the movement together.[4] In this circular process the SA played a crucial role, for the storm troopers bore the lion's share of the burden necessitated by the frenetic propaganda campaigns which so impressed contemporaries and have drawn the attention of historians ever since. Yet the contribution of the storm troopers was not limited to the *dissemination* of propaganda. In a very real sense the storm troopers themselves *were* Nazi propaganda, as well as its distributors. The Nazi movement did not attract support simply through the distribution of leaflets or the *Völkischer Beobachter* or the repetition of hackneyed nationalist rhetoric by the hundreds of speakers trained by the NSDAP. It also attracted support by generating an image of a young, virile, uncompromising political movement – an image which was embodied in the SA.[5] And this image was no less important for the storm troopers themselves than for those who cast their votes for the Nazi Party. There is little doubt that the SA, rather than the NSDAP itself, drew large numbers of young men to the movement in the early 1930s. Whether the prime attraction was the male cameraderie, the opportunity to demonstrate their toughness, the soup kitchens and the SA hostels, or the chance to march around in uniform, it is clear that many men joined the Nazi Party because (before 1933) to do so generally went hand in hand with joining the SA.

Obviously the image created by the SA and the attraction it held for its members, as well as the nature of its activities, revolved around the fact that it was an all-male organisation. Much of the storm troopers' actions can be explained as the behaviour of young men out to prove their toughness. This was particularly the case in the confrontations between Nazis and Communists, who were the most willing to meet the SA on its own terms. In many respects the activities of the SA took on almost ritual forms: the honouring of the movement's martyrs, the torchlight parades (especially in the wake of Hitler's appointment as Reich Chancellor), the salutes, the ridiculing of opponents. Many of the confrontations in which the SA was involved can be seen almost as virility contests, in which the storm troopers had to 'prove themselves'. Challenges had to be answered (a good example of this is the Schweidnitz incident described above);[6] insults could not be allowed to pass; scores had to be settled; opponents had to be humiliated; territory had to be defended. The SA was maschismo in uniform, the channelling into politics of behaviour which most western societies expect of their young men but which they usually get in unfocussed gang violence or in countless individual incidents. In a sense the SA represented a distillation of the social values which German society had instilled in its young men: that they be tough, that they not shy away from violence, that they stand their ground and fight when challenged; that they be ready to prove themselves. Individual doubts about whether one would live up to this image of manliness could be submerged in the cameraderie of the SA group. The SA offered a certain solidarity, a form of sociability which promised support and reinforcement for young men who felt the need to prove their toughness in a world which expected young men to be tough. The SA therefore was not simply the expression of military values in civilian life (although it was that too);[7] it was an expression of wider social values which were basic to German (and western) society.

As Natalie Davis has pointed out in a very different context, 'violence is intense' when 'it connects intimately with the fundamental roles and self-definition of a community'.[8] It was this which gave SA violence its intensity and made it so effective – that it was an expression of commonly accepted social roles and values. The violence of the young man out to prove his virility, clothed in and justified by the language of radical nationalism and anti-Marxism, proved a powerful political weapon. Thus the SA should not be seen as the product of some sort of 'deviant' culture or of the personal frustrations and aggressions of disturbed 'individuals of violent propensity'.[9] It was able to attract hundreds of thousands of members in large measure because it was an effective expression of mainstream social values. Looked at from this angle, the SA was not essentially a manifestation of rebellion against bourgeois values, even though many of its members no doubt saw their participation in the organisation in such a light, but rather a confirmation of those values in the political arena. To be sure, the behaviour of the storm troopers was anti-social; but it was anti-social behaviour of a sort which confirmed dominant social values, and for that reason was all the easier to channel into a movement which (initially, at least) was defending, not destroying, the existing social order.

The SA came unstuck where it transgressed commonly accepted social and moral codes – where its members went too far during 1933 and 1934. Youthful violence was acceptable as long as it remained within bounds. But when the storm troopers seemed to threaten not only Jews, 'Marxists' and other pariahs but also members of the general public and when they came to pose a problem for the police of the emerging Nazi state, then they had lost touch with 'the fundamental roles and self-definition of a community' upon which the success of the SA had been based. Once that had happened, the SA was isolated and easily destroyed as a political force. The prominence of the charges of homosexuality against SA leaders in July 1934 and the degree to which these accusations brought approval from the German public form just one indication of the failure of the SA to keep in step with the values of the society within which it operated.

Although it was an expression of an unexceptionally violent culture, the behaviour of the storm troopers, fortunately, remains exceptional. It required the specific social and economic context of Weimar Germany to allow a political movement of the character of National Socialism to grow and to channel the energy of hundreds of thousands of people. A number of factors made possible the transfer into the political arena of the violent impulses of so many young men. Chief among these was mass unemployment. It is perhaps a fairly obvious point, but one which bears repeating, that the violent street politics of the early 1930s and the growth of the SA hardly would have been possible, certainly not on such a scale, had work been available for young Germans. The activities of the storm troopers – the seemingly never-ending succession of marches, rallies, fights, meetings – presupposed that the young men who formed the activist core of the Nazi movement had a great deal of time on their hands. Indeed, as we have seen, it was this activist core who became full-time 'political soldiers', often housed in SA barracks and fed in SA soup kitchens, and who did so much to form the picture of the tireless Nazi 'fanatic'. The combination of mass unemployment (and, particularly in the rural districts of eastern Germany, underemployment), a breakdown of traditional poltical allegiances and a culture which embraced violent aggressive values combined to lift the SA from relative obscurity during the mid-1920s to become the largest active party army in Germany on the eve of Hitler's appointment as Reich Chancellor .

Yet the fundamental instability of the SA prevented it, perhaps inevitably, from becoming a political force in the 'Third Reich'. The SA possessed no really effective bond to hold its members, and after the victories of early 1933 the organisation became more, not less, volatile and increasingly ill-suited to filling an important place in the emerging power structures. One may be amazed at the political illiteracy of many SA leaders, such as Hans Ramshorn or Edmund Heines, as they persisted with behaviour destined to put them before a firing squad. But whatever they did, their ambitions were bound to be frustrated. It is indicative of the SA that it did not provide a springboard for prominent careers in the 'Third Reich'. The most prominent SA leaders received their reward from Adolf Hitler in the Stadelheim prison in Munich. Politically astute Nazi veterans saw that the path to power lay elsewhere. The politics of violence may have made the 'Third Reich' possible, but it could not provide a basis for the politics of dictatorship.

Notes

Notes to the Introduction

1. *OVS*, 10 Aug. 1931, 'Zweites Blatt'.
2. See Eve Rosenhaft, 'Gewalt in der Politik: Zum Problem des "Sozialen Militarismus" ', in Klaus-Jürgen Müller and Eckardt Opitz (eds.), *Militär und Militarismus in der Weimarer Republik* (Düsseldorf, 1978), esp. pp. 253–7; Eve Rosenhaft, *Beating the Fascists? The German Communists and Political Violence 1929–1933* (Cambridge, 1983), Chapter III.
3. BA, R 43 I/2683, ff. 297–303: *Terror-Abwehrstelle beim Parteivorstand der* SPD to *Reichsminister* Groener, Berlin, 1 Feb. 1931.
4. Still unequalled as a source of information about the violence of this period is Emil Julius Gumbel, *Vier Jahre politischer Mord* (Berlin, 1922). For the campaigns of the *Freikorps*, see Robert G. L. Waite, *Vanguard of Nazism. The Free Corps Movement in Postwar Germany 1918–1923* (Cambridge, Mass., 1952); Hagen Schulze, *Freikorps und Republik 1918–1920* (Boppard/Rhein, 1969). For a general study of paramilitary formations during the Weimar period, see James M. Diehl, *Paramilitary Politics in Weimar Germany* (Bloomington and London, 1977).
5. According to Kurt Finker, between 1924 and 1927 three members of the KPD, one member of the Communist RFB and six members of the largely Social-Democratic *Reichsbanner* were killed in confrontations with members of the *Stahlhelm* and other right-wing organisations. See Kurt Finker, 'Die militaristischen Wehrverbände in der Weimarer Republik und ihre Rolle bei der Unterdrückung der Arbeiterklasse und bei der Vorbereitung eines neuen imperialistischen Krieges (1924–1929)' (Pädagogische Hochschule Potsdam Phil. Habil., 1964), p. 457.
6. See Diehl, *Paramilitary Politics,* pp. 276–85; Richard Bessel, 'Militarismus im innenpolitischen Leben der Weimarer Republik: Von den Freikorps zur SA', in Müller and Opitz (eds.', *Militär und Militarismus in der Weimarer Republik,* pp. 197–202, 207–15.
7. The phrase is Trotsky's. See Leon Trotsky, 'The German Catastrophe: The Responsibility of the Leadership' (from 28 May 1933), in Leon Trotsky, *The Struggle against Fascism in Germany* (Harmondsworth, 1975), p. 397.
8. Among the most important contributions remain Alan Bullock's biography, *Hitler. A Study in Tyranny* (Harmondsworth, 1962), and the classic studies by Karl Dietrich Bracher and his associates: Karl Dietrich Bracher, *Die Auflösung der Weimarer Republik. Eine Studie zum Problem des Machtverfalls in der Demokratie* (4th edn., Villingen, 1964), and Karl Dietrich Bracher, Wolfgang Sauer and Gerhard Schulz, *Die nationalsozialistische Machtergreifung. Studien zur Errichtung des totalitären Herrschaftssystems in Deutschland 1933/34* (2nd edn., Cologne and Opladen, 1962). See also the collection edited by Gotthard Jasper, *Von Weimar zu Hitler 1930–1933* (Cologne and Berlin, 1968).
9. Joseph Nyomarkay, *Charisma and Factionalism in the Nazi Party* (Minneapolis, 1967); Dietrich Orlow, *The History of the Nazi Party 1919–1933* (Pittsburgh, 1969).
10. Among the earliest attempts to provide outlines of the Nazi rise at local level were studies of Braunschweig and Hamburg. See Ernst-August Roloff, *Bürgertum und Nationalsozialismus 1930–1933. Braunschweigs Weg ins Dritte Reich* (Hannover, 1961), and

Werner Jochmann, *Nationalsozialismus und Revolution. Ursprung und Geschichte der NSDAP in Hamburg 1922–33. Dokumente* (Frankfurt/Main, 1963).

11. The research for this 'sociography' of the Nazi rise was completed in 1934 but not published until after the War. An abbreviated version was published in English in 1945 and republished in 1970: Rudolf Heberle, *From Democracy to Nazism. A Regional Case Study on Political Parties in Germany* (2nd edn., New York, 1970). The original German manuscript was published in 1963: Rudolf Heberle, *Landbevölkerung und Nationalsozialismus. Eine soziologische Untersuchung der politischen Willensbildung in Schleswig-Holstein 1918–1932* (Stuttgart, 1963).

12. William Sheridan Allen, *The Nazi Seizure of Power. The Experience of a Single German Town 1930–1935* (Chicago, 1965).

13. Bogusław Drewniak, *Początki ruchu hitlerowskiego na Pomorzu Zachodnim 1923–1934* (Poznań, 1962).

14. Jeremy Noakes, *The Nazi Party in Lower Saxony 1921–1933* (London, 1971).

15. Eberhart Schön, *Die Entstehung des Nationalsozialismus in Hessen* (Meisenheim/Glan, 1972).

16. Geoffrey Pridham, *Hitler's Rise to Power. The Nazi Movement in Bavaria 1923–1933* (London, 1973); Falk Wiesemann, *Die Vorgeschichte der nationalsozialistischen Machtübernhme in Bayern 1932/33* (Berlin, 1975).

17. Herbert S. Levine, *Hitler's Free City: A History of the Nazi Party in Danzig, 1925–1939* (Chicago, 1973).

18. Wilfried Böhnke, *Die NSDAP im Ruhrgebiet 1920–1933* (Bonn-Bad Godesberg, 1974).

19. Johnpeter Horst Grill, 'The Nazi Party in Baden, 1920–1945' (Univ. of Michigan Ph.D. thesis 1975).

20. Rainer Hambrecht, *Der Aufstieg der NSDAP in Mittel- und Oberfranken (1925–1933)* (Nürnberg, 1976).

21. Zdenek Zofka, *Die Ausbreitung des Nationalsozialismus auf dem Lande. Eine regionale Fallstudie zur politischen Einstellung der Landbevölkerung in der Zeit des Aufstiegs und der Machtergreifung der NSDAP 1928–1936* (Munich, 1979).

22. Rudy Koshar, 'Organisation Life and Nazism: A Study of Mobilization in Marburg an der Lahn, 1918–1935' (Univ. of Michigan Ph.D. thesis 1979). See also Rudy Koshar, 'Two "Nazisms": the Social Context of Nazi Mobilization in Marburg and Tübingen', *Social History,* vii (1982).

23. The basic study of voting behaviour in Weimar Germany remains Alfred Milatz, *Wähler und Wahlen in der Weimarer Republik* (Bonn, 1965). See also Thomas Childers, 'The Social Bases of the National Socialist Vote', *Journal of Contemporary History,* xi (1976); and, most recently, Richard F. Hamilton, *Who Voted for Hitler?* (Princeton, 1982).

24. Reichsorganisationsleiter der NSDAP (ed.), *Partei-Statistik* (1935).

25. See Michael H. Kater, 'Sozialer Wandel in der NSDAP im Zuge der nationalsozialistischen Machtergreifung', in Wolfgang Schieder (ed.), *Faschismus als soziale Bewegung. Deutschland und Italien im Vergleich* (Hamburg, 1976).

26. See the recent collection edited by Reinhard Mann, *Die Nationalsozialisten. Analysen faschistischer Bewegungen* (Stuttgart, 1980).

27. Dee Richard Wernette, 'Political Violence and German Elections: 1930 and July 1932' (Univ. of Michigan Ph.D. thesis 1974). Unfortunately, Wernette's examination of political violence consists essentially of the tabulation of information extracted from a single newspaper.

28. The occasion of the first studies was the twentieth anniversary of the "Röhm affair". See Helmut Krausnick, 'Der 30. Juni 1934. Bedeutung – Hintergründe – Verlauf', *Aus Politik und Zeitgeschichte. Beilage zur Wochenzeitung Das Parlament,* xxv/1954; Hermann Mau, 'Die "Zweite Revolution" – Der 30. Juni 1934', *Vierteljahrshefte für Zeitgeschichte,* i (1953).

29. Wolfgang Sauer, 'Die Mobilmachung der Gewalt', in Bracher/Sauer/Schulz, *Die nationalsozialistische Machtergreifung.*

30. Heinrich Bennecke, *Hitler und die SA* (Munich and Vienna, 1962).

31. Kurt Gossweiler, 'Die Rolle des Monopolkapitals bei der Herbeiführung der Röhm-Affäre' (Humbolt Univ. Berlin Phil. Diss. 1963).

32. Charles Bloch, *Die SA und die Krise des NS-Regimes 1934* (Frankfurt/Main, 1970).

33. Andreas Werner, 'SA und NSDAP. SA: "Wehrverband", "Parteitruppe" oder "Revolutionsarmee"? Studien zur Geschichte der SA und der NSDAP 1920 bis 1933' (Univ. Erlangen Phil. Diss. 1964).
34. See, for example, Drewniak, *Początki ruchu hitlerowskiego,* pp. 61–71; Noakes, *The Nazi Party in Lower Saxony,* pp. 187–7; Schön, *Die Entstehung des Nationalsozialismus,* pp. 116–42; Hambrecht, *Der Aufstieg der NSDAP,* pp. 317–27.
35. On the social composition of the SA nationwide, see Conan Fischer, 'The Occupational Background of the SA's Rank and File Membership during the Depression Years, 1929 to mid-1934', in Peter D. Stachura (ed.), *The Shaping of the Nazi State* (London, 1978); and Conan Fischer, *Stormtroopers. A Social, Economic and Ideological Analysis, 1929–35* (London, 1983). See also Michael H. Kater, 'Ansätze zu eine Soziologie der SA bis zur Röhm-Krise', in Ulrich Engelhardt, Volker Sellin and Horst Stuke (eds.), *Soziale Bewegung und politische Verfassung* (Stuttgart, 1976); and Peter H. Merkl, *The Making of a Storm-trooper* (Princeton, 1980). For a detailed investigation of the composition of the SA leadership, see Mathilde Jamin, 'Zwischen den Klassen. Eine quantitative Untersuchung zur Sozialstruktur der SA-Führerschaft' (Ruhr Univ. Bochum Phil. Diss. 1982).
36. Eric G. Reiche, 'The Development of the SA in Nuremberg, 1922 to 1934' (Univ. of Delaware Ph.D. thesis 1972); Eric G. Reiche, 'From "Spontaneous" to Legal Terror: SA, Police, and the Judiciary in Nürnberg, 1933–34', *European Studies Review,* ix (1979).
37. See note 2 above. See also Eve Rosenhaft, 'Working-Class Life and Working-Class Politics: Communists, Nazis and the State in the Battle for the Streets, Berlin 1928–1932', in Richard Bessel and E. J. Feuchtwanger (eds.), *Social Change and Political Development in Weimar Germany* (London, 1981).

Notes to Chapter I

1. For example, G. Schneider, 'Die grenzpolitische Bedeutung Oberschlesiens als Provinz', in Presse-, Statistisches und Verkehrsamt der Provinzverwaltung von Oberschlesien (ed.), *Zehn Jahre Provinz Oberschlesien* (Ratibor, 1929), p. 10.
2. In East Prussia the district around Soldau, in the south of the province, was ceded to Poland, and to the north the Memelland was placed initially under Allied administration and occupied by Lithuanian troops in early 1923. Poland was granted a 'corridor' to the sea consisting of territory of the pre-war province of West Prussia, and Danzig and the surrounding countryside became a 'Free City'.
3. See Gotthold Rhode, 'Staatliche Entwicklung und Grenzziehung', in Gotthold Rhode (ed.), *Die Ostgebiete des Deutschen Reiches* (3rd edn., Würzburg, 1956), pp. 122–3; Kurt Fortreuter, 'Ostpreußen', in *Die deutschen Ostgebiete zur Zeit der Weimarer Republik* (*Studien zum Deutschtum im Osten,* iii, Cologne and Graz, 1966), p. 18; Dieter Hertz-Eichenrode, *Politik und Landwirtschaft in Ostpreußen 1919 bis 1930. Untersuchung eines Strukturproblems in der Weimarer Republik* (Cologne and Opladen, 1969), pp. 14–15.
4. For accounts of the post-war events in Upper Silesia see Karl Bergerhoff, *Die Schwarze Schar in O/S. Ein historischer Abschnitt aus Oberschlesiens Schreckenstagen* (Gleiwitz, 1932); Karl Hoeser, *Oberschlesien in der Aufstandszeit 1918–1921. Erinnerungen und Dokumente* (Berlin, 1938); Ernst Birke, 'Schlesien', in *Die deutschen Ostgebiete zur Zeit der Weimarer Republik,* pp. 150–86; Wilhelm Matull, *Ostdeutschlands Arbeiterbewegung. Abriß ihrer Geschichte, Leistung und Opfer* (Würzburg, 1973), pp. 193–214. For a balance sheet of Germany's territorial, population and economic losses in the East see Roland Baier, *Der deutsche Osten als soziale Frage. Eine Studie zur preußischen und deutschen Siedlungs- und Polenpolitik in den Ostprovinzen während des Kaiserreichs und der Weimarer Republik* (Cologne and Vienna, 1980), pp. 156–61.
5. See Waite, *Vanguard of Nazism,* pp. 285–96. For details of the various right-wing organisations active in the struggle against the Poles, see Karol Fiedor, *Antypolskie organizacje w Niemczech 1918–1933* (Wrocław, 1973).
6. For the numbers of the refugees and where they re-settled, see Heinz Rogmann, *Die Bevölkerungsentwicklung im preußischen Osten in den letzten hundert Jahren* (Berlin, 1937), pp. 120–2.
7. Landeshauptleute der Provinzen Ostpreußen, Grenzmark Posen-Westpreußen, Pommern,

Brandenburg, Niederschlesien und Oberschlesien (eds.), *Die Not der preußischen Ost-provinzen* (Königsberg, 1930), p. 30.

8. Knut Borchardt, 'The Industrial Revolution in Germany 1700–1914', in Carlo M. Cipolla (ed.), *The Fontana Economic History of Europe. The Emergence of Industrial Societies — 1* (Glasgow, 1973), p. 139.

9. See Rogmann, *Die Bevölkerungsentwicklung in preußischen Osten,* pp. 128, 244–5; Hans Raupach, 'Der interregionale Wohlfahrtsausgleich als Problem der Politik des Deutschen Reiches', in Werner Conze and Hans Raupach (eds.), *Die Staats- und Wirtschaftskrise des Deutschen Reiches 1929/33* (Stuttgart, 1967), p. 15; Borchardt, 'The Industrial Revolution in Germany', p. 123.

10. Rudolf Neumann, 'Die ostdeutsche Wirtschaft', in Rhode (ed.), *Die Ostgebiete des Deut-schen Reiches,* p. 166. The figures used refer to Germany east of the Oder-Neiße, and give the value of eastern German industrial production in 1936. However, since there was little investment in Germany during the economic crisis, these figures can be regarded as reason-ably indicative of the relative importance of eastern German industry during the 1920s and early 1930s.

11. For the prices of agricultural produce and property, see Dieter Gessner, *Agrarverbände in der Weimarer Republik. Wirtschaftliche und sozialer Voraussetzungen agrarkonservativer Politik vor 1933* (Düsseldorf, 1976), pp. 86, 89.

12. Dieter Petzina, 'Hauptprobleme der deutschen Wirtschaftspolitik 1932/33', *Vierteljahrs-hefte für Zeitgeschichte,* xv (1967), p. 31.

13. Hans Gladosch, 'Untersuchungen über die Notwendigkeit, Maßnahmen und Ergebnisse der Osthilfe in Oberschlesien' (Univ. Heidelberg Phil. Diss. 1933), pp. 10–12.

14. See Forstreuter, 'Ostpreußen', p. 28.

15. For detailed descriptions of the aid programmes to eastern Germany, see Heinrich Niehaus, 'Die Osthilfe', in *Die deutschen Ostegebiete zur Zeit der Weimarer Republik,* pp. 187–211; Bruno Buchta, *Die Junker und die Weimarer Republik. Charakter und Bedeutung der Osthilfe in den Jahren 1928–1931* (Berlin, 1959); Gerhard Schulz, 'Staatliche Stüt-zungsmaßnahmen in den deutschen Ostgebieten', in Ferdinand A. Hermens and Theodor Schieder (eds.), *Staat Wirtschaft und Politik in der Weimarer Republik. Festschrift für Heinrich Brüning* (Berlin, 1967), pp. 141–204; Heinrich Muth, 'Agrarpolitik und Par-teipolitik im Frühjahr 1932', in Hermens and Schieder (eds.), *Staat Wirtschaft und Politik,* pp. 317–60; Hertz-Eichenrode, *Politik und Landwirtschaft in Ostpreußen,* pp. 159–337; Karol Fiedor, 'The Character of State Assistance to the German Eastern Provinces in the Years 1919–1933', *Polish Western Affairs,* xii (1971), pp. 309–26; Bogusław Olszewski, '*Osthilfe' interwencjonizm państwowy w rolnictwie śląskim w latach 1919–1939* (Wrocław, 1974); Hans-Peter Ehni, *Bollwerk Preußen? Preußen-Regierung, Reich-Länder-Problem und Sozialdemokratie 1928–1932* (Bonn-Bad Godesberg, 1975), pp. 56–76; Richard Bes-sel, 'Eastern Germany as a Structural Problem in the Weimar Republic', *Social History,* iii (1978), pp. 210–13.

16. *StJDR 1932,* pp. 376–7.

17. For discussions of how the Nazi Party took advantage of this situation, see Horst Gies, 'NSDAP und landwirtschaftliche Organisationen in der Endphase der Weimarer Republik', *Vierteljahrshefte für Zeitgeschichte,* xv (1967), pp. 341–76; J. E. Farquharson, *The Plough and the Swastika. The NSDAP and Agriculture in Germany 1928–1945* (London and Beverly Hills, 1976), pp. 1–42.

18. For an example of how the SPD sought to identify itself with the national struggle along the border, see E. Janotta, 'Sozialdemokratie und Provinz Oberschlesien', in *Zehn Jahre Provinz Oberschlesien,* p. 6.

19. See Heinrich August Winkler, *Mittelstand Demokratie und Nationalsozialismus. Die politische Entwicklung von Handwerk und Kleinhandel in der Weimarer Republik* (Cologne, 1972).

20. Gessner, *Agrarverbände in der Weimarer Republik,* pp. 248–9.

21. Wilhelm Dittmann, *Das politische Deutschland vor Hitler* (Zürich and New York, 1945); Milatz, *Wähler und Wahlen in der Weimarer Republik.*

22. See, for example, StAG, Rep. 240/C.64.b: letter to the NSDAP *Ortsgruppe* in Neidenburg, Schweidnitz, 19 March 1932.

Notes to Chapter II

1. For an account of the early development of the NSDAP, see Werner Maser, *Die Frühgeschichte der NSDAP. Hitlers Weg bis 1924* (Frankfurt/Main and Bonn, 1965). For a discussion of the Prussian ban of the NSDAP, see Gotthard Jasper, *Der Schutz der Republik. Studien zur staatlichen Sicherung der Demokratie in der Weimarer Republik 1922–1930* (Tübingen, 1963), pp. 301–4.
2. Maser, *Die Frühgeschichte der NSDAP*, p. 319; Böhnke, *Die NSDAP im Ruhrgebiet*, pp. 40–1; Noakes, *The Nazi Party in Lower Saxony*, pp. 14–20.
3. See, for example, the account of the formation of *völkisch* groupings in the Upper Silesian border city of Hindenburg during the early 1920s in Hans Paschke, *Chronik der Stadt Hindenburg in Oberschlesien* (Berlin, 1941), p. 69.
4. See, for example, StAG, Rep. 240/C.76.a.: a history of the Nazi movement in Tilsit, unsigned.
5. StAG, Rep. 240/C.51.a.: a history of the Nazi movement in *Kreis* Insterburg, unsigned.
6. WAP Opole, OPO/989, f. 200: The *Polizeipräsident* to the *Oberpräsident*, Gleiwitz, 10 Mar. 1925.
7. Klaus Gundelach, *Vom Kampf und Sieg der schlesischen SA* (Breslau, 1934), p. 49. The original 'Bund Oberland' had been among the more important groups involved in the fighting in Upper Silesia during 1921. See Waite, *Vanguard of Nazism*, pp. 228–9, 232.
8. StAG, Rep. 240/C.53.a.(2): 'Die ersten politischen Marschkolonnen'. By the time of the Munich *Putsch* there were roughly 30 to 40 'individual' NSDAP members in Königsberg. See StAG, Rep. 240/C.53.a(1): a history of the NSDAP in Königsberg, signed by W. Stich.
9. Maser, *Die Frühgeschichte der NSDAP*, p. 320.
10. Herbert Gaede, *Pommern* (Berlin, 1940), p. 13; Drewniak, *Początki ruchu hitlerowskiego*, p. 17.
11. Gundelach, *Vom Kampf und Sieg der schlesischen SA*, pp. 47–9.
12. Ibid., p. 49; Edward Mendel, *Stosunki społeczne i polityczne w Opolu w latach 1919–1933* (Warsaw and Wrocław, 1975), pp. 94–5.
13. For accounts of the rebirth of the NSDAP in 1925, see Bullock, *Hitler*, pp. 120–35; Orlow, *The History of the Nazi Party 1919–1933*, pp. 53–8; Noakes, *The Nazi Party in Lower Saxony*, pp. 64–5.
14. See p. 27.
15. Paschke, *Chronik der Stadt Hindenburg*, pp. 69–70.
16. Drewniak, *Początki ruchu hitlerowskiego*, p. 17.
17. The core of this Königsberg group consisted of NSDAP members from before 1923. See StAG, Rep. 240/C.53.a.(2): 'Die ersten politischen Marschkolonnen'; StAG, Rep. 240/B.31.c.: 'Erste Anfänge der SA in Ostpreußen'; BA, Sammlung Schumacher/207, vol. 1, ff. 261–2: Wilhelm Stich to the *Parteileitung der* NSDAP, Königsberg, 10 Mar. 1925; Fritz Gause, *Die Geschichte der Stadt Königsberg in Preußen*, iii, (Cologne, 1971), p. 111.
18. BA, Sammlung Schumacher/208, vol. 2, ff. 42–3: Helmuth Brückner to Adolf Hitler, Breslau, 6 Mar. 1925; ibid., f. 44: letter to members of the NSFB, Breslau, 7 Mar. 1925. The DVFP, founded in December 1922 by breakaway members of the DNVP, had been a focus of *völkisch* politics in northern Germany after the Prussian government banned the NSDAP. See Albrecht Tyrell, *Führer befiehl . . . Selbstzeugnisse aus der 'Kampfzeit' der NSDAP* (Düsseldorf, 1969), pp. 68–94; Orlow, *The History of the Nazi Party 1919–1933*, pp. 46–58; Noakes, *The Nazi Party in Lower Saxony*, pp. 28–63.
19. Paul-Willy Jakubaschk, '8 Jahre schlesische Hitlerbewegung', in *NSST*, 15 Mar. 1933, pp. 1–2; Marek Maciejewski, 'Uwagi o genezie partii narodowych socjalistów i jej ideologii na Śląsku Opolskim (1925–1932)', *Studia Śląskie*, xxiv (1973), p. 190; Mirosław Cygański, *Hitlerowskie organizacje dywersyjne w województwie śląskim 1931–1936* (Katowice, 1971), p. 15. Cygański mistakenly lists Rosikat as the first *Gauleiter* of the Silesian NSDAP, followed by Brückner in 1928. In fact, Brückner remained *Gauleiter* without interruption from March 1925 to the end of 1934.
20. BA, Sammlung Schumacher/207, vol. 2, f. 112: Philip Bouhler to Theodor Vahlen, Munich, 3 Apr. 1925; Gaede, *Pommern*, p. 13; Robert Henry Frank, 'Hitler and the National Socialist Coalition: 1924–1932' (Johns Hopkins Univ. Ph.D. thesis 1969), pp. 91–2. Vahlen became associated with the 'left wing' of the NSDAP, and was the only

Gauleiter in eastern Germany to cooperate closely with the 'Arbeitsgemeinschaft' formed by north-western German *Gauleiter* in September 1925. See Peter Hüttenberger, *Die Gauleiter. Studie zum Wandel des Machtgefüges in der NSDAP* (Stuttgart, 1969), pp. 28–33.

21. StAG, Rep. 240/B.31.c.: 'Erste Anfänge der SA in Ostpreußen'.
22. StAG, Rep. 240/C.53.a.(2): 'Die ersten politischen Marschkolonnen'.
23. See Bracher/Sauer/Schulz, *Die nationalsozialistische Machtergreifung,* p. 838; Frank, 'Hitler and the National Socialist Coalition', pp. 209–10.
24. StAG, Rep. 240/B.31.c.: 'Erste Anfänge der SA in Ostpreußen'; Gause, *Die Geschichte der Stadt Königsberg,* iii, p. 111.
25. BA, Sammlung Schumacher/207, vol. 2, ff. 244–5: Willy Behnke to the *Leitung der* NSDAP, Stettin, 11 June 1926; ibid., f. 246: Willy Behnke to the *Leitung der* NSDAP, Stettin, 21 June 1926.
26. Drewniak, *Początki ruchu hitlerowskiego,* p. 47.
27. Paul-Willi Jakubaschk, *Helmuth Brückner. Sein Kampf und Sieg in Schlesien* (Hirschberg, 1933), pp. 59–60.
28. Paschke, *Chronik der Stadt Hindenburg,* pp. 69–70.
29. See, for example, G. Riedel, 'Die Entwicklung der NSDAP im Kreise Oppeln', in *Oppelner Heimat Kalender für Stadt und Land 1934* (Oppeln, 1934), pp. 40–2.
30. See above, p. 11.
31. BA, NS 26/156: NSDAP *Gaupresseamt Schlesien to the NSDAP Hauptarchiv,* Breslau, 20. Mar. 1937.
32. BA, Sammlung Schumacher/208, vol. 2, f. 64: Helmuth Brückner to the *Reichsleitung der* NSDAP, Breslau, 15 Feb. 1927.
33. WAP Wrocław, RO I/1800, ff. 81–6: The *Polizeipräsident* to the *Regierungspräsident,* Gleiwitz, 21 July 1927.
34. BA, Sammlung Schumacher/208, vol. 2, f. 64.
35. BDC, AOPG, Helmuth Brückner: Arthur Niedergesäß to Major Buch, Breslau, 20 May 1928, with an accompanying 'Denkschrift über die Ursachen zur Gründung der National-sozialistischen Arbeitsgemeinschaft Groß-Breslau'; ibid.: Helmuth Brückner to the *Reichsleitung der* NSDAP, Breslau, 17 June 1928.
36. Ibid.: 'Meldung', signed by Lang, 'former SA leader in Breslau', Breslau, 10 May 1928.: Kurt Geyer to the USchlA *der Reichsleitung der* NSDAP, Breslau, 16 June 1928.
37. Ibid.: 'Bekanntmachung', undated (probably from June 1928), signed by Helmuth Brückner; ibid.: Richard Linke to Adolf Hitler, Breslau, 28 July 1928.
38. Ibid.: *Bezirksleiter* Kremser to the *Gauleitung Schlesien der* NSDAP, Ratibor, 11 June 1928.
39. StAG, Rep. 10/28, f. 99: 'Bericht über die Mitgliederversammlung der nationalsozialisti-schen deutschen Arbeiterpartei am 25. Juni 1926', Königsberg, 30 June 1926.
40. StAG, Rep. 240/C.53.a.(2): 'Die ersten politischen Marschkolonnen'.
41. StAG, Rep. 10/28, f. 128: report dated Königsberg, 13 Apr. 1927; StAG, Rep. 10/33, f. 6: The *Polizeipräsident* to the *Regierungspräsident*, Königsberg, 26 Jan. 1930.
42. See StAG, Rep. 240/B.7.b.: NSDAP *Gau Ostpreußen,* 'Rundschreiben an alle Ortsgrup-pen und Einzelmitglieder des Gaues Ostpreußen', Königsberg, 23 Sept. 1926; ibid.: NSDAP *Gau Ostpreußen,* '2. Rundschreiben an alle Ortsgruppen und Einzelmitglieder', Königsberg, 8 Oct. 1926; StAG, Rep. 240/C.53.a.(2): 'Die ersten politischen Marschkolonnen'.
43. The memberships of the local groups were as follows: Königsberg, 109; Insterburg, 61; Tilsit, 27; Allenstein, 20; and Artam, 16. In addition a group of 18 members was forming in Gerdauen. See ibid.: report of the 'Gautagung des Gaues Ostpreußen der Nationalsozialist-ischen Deutschen Arbeiterpartei am 18. März 1928 in Königsberg (Pr.)'.
44. BA, Sammlung Schumacher/207, vol. 2, f. 14: 'Mitgliederstand des Gaues Ostpreußen der NSDAP'.
45. StAG, Rep. 240/C.53.a.(2): report of the 'Gautagung des Gaues Ostpreußen der Nationalsozialistischen Deutschen Arbeiterpartei am 18. März 1928 in Königsberg (Pr.)'.
46. Ibid.: 'Die ersten politischen Marschkolonnen'; Gause, *Die Geschichte der Stadt Königs-berg,* iii, p. 112.
47. BA, Sammlung Schumacher /374: 'Die Entwicklung der NSDAP in Preußen in den Jahren 1928–1930', Berlin, 11 Nov. 1930.

48. Hertz-Eichenrode, *Politik und Landwirtschaft in Ostpreußen,* p. 67.
49. BA, Sammlung Schumacher/374: 'Die Entwicklung der NSDAP in Preußen in den Jahren 1928–1930'; IfZ, MA 198/5, microfilm of ZStAM, Rep. 77, tit. 4043, Nr. 283, f. 26: 'Wahlerfolge der NSDAP in Preußen bei den Landtagswahlen am 20. Mai 1928 und in den Provinziallandtagswahlen am 17. November 1929'.
50. StAG, Rep. 240/C.53.a.(1): 'Versammlungsbericht', Königsberg, 28 Jan. 1929.
51. See, for example, StAG, Rep. 14/B.I.2.: reports of NSDAP propaganda activities in the Reg. Bez. Allenstein; StAG, Rep. 14/B.III.2., f. 10: *Landeskriminalpolizei* Allenstein to the *Kriminal- und Grenzkommissariate* in Prostken, Dlottowen, Ortelsburg, Neidenburg and Gilgenburg, Allenstein, 14 Sept. 1929; WAP Olsztyn, Magistrat Johannisburg/217: 'Lageberichte' from 1929 and 1930; StAG, Rep. 10/17, ff. 433–9: The *Regierungspräsident* to the *Oberpräsident,* Marienwerder, 16 Apr. 1930; StAG, Rep. 240/C.74.b.: The *Landrat* to the *Regierungspräsident,* Sensburg, 25 Mar. 1930.
52. See StAG, Rep. 10/17, ff. 441–9: The *Regierungspräsident* to the *Oberpräsident,* Marienwerder, 18 July 1930; WAP Szczecin, RS/10, f. 102: The *Landrat* to the *Regierungspräsident,* Demmin, 31 Jan. 1931; WAP Szczecin, RS/17, ff. 37–41: The *kom. Landrat* to the *Regierungspräsident,* Greifenhagen, 1 Feb. 1931; WAP Szczecin, RS/3, ff. 57–9: The *Landrat* to the *Regierungspräsident,* Anklam, 6 Feb. 1931; WAP Szczecin, RS/8, ff. 515–16: The *Landrat* to the *Regierungspräsident,* Cammin, 4 Mar. 1931.
53. StAG, Rep. 10/31, ff. 26–7: The *Oberpräsident* to the *Regierungspräsident,* Königsberg, 21 Jan. 1930. For details of Darré's early efforts to form a nationwide organisation, see Gies, 'NSDAP und landwirtschaftliche Organisation', pp. 341–6, and Farquharson, *The Plough and the Swastika,* pp. 15–19.
54. StAG, Rep. 240/B.9.a.: 'Lagebericht der Gauleitung', Königsberg, 20 Jan. 1930.
55. Richard Bessel, 'The Rise of the NSDAP and the Myth of Nazi Propaganda', *The Wiener Library Bulletin,* xxxiii, nos. 51/52 (1980), pp. 22–3. See also Zofka, *Die Ausbreitung des Nationalsozialismus auf dem Lande,* pp. 78–80.
56. For the growth in the 'Ostmark', see Kurt Pätzold and Manfred Weißbecker, *Geschichte der NSDAP 1920–1945* (Cologne, 1981), p. 134. For the growth in Silesia, see BA, NS 22/1068: Helmuth Brückner to Gregor Straßer, Breslau, 3 Nov. 1931. On 1 October 1931 the membership of the NSDAP in Silesia was said to be 26,800.
57. WAP Wrocław, RO I/1830, ff. 191–227: 'Bericht Nr. 2 über die Provinz Oberschlesien in der Zeit vom 1. Juli bis 30. September 1930', Oppeln, 20 Oct. 1930; ibid., ff. 293–301: 'Bericht über die politische Lage im Bereich der Landespolizeistelle für die Provinz Oberschlesien in der Zeit vom 1.10 bis zum 31.12.30', Oppeln, 28 Jan. 1931.
58. Ibid., ff. 367–73: 'Bericht über die politische Lage im Bereich der Landespolizeistelle für Provinz Oberschlesien in der Zeit vom 1.1 bis zum 31.3.1931', Oppeln, 30 Apr. 1931; ibid, ff. 421–7: 'Bericht über die politische Lage im Bereich der Landespolizeistelle für die Provinz Oberschlesien in der Zeit vom 1. April bis zum 30. Juni 1931', Oppeln, 23 July 1931; ibid., ff. 571–7: 'Bericht über die politische Lage im Bereich der Landespolizeistelle für die Provinz Oberschlesien für die Zeit vom 1. Oktober bis 31. Dezember 1931', Oppeln, 25 Jan. 1932.
59. See, for example, StAG, Rep. 240/C.39.d.: text of an article from the *Ostdeutscher Beobachter,* 29 Sept. 1929.
60. See Gies, 'NSDAP und landwirtschaftliche Organisation'; Gessner, *Agrarverbände in der Weimarer Republik,* pp. 241–51.
61. WAP Szczecin, RS/3, ff. 57–9: The *Landrat* to the *Polizeipräsident* in Stettin, Anklam, 6 Feb. 1931; *VB,* 24 Oct. 1930, p. 2.
62. WAP Poznań, OPS/368, f. 498: *Landwirtschaftskammer für die Grenzmark Posen-Westpreußen* to the *Oberpräsident,* Schneidemühl, 3 Dec. 1932.
63. Kube, who was active in the DNVP in the early 1920s and became a *Reichstag* deputy of the NSFB in 1924, was expelled in 1927 from the Reich leadership of the DVFB and joined the NSDAP in 1928. He became *Gauleiter* of the 'Ostmark' in September 1928. See Hüttenberger, *Die Gauleiter,* pp. 215–16.
64. Ibid., pp. 222–3; BA, Sammlung Schumacher/207, vol. 2, f. 386: Adolf Hitler, 'Anordnung', Munich, 1 Apr. 1931; ibid., f. 387: Walther von Corswandt, Cuntzow, 4 Mar. 1931; BA, NS 26/152, f. 484: *Gaupresseamt* to the *Hauptarchiv der* NSDAP, Stettin, 27 Jan. 1937.
65. For a detailed description of this development in Lower Saxony, see Noakes, *The Nazi*

Party in Lower Saxony, pp. 156–200.
66. See, for example, the lists of the *Gau* organisations and advisors in East Prussia and Silesia in BA, NS 22/1065, and BA, NS 22/1068.
67. BA, NS 26/951: R. Walther Darré to the *landwirtschaftliche Fachberater der Gauleitungen,* Munich, 20 Nov. 1930; BA, NS 26/949: undated report (*c.* Dec. 1930).
68. StAG, Rep. 240/B.29.c.: 'Boykottfälle'.
69. WAP Wrocław, RO I/1806, ff. 939–41: The *komm. Polizeipräsident* to the *Regierungspräsident,* Gleiwitz, 14 Nov. 1932.
70. IfZ, Fa 107, ff. 33–5: GRUSA II, Munich, 31 May 1927; Peter D. Stachura, *Nazi Youth in the Weimar Republic* (Santa Barbara and Oxford, 1975), pp. 25–7. According to the 1927 scheme, which never was realised, the SA was to consist of three sections: for men, women and youth.
71. Ibid., pp. 25–38, 133–6.
72. See WAP Wrocław, RO I/1800, f. 1021: The *Polizeipräsident* to the *Regierungspräsident,* Oppeln, 14 June 1930; WAP Wrocław, RO I/1830, ff. 293–301.
73. Stachura, *Nazi Youth in the Weimar Republic,* pp. 30–1, 185, 261–2.
74. Ibid., pp. 179–85, 267–9.
75. Ibid., pp. 267–9; WAP Wrocław, RO I/1830, ff. 293–301.
76. See StAG, Rep. 240/C.64.b.: *Gauleitung* Schlesien to the *Ortsgruppe der* NSDAP Neidenburg, Schweidnitz, 19 Mar. 1932.
77. StDR, ccccxxxiv *(Die Wahlen zum Reichstag am 31. Juli und 6. November 1932 und am 5. März 1933)* (Berlin, 1935), pp. 8, 9, 43, 45–8, 76–7, 111, 113–16, 142–3, 166, 172–180.
78. StAG, Rep. 240/C.59.b: 'Vierteljährliche Organisationsmeldungen' from 21 Oct. 1932 and 31 Dec. 1932.
79. See, for example, StAG, Rep. 240/C.54.b.: 'Chronik der NSDAP Ortsgruppe Roßgarten, Kreis Königsberg/Pr.'. For a more detailed discussion of the crisis in late 1932, and especially the role played by the SA, see pp. 92–5.
80. See, for example, StAG, Rep. 240/C.61.a.: 'Vierteljährliche Organisationsmeldungen' for the period July 1932–May 1933.
81. In Pomerania Karl von Halfern, *Oberpräsident* since June 1930, remained at his post until October 1933. He was not replaced until July 1934, when Franz Schwede, Karpenstein's successor as *Gauleiter,* became *Oberpräsident.* See Robert Thévoz, Hans Branig and Cécile Lowenthal-Hensel, *Pommern 1934/35 im Spiegel von Gestapo-Lageberichten und Sachakten (Darstellung)* (Cologne and Berlin, 1974), pp. 45, 289.
82. *VB,* 26 Feb. 1925, p. 2. The text of Hitler's 'Basic guidelines for the re-activation of the National Socialist German Workers' Party' is published in Tyrell, *Führer befiehl,* pp. 105–7. See also Adolf Hitler, *Mein Kampf* (213/217 edn., Munich, 1936), pp. 619–20.
83. See Werner, 'SA und NSDAP', p. 320; Bennecke, *Hitler und die SA,* pp. 119–32; Nyomarkay, *Charisma and Factionalism,* pp. 110–13; Wolfgang Horn, *Führerideologie und Parteiorganisation in der NSDAP (1919–1933)* (Düsseldorf, 1972), pp. 226–30.
84. For a detailed discussion of the organisation of the SA, as developed by von Pfeffer, see Werner, 'SA und NSDAP', pp. 356–403.
85. Bennecke, *Hitler und die SA,* pp. 131–2, 247–8; Noakes, *The Nazi Party in Lower Saxony,* p. 182.
86. The organisational structure was fixed as follows:

6–12 men	= 1 'Gruppe' (later revised to 3–12 men)
5–8 'Gruppen'	= 1 'Trupp'
2–4 'Trupps'	= 1 'Sturm'
2–5 'Stürme'	= 1 'Standarte'
2–5 'Standarten'	= 1 'Brigade'

All the 'Brigaden' within a *Gau* formed a 'Gausturm'.
All the 'Gaustürme' together formed the SA.

See IfZ, Fa 107, ff. 19–20: SABE 6, Munich, 6 Nov. 1926; ibid., f. 27: SABE 14, Munich, 14 Nov. 1926; ibid., ff. 37–8: GRUSA IA, Munich, 4 June 1927.
87. WAP Wrocław, RO I/1800, ff. 29–65: reports from district officials throughout Upper Silesia concerning the size of local Nazi groups, dated late February 1927.
88. Ibid., f. 171: The *Oberbürgermeister* to the *Regierungspräsident,* Oppeln, 27 Oct. 1927.

89. In October a 'Schutzstaffel' with 17 members was reported in Ratibor as well. See ibid., f. 139: The *Oberbürgermeister* to the *Regierungspräsident*, Ratibor, 6 Oct. 1927.
90. Ibid., ff. 198–9: 'Nachweisung der Schutzstaffeln und Sportabteilungen der NSDAP in der Provinz Oberschlesien nach dem Stande vom Januar 1928'.
91. Ibid., f. 491: The *Polizeipräsident* to the *Regierungspräsident*, Oppeln, 26 Apr. 1929.
92. See BA, NS 22/1068: 'Beschaffenheitsbericht Mitte März bis Pfingsten 29', Schweidnitz, 14 May 1929; BA, Sammlung Schumacher/208, vol. 2, f. 73.
93. See WAP Wrocław, RO I/1829, ff. 3–75: 'Lagebericht für die politische Bewegung im Präsidialbezirk Oppeln für die Zeit vom 1. Okt. bis 31. Dez. 1929', Oppeln, 7 Jan. 1930.
94. In the first quarter of 1930 the police reported the size of the SA units in the region as follows: Oppeln, 68; Kreuzburg, 18; Hindenburg, 45; Ratibor, 52; Gleiwitz, 28; and Beuthen, 37. See ibid., ff. 523–73: 'Bericht über die politische Lage im Dienstbereich des Polizeipräsidiums Gleiwitz für die Zeit vom 1. Januar bis 31. März 1930', Gleiwitz, 11 Apr. 1930.
95. WAP Wrocław, RO I/1802, ff. 283–9: 'Nachweisung über die Organisation der NSDAP'. The number of men in the groups listed was 457, but this seems not to have covered the entire SA membership.
96. WAP Wrocław, RO I/1830, ff. 293–301.
97. Ibid., ff. 421–31.
98. Ibid., ff. 571–7. This figure was corroborated by Upper Silesian SA leader Andreas von Flotow, who revealed in December 1931 that the SA numbered roughly 3,500 men in the province. See BDC, SA-Akte, Andreas von Flotow: 'Sonderbericht über die Lage der Provinz Oberschlesien im Dezember 1931'. According to the Munich headquarters, the SA in Upper Silesia numbered 4,295 men in December 1931 (and 4,675 in January 1932). See BA, Sammlung Schumacher/415: 'Stand der SA nach dem Stande der letzten Stärkemeldung (15.2.32)', Munich, 27 Feb. 1932.
99. WAP Wrocław, RO I/1830, ff. 571–7.
100. Ibid., ff. 645–53: 'Bericht über die politische Lage im Bereich der Landespolizeistelle für die Provinz Oberschlesien für die Zeit vom 1. Januar bis 30. April 1932', Oppeln, 10 May 1932.
101. Ibid., ff. 723–31: 'Bericht über die politische Lage im Bereich der Landespolizeistelle für die Provinz Oberschlesien für die Zeit vom 1. Mai bis 30. Juni 1932', Oppeln, 1 Aug. 1932; ibid., ff. 791–9: 'Bericht über die politische Lage im Bereich der Landespolizeistelle für die Provinz Oberschlesien für die Zeit vom 1. Juli bis 10. November 1932', Oppeln, 11 Nov. 1932.
102. Ibid., ff. 853–69: 'Bericht über die politische Lage im Bereich der Landespolizeistelle für die Provinz Oberschlesien für die Zeit vom 6. November 1932 bis Mitte Januar 1933', Oppeln, 26 Jan. 1933.
103. StAG, Rep. 10/29, f. 37: The *Polizeipräsident* to the *Regierungspräsident*, Königsberg, 11 Apr. 1929; StAG, Rep. 10/30, ff. 109–16: The *Polizeipräsident* to the *Regierungspräsident*, Königsberg, 1 Oct. 1930; ibid., ff. 145–7: The *Polizeipräsident* to the *Regierungspräsident*, Königsberg, 29 June 1931.
104. StAG, Rep. 14/B.I.3., f. 899: *Kriminal- und Grenzkommissariat* Allenstein to the *Polizeipräsident* in Königsberg, Allenstein, 14 Dec. 1931; ibid., ff. 885–98: 'Zusammenstellung über die im Regierungsbezirk Allenstein vorhandene SA der NSDAP nach dem Stande vom 10. Dezember 1931'.
105. For example, at the end of 1932 (when Nazi fortunes were at low ebb) strengths of political groups in the East Prussian *Kreis* Lötzen were as follows: NSDAP, 836 members; SA, 490; *Reichsbanner,* 96; SPD, 202; ADGB, 83; KPD, 113; DNVP, 101; DVP, 34; *Staatspartei,* 13; and *Stahlhelm,* 283. See WAP Olsztyn, Landratsamt Lötzen/242, ff. 12–51: The *Landrat* to the *Regierungspräsident*, Lötzen, 3 Dec. 1932.
106. BA, Sammlung Schumacher/415: 'Stärke der SA & SS nach dem Stande vom 1.4.1931', Munich, 18 May 1931; ibid.: 'Aufstellung über die Stärke der SA und deren Anwachsen in einem Monat gemäß der Stärkemeldungen für Dezember 1931 (15.11.–15.12.31)', Munich, 1 Feb. 1932; ibid.: 'Stand der SA nach dem Stande der letzten Stärkemeldungen (15.2.32)', Munich, 27 Feb. 1932; BA, NS 26/307: The *Oberster* SA-*Führer,* Munich, 11 Jan. 1932; WAP Szczecin, RS/212 I, ff. 221–37: 'Standorte, Führer und Stärken der Sturmabteilungen (SA) der NSDAP im Gausturm Pommern nach dem Stande von etwa

September 1931'; WAP Poznań, OPS/166, ff. 356–7: 'Gliederung der SA in der Grenzmark Posen-Westpreußen. Stand: 19.9.1931'.

107. BA, NS 23/474, ff. 105060–2: The *Führer der Standarte 5* to the *Oberster* SA-*Führer,* Danzig, 24 Sept. 1932.

108. For discussion of von Pfeffer's resignation in the summer of 1930, see IfZ, Fa 107, f. 58: Adolf Hitler to the SA and SS, Munich, 2 Sept. 1930; Bennecke, *Hitler und die SA,* pp. 147–9; Werner, 'SA und NSDAP', pp. 470–85; Nyomarkay, *Charisma and Factionalism,* pp. 116–17; Frank, 'Hitler and the National Socialist Coalition', pp. 360–98.

109. The new structure was as follows:

4–12 SA men	= 1 'Schar'	
3–6 'Scharen'	= 1 'Trupp'	= 20–60 men
2 or more 'Trupps'	= 1 'Sturm'	= 70–100 men
3 or more 'Stürme'	= 1 'Sturmbann'	= 250–600 men
2 or more 'Sturmbannen'	= 1 'Standarte'	= 1,200–3,000 men
all 'Standarten' in a particular region	= 1 'Untergruppe'	
'Untergruppen' joined together	= 1 'Gruppe'	= about 15,000 men

See WAP Poznań, OPS/166, f. 195: The *Regierungspräsident,* Frankfurt/Oder, 28 Apr. 1931; ibid., f. 196: The *staatl. Polizeidirektor* to the *Oberpräsident,* Schneidemühl, 8 May 1931; IfZ, Fa 107, ff. 205–9: excerpts from a Nazi history of the SA, undated.

110. WAP Poznań, OPS/166, ff. 356–7; WAP Szczecin, RS/212 I, ff. 221–37.

111. StAG, Rep. 240/C.33.a.: 'Nachrichtenblatt des Bezirks Groß Königsbergs Pr. der Nationalsozialistischen Deutschen Arbeiterpartei', Königsberg, 11 May 1929.

112. For example, in Stettin in September 1931 the SA had 485 members altogether, of whom only 128 were in the Reserve. See WAP Szczecin, RS/212 I, ff. 87–91: The *Polizeipräsident* to the *Oberpräsident,* Stettin, 15 Sept. 1931. In his study of the Nürnberg SA, Eric Reiche noted the same pattern; in May 1930 the Nuremberg SA numbered 350 men, and the Reserve an additional 70. See Reiche, 'The Development of the SA in Nuremberg', p. 125.

113. StAG, Rep. 240/C.73.c.: The *Gaugeschäftsführer* to the *Ortsgruppe* Rößel, Königsberg, 15 Sept. 1931; WAP Wrocław, RO I/1806, ff. 11–12: The *Polizeipräsident* to the *Oberpräsident,* Oppeln, 6 Sept. 1932.

114. See WAP Szczecin, RS/212 II, ff. 17–61: The *Polizeipräsident* to the *Oberpräsident,* Stettin, 11 Apr. 1932; StAG, Rep. 10/30, f. 283: The *Polizeipräsident* to the *Regierungspräsident,* Königsberg, 23 Dec. 1932.

115. StAG, Rep. 14/B.I.3., f. 394: The *Polizeipräsident* to the *Regierungspräsident* in Allenstein, Königsberg, 25 Mar. 1931; WAP Wrocław, RO I/1804, ff. 477–84: The *Polizeipräsident* to the *Regierungspräsident* in Oppeln, Breslau, 9 Dec. 1931; Frank, 'Hitler and the National Socialist Coalition', p. 428.

116. WAP Szczecin, RS/212 I, ff. 245–51: The *Polizeipräsident* to the *Oberpräsident,* Stettin, 24 Feb. 1932; ibid., ff. 257–8: The *Regierungspräsident* to the *Landräte des Bezirks,* Stettin, 21 Apr. 1932.

117. StAG, Rep. 10/30, f. 271: The *Polizeipräsident* to the *Regierungspräsident,* Königsberg, 26 Mar. 1932.

118. WAP Wrocław, RO I/1806, ff. 1037–8: The *komm. Polizeipräsident* to the *Regierungspräsident,* Oppeln, 21 Dec. 1932. See also p. 95.

Notes to Chapter III

1. For a recent survey of research in this area, see Peter D. Stachura, 'Who Were the Nazis? A Socio-Political Analysis of the National Socialist *Machtübernahme', European Studies Review,* xi (1981), pp. 293–324.

2. Reichsorganisationsleiter der NSDAP (ed.), *Partei-Statistik (1935),* i, pp. 70–1: Martin Broszat, *Der Staat Hitlers* (Munich, 1969), p. 51. The differences between the NSDAP membership and the German working population become even more striking when it is considered that the former was almost 95% male.

3. BA, Sammlung Schumacher/376. This table is reproduced, in reduced form, in Tyrell, *Führer befiehl.*

4. Michael H. Kater, 'Sozialer Wandel in der NSDAP im Zuge der nationalsozialistischen Machtergreifung', in Wolfgang Schieder (ed.), *Faschismus als soziale Bewegung. Deutschland und Italien im Vergleich* (Hamburg, 1976), pp. 29–32; Lawrence D. Stokes, 'The Social Composition of the Nazi Party in Eutin, 1925–32', *International Review of Social History,* xxii (1978), pp. 1–32.

5. Detlev Mühlberger, 'The Sociology of the NSDAP: The Question of Working-Class Membership', *Journal of Contemporary History,* xv (1980), pp. 493–511.

6. *Partei-Statistik,* i, pp. 146, 148. Since the NSDAP in the Border Province formed part of the 'Gau Ostmark', separate figures were not compiled for it. There is, however, an analysis of the structure of the NSDAP in the province (compiled by the police in late 1931), in which the occupations of the local party leadership are listed; see WAP Poznań, OPS/166, ff. 331–5: 'Gliederung der NSDAP im Lkp.-Bezirk Schneidemühl. Stand 1.10.1931'.

7. *Der SA-Mann,* 7 Jan. 1933, p. 4.

8. BA, R 43 I/2682, ff. 645–7: The *Polizeipräsident* to the *Minister des Innern,* Berlin, 2 Mar. 1931.

9. Reiche, 'The Development of the SA in Nuremberg', p. 256.

10. Peter H. Merkl, *Political Violence under the Swastika. 581 Early Nazis* (Princeton, 1975), p. 595. In his second re-working of the Abel materials, however, Merkl claims that 38.5% of the SA men in this group were 'skilled and unskilled workers'; see Merkl, *The Making of a Stormtrooper,* p. 99.

11. Kater, 'Ansätze zu einer Soziologie der SA', pp. 801–2.

12. Stokes, 'The Social Composition of the Nazi Party in Eutin', p. 27.

13. See the tables showing the social composition of the leadership for the pre-1918, 1918–24, 1925–29, 1930–33 and 1933–36 periods in Jamin, 'Zwischen den Klassen', Chapter IV.

14. Fischer, 'The Occupational Background of the SA's Rank-and-File Membership', p. 138. See also Fischer, *Stormtroopers,* pp. 25–32. Among the problems with Fischer's work are that his statistical 'sample' is not really a sample, and that his analysis of the pre-1933 SA is based largely upon materials describing storm troopers in Munich in 1931. For a critique of Fischer, see Richard Bessel and Mathilde Jamin, 'Nazis, Workers and the Uses of Quantitative Evidence', *Social History,* iv (1979), pp. 111–16. For Fischer's response, see Conan Fischer and Carolyn Hicks, 'Statistics and the Historian: the Occupational Profile of the SA of the NSDAP', *Social History,* v (1980), pp. 131–8.

15. 73.1% of the 18-19-year-old males, 69.5% of those aged 20–24 and 64.5% of those aged 25–29 were workers. See Jamin, 'Zwischen den Klassen', Chapter IV.

16. This point has been underlined recently by Christoph Schmidt. Through a systematic analysis of 74 life-histories of early NSDAP members in Hessen-Nassau, Schmidt has demonstrated that the occupational data given in the BDC card files and lists of party members can be quite unreliable. See Christoph Schmidt, 'Zu den Motiven "alter Kämpfer" in der NSDAP', in Detlev Peukert and Jürgen Reulecke (eds.), *Die Reihen fast geschlossen. Beiträge zur Geschichte des Alltags unterm Nationalsozialismus* (Wuppertal, 1981), pp. 22–5.

17. BA, Kleine Erwerbungen/569: Heinrich Bennecke, 'Die SA in Sachsen vor der "Machtübernahme" ', p. 25.

18. Copies of this memorandum were found among files from Oppeln and Königsberg. See WAP Wrocław, RO I/1801, ff. 69–70; and StAG, Rep. 10/30, f. 106: The *Preußische Minister des Innern* to the *Ober-* and *Regierungspräsidenten* and the *Polizeipräsident* in Berlin, Berlin, 20 Aug. 1930.

19. Ibid., f. 109: The *Polizeipräsident* to the *Regierungspräsident,* Königsberg, 1 Oct. 1930.

20. Ibid., f. 145: The *Polizeipräsident* to the *Regierungspräsident,* Königsberg, 29 June 1931.

21. StAG, Rep. 14/B.I.3., f. 556: The *Regierungspräsident* to the *Polizeipräsident* in Königsberg, Allenstein, 19 June 1931.

22. In 1925, 26.6% of the male labour force in Königsberg were classified as workers in industry and crafts. See *StDR,* cccciii ('Volks-, Berufs- und Betriebszählung vom 16. JuPolitical Violence—5

21. StAG, Rep. 14/B.I.3., f. 556: The *Regierungspräsident* to the *Polizeipräsident* in Königsberg, Allenstein, 19 June 1931.

22. In 1925, 26.6% of the male labour force in Königsberg were classified as workers in industry and crafts. See *StDR,* cccciii *(Volks-, Berufs- und Betriebszählung vom 16. Juni 1925. Die berufliche und soziale Gliederung der Bevölkerung in den Ländern und Landesteilen)* (Berlin, 1929), i, p. 2/65.
23. Ibid., p. 2/64.
24. Ibid., p. 2/64.
25. Ibid., p. 2/76.
26. The figures for the *Regierungsbezirke* Königsberg and Allenstein, derived from the 1925 census data, were 15.7% and 12.1% respectively. See ibid., pp. 2/64, 2/76.
27. StAG, Rep. 240/C.68.a.: NSDAP *Kreisleitung* Osterode to the *Gauleitung,* Kraplau, 7 Nov. 1932. Similar conclusions are reached by Geoffrey Pridham in his examination of the Nazi rise in rural Franconia. See Pridham, *Hitler's Rise to Power,* p. 233.
28. See Noakes, *The Nazi Party in Lower Saxony,* p. 127.
29. StAG, Rep. 14/B.I.3., ff. 313–14: The *Landrat* to the *Regierungspräsident,* Johannisburg, 9 Feb. 1931; ibid., ff. 541–3: The *Landrat* to the *Regierungspräsident,* Johannisburg, 8 June 1931; ibid., ff. 755–6: The *Landrat* to the *Regierungspräsident,* Johannisburg, 10 Sept. 1931.
30. Heberle, *Landbevölkerung und Nationalsozialismus,* p. 44.
31. Organisational analyses, including the strengths of SA units and the names and occupations of their leaders, were coupled to the statistical reports from October 1930 and June 1931. See StAG, Rep. 10/30, ff. 111–16, 146–66.
32. WAP Szczecin, RS/212 I, ff. 77–85: The *Polizeipräsident* to the *Polizeipräsident* in Berlin, Stettin, 2 July 1931.
33. See p. 64.
34. WAP Szczecin, RS/212 I, ff. 221–37: 'Standarte, Führer und Stärken der Sturmabteilungen (SA) der NSDAP in Gausturm Pommern nach dem Stande von etwa September 1931'.
35. WAP Wrocław, RO I/1829, ff. 569–73.
36. WAP Wrocław, RO I/1802, ff. 283–9: 'Nachweisung über die Organisation der NSDAP', Oppeln, 13 Sept. 1930.
37. Cuno Horkenbach (ed.), *Das Deutsche Reich von 1918 bis heute* (Berlin, 1930), p. 693.
38. WAP Poznań, OPS/166, f. 196: The *staatl. Polizeidirektor* to the *Oberpräsident,* Schneidemühl, 8 May 1931.
39. WAP Szczecin, RS/212 I, ff. 55–61: The *Polizeipräsident* to the *Oberpräsident,* Stettin, 6 May 1931.
40. WAP Wrocław, RO I/1800, f. 29: The *Oberbürgermeister* to the *Regierungspräsident,* Ratibor, 19 Mar. 1929.
41. Waite, *Vanguard of Nazism,* p. 289.
42. Ibid., p. 292.
43. WAP Szczecin, RS/207, ff. 55–69: 'Auszug aus dem Personalakt des Kaufmanns Edmund Heines, geb. 21.7.97 in München', Munich, 25 Jan. 1928. This report, which was prepared for the '*Feme*' trial in Stettin in 1928, is published in Drewniak, *Poczatki ruchu hitlerow-.kiego,* pp. 266–70. See also BA, NS 26/1348: The *Polizeipräsident* to the *Polizeipräsident* in Bielefeld, Berlin, 15 May 1931.
44. For an extremely perceptive discussion of the *Freikorps* and of the relationship of sexuality to politics, see the recent study by Klaus Theweleit, *Männerphantasien 1. Frauen, Fluten, Körper, Geschichte* (Frankfurt/Main, 1977), and *Männerphantasien 2. Männerkörper. Zur Psychoanalyse des weißen Terrors* (Frankfurt/Main, 1978). See also Lutz Niethammer, 'Male Fantasies: an Argument for and with an important new Study in History and Psychoanalysis', *History Workshop. A Journal of Socialist Historians,* no. 7 (1979), pp. 176–86.
45. StAG, Rep. 240/B.9.a.: 'Lagebericht der Gauleitung', Königsberg, 20 Jan. 1930.
46. WAP Szczecin, RS/225, f. 39: an appeal to join the SA by Ernst Gensch, Podejuch.
47. StAG, Rep. 240/C.33.: 'Tätigkeitsbericht für Monat März 1931', Insterburg, 1 Apr. 1931.
48. BA, NS 23/474, ff. 105185-90: The *Führer der Untergruppe O-S* to Ernst Röhm, Oppeln, 22 Sept. 1932.
49. StAG, Rep. 240/C.81.c.: Berhard Schlie to Erich Koch, Rosenberg, 17 Dec. 1930.
50. StAG, Rep. 240/C.69.b.: 'Tätigkeitsbericht', Kussen, Kr. Pillkallen, 26 Nov. 1930.

51. BA, NS 23/474, ff. 105182–3: The *Führer der Standarte 11* to the *Chef des Stabes*, Breslau, 22 Sept. 1932.

52. Gundelach, *Vom Kampf und Sieg der schlesischen SA*, p. 137.

53. For evidence of unemployment among SA members in other regions, see BA, Kleine Erwerbungen/569: Bennecke, 'Die SA in Sachsen vor der "Machtübernahme" ', pp. 52–3; Reiche, 'The Development of the SA in Nuremberg', pp. 144–5; Böhnke, *Die NSDAP im Ruhrgebiet,* pp. 154, 158; Fischer, 'The Occupational Background of the SA', pp. 147–9; Fischer, *Stormtroopers,* pp. 45–8, 82–109. See also Timothy W. Mason, *Sozialpolitik im Dritten Reich. Arbeiterklasse und Volksgemeinschaft* (Opladen, 1977), pp. 66–7.

54. WAP Szczecin, RS/17, ff. 19–23: The *kom. Landrat* to the *Regierungspräsident,* Greifenhagen, 20 Dec. 1930.

55. See pp. 49–53.

56. See the age distribution graphs in *Schlag nach! Wissenswerte Tatsachen aus allen Gebieten* (2nd end., Leipzig, 1939), p. 191; *Statistisches Handbuch für die Provinz Ostpreußen* (Schloßberg and Leipzig, 1938), p. 37.

57. This point is emphasised by Merkl in *The Making of a Stormtrooper,* pp. 185–90.

58. See ibid., pp. 190–4.

59. See esp. pp. 47, 150–4.

60. Fischer, on the other hand, stresses the social differences. See Fischer, *Stormtroopers,* esp. pp. 25–32, 169, 194–6.

61. IfZ, Fa 107, ff 33–5: GRUSA II, Munich, 31 May 1927.

62. For accounts of Nazi propaganda activities in western and southern Germany, see Allen, *The Nazi Seizure of Power,* pp. 23–138; Noakes, *The Nazi Party in Lower Saxony,* pp. 142–3, 201–21; Pridham, *Hitler's Rise to Power,* pp. 133–8; Böhnke, *Die NSDAP im Ruhrgebiet,* pp. 145–54.

63. See, for example, WAP Wrocław, RO I/1830, ff. 191–227; StAG, Rep. 240/C.50.b.: NSDAP *Ortsgruppe* Heilsberg, 'Parteigeschichte', Heilsberg, 20 June 1935.

64. For discussion of how the lives of unemployed Nazis were structured by the movement, see Schmidt, 'Zu den Motiven "alter Kämpfer" ', pp. 30–1.

65. For the politics of taverns in Berlin during the late Weimar period, see the perceptive comments of Eve Rosenhaft in 'Working-Class Life and Working-Class Politics', esp. pp. 230–4.

66. StAG, Rep. 240/C.37.b.: The *Gaukommissar Ost* to the *Gauleitung,* Kiauten, 1 Aug. 1931.

67. StAG, Rep. 14/B.I.3., f. 677: *Kriminal- und Grenzkommissariat* to the *Regierungspräsident,* Prostken, 16 Oct. 1931. Investigations of the SA in Northeim and Nürnberg confirm the impression that SA men often did not become NSDAP members. See Allen, *The Nazi Seizure of Power,* p. 73; Reiche, 'The Development of the SA in Nuremberg', pp. 267–8.

68. StAG, Rep. 240/C.61.b.(1): 'Die Geschichte der Bewegung der NSDAP Ortsgruppe Widminnen'.

69. BA, NS 23/474, ff. 105178–81: Hans Hayn to the *Oberste* SA-*Führung,* Breslau, 22 Sept. 1932.

70. In his study of the SA, Merkl also downplays the storm troopers' commitment to Nazi ideology. See Merkl, *The Making of a Stormtrooper,* esp. pp. 170–2.

71. For an example of how rallies helped expand the Nazi organisation, see the account of a meeting in February 1931 in Langkischken, *Kreis* Goldap (East Prussia), which brought to the NSDAP '19 new members, 16 of them for the SA', in StAG, Rep. 240/C.47.b.: Richard Georges to the *Bezirksleitung der NSDAP in Insterburg,* Kiauten, 24 Feb. 1931.

72. Friedrich Franz von Unruh, *Nationalsozialismus* (Frankfurt/Main, 1931), p. 19.

73. See StAG, Rep. 10/17, ff. 441–9: The *Regierungspräsident* to the *Oberpräsident,* Marienwerder, 18 July 1930.

74. See Allen, *The Nazi Seizure of Power,* pp. 73–5.

75. See, for example, WAP Szczecin, RS/17, ff. 37–41: The *kom. Landrat* to the *Regierungspräsident,* Greifenhagen, 1 Feb. 1931.

76. WAP Szczecin, RS/212 I, f. 43: 'Geheimbefehl der OSAF O', Berlin, 26 Feb. 1931.

77. WAP Opole, OPS/1020, f. 143: Preußisches Polizeiinstitut, 'Denkschrift über Vorbereitung und Kampfgrundsätze radikaler Organisationen' (1931).

78. See p. 95.

79. BA, NS 23/474, ff. 105175–7: The *Führer der Untergruppe Mittelschlesien Süd* to the

Oberste SA-*Führung,* Reichenbach (Eulengeb.), 26 Sept. 1932.

80. Frank, 'Hitler and the National Socialist Coalition', p. 428. For a description of the course in East Prussia, see StAG, 14/B.I.3., f. 394: The *Polizeipräsident* to the *Regierungspräsident* in Allenstein, Königsberg, 25 Mar. 1931.
81. WAP Wrocław, RO I/1804, ff. 477–84: The *Polizeipräsident* to the *Regierungspräsident,* Breslau, 9 Dec. 1931.
82. BA, Sammlung Schumacher/207, vol. 2, f. 339: NSDAP *Gau Pommern,* 'Tätigkeitsbericht für den Monat August 1928'.
83. StAG, Rep. 240/C.53.a.(1): *Prop. Obmann* to the *Prop. Abtl. d.* NSDAP in Munich, Königsberg, 20 Aug. 1928.
84. StAG, Rep. 240/C.33.a.: *Bezirksleiter* Heidrich to all *Parteigenossen,* SA and SS Members, Königsberg, 15 Aug. 1929.
85. StAG, Rep. 10/17, ff. 441–9.
86. WAP Szczecin, RS/8, f. 9: The *Polizeiverwaltung,* Cammin, 28 July 1930.
87. *VB,* 19 July 1932, p. 1.
88. More than 400 SA and SS men made the trip from Upper Silesia alone. See WAP Wrocław, RO I/1804, f. 43: The *Polizeipräsident* to the *Regierungspräsident,* Oppeln, 30 Oct. 1931.
89. Werner, 'SA und NSDAP', p. 417.
90. StAG, Rep. 240/C.54.b.: 'Chronik der NSDAP Ortsgruppe Roßgarten Kreis Königsberg/Pr.'.
91. WAP Wrocław, RO I/1830, ff. 423–7.
92. Ibid., ff. 489–95: 'Bericht über die politische Lage im Bereich der Landespolizeistelle für die Provinz Oberschlesien für das verflossene Vierteljahr', Oppeln, 30 Nov. 1931.
93. See Bennecke, *Hitler und die SA,* p. 175.
94. StAG, Rep. 10/30, f. 207: The *Preußische Minister des Innern,* Berlin, 4 Sept. 1931.
95. WAP Wrocław, RO I/1830, ff. 489–95.
96. StAG, Rep. 240/C.54.b: 'Chronik der NSDAP Ortsgruppe Roßgarten Kreis Königsberg/Pr.'.
97. WAP Wrocław, RO I/1803, ff. 891–3: The *Polizeipräsident* to the *Regierungspräsident,* Oppeln, 12 Oct. 1931.
98. In Silesia, for example, a major crackdown came in January 1932, when *Heime* in Gleiwitz, Hindenburg, Konstadt and Lüben were shut. See WAP Wrocław, RO I/1804, ff. 435–6: The *Polizeipräsident* to the *Regierungspräsident,* Gleiwitz, 11 Jan. 1932; ibid., ff. 518–19: The *Polizeipräsident* to the *Regierungspräsident,* Gleiwitz, 15 Jan. 1932; ibid., ff. 709–10: letter to the *Ortspolizeibehörde* in Konstadt (undated, from Jan. 1932); WAP Wrocław, RO I/1806, f. 469: The *Landrat* to Dr Wagner, Kreuzburg, 18 Feb. 1932; *SZ,* 12 Jan. 1932, p. 3; ibid., 14 Jan. 1932, p. 3.
99. WAP Wrocław, RO I/1803, f. 841: The *Polizeipräsident* to the *Regierungspräsident,* Oppeln, 21 Aug. 1931.
100. See, for example, the report of the closing of the SA-*Heim* in Tilsit, in *VB,* 11 Nov. 1931, p. 1.
101. For example, in Kreuzburg in Upper Silesia a stable owned by the propaganda chief of the local NSDAP became an SA-*Heim* housing 8 or 9 SA men. See WAP Wrocław, RO I/1803, f. 843: The *Polizeipräsident* to the *Regierungspräsident,* Oppeln, 28 Sept. 1931; ibid., f. 845: The *Polizeipräsident* to the *Regierungspräsident,* Oppeln, 25 Jan. 1932.
102. StAG, Rep. 10/30, ff. 226–7: The *Regierungspräsident* to the *Pr. Minister des Innern,* Königsberg, 3 Oct. 1931.
103. WAP Wrocław, RO I/1803, f. 569: clipping from *ST,* 24 Aug. 1931.
104. Ibid., ff. 575–7: The *Polizeipräsident* to the *Regierungspräsident,* Oppeln, 27 Aug. 1931.
105. The real reason for terminating the agreement appears to have been concern by Schultheiss that it was losing business because it rented property to the Nazis. See ibid., ff. 1105–6: The *Polizeipräsident* to the *Regierungspräsident,* Oppeln, 22 Oct. 1931.
106. Ibid., f. 47: The *Polizeipräsident* to the *Regierungspräsident,* Oppeln, 22 May 1931.
107. Ibid., ff. 513–14: The *Polizeipräsident* to the *Regierungspräsident,* Oppeln, 7 Aug. 1931.
108. WAP Wrocław, RO I/1804, f. 71: The *Polizeipräsident* to the *Regierungspräsident,* Oppeln, 8 Nov. 1931. See also WAP Wrocław, RO I/1830, ff. 571–7.
109. Ibid., ff. 571–7.

Notes to Chapter IV

1. For an analysis of the self-financing of a Nazi *Gau* organisation, see Horst Mazerath and Henry A. Turner, 'Die Selbstfinanzierung der NSDAP 1930–1933', *Geschichte und Gesellschaft*, iii (1977), pp. 59–82. The only evidence found of support by large firms for the Nazi movement in eastern Germany was the readiness of the Borsig factory in Hindenburg to provide a site for a Hitler rally free of charge. See BA, NS 22/1068: Wilhelm Hüttmann to Gregor Straßer, Oppeln, 4 July 1932.
2. For a discussion of the role of political rallies in financing local party groups, see Bessel, 'The Rise of the NSDAP', pp. 25–6. See also Theodor Heuß, *Hitlers Weg. Eine historisch-politische Studie über den Nationalsozialismus* (Stuttgart, Berlin and Leipzig, 1932), pp. 123–4.
3. BA, NS 1/511: *Reichsschatzmeister,* 'Rundschreiben an sämtliche Gauleitungen der NSDAP', Munich, 6 Sept. 1932; ibid.: *Reichsschatzmeister,* 'Rundschreiben an sämtliche Gauleitungen der NSDAP', Munich, 17 Oct. 1932.
4. For details of the SA insurance scheme, see Werner, 'SA und NSDAP', pp. 408–14. During the 1920s this insurance business was handled by private firms, but in 1929, after disputes over rising premiums, it was taken over directly by the NSDAP; its director was Martin Bormann. See BA, NS 1/393.
5. In October 1930, for example, a brown shirt cost 6.80 RM, the cheapest brown trousers 7.50, an SA cap 3.10 RM, and a shoulder strap 1.70 RM. See *Illustrierter Beobachter,* 11 Oct. 1930, p. 713: advertisement of the *Sporthaus* 'Scharnhorst', Hamburg.
6. See Werner, 'SA und NSDAP', p. 362.
7. Ibid., pp. 361–2.
8. See BA, NS 23/474, ff. 105178–81: Hans Hayn to the *Oberste* SA-*Führung,* Breslau, 22 Sept. 1932.
9. Ibid., ff. 105182–3: The *Führer der Standarte 11* to the *Chef des Stabes,* Breslau, 22 Sept. 1932; ibid., ff. 105186–90: The *Führer der Untergruppe* O/S to the *Chef des Stabes,* Oppeln, 22 Sept. 1932.
10. In Breslau, the proceeds from 'Sturm' cigarettes brought the *Standarte* 50 RM in July 1932 and 595 RM in August. See ibid., ff. 105182–3.
11. The monthly salary of *Gau* SA leaders before 1933 was roughly 300 RM. See *TMWC* (Nürnberg, 1947), xxi, p. 130; testimony of Max Jüttner, from 1 Nov. 1945. Many regional SA leaders had other sources of income, however, either as *Reichstag* deputies (Heines and Ramshorn) or provincial assembly deputies (Manthey), or from independent means (Litzmann).
12. See StAG, Rep. 240/C.66.e: Georg Heidrich to Ernst Linkies, Königsberg, 30 Oct. 1930; BA, NS 23/474, ff. 105094–5: The *Führer der Gruppe Ostsee* to the *Chef des Stabes,* Stettin, 22 Sept. 1932; ibid., ff. 105066–9: The *Führer der Untergruppe Pommern-Ost* to the *Chef des Stabes,* Berlin, 22 Sept. 1932.
13. BA, Sammlung Schumacher/403: 'Bericht über Aussprache der SAF mit Herrn Reichsschatzmeister Schwarz über Finanzierung der SA', Munich, 30 Nov. 1930.
14. On 12 September, the Friday before the *Reichstag* elections, Hitler spoke before an estimated 30,000 people in Breslau. See *SZ,* 13 Sept. 1930, p. 2.
15. See, for example, BA, NS 23/474, ff. 105174–7: Hans Hayn to the *Oberste* SA-*Führung,* Reichenbach (Eulengeb.), 26 Sept. 1932.
16. Ibid., ff. 105066–9.
17. Ibid., ff. 105096–101: The *Führer der Untergruppe Pommern-West* to the *Chef des Stabes,* Stettin, 22 Sept. 1932.
18. StAG, Rep. 240/C.70.b.: Otto Fuchs to the *Gauleitung in* Königsberg, Landsberg, 10 Dec. 1931. Fuchs was placed in considerable difficulties when, by December, he still had not been repaid.
19. IfZ, Fa 107, f. 15: SABE 2, Munich, 2 Nov. 1926.
20. See Nyomarkay, *Charisma and Factionalism,* pp. 110–15; Rudolf Diels, *Lucifer ante Portas. Zwischen Severing und Heydrich* (Zürich (1950), p. 153.
21. See above, p. 19.
22. BA, NS 22/1068: Helmuth Brückner to the *Reichsleitung der* NSDAP, Schweidnitz, 10 May 1930.

23. BA, Sammlung Schumacher/208, vol. 2, f. 75: Otto Wagener to Helmuth Brückner, Munich, 5 Nov. 1930.
24. BDC, AOPG, Max Wieschalla: The USchlA *Vorsitzender* to Ferdinand von Hiddessen, Munich, 16 Dec. 1930.
25. See pp. 63–5.
26. See BA, NS 26/152, f. 484; Gaede, *Pommern*, pp. 13–15.
27. BDC, SA-Akte, Hans Friedrich: *Stabsleiter* Krüger to the *Oberster* SA-*Führer*, Berlin, 7 Aug. 1931; ibid.: Hans Friedrich to the *Oberster* SA-*Führer*, Munich, 13 Aug. 1931; ibid.: *Stabsleiter* Krüger to the *Chef des Stabes*, Berlin, 28 Aug. 1931; ibid.: 'Stellungnahme zum Rechenschaftsbericht des Oberführer Friedrich'; ibid.: SS-*Oberführer* Erbprinz zu Waldeck to the *Oberste* SA-*Führung*, Munich, 18 Aug. 1931; ibid.: Hans Friedrich to the *Chef des Stabes*, Demmin, 29 Aug. 1931.
28. BA, NS 23/474, ff. 105096–101.
29. Ibid., ff. 105066–8, 105094–5.
30. See Hüttenberger, *Die Gauleiter*, pp. 72–3.
31. BDC, Partei-Kanzlei Korrespondenz, Georg Usadel: report of the hearing of the *Gau* USchlA in Königsberg on 28 May 1931; ibid.: Erich Koch to Major Buch, Königsberg, 30 May 1931.
32. BA, NS 22/1065: Erich Koch to Gregor Straßer, Königsberg, 23 July 1931.
33. Ibid.: Erich Koch to Gregor Straßer, Königsberg, 9 Nov. 1931; ibid.: Erich Koch to Gregor Straßer, Königsberg, 21 Dec. 1931.
34. Ibid.: Karl-Siegmund Litzmann to Erich Koch, 29 Dec. 1931.
35. StAG, Rep. 10/34, ff. 102–3: The *Polizeipräsident* to the *Regierungspräsident*, 5 Jan. 1932.
36. See, for example, StAG, Rep. 240/C.61.b.(1): 'Die Geschichte der Bewegung der NSDAP Ortsgruppe Widminnen'; StAG, Rep. 240/C.73.b.: W. Mayer to the *Gauleitung*, Bischofsburg, 9 Nov. 1932.
37. BDC, AOPG, Konrad Ritsch: The *Führer der Standarte 58* to the *Untergruppe NS* in Liegnitz, Beuthen a.O., 21 Jan. 1932.
38. StAG, Rep. 240/C.33.b.: Gerhard Albin to Georg Heidrich, Korschen, 25 Nov. 1930.
39. StAG, Rep. 240/C.34.b.: Anton Arendt to the *Gauleitung*, Tannenhof, 3 Mar. 1930; StAG, Rep. 240/C.67.e.: Arno Lissak to Georg Heidrich, Ortelsburg, 12 Sept. 1931.
40. StAG, Rep. 240/C.62.b.: Erich Budday to the *Gauleitung*, Lyck, 11 Dec. 1931.
41. BA, NS 22/1068: letter to *Gauleiter* Brückner, signed by 13 local NSDAP members, Görlitz, 25 Nov. 1930.
42. StAG, Rep. 240/C.34.c.: *Bezirksleiter* Martini to the *Gauleitung*, Sensburg, 17 Feb. 1931.
43. On the integrative function within the Nazi movement of Hitler's leadership, see Horn, *Führerideologie und Parteiorganisation*, and Nyomarkay, *Charisma and Factionalism*.
44. See, for example, Mau, 'Die "Zweite Revolution"', p. 122; Kater, 'Ansätze zu einer Soziologie der SA', pp. 806–7.
45. For perceptive comments along these lines, see Tim Mason, 'Intention and Explanation: A Current Controversy about the Interpretation of National Socialism', in Gerhard Hirschfeld and Lother Kettenacker (eds.), *Der 'Führerstaat'. Mythos und Realität* (Stuttgart, 1981), pp. 39–40.
46. See Werner, 'SA und NSDAP, pp. 445–7: Tyrrell, *Führer befiehl*, pp. 227, 252.
47. For accounts of the Berlin SA revolts, see Werner, 'SA und NSDAP', pp. 462–85, 524–31; Frank, 'Hitler and the National Socialist Coalition', pp. 360–98, 477–504; Charles Drage, *The Amiable Prussian* (London, 1958), pp. 72–6, 82–4; Bennecke, *Hitler und die SA*, pp. 148–50, 164–5; Nyomarkay, *Charisma and Factionalism*, pp. 116–21; Orlow, *The History of the Nazi Party 1919–1933*, pp. 212, 216–20; Julek Karl von Engelbrechten, *Eine braune Armee entsteht. Die Geschichte der Berlin-Brandenburger SA* (Munich, 1937), pp. 138–9.
48. See Bracher/Sauer/Schulz, *Die nationalsozialistische Machtergreifung*, p. 852; Bennecke, *Hitler und die SA*, p. 164.
49. Tyrell, *Führer befiehl*, pp. 342–3.
50. BA, NS 26/325: 'Erklärung und Aufruf', signed by leaders of the Pomeranian SA.
51. WAP Szczecin, RS/212 I, ff. 77–9: The *Polizeipräsident* to the *Polizeipräsident* in Berlin, Stettin, 2 July 1931.
52. Ibid., ff. 55–61: The *Polizeipräsident* to the *Oberpräsident*, Stettin, 6 May 1931.
53. *VB*, 4 Apr. 1931, 'Erstes Beiblatt'. See also *SZ*, 4 Apr. 1931, p. 1; *PT*, 3 Apr. 1931, p. 3.

54. *VB,* 20 May 1931, p. 3.
55. WAP Szczecin, RS/212 I, ff. 55–61.
56. See WAP Wrocław, RO I/1803, f. 469: The *Polizeipräsident* to the *Oberpräsident,* Oppeln, 18 June 1931; Frank, 'Hitler and the National Socialist Coalition', p. 495. Frank's account is based on an interview with Kurt Kremser in 1963.
57. BA, NS 23/474, ff. 105182–3.
58. WAP Szczecin, RS/212 I, ff. 55–61.
59. *SB,* 8 Apr. 1931, p. 1; *Schlesischer Beobachter,* 11 Apr. 1931, p. 7; Jakubaschk, *Helmuth Brückner,* p. 62.
60. WAP Wrocław, RO I/1800, f. 33: The *Landrat* to the *Regierungspräsident,* Gleiwitz, 21 Mar. 1927; ibid., ff. 198–9: 'Nachweisung der Schutzstaffeln und Sportabteilungen der NSDAP in der Provinz Oberschlesien nach dem Stande von Januar 1928'. See also Frank, 'Hitler and the National Socialist Coalition', p. 471; Mirosław Cygański, 'SS w pruskich prowincjach Śląska w latach 1929–1935', *Studia Śląskie,* xxv (1974), pp. 208–9.
61. Even then the development of the SS remained slow. When Röhm presented guidelines for SS recruitment in December 1931 — guidelines aimed primarily at bringing the SS up to strength, not limiting its growth — the actual size of the SS in the East was far below target. See BA, NS 26/306: The *Chef des Stabes* to *sämtliche Gruppenführer,* RFSS, *Generalinspekteur,* Munich, 2 Dec. 1931.
62. For a general account of the relations between the SA and the SS, see Kater, 'Zum gegenseitigen Verhältnis von SA und SS'.
63. Ibid., pp. 351–2.
64. Werner, 'SA und NSDAP', p. 499; StAG, Rep. 14/B.I.3., ff. 232–3: The *Chef des Stabes,* 'SA-Befehl', Munich, 16 Jan. 1931.
65. See StAG, Rep. 10/29, ff. 43–135: reports from the *Polizeipräsident* in Königsberg to the *Regierungspräsident,* dated between 10 Jan. 1930 and 3 Jan. 1933.
66. Michael Kater confirms that this pattern was true for the SS in the Reich as a whole. See 'Zum gegenseitigen Verhältnis von SA und SS', p. 349.
67. Ibid., pp. 353–7.
68. See, for example, StAG, Rep. 10/29, f. 130: The *Polizeipräsident,* Königsberg, 3 Jan. 1933.
69. StAG, Rep. 14/B.I.3., f. 197: *Kriminal- und Grenzkommissariat,* Ortelsburg, 6 Feb. 1931.
70. See Mathilde Jamin, 'Zur Rolle der SA im Nationalsozialistischen Herrschaftssystem', in Hirschfeld and Kettenacker (eds.), *Der 'Führerstaat',* p. 330.
71. StAG, Rep. 10/29, f. 113: The *Polizeipräsident* to the *Regierungspräsident,* Königsberg, 24 Feb. 1932.

Notes to Chapter V

1. 'Denkschrift des Reichswehrministers Groener zur wehrpolitischen Lage des Deutschen Reiches Ende 1928', in Otto Ernst Schüddekopf, *Das Heer und die Republik. Quellen zur Politik der Reichswehrführung 1918 bis 1933* (Hannover and Frankfurt/Main, 1955), pp. 251–4. See also Waldemar Erfurth, *Die Geschichte des deutchen Generalstabes 1918–1945* (Göttingen, 1957), pp. 85–6; Thilo Vogelsang, *Reichswehr Staat und NSDAP* (Stuttgart, 1962), pp. 16–22; Francis L. Carsten, *The Reichswehr and Politics 1918–1933* (Oxford, 1966), pp. 147–52, 268–72, 350–3; Rainer Wohlfeil and Edgar Graf von Matuschka, *Reichswehr und Republik (1918–1933)* (Frankfurt/Main, 1970), pp. 199–200; Edward W, Bennett, *German Rearmament and the West, 1932–1933* (Princeton, 1979), pp. 27–9.
2. For a discussion of the organisation of the *Grenzschutz,* see Georges Castellan, *Le réarmament clandestin du Reich 1930–1935 vue par le 2ᵉ Bureau de l'État-Major Français* (Paris, 1954), pp. 397–403. For discussion of Reichswehr planning for civilian participation in border defence, see esp. Michael Geyer, *Aufrüstung oder Sicherheit. Die Reichswehr in der Krise der Machtpolitik 1924–1936* (Wiesbaden, 1980), pp. 97–112.
3. Kurt Schützle, *Reichswehr wider die Nation. Zur Rolle der Reichswehr bei der Vorbereitung und Errichtung der faschistischen Diktatur in Deutschland (1929–1933)* (Berlin, 1963), p. 100; Erfurth, *Die Geschichte des deutschen Generalstabes,* p. 139; Michael Geyer, 'Professionals and Junkers: German Rearmament and Politics in the Weimar Republic', in Bessel and Feuchtwanger (eds.), *Social Change and Political Development,* pp. 108–9.

4. See Volker R. Berghahn, *Der Stahlhelm Bund der Frontsoldaten 1919–1935* (Düsseldorf, 1966), pp. 55–63; Alois Klotzbücher, 'Der politische Weg des Stahlhelms, Bund der Frontsoldaten, in der Weimarer Republik. Ein Beitrag zur Geschichte der 'Nationalen Opposition' 1918–1933' (Univ. Erlangen Phil. Diss. 1964), pp. 19–22; Finker, 'Die militaristischen Wehrverbande in der Weimarer Republik', pp. 171–9; Hertz-Eichenrode, *Politik und Landwirtschaft in Ostpreußen*, pp.74–5.

5. See Vogelsang, *Reichswehr Staat und NSDAP*, p. 157.

6. Albert Grzesinski, *Inside Germany* (New York, 1939), p. 135. See also Thilo Vogelsang, 'Hitlers Brief an Reichenau vom 4. Dezember 1932', *Vierteljahrshefte für Zeitgeschichte*, vii (1959), pp. 429–30.

7. Vogelsang, *Reichswehr Staat und NSDAP*, pp. 157–8; Carsten, *The Reichswehr and Politics*, p. 352. During the late 1920s cooperation with the *Reichsbanner* had been promoted by the Chief of Staff of the *Wehrkreis I*, Colonel Erich von Bonin. See Karl Rohe, *Das Reichsbanner Schwarz–Rot–Gold. Ein Beitrag zur Geschichte und Struktur der politischen Kampfverbände zur Zeit der Weimarer Republik* (Düsseldorf, 1966), p. 180.

8. Bracher/Sauer/Schulz, *Die nationalsozialistische Machtergreifung*, pp. 713–14.

9. StAG, Rep. 14/B.I.3., f. 193: *Kriminal– und Grenzkommissariat* to the *Landespolizeistelle* in Allenstein, Prostken, 4 Feb. 1931; ibid., f. 466: The *Landrat* to the *Regierungspräsident*,, Lötzen, 18 Oct. 1930; ibid., f. 471: *Wehrkeiskommando I* to the *Regierungspräsident* in Allenstein, Königsberg, 5 Nov. 1930.

10. Christian Kinder, *Neue Beiträge zur Geschichte der evangelischen Kirche im Schleswig–Holstein und im Reich 1924–1945* (Flensburg, 1966), p. 45; BA, NS 22/1065: Erich Koch to Gregor Straßer, Königsberg, 22 July 1931.

11. See Vogelsang, *Reichswehr Staat und NSDAP*, pp. 118–19; Carsten, *The Reichswehr and Politics*, pp. 332–3; Bennett, *German Rearmament and the West*, p. 65.

12. BA, NS 22/1065: *Reichsorganisationleiter* to *Gauleiter* Koch, Munich, 21 May 1931.

13. StAG, Rep. 14/B.I.3., f. 909: *Kriminal– und Grenzdienststelle* to the *Regierungspräsident*, Prostken, 8 Mar. 1932.

14. Ibid. f. 193; BA, NS 22/1065: Erich Koch to Gregor Straßer, Königsberg, 22 July 1931; Kinder, *Neue Beiträge zur Geschichte der evangelischen Kirche*, p. 45.

15. Peter Bor, *Gespräche mit Halder* (Wiesbaden, 1950), p. 105.

16. WAP Poznań, OPS/113, f. 204: The *staatl. Polizeidirektor* to the *Oberpräsident*, Schneidemühl, 28 Apr. 1930. For a discussion of the attitudes of the SPD and the Prussian Interior Ministry toward the Reichswehr, *Grenzschutz* and Nazi involvement in border defence, see Bennett, *German Rearmament and the West*, pp. 22–35.

17. WAP Poznań, OPS/113, f. 221: The *Chef des Stabes*, 2. Division *(Wehrkreiskommando II)*, to the *Oberpräsident*, Stettin, 27 June 1930.

18. Ibid., f. 209: The *Polizeipräsident* to the *Minster des Innern*, Berlin, 31 May 1930: ibid., ff. 212–14: The *staatl. Polizeidirektor* to the *Oberpräsident*, Schneidemühl, 27 June 1930.

19. Ibid., ff. 321–3: The *Polizeidirektor* to the *Oberpräsident*, Schneidemühl, 16 Nov. 1931.

20. Ibid. ff. 327–34: The *Chef des Stabes*, 2. Division *(Wehrkreiskommando II)*, to the *Reichswehrministerium, Wehrmachtsabteilung, Abwehrabteilung*, Stettin, 14 Dec. 1931.

21. *SB*, 22 July 1932, p. 1. See also Bessel, 'Militarismus im Innenpolitischen Leben', pp. 195–6.

22. WAP Poznań, OPS/169, f. 169: The *Regierungspräsident* to the *Oberpräsident der Provinz Grenzmark Posen–Westpreuß*en, Frankfurt/Oder, 3 Feb. 1933.

23. See Vogelsang, *Reichswehr Staat und NSDAP*, p. 158; Carsten, *The Reichswehr and Politics*, pp. 351–2.

24. Frank, 'Hitler and the National Socialist Coalition', p. 349f.

25. See Thilo Vogelsang, 'Neue Dokumente zur Geschichte der Reichswehr 1930–1933', *Vierteljahrshefte für Zeitgeschichte*, ii (1954), p. 423; Carsten, *The Reichswehr and Politics*, p. 352.

26. See Geyer, 'Professionals and Junkers', pp. 108–9, 130, esp. note 88.

27. BA, NS 23/474, ff. 105066–9; ibid., ff. 105096–101.

28. WAP Szczecin, RS/212 I, ff. 289–91: The *Polizeipräsident* to the *Oberpräsident*, Stettin, 5 Aug. 1932.

29 Frank, 'Hitler and the National Socialist Coalition', p. 349f.

30. Vogelsang, *Reichswehr Staat und NSDAP*, p. 159; Carsten, *The Reichswehr and Politics*,

pp. 352–3.
31. BDC, SA–Akte, Andreas von Flotow: 'Sonderbericht über die Lage der Provinz Oberschlesien im Dezember 1931'. The *Landesschützenverband* was a right-wing paramilitary organisation, politically close to the DNVP, headquartered in Oppeln and Breslau; the *Selbstschutz (Der Bund ehemaliger Selbstschutzkämpfer Oberschlesiens)* was founded in September 1931 and was composed largely of discontented SA men in Hindenburg. See Fiedor, *Antypolskie organizacje w Niemczech*, pp. 172, 220–1.
32. Carsten, *The Reichswehr and Politics*, p. 353.
33. BA, NS 23/474, ff. 105186–90.
34. Ibid., ff. 105182–3.
35. Ibid., ff. 105184–5.
36. Ibid., ff. 105178–81.

Notes to Chapter VI

1. Joseph Goebbels, *Kampf um Berlin* (9th edn., Munich, 1936), p. 30.
2. At times this posed problems for Nazi leaders, when they had to comment publicly on the excesses of their followers. This dilemma was most striking in the case of the Potempa Murder. See Richard Bessel, 'The Potempa Murder', *Central European History*, x (1977).
3. See Ian Kershaw, *Der Hitler-Mythos. Volksmeinung und Propaganda im Dritten Reich* (Stuttgart, 1980), pp. 48–9.
4. For extremely perceptive accounts of the struggles between the Communists and the SA in Berlin, see Rosenhaft, *Beating the Fascists?*, and Rosenhaft, 'Working-Class Life and Working-Class Politics'.
5. I am indebted to James Wickham for sharpening my thinking on this point.
6. Hans Volz, *Die Geschichte der SA* (Berlin, 1934), p. 63.
7. *Halbmast. Ein Heldenbuch der SA und SS* (Munich, 1932).
8. BA, Sammlung Schumacher/374: 'Ehrenliste der Ermordeten der Bewegung'.
9. *VB*, 2 Dec. 1931, p. 2.
10. IfZ, MA 198/5, microfilm of ZStAM, Rep. 77, tit. 4043, Nr. 126: The *Minister des Innern*, Berlin, 23 Nov. 1932; Broszat, *Der Staat Hitlers*, p. 44.
11. The *Kampfbund* numbered roughly 38,000 nationwide by the end of 1930, and the total membership hovered around 100,000 during 1931. See Hermann Weber, *Die Wandlung des deutschen Kommunismus. Die Stalinisierung der KPD in der Weimarer Republik. Studienausgabe* (Frankfurt/Main, 1969), pp. 364–5; James J. Ward, '"Smash the Fascists . . ." German Communist Efforts to Counter the Nazis, 1930–31', *Central European History*, xiv (1981), pp. 55–6. For details of the early growth of the *Kampfbund* in eastern Germany, see WAP Szczecin, RS/157, ff. 139–45: The *Polizeipräsident* to the *Polizeipräsident* in Berlin, Stettin, 21 Oct. 1930; Stefan Migdał, *Opolszczyzna przeciw faszyzmowi w przededniu dojścia Hitlera do władzy* (Katowice, 1960), p. 76.
12. See Rosenhaft, 'Gewalt in der Politik', pp. 253–7.
13. IfZ, MA 198/5, microfilm of ZStAM, Rep. 77, tit. 4043, Nr. 126: The *Minister des Innern*, Berlin, 22 Nov. 1932; ibid.: The *Minister des Innern*, Berlin, 7 Dec. 1932.
14. StAG, Rep. 240/C.78.a.: *Kreisleiter* Marenski to the *Gauleitung* in Königsberg, Treuburg, 1 Sept. 1930.
15. See, for example, StAG, Rep. 240/C.38.c.1: *Gaukommissar* Dargel to the *Gauleitung* in Königsberg, Marienburg, 25 June 1931.
16. WAP Opole, OPO/1025, f. 1: The *Regierungspräsident* to the *Oberpräsident*, Oppeln, 7 Jan. 1931.
17. StAG, Rep. 240/C.34.d.: NSDAP *Bezirk Westpreußen* to the NSDAP *Gau Ostpreußen*, Riesenburg, 14 Mar. 1931.
18. The police dutifully reported that 103 window panes, 107 chairs, 57 beer glasses, 37 other glasses, 27 plates, 22 bottles and 17 teaspoons, as well as a number of hanging electric lights and tablecloths, had been destroyed. See WAP Szczecin, RS/28, ff. 125–45: *Landeskriminalpolizeistelle* to the *Regierungspräsident*, Stettin, 12 Mar. 1931.
19. WAP Szczecin, RS/16, ff. 265–8: The *Landrat* to the *Regierungspräsident* in Stralsund, Grimmen, 2 Oct. 1931.

20. See, for example, WAP Wrocław, RO I/1804, f. 223: The *Polizeipräsident* to the *Regierungspräsident*, Oppeln, 1 Apr. 1931; StAG, Rep. 14/B.I.3., f. 196: *Kriminal- und Grenzkommissariat* to the *Landeskriminalpolizeistelle* in Allenstein, Prostken, 6 Feb. 1931.
21. See BA, R 43 II/1221, f. 2: 'Straßenterror'.
22. See, for example, StAG, Rep. 10/17, ff. 433-9: The *Regierungspräsident* to the *Oberpräsident*, Marienwerder, 16 Apr. 1930; WAP Wrocław, RO I/1804, f. 147: The *Polizeipräsident* to the *Regierungspräsident*, Oppeln, 2 Dec. 1931.
23. See BA, R 43 II/1221, f. 2.
24. WAP Poznań, OPS/148, ff. 218-19: 'Bericht über den Verlauf der öffentlichen Versammlung des Tannenbergbundes am 26. Oktober 1932 in Schneidemühl, Lokal Reichsadler', Schneidemühl, 27 Oct. 1932.
25. WAP Wrocław, RO I/1804, ff. 915-17: The *Polizeipräsident* to the *Regierungspräsident*, Oppeln, 4 Aug. 1931.
26. *SB*, 28 Sept. 1932, p. 1. In October 1932 the SA leadership prohibited the disruption of DNVP meetings, noting that the SA merely filled the halls for the conservatives and offered the government an excuse to suppress the NSDAP. See BA, NS 22/853: The *Oberste SA-Führer*, Munich, 13 Oct. 1932.
27. BA, R 43 II/1218, ff. 2-3: 'Straßenterror'.
28. *VBS*, 9 Mar. 1932; WAP Szczecin, RS/15, ff. 15-19: The *Regierungspräsident* to the *Minister des Innern*, Stralsund, 9 Mar. 1932; Karl-Heinz Jahnke, 'Die Geschichte der revolutionären Arbeiterbewegung in Stralsund von ihren Anfängen bis zur Gründung der SED (1891-1946)' (Univ. Greifswald Phil. Diss. 1960), p. 284.
29. *VWB*, 4 July 1932, p. 1; *SB*, 5 July 1932, p. 1.
30. Ibid.
31. *VWB*, 9 July 1932, p. 1.
32. GStA, Rep. 84a/11770, ff. 2-3: 'Strafverfahren gegen Rechts wegen politischer Ausschreitungen'; WAP Wrocław, RO I/1805, ff. 1199-200: The *Polizeipräsident* to the *Oberpräsident*, Oppeln, 8 Aug. 1932.
33. *SB*, 23 July 1932, p. 1; *AZ*, 12 Aug. 1932, p. 3.
34. See StAG, Rep. 240/B.31.c.: 'Wie kam es nun zum 1. August 1932?'; Kurt Sabatzky, 'Meine Erinnerungen an den Nationalsozialismus' (unpublished MS in the Wiener Library, London); *KV*, 1-10 Aug. 1932; ibid., 1-2 Nov. 1932. For details of the terror in East Prussia and Silesia during July and August 1932, see pp. 87–92.
35. See, for example, *VB*, 18 Aug. 1932, p. 1; G. Riedel, 'Die Entwicklung der NSDAP im Kreise Oppeln', in *Oppelner Heimat Kalender 1934*, pp. 40-2.
36. WAP Wrocław, RO I/1805, ff. 1443-4: The *Polizeipräsident* to the *Oberpräsident*, Oppeln, 21 Aug. 1932.
37. See *VBS*, 13 Jan. 1932, '2. Beilage zum "Volksbote"'.
38. See, for example, WAP Szczecin, RS/10, f. 202: The *Landrat* to the *Regierungspräsident*, Stettin, 10 Mar. 1931.
40. See, for example, StAG, Rep. 240/C.38.c.1.: *Gaukommissar* Dargel to the *Gauleitung* in Königsberg, Marienburg, 26 Aug. 1931; WAP Opole, OPO/1039, f. 17: The *Regierungspräsident* to the *Preußischer Minister des Innern*, Oppeln, 5 May 1931.
41. For discussion of the ban, and of the intrigues which led up to it, see Bracher, *Die Auflösung der Weimarer Republik*, pp. 481-99, 548-9; Bennecke, *Hitler und die SA*, pp. 176-82, 187-8.
42. See, for example, *VB*, 20 Jan. 1931, p. 3.
43. StAG, Rep. 240/C.65.b.: Emil (?, signature illegible) to Erich Koch, Alt-Buttkischken, 5 Apr. 1930.
44. WAP Wrocław, RO I/1805, ff. 1243-5: The *Polizeipräsident* to the *Regierungspräsident*, Gleiwitz, 6 Mar. 1931.
45. StAG, Rep. 240/C.33.d.1.: H. Berg to the *Gauleitung* in Königsberg, Tilsit, 19 Feb. 1929.
46. StAG, Rep. 240/C.33.a.: *Bezirkspropagandaleiter* Fuchs to the *Gauleitung, Abteilung Propaganda*, Insterburg, 4 Mar. 1931.
47. WAP Wrocław, RO I/1806, ff. 939-41: The *komm. Polizeipräsident* to the *Regierungspräsident*, Gleiwitz, 14 Nov. 1932.
48. For example, WAP Wrocław, RO I/1803, f. 209: SPD *Unterbezirk* Oppeln to *Vize-Präsident* Müller, Oppeln, 10 June 1931; ibid., f. 913: *Reichsbanner Gau Oberschlesien* to

Pr. Innenminister Severing, Hindenburg, 8 Apr. 1931.
49. WAP Wrocław, RO I/1805, ff. 453-4: The *Polizeipräsident* to the *Regierungspräsident*, Gleiwitz, 19 Apr. 1932; WAP Szczecin, RS/212 II, f. 105: The *Landrat*, Demmin, 14 Apr. 1932; WAP Poznań, OPS/168, f. 112: The *Landrat* to the *Regierungspräsident*, Flatow, 14 Apr. 1932; StAG, Rep. 14/B.I.3., f. 1005: *Kriminal- und Grenzdienststelle* to the *Kriminal- und Grenzkommissariat* in Allenstein, Ortelsburg, 14 Apr. 1932.
50. Similar tactics were used by Fascist squads in Italy during 1921 and 1922. See Angelo Tasca, *Naissance du Fascisme. L'Italie de l'armistice à la marche sur Rome* (Paris, 1967), pp. 129-47; Adrian Lyttelton, *The Seizure of Power. Fascism in Italy 1919-1929* (London, 1973), pp. 53-4; Paul Corner, *Fascism in Ferrara 1915-1925* (London, 1975), pp. 139-42.
51. The Communists defended themselves rather more effectively. In *Kreis* Fraustadt (Border Province) they formed squads of 35 to 40 men who attacked the lorry-loads of Nazis as they left the towns. See WAP Poznań, OPS/167, ff. 156-7: The *Landrat* to the *Oberpräsident*, Fraustadt, 4 May 1931.
52. WAP Szczecin, RS/28, ff. 55-71: The *Regierungspräsident* to the *Preußischer Minister des Innern*, Stralsund, 24 Dec. 1931.
53. WAP Wrocław, RO I/1803, f. 913; ibid., ff. 955-6: The *Landrat* to the *Regierungspräsident*, Groß-Strehlitz, 19 July 1931.
54. WAP Wrocław, RO I/1805, f. 1331: *Reichsbanner Gau Oberschlesien* to the *Regierungspräsident*, Hindenburg, 8 Mar. 1932; ibid., ff. 1345-55: The *Polizeipräsident* to the *Regierungspräsident*, Oppeln, 12 Apr. 1932.
55. See *VWB*, 23 June 1932, p. 1; *VBS*, 24 June 1932, p. 1. Naturally the Nazis saw the situation rather differently; according to Heines, the SA had been the victim of 'Marxist' attacks. See *VB*, 24 June 1932, p. 1.
56. See BA, NS 22/1068: unsigned Nazi account of the incident, Schweidnitz, 11 Oct. 1929; ibid.: unsigned police account, dated 3 Oct. 1929; *SB*, 28 Sept. 1929, p. 1; *Illustrierter Beobachter*, 21 Dec. 1929, p. 691; Gundelach, *Vom Kampf und Sieg der schlesischen SA*, pp. 55-8.
57. *SB*, 28 Sept. 1929, p. 1.
58. *Illustrierter Beobachter*, 21 Dec. 1929, p. 691; Gundelach, *Vom Kampf und Sieg der schlesischen SA*, p. 56.
59. Ibid., p. 57; *VB*, 21/22 Feb. 1932, p. 3.
60. From March 1929 until December 1931 the Silesian *Gau* headquarters was situated in Schweidnitz. See BA, NS 26/156: NSDAP *Gaupresseamt* Schlesien to the NSDAP *Hauptarchiv*, Breslau, 20 Mar. 1937.
61. For accounts of the confrontation, see *VWB*, 11 July 1932, pp. 1-2; ibid., 12 July 1932, pp. 1-2; *SB*, 12 July 1932, p. 1; *Deutsche Ostfront*, 11 July 1932, p. 1; *VB*, 13 July 1932, p. 1.
62. Bessel, 'The Potempa Murder', p. 251.
63. See, for example, *VB*, 24 Aug. 1932, p. 2.
64. For accounts of the Greifswald incident, see WAP Szczecin, RS/15, ff. 53-5: The *Regierungspräsident* to the *Minister des Innern*, Stralsund, 20 July 1932; ibid., ff. 69-186: The *Regierungspräsident* to the *Minister des Innern*, Stralsund, 18 July 1932, followed by statements about the incident taken by the police; *PZ*, 19 July 1932; *VB*, 19 July 1932, p. 1; ibid., 20 July 1932, p. 2; Jahnke, 'Die Geschichte der revolutionären Arbeiterbewegung in Stralsund', p. 289. For the relative strengths of political groups in Greifswald in late 1932, see WAP Szczecin, RS/15, ff. 193-4: The *Oberbürgermeister* to the *Regierungspräsident* in Stettin, Greifswald, 19 Dec. 1932.
65. WAP Szczecin, RS/15, ff. 53-5.
66. StAG, Rep. 240/B.31.a: 'Wie kam es nun zum 1. August 1932?'
67. Ibid. See also *KV*, 1 Aug. 1932; Gause, *Die Geschichte der Stadt Königsberg*, iii, pp. 114-15; Wilhelm Matull, *Ostpreußens Arbeiterbewegung. Geschichte und Leistung im Überblick* (Würzburg, 1970), p. 115; Sabatzky, 'Meine Erinnerungen', pp. 19-20.
68. Matull, *Ostpreußens Arbeiterbewegung*, p. 115; *KV*, 2-10 Aug. 1932; ibid., 1-2 Nov. 1932; *VB*, 4 Aug. 1932, p. 1; StAG, Rep. 240/C.67.a.: history of the NSDAP in *Kreis* Ortelsburg.
69. StAG, Rep. 240/C.53.a.(1): 'Die Geschichte der jetzigen Ortsgruppe Königstraße (Königsberg)'; StAG, Rep. 240/B.31.c.: 'Wie kam es nun zum 1, August 1932?'; Gause, *Die Geschichte der Stadt Königsberg*, iii, pp. 114-15.

70. See p. 93.

71. *RGB1*, 1932, I, p. 389.

72. BDC, AOPG, Paul Lachmann, ff. 43-5: *Kreisgeschäftsführer* Blachnik to the *stellvertretender Gauleiter* Bracht, Gleiwitz, 7 Aug. 1939.

73. BA, NS 23/474, ff. 105186-90; ibid., f. 105241: The *Führer der Untergruppe MS-Nord* to the *Oberste SA-Führung*, Schloß Kleinöls, 24 Sept. 1932.

74. NAM, T-253, roll 23, frame 1473875: The *Gruppenführer Schlesien*, 'Gruppenbefehl Nr. 5', Reichenbach, 3 Aug. 1932.

75. A member of the *Sturm* which carried out the Potempa raid — but not a member of the murder expedition — wrote years later that the Potempa killing and the wave of bombings and shootings in August 1932 were consequences of '*Terrorparolen*' and orders from higher up. See BDC, AOPG, Paul Lachmann, ff. 43-5. See also NAM, T-253, roll 23, frames 1474527-8: Walter Luetgebrune to Ernst Röhm, Berlin, 1 Dec. 1932, Bennecke, *Hitler und die SA*, pp. 194-5.

76. *BUA*, 2 Aug. 1932, p. 1; *VB*, 4 Aug. 1932, p. 1; *AZ*, 12 Aug. 1932, p. 3.

77. *BUA*, 6 Aug. 1932, p. 1; *AZ*, 12 Aug. 1932, p. 3; ibid., 17 Aug. 1932, p. 3. Eckstein had been chairman of the Breslau SPD until October 1931, when he helped form the breakaway Socialist Workers' Party. He survived the attempt on his life in 1932, but was arrested in February 1933 and taken to the SA concentration camp at Dürrgoy near Breslau and on 8 May 1933 died as a result of his treatment there. See Matull, *Ostdeutschlands Arbeiterbewegung*, pp. 106, 128-30; Kurt Koszyk, 'Die Presse der schlesischen Sozialdemokratie', *Jahrbuch der schlesischen Friedrich-Wilhelms-Universität zu Breslau*, v (1960), p. 248.

78. *SB*, 8 Aug. 1932, pp. 1-3; *VB*, 9 Aug. 1932, p. 2; ibid., 10 Aug. 1932, p. 2; *AZ*, 17 Aug. 1932, p. 3.

79. *VWB*, 9 Aug. 1932, p. 1; *SB*, 10 Aug. 1932, p. 1; *VB*, 11 Aug. 1932, p. 2; *AZ*, 17 Aug. 1932, p. 3. For accounts of the Reichenbach incident and the resulting trial, in which Edmund Heines was convicted of encouraging the assassination attempt, see Gundelach, *Vom Kampf und Sieg der schlesischen SA*, p. 159; IfZ, Sammlung Carl Paeschke/17, ff. 29-31: Carl Paeschke to *Justizrat* Bandmann, Reichenbach, 23 Sept. 1932; IfZ, Sammlung Carl Paeschke/18, ff. 19, 92, 113, 116: various newspaper clippings.

80. *AZ*, 17 Aug. 1932, p. 3; *Deutsche Ostfront*, 10 Aug. 1932, p. 1; Otis Mitchell, 'An Institutional History of the National Socialist SA: A Study of the SA as a Functioning Organisation within the Party Structure (1931-1934)' (Univ. of Kansas Ph.D. thesis 1964), pp. 133-40. For accounts of the Potempa murder and the resulting trial, see Paul Kluke, 'Der Fall Potempa', *Vierteljahrshefte für Zeitgeschichte*, v (1957), pp. 279-82; Heinrich Hannover and Elisabeth Hannover-Drück, *Politische Justiz 1918-1933* (Frankfurt/Main, 1966), pp. 301-10; Bessel, 'The Potempa Murder', pp. 241-54.

81. *RGB1*, 1932, I, pp. 403-7. See also Kluke, 'Der Fall Potempa', pp. 279-82; Vogelsang, *Reichswehr Staat und NSDAP*, p. 259.

82. NAM, T-253, roll 23, frames 1474376-82: The *Oberstaatsanwalt* to the *Sondergericht*, Görlitz, 19 Nov. 1932.

83. For a description of how the assaults were carried out, see ibid., frames 1474343-50: The *Oberstaatsanwalt* to the *Sondergericht*, Görlitz, 28 Nov. 1932.

84. BA, NS 23/474, f. 105179. See also *SB*, 19 Oct. 1932, p. 1; ibid., 22 Oct. 1932, p. 1.

85. BA, NS 23/474, ff. 105186-90.

86. See Bessel, 'The Potempa Murder', pp. 242, 251-2.

87. See the table above, p. 25.

88. StAG, Rep. 240/B.7.d.: 'Stimmungsbericht der Gau-Propaganda Ostpreußen über die Wahlen vom 6. November 1932', Königsberg, 10 Nov. 1932.

89. StAG, Rep. 240/C.78.a.: NSDAP *Kreisleitung* Treuburg to the *Gauleitung, Abt. Propaganda*, Treuburg, 8 Nov. 1932.

90. StAG, Rep. 240/C.47.e.: NSDAP *Ortsgruppe* Blindgallen to the *Gauleitung*, Blindgallen, 8 Nov. 1932.

91. StAG, Rep. 240/C.39.b.: NSDAP *Kreisleitung* Allenstein to the *Gau-Propagandaleitung*, Allenstein, 8 Nov. 1932.

92. StAG, Rep. 240/C.68.a.: NSDAP *Kreisleitung* Osterode to the *Gauleitung, Abt. Propaganda*, Kraplau, 7 Nov. 1932.

93. BA, NS 22/1: 'Stimmungsbericht der Reichspropagandaleitung', undated (from late

November 1932).

94. Ibid.
95. WAP Szczecin, RS/83, f. 287: notice issued by the *Polizeipräsident* in Stettin; *VB*, 9 Aug. 1932, p. 2; ibid., 11 Aug. 1932, p. 2; ibid., 9 Jan. 1933, p. 2; *VBS*, 8 Jan. 1933, p. 1.
96. See *VB*, 9 Jan. 1933. Leuschner resurfaced within the Nazi movement soon after 30 January.
97. StAG, Rep. 240/C.54.b.: 'Chronik der Ortsgruppe Steindamm', p. 36.
98. See, for example, StAG, Rep. 240/C.39.b.: NSDAP *Kreisleitung* Allenstein to the *Gau-Propagandaleitung*, Allenstein, 8 Nov. 1932.
99. BA, NS 22/1064: Wilhelm Kube to the *Reichsleitung der* NSDAP, Berlin, 21 Nov. 1932.
100. See StAG, Rep. 240/B.7.d.: 'Stimmungsbericht der Gau-Propaganda Ostpreußen über die Wahlen vom 6. November 1932'.
101. See, for example, BA, NS 23/474, ff. 105094-5; ibid., ff. 105096-101.
102. Ibid., ff. 105182-3.
103. Ibid., ff. 105186-90.
104. WAP Wrocław, RO I/1806, ff. 1037-8.
105. Ibid., ff. 1043-4: The *Polizeipräsident* to the *Regierungspräsident*, Oppeln, 3 Jan. 1933.
106. BA, NS 22/1: 'Stimmungsbericht der Reichspropagandaleitung'.

Notes to Chapter VII

1. The phrase comes from Bullock, *Hitler*, p. 253.
2. See, especially, Mason, *Sozialpolitik im Dritten Reich*, pp. 81-8.
3. Mathilde Jamin, 'Zur Rolle der SA im nationalsozialistischen Hersschaftssystem', in Gerhard Hirschfeld and Lothar Kettenacker (eds.), *Der 'Führerstaat'. Mythos und Realität* (Stuttgart, 1981), pp. 332-4.
4. BA, NS 23/9: The *Oberster* SA-*Führer*, Munich, 27 Mar. 1934.
5. For the immediate reactions of the Social Democratic leadership to the events of 30 January, see Erich Matthias, 'Die Sozialdemokratische Partei Deutschlands', in Erich Matthias and Rudolf Morsey (eds.), *Das Ende der Parteien 1933* (Düsseldorf, 1960), pp. 158-60; Hagen Schulze (ed.), *Anpassung oder Widerstand? Aus den Akten des Parteivorstandes der deutschen Sozialdemokratie 1932/33* (Bonn-Bad Godesberg, 1975), pp. 131-53. For a general discussion of the vacillating politics of the ADGB in early 1933, see Gerard Braunthal, *Socialist Labor and Politics in Weimar Germany. The General Federation of German Trade Unions* (Hamden, Conn., 1978), pp. 74-83. For a recent discussion of Communist responses to Hitler's appointment as Reich Chancellor, see Detlev Peukert, *Die KPD im Widerstand. Verfolgung und Untergrundarbeit an Rhein und Ruhr 1933 bis 1945* (Wuppertal, 1980), pp. 30-6.
6. *VWB*, 1 Feb. 1933, 'Beilage'.
7. Despite his zeal in combatting the Communists, Police President Thaiß was forced to resign only two weeks later.
8. *Schlesischer N.S. Beobachter*, 4 Feb. 1933, p. 5.
9. WAP Opole, OPO/1021, ff. 381-3: The *komm. Polizeipräsident* to the *Oberpräsident*, Oppeln, 2 Feb. 1933.
10. WAP Poznań, OPS/169, f. 148: 'Bericht über den Verlauf des Fackelzuges der SA, SS and HJ sowie des Stahlhelms, Ortsgruppe Schneidemühl, am 31. Januar 1933', Schneidemühl, 1 Feb. 1933.
11. See WAP Opole, OPO/1021, ff. 381-3; *VWB*, 1 Feb. 1933, 'Beilage'; Günther Schmerbach, 'Der Kampf der Kommunistischen Partei Deutschlands gegen Faschismus und Kriegsgefahr im Berzirk Oberschlesien 1932/33' (Univ. Jena Phil. Diss. 1957), pp. 186-8. For a discussion of the terror against Communists in the Ruhr during this period, see Peukert, *Die KPD im Widerstand*, pp. 79-83.
12. Bracher/Sauer/Schulz, *Die nationalsozialistische Machtergreifung*, pp. 70-1.
13. See, for example, *VWB*, 3 Feb. 1933, 'Beilage zur Volkswacht'; *VWS*, 11 Feb. 1933, p. 2; WAP Opole, OPO/1021, ff. 379-80: The *komm. Polizeipresident* to the *Oberpräsident*, Oppeln, 15 Feb. 1933.
14. WAP Wrocław, RO I/1797, f. 1: The *Pr. Minister des Innern* to the *Ober- und*

Regierungspräsidenten and the *Polizeipräsident* in Berlin, Berlin, 15 Feb. 1933.

15. See Bracher/Sauer/Schulz, *Die nationalsozialistische Machtergreifung*, pp. 72-3, 864-5.
16. Ibid., p. 66. For a discussion of the *Hilfspolizei* in eastern Germany, see pp. 112–14.
17. See *KV*, 22 Feb. 1933, p. 3.
18. See *OK*, 27 Feb. 1933, p. 6; *VWB*, 27 Feb. 1933, p. 5.
19. See *VWB*, 23 Feb. 1933, p. 1.
20. StAG, Rep. 240/C.39.e.: NSDAP *Kreis* Allenstein *Land*, 'Tätigkeitsbericht für den Monat Februar 1933', Allenstein, 13 Mar. 1933.
21. StAG, Rep. 240/C.46.a.: NSDAP *Kreis* Gerdauen, 'Tätigkeitsbericht für den Monat Februar/März 1933', Gerdauen, 14 Mar. 1933.
22. Matull, *Ostdeutschlands Arbeiterbewegung*, pp. 357-9; *Braunbuch über Reichstagsbrand und Hitlerterror* (Basel, 1933), pp. 133-4.
23. IfZ, MA 198/5, microfilm of ZStAM, Rep. 77, tit. 4043, Nr. 127: report of the incident in Breslau on 8 March 1933; GStA, Rep. 77/23: *Ortsausschuß* Breslau *des* ADGB to *Vize-Kanzler* von Papen, Breslau, 8 Mar. 1933; GStA, Rep. 77/29: Helmuth Brückner to Hermann Göring, Breslau, 9 Mar. 1933; *ST*, 9 Mar. 1933, p. 1; Walter Tausk, 'Tagebuch 19' (MS in the University Library, Wrocław, Ako. 1949 KN 1351), pp. 28-30; Walter Tausk, *Breslauer Tagebuch 1933-1940* (Berlin, 1975), pp. 32-4; Bracher/Sauer/Schulz, *Die nationalsozialistische Machtergreifung*, p. 441.
24. GStA, Rep. 77/32, ff. 64-5: The *Kreisleiter der* NSDAP Liegnitz Stadt-Land to the *Untergauleiter der* NSDAP *Niederschlesien*, Liegnitz, 12 Mar. 1933.
25. Matull, *Ostdeutschlands Arbeiterbewegung*, p. 292; Thévoz/Branig/Lowenthal-Hensel, *Pommern 1934/35 (Darstellung)*, pp. 29-30.
26. BA, R 43 II/531, ff. 37-43: The *Vorstand des* ADGB to *Reichspräsident* von Hindenburg, Berlin, 5 Apr. 1933; WAP Poznań, OPS/152, ff. 280-2: ADGB *Ortsausschuß* Schneidemühl to the *Oberpräsident*, Schniedemühl, 13 Mar. 1933; ibid., f. 283: The *Polizeidirektor* to the *Oberpräsident*, Schneidemühl, 27 Mar. 1933.
27. WAP Szczecin, RS/35, f. 113: *Allgemeiner Freier Angestelltenbund, Bezirkskartell Pommern und Mecklenburg-Strelitz*, to the *Regierungspräsident*, Stettin, 28 Mar. 1933; ibid., ff. 117-18: *Deutscher Landarbeiter-Verband, Gau* Stettin, to the *Regierungspräsident*, Stettin, 25 Mar. 1933; ibid., f. 119: *Deutscher Landarbeiter-Verband, Kreisgruppe* Pyritz-Saatzig, to the *Gauleitung des Deutschen Landarbeiter-Verbandes* in Stettin, Stargard, 22 Mar. 1933; ibid., ff. 125-9: ADGB, *Bezirk Pommern und Mecklenburg-Strelitz*, to the *Regierungspräsident*, Stettin, 25 Mar. 1933.
28. BA, R 43 II/531, ff. 37-43; WAP Szczecin, RS/15, ff. 371-2: The *Oberbürgermeister* to the *Regierungspräsident*, Greifswald, 29 Mar. 1933; ibid., f. 375: The *Führer der* SA-*Untergruppe Pommern-West* to the *Regierungspräsident*, Stettin, 6 Apr. 1933; ibid., ff. 377-8: The *Oberbürgermeister* to the *Regierungspräsident*, Greifswald, 7 Apr. 1933.
29. Evidence of SA violence against the Catholic trade unions in eastern Germany could not be found, and this aspect of the Nazi campaign against organised labour remains to be investigated. Jürgen Aretz, in his study of the Catholic trade-union movement in western Germany, unfortunately has little to say about the role of Nazi terror in suppressing such organisations at local level. See Jürgen Aretz, *Katholische Arbeiterbewegung und Nationalsozialismus. Der Verband katholischer Arbeiter- und Knappenvereine Westdeutschlands 1923-1945* (Mainz, 1978), pp. 69-88.
30. For discussion of the importance of this campaign, see Gerhard Beier, *Das Lehrstück vom 1. und 2. Mai 1933* (Frankfurt/Main and Cologne, 1975); Mason, *Sozialpolitik im Dritten Reich*, pp. 82-8.
31. See p. 117.
32. WAP Wrocław, RO I/1845, ff. 5-33: letters of the *komm. Polizeipräsident* to the *Regierungspräsident*, dated between 17 Mar. and 8 July 1933.
33. *ST*, 9 Apr. 1933, p. 1; *VB*, 10 Apr. 1933, p. 1; Tausk, 'Tagebuch 19', pp. 101-2; Tausk, *Breslauer Tagebuch*, pp. 61-2.
34. StAG, Rep. 240/C.46.a.: NSDAP *Kreis* Gerdauen, 'Tätigkeitsbericht für den Monat Februar/März 1933', Gerdauen, 14 Mar. 1933.
35. StAG, Rep. 240/C.43.a.: NSDAP *Kreis* Darknehmen, 'Tätigkeitsbericht für den Monat Februar/März 1933', Darknehmen, 15 Mar. 1933.
36. StAG, Rep. 240/C.39.c.: NSDAP *Kreis* Allenstein Stadt, 'Tätigkeitsbericht für die Zeit

vom 13. bis 31 März 1933', Allenstein, 8 Apr. 1933; ibid.: NSDAP *Kreis* Allenstein Stadt, 'Tätigkeitsbericht für die Zeit vom 1. bis 30.4.1933', Allenstein, 6 May 1933.
37. StAG, Rep. 240/C.67.d.: NSDAP *Kreisleitung* Ortelsburg, 'Tätigkeitsbericht für den Monat April 1933', Ortelsburg, 2 May 1933.
38. For a perceptive recent discussion of this process in a Ruhr mining community, see Michael Zimmermann. '"Ein schwer zu bearbeitendes Pflaster"': der Bergarbeiterort Hochlarmark unter dem Nationalsozialismus', in Peukert and Reulecke (eds.), *Die Reihen fast geschlossen*, pp. 72-4.
39. Mason, *Sozialpolitik im Dritten Reich*, pp. 84-6. See also pp. 122–4.
40. *RGB1*, 1933, I, p. 191; Bracher/Sauer/Schulz, *Die nationalsozialistische Machtergreifung*, p. 181.
41. BA, Sammlung Schumacher/235: NSDAP *Reichsleitung*, *Stabsleiter* Robert Ley, 'Rundschreiben Nr. 6/33', Munich, 21 Apr. 1933; Hans-Gerd Schumann, *Nationalsozialismus und Gewerkschaftsbewegung* (Hannover and Frankfurt/Main, 1958), pp. 69-74; Bracher/Sauer/Schulz, *Die nationalsozialistische Machtergreifung*, pp. 181-3; Braunthal, *Socialist Labor and Politics*, pp. 74-83.
42. Joseph Goebbels, *Vom Kaiserhof zur Reichskanzlei* (Munich, 1934), p. 307.
43. Rohe, *Das Reichsbanner*, p. 463; Matull, *Ostdeutschlands Arbeiterbewegung*, p. 293.
44. Ibid., p. 359; Matull, *Ostpreußens Arbeiterbewegung*, pp. 126-7.
45. WAP Poznań, RP/59, f. 92: *Staatspolizeistelle* to the *Oberpräsident*, Schneidemühl, 18 May 1933.
46. WAP Wrocław, RO I/1806, ff. 929-30: The *Landrat* to the *Polizeipräsident* in Oppeln, Cosel, 23 Feb. 1933.
47. It was not until the eve of the *Reichstag* elections that Walter Tausk, a Jewish businessman in Breslau, first noted that the Nazis were turning their attentions to the Jews. See Tausk, 'Tagebuch 19', pp. 1-25.
48. Kurt Pätzold, *Faschismus Rassenwahn Judenverfolgung. Eine Studie zur politischen Strategie und Taktik des faschistischen deutschen Imperialismus (1933-1945)* (Berlin, 1975), p. 40.
49. WAP Szczecin, RS/20, ff. 191-3: The *Bürgermeister*, Gollnow, 14 Mar. 1933.
50. The mayor of Pasewalk decided not to call for police intervention, citing Göring's speech as his justification. See WAP Szczecin, RS/36, f. 411: The *Bürgermeister* to the *Landrat* in Uekermünde, Pasewalk, 13 Mar. 1933.
51. StAG, Rep. 240/B.29.f.: Fräulein Itzig to *Reichsminister* (sic) *des Innern* Göring, Arys, 15 Mar. 1933; ibid.: *Centralverein deutscher Staatsbürger jüdischen Glaubens* to the *Landesverband des C.V.*, Berlin, 23 Mar. 1933.
52. Tausk, 'Tagebuch 19', pp. 42-4; Tausk, *Breslauer Tagebuch*, pp. 38-9; Comité des Délégations Juives (ed.), *Das Schwarzbuch. Tatsachen und Dokumente. Die Lage der Juden in Deutschland 1933* (Paris, 1934), pp. 94-105; Horst Göppinger, *Die Verfolgung der Juristen jüdischer Abstammung durch den Nationalsozialismus* (Villingen, 1963), pp. 21-2; Helmut Krausnick, 'The Persecution of the Jews', in Helmut Krausnick, Hans Buchheim, Martin Broszat and Hans-Adolf Jakobsen, *Anatomy of the SS State* (London, 1968), p. 24; Pätzold, *Faschismus Rassenwahn Judenverfolgung*, pp. 43-6.
53. Karl Schleunes, *The Twisted Road to Auschwitz. Nazi Policy toward German Jews* (London, 1972), p. 73.
54. StAG, Rep. 240/B.29.f.: 'Mitteilungen des C.V.-Syndikats', by Alfred Levi, Berlin, undated but probably written in late March 1933; ibid.: *Centralverein deutscher Staatsbürger jüdischen Glaubens Ostpreußen* to the *Centrale* Berlin, Königsberg, 27 Mar. 1933. See also Gause, *Die Geschichte der Stadt Königsberg*, iii, p. 117; and Gerhard Reifferscheid, *Das Bistum Ermland und das Dritte Reich* (Cologne and Vienna, 1975), p. 22.
55. For other accounts of the mounting pressure on the Jews, see Schleunes, *The Twisted Road to Auschwitz*, pp. 62-91; Uwe Dietrich Adam, *Judenpolitik im Dritten Reich* (Düsseldorf, 1972), pp. 46-9; Helmut Genschel, *Die Verdrängung der Juden aus der Wirtschaft im Dritten Reich* (Göttingen, 1966), pp. 44-5; Pätzold, *Faschismus Rassenwahn Judenverfolgung*, pp. 41-7; Falk Wiesemann, 'Juden auf dem Lande: die wirtschaftliche Ausgrenzung der jüdischen Viehhändler in Bayern', in Peukert and Reulecke (eds.), *Die Reihen fast geschlossen*, pp. 382–3.
56. BA, R 43 II/1195, f. 61: 'Aufruf Adolf Hitlers an SA und SS', Berlin, 10 Mar. 1933.

57. StAG, Rep. 240/B.29.f.: 'Mitteilungen des C.V.-Syndikats'; OT Gliwice, Landratsamt Gleiwitz/G63, f. 147: The *Reichsminister des Innern* to the *Innenministerien der Länder* and the *Reichskommissare*, Berlin, 13 Mar. 1933; *VB*, 14 Mar. 1933, p. 2; Heinrich Uhlig, *Die Warenhäuser im Dritten Reich* (Cologne and Opladen, 1956), p. 196; Genschel, *Die Verdrängung der Juden*, pp. 45-6; Mason, *Sozialpolitik im Dritten Reich*, pp. 84-5.
58. Goebbels, *Vom Kaiserhof zur Reichskanzlei*, p. 288; Genschel, *Die Verdrängung der Juden*, pp. 46-61; Pätzold, *Faschismus Rassenwahn Judenverfolgung*, pp. 51-9; Schleunes, *The Twisted Road to Auschwitz*, pp. 75-6.
59. StAG, Rep. 240/C.46.a.: 'Tätigkeitsbericht für den Monat März 1933', Gerdauen, 5 Apr. 1933.
60. WAP Szczecin, RS/35, f. 109: *Centralverein deutscher Staatsbürger jüdischen Glaubens, Landesverband Pommern-Grenzmark/Ortsgruppe* Stettin, to the *Regierungspräsident*, Stettin, 28 Mar. 1933.
61. WAP Szczecin, RS/38, f. 352: *Centralverein deutscher Staatsbürger jüdischen Glaubens, Landesverband Pommern-Grenzmark/Ortsgruppe* Stettin, to the *Regierungspräsident*, Stettin, 28 Mar. 1933; WAP Szczecin, RS/92, ff. 107-9: The *Landrat* to the *Regierungspräsident*, Swinemünde, 31 Mar. 1933.
62. *ST*, 31 Mar. 1933, p. 7; Pätzold, *Faschismus Rassenwahn Judenverfolgung*, p. 65.
63. StAG, Rep. 240/C.46.a.: 'Tätigkeitsbericht für den Monat März 1933', Gerdauen, 5 Apr. 1933; *Der SA-Mann*, 8 Apr. 1933, p. 2: *Das Schwarzbuch*, pp. 302-14; Schleunes, *The Twisted Road to Auschwitz*, pp. 84-6.
64. Gause, *Die Geschichte der Stadt Königsberg*, iii, p. 147; StAG Rep. 240/C.54.b.: 'Chronik der Ortsgruppe Steindamm (Königsberg-Stadt)'; Pätzold, *Faschismus Rassenwahn Judenverfolgung*, p. 75.
65. *BUA*, 1 Apr. 1933, p. 1; Tausk, 'Tagebuch 19', pp. 78-86; Tausk, *Breslauer Tagebuch*, pp. 52-6.
66. *BUA*, 1 Apr. 1933, p. 1; *VB*, 3 Apr. 1933, p. 1.
67. Tausk, *Breslauer Tagebuch*, pp. 51-2.
68. StAG, Rep. 240/C.39.e.: NSDAP *Kreis* Allenstein-Land, 'Tätigkeitsbericht für den Monat März 1933', Allenstein, 8 Apr. 1933.
69. Genschel, *Die Verdrängung der Juden*, pp. 53-4; *OK*, 1 Apr. 1933, p. 1; *ST*, 4 Apr. 1933, p. 1.
70. See Pätzold, *Faschismus Rassenwahn Judenverfolgung*, pp. 75-6; Schleunes, *The Twisted Road to Auschwitz*, p. 87.
71. WAP Szczecin, RS/38, f. 358: *Centralverein deutscher Staatsbürger jüdischen Glaubens, Landesverband Pommern-Grenzmark/Ortsgruppe* Stettin, to the *Regierungspräsident*, Stettin, 3 Apr. 1933.
72. Karl Schleunes reaches similar conclusions. See Schleunes, *The Twisted Road to Auschwitz*, p. 71.
73. *OK*, 22 Feb. 1933, p. 1.
74. OT Gliwice, *Landratsamt* Gleiwitz/G64, ff. 8-9: The *Magistrat* to the *Landrat* in Gleiwitz, Peiskretscham, 23 Feb. 1933.
75. WAP Opole, OPO/1025, ff. 324-5: *Magistrat* Brzezinka to *Oberpräsident* Lukaschek, Gleiwitz, 10 Mar. 1933; *OK*, 10 Mar. 1933, p. 1; Gerhard Webersinn, 'Prälat Karl Ulitzka', *Jahrbuch der schlesischen Friedrich-Wilhelms-Universität zu Breslau*, xv (1970), p. 191.
76. WAP Poznań, OPS/152, f. 315: *Landjäger Oberleutnant* Schnalke to the *Landrat*, Flatow, 21 Apr. 1933; ibid., f. 313: The *Landrat* to the *Oberpräsident*, Flatow, 29 Apr. 1933; WAP Poznań, OPS/169, f. 293: *Kriminal- und Grenzkommissariat* to the *Staatspolizeistelle* Schneidemühl, Neu Bentschen, 5 Apr. 1933.
77. Ibid., f. 374: The *Regierungspräsident* to SA *Brigadeführer* Manthey, Schneidemühl, 19 Apr. 1933.
78. WAP Poznań, RP/49, f. 45: The *Regierungspräsident* to the *Landräte des Bezirks*, Schneidemühl, [?] Apr. 1933; GStA, Rep. 77/14, f. 3: 'Entwurf Telegramm an alle SA, SS und Stahlhelm Formationen von Ostpreußen, Schlesien und Grenzmark'; ibid., f. 2: The *Gruppenführer* Schlesien, 'Gruppenbefehl Nr. 32', Breslau, 24 Apr. 1933; WAP Wrocław, RO/1797, f. 79: The *Oberste SA-Führer*, Munich, 2 May 1933; Karol Jonca, *Polityka narodowościowa Trzeciej Rzeszy na Śląsku Opolskim (1933-1940). Studium polityczno-prawne* (Katowice, 1970), p. 149.

79. See *NSST*, 25 Nov. 1930, p. 5.
80. Tausk, *Breslauer Tagebuch*, pp. 35-6; Schleunes, *The Twisted Road to Auschwitz*, pp. 71-2.
81. *ST*, 31 Mar. 1933, p. 6.
82. WAP Szczecin, RS/32, ff. 77-9: A. Wertheim GmbH to the *Regierungspräsident* in Stettin, Berlin, 2 June 1933; ibid., ff. 103-5: A. Wertheim GmbH to the *Pr. Minister des Innern*, Berlin, 9 May 1933.
83. However, soon thereafter the provincial administration secured a promise from Upper Silesian SA leader Ramshorn that further actions against the store would not be permitted. See WAP Wrocław, RO/1738, f. 29: *Hava, Haus der vielen Artikeln*, to the *Oberpräsident*, Neisse, 11 Mar. 1933.
84. *ST*, 31 Mar. 1933, p. 7; ibid., 7 May 1933, p. 9.
85. Elsewhere in Germany, however, banks were a target for the SA. See Jamin, 'Zur Rolle der SA', pp. 335-8.
86. For a discussion of this in Germany as a whole, see Horst Mazerath, *Nationalsozialismus und kommunale Selbstverwaltung* (Stuttgart, 1970), pp. 66-72.
87. Tausk, *Breslauer Tagebuch*, pp. 31-2.
88. WAP Szczecin, RS/20, ff. 187-8: The *Bürgermeister*, Naugard, 11 Mar. 1933.
89. The precise motive is unclear, although the man who led the raid was himself a city employee. See WAP Wrocław, RO I/1806, f. 1103: The *Oberbürgermeister* to the *Pr. Minister des Innern*, Hindenburg, 9 Mar. 1933; ibid., ff. 1105-15: police statements and reports of the incident.
90. WAP Poznań, RP/59, f. 62: *Oberpostdirektion* to the *Regierungspräsident* to the *Präsident der Oberpostdirektion* Köslin, Schneidemühl, [?] Apr. 1933.
91. WAP Wrocław, RO I/1806, f. 1091: The *Führer der Untergruppe OS* to the *Oberpräsident*, Oppeln, 12 Mar. 1933.
92. The efforts of the Schneidemühl SA leader were deflected by the provincial administration, which claimed that these matters could not be settled until work connected with the 'Law for the Re-Establishment of the Professional Civil Service' was finished. See WAP Poznań, OPS/152, f. 376: report of a visit by 'Stabsführer Müller', Schneidemühl, 25 Apr. 1933; ibid., f. 381: The *Oberpräsident* to the SA *Untergruppe* Grenzland, Schneidemühl, 29 June 1933.
93. See Jane Caplan, 'Civil Service Support for National Socialism: An Evaluation', in Hirschfeld and Kettenacker (eds.), *Der 'Führerstaat'*, pp. 176-7.
94. On this point, see Timothy W. Mason, 'Die Bändigung der Arbeiterklasse im national-sozialistischen Deutschland', in Carola Sachse, Tilla Siegel, Hasso Spode and Wolfgang Spohn, *Angst, Belohnung, Zucht und Ordnung* (Opladen, 1982), pp. 48-9.
95. See Roloff, *Bürgertum und Nationalsozialismus*, p. 113.
96. For Liegnitz, WAP Wrocław, RO I/1797, ff. 13-15: The *Regierungspräsident*, 'Rundver-fügung betreffend Hilfspolizei', Liegnitz, 20 Feb. 1933; for Breslau and Oppeln, ibid., ff. 17-19: *Stahlhelm, Landesamt Schlesien*, to the *Gaue*, Breslau, 21 Feb. 1933.
97. See Konrad Heiden, *Geburt des dritten Reiches. Die Geschichte des Nationalsozialismus bis Herbst 1933* (Zürich, 1934), pp. 117-18; Broszat, *Der Staat Hitlers*, p. 95.
98. BA, R 43 II/395, ff. 20-1: The *Reichsminister des Innern* to the *Bayerisches Staatsmini-sterium des Innern*, Berlin, 12 May 1933.
99. WAP Szczecin, RS/92, ff. 111-13: The *Landrat* to the *Regierungspräsident*, Uekermünde, 31 Mar. 1933; Engelbrechten, *Eine braune Armee entsteht*, p. 266.
100. GStA, Rep. 77/28: The *Polizeipräsident* to the *Pr. Minister des Innern*, Breslau, 25 Apr. 1933.
101. WAP Szczecin, RS/92, ff. 51-5: The *Landrat* to the *Regierungspräsident*, Uekermünde, 15 Mar. 1933.
102. Lists of auxiliary police recruits in WAP Poznań, RP/705 (for *Kreis* Bomst); WAP Poznań, RP/706 (for *Kreis* Deutsch Krone); and WAP Poznań, RP/707 (for *Kreis* Meseritz).
103. WAP Poznań, OPS/169, f. 162: The *Führer der Gruppe* Ostmark, 'Gruppenbefehl Nr. 19', Frankfurt/Oder, 27 Feb. 1933; WAP Poznań, RP/59, f. 92: *Staatspolizeistelle* to the *Oberpräsident*, Schneidemühl, 18 May 1933.
104. WAP Wrocław, RO I/1797, f. 91: The *Pr. Minister des Innern* to *sämtl. Polizeischulen und*

sämtl. Regierungspräsidenten, Berlin, 2 Aug. 1933.

105. OT Gliwice, *Landratsamt* Gleiwitz/G92, ff. 37-8: The *Landrat* to the *Landjägerhaupt-mann* Seeliger, Gleiwitz, 23 Aug. 1933; ibid., f.40: The *komm. Landrat* to the *Regierungspräsident* in Oppeln, Gleiwitz, 30 Oct. 1933.

106. BA, Sammlung Schumacher/406: The *Chef des Stabes*, 'Wahrung der Disziplin', Munich, 25 Feb. 1933. In October 1933 the 'Special Commissar' posts were superseded by the posts of 'Special Plenipotentiaries' *(Sonderbevollmächtigte)* for those who maintained contacts with the *Oberpräsidenten*, and 'Special Commissioners' *(Sonderbeauftragte)* for those appointed to maintain contacts with the *Regierungspräsidenten* and *Landräte*. See Bracher/ Sauer/Schulz, *Die nationalsozialistische Machtergreifung*, pp. 512-13.

107. BA, Sammlung Schumacher/409: The *Chef des Stabes*, 'Sonderkommissare', Munich, 12 May 1933.

108. For details, see author's thesis, 'The S.A. in the Eastern Regions of Germany, 1925-1934' (Univ. Oxford D.Phil. thesis 1980), p. 262.

109. For example, in June 1933 von Woyrsch banned a number of *Stahlhelm* groups, an exercise of the post of Special Commissar not attempted by any of the SA leaders. See WAP Wrocław, RO I/1797, f. 405: Von Woyrsch to the *Oberpräsident*, Brieg, 23 June 1933; WAP Opole, OPO/998, f. 87: clipping from the *Neue Breslauer Zeitung*, 28 June 1933.

110. This has been suggested by Edward N. Peterson, *The Limits of Hitler's Power* (Princeton, 1969), pp. 90-1.

111. WAP Szczecin, RS/186, ff. 283-311: *Staatspolizeistelle* to the *Geheimes Staatspolizeiamt* in Berlin, Stettin, 8 Dec. 1933. In other areas of Germany, such as Württemberg and Bavaria, the *Sonderkommissare* caused considerable friction. See Hüttenberger, *Die Gauleiter*, pp. 83-4.

112. BA, Sammlung Schumacher/409: The *Chef des Stabes*, 'Sonderbevollmachtigte der Obersten SA-Führung', Munich, 10 July 1934.

113. See Thévoz/Branig/Lowenthal-Hensel, *Pommern 1934/35 (Darstellung)*, pp. 20-35. Engel was dismissed in the wake of the scandal arising from conditions at the SS concentration camp set up in the Stettin docks. See p. 118.

114. Kasche had been offered the position of *Regierungspräsident* in Frankfurt/Oder but turned it down because his 'primary talent lay in the military field'. See GStA, Rep. 77/2: Wilhelm Kube to Hermann Göring, Berlin, 1 Apr. 1933.

115. See Gause, *Die Geschichte der Stadt Königsberg*, iii, p. 128; Hugo Linck, *Der Kirchenkampf in Ostpreußen* (Munich, 1968), pp. 110, 243.

116. Gause, *Die Geschichte der Stadt Königsberg*, iii, p. 129; Bracher/Sauer/Schulz, *Die nationalsozialistische Machtergreifung*, pp. 436-7.

117. GStA, Rep. 77/32, ff. 3-4: Helmuth Brückner to Hermann Göring, Breslau, 1 Mar. 1933.

118. GStA, Rep. 77/29: Hans Ramshorn to Edmund Heines, Oppeln, 11 Mar. 1933.

119. Ibid.: *Gruppenstabsführer* Graf Pückler to SS-*Gruppenführer Staatskommissar* Daluege, Breslau, 14 Mar. 1933.

120. *OVS*, 26 Mar. 1933, p. 1; *NSST*, 27 Mar. 1933, p. 1.

121. See Tausk, *Breslauer Tagebuch*, p. 122.

122. BA, Sammlung Schumacher/271: The *Pr. Minister des Innern* to the *Reichsminister des Innern*, Berlin, [?] June 1933; Diels, *Lucifer ante Portas*, p. 190.

123. Matull, *Ostdeutschlands Arbeiterbewegung*, p. 292.

124. Diels, *Lucifer ante Portas*, p. 190.

125. BA, Sammlung Schumacher/271: The *Pr. Minister des Innern* to the *Reichsminister des Innern*, Berlin, [?] June 1933; Martin Broszat, 'The Concentration Camps 1933-45', in *Anatomy of the SS State*, pp. 409-10.

126. Thévoz/Branig/Lowenthal-Hensel, *Pommern 1934/35 (Darstellung)*, p. 31; WAP Poznań, OPS/177, f. 93: The *Pr. Minister des Innern* to the *Oberpräsident* in Schneidemühl and the *Polizeipräsident* in Berlin, Berlin, 4 July 1933; ibid., f. 109: The *Lagerkommandant* to the *Oberpräsident*, Hammerstein, 10 July 1933. Other prisoners from Pomerania were sent to the much larger camp at Sonnenburg, for which the Prussian authorities had given 170,000 RM and which was run primarily by the SS.

127. Günther Schmerbach, 'Dokumente zum faschistischen Terror gegen die Arbeiterbewegung (1933 und 1934)', *Zeitschrift für Geschichtswissenschaft*, iii (1955), p. 441.

128. Ibid., p. 441; Matull, *Ostdeutschlands Arbeiterbewegung*, pp. 130-2; Gundelach, *Vom*

Kampf und Sieg der schlesischen SA, pp. 171-2.

129. Diels, *Lucifer ante Portas*, pp. 190, 194-5.

130. For accounts of life in the camp, see Paul Löbe, *Erinnergungen eines Reichstagspräsidenten* (Berlin, 1949), pp. 152-60; Karol Fiedor, 'Oboz koncentracyjny we Wrocławiu w 1933 r', *Slaşki Kwartalnik Historyczny Sobótka*, i (1967), pp. 170-90. Fiedor's account is based largely on the diary of a prisoner of the camp, Helmut Friese, deposited with the SED Party Archive in Berlin, and on the oral account of another prisoner, Kurt Skupin.

131. Löbe, *Erinnerungen*, p. 158; Gerhard Rossbach, *Mein Weg durch die Zeit. Erinnerungen und Bekenntnisse* (Weilberg-Lahn, 1950), pp. 139-41.

132. Diels, *Lucifer ante Portas*, p. 195.

133. Drewniak, *Początki ruchu hitlerowskiego*, pp. 105-8, 156-62, 287; Thévoz/Branig/ Lowenthal-Hensel, *Pommern 1934/35 (Darstellung)*, pp. 29-35, 287.

134. Diels, *Lucifer ante Portas*, pp. 287-9; Drewniak, *Początki ruchu hitlerowskiego*, pp. 178-86; Thévoz/Branig/Lowenthal-Hensel, *Pommern 1934/35 (Darstellung)*, pp. 31-5; Thévoz/Branig/Lowenthal-Hensel, *Pommern 1934/35 (Quellen)*, pp. 268-78.

Notes to Chapter VIII

1. Berghahn, *Der Stahlhelm*, p. 252. Not all *Stahlhelm* groups obeyed, however. See, for example, WAP Szczecin, RS/20, ff. 187-8: The *Bürgermeister*, Naugard, 11 Mar. 1933.

2. For example, StAG, Rep. 240/C.49.a.: 'Tätigkeitsbericht für die Zeit vom 1.2. bis 12.3.1933', Heiligenbeil, 29 Mar. 1933.

3. WAP Wrocław, RO I/1777, ff. 361-2: The *Stahlhelm, Landesverband Schlesien, Gauleitung Oberschlesien*, to the *Regierungspräsident*, Gleiwitz, 29 Mar. 1933; StAG, Rep. 240/ B.10.d.: The *Höhere Polizeiführer Ost* to the *Gauleitung der* NSDAP, Königsberg, 7 Apr. 1933.

4. Walter Görlitz, *Die Junker. Adel und Bauer im deutschen Osten* (Glücksburg, 1956), pp. 393-3. According to Görlitz, when Heines heard of Zitzewitz' remarks he came to Pomerania with a squad of SA men to jail 'that pig Zitzewitz' for life, but was dissuaded when, upon arriving in Kolberg to arrest the conservative leader, he was met by an armed *Stahlhelm* unit.

5. WAP Poznań, OPS/172, f. 120: The *Polizeidirektor* to the *Oberpräsident*, Schneidemühl, 10 June 1933; ibid., ff. 121-2: *Staatspolizeistelle* to the *Geheimes Staatspolizeiamt* in Berlin, Schneidemühl, 16 June 1933.

6. See Roloff, *Bürgertum und Nationalsozialismus*, pp. 147-9; Berghahn, *Der Stahlhelm*, pp. 263-5.

7. WAP Szczecin, RS/187, ff. 73-91: *Gauleitung Pommern der* NSDAP, 'Bericht über den Übertritt ehemaliger Marxisten in nationale Verbände in Sonderheit in den Stahlhelm', Stettin, 29 May 1933; ibid., ff. 93-5: The *Führer der* SA *Gruppe Pommern* to the *Regierungspräsident*, Stettin, 29 May 1933; WAP Szczecin, RS/186, ff. 33-5: 'Ergebnis der Feststellungen in Sachen "Neuaufnahmen in den Stahlhelm und Durchsetzung desselben mit Marxisten in Vorpommern und auf Rügen"', Stettin, 25 June 1933; ibid., ff. 39-41: 'Ergebnis der Festellungen in Sachen "Neuaufnahmen in den Stahlhelm und Durchsetzung desselben mit Marxisten in Hinterpommern und Usedom-Wollin"', Stettin, 26 June 1933. Similar concern was registered in East Prussia. See StAG, Rep. 240/C.40.a.: 'Tätigkeitsbericht für die Zeit vom 13.3. bis 31.3.33', Angerburg, 4 Apr. 1933.

8. For details of the gradual takeover of the *Stahlhelm* by the SA, see Berghahn, *Der Stahlhelm*, pp. 257-70; Bracher/Sauer/Schulz, *Die nationalsozialistische Machtergreifung*, pp. 886, 890-2; Karl Martin Graß, 'Edgar Jung, Papenkreis und Röhmkrise 1933/34' (Univ. Heidelberg Phil. Diss. 1966), pp. 105-9. See also the testimony of Theodor Gruss, the national treasurer of the *Stahlhelm* in 1933, at the Nuremberg trials in 1946, in *TMWC*, xxi, pp. 107-11; Theodor Duesterberg, *Der Stahlhelm und Hitler* (Wolfenbüttel and Hannover, 1949), pp. 138-42.

9. *TMWC*, xxi, p. 109.

10. BDC, AOPG, Edmund Heines: report sent to *Ministerialdirektor* Daluege, Berlin, 24 June 1933.

11. WAP Wrocław, RO I/1777, f. 377: 'Amtlicher Preußischer Pressedienst vom 26.6.33'. See

also WAP Szczecin, RS/186, f. 31: The *Polizeipräsident, Staatspolizeistelle*, to the *Regierungspräsident*, Stettin, 26 July 1933; ibid., f. 71: The *Stahlhelm, Landesverband Pommern-Grenzmark, to the Regierungspräsident*, Stettin, 24 July 1933.

12. See above, Chapter VII, note 109.
13. WAP Szczecin, RS/186, ff. 469-71: *Staatspolizeistelle* to the *Landräte des Bezirks* and *Oberbürgermeister der kreisfreien Städte*, Stettin, 29 May 1934; Thévoz/Branig/Lowenthal-Hensel, *Pommern 1934/35 (Darstellung)*, p. 82; Thévoz/Branig/Lowenthal-Hensel, *Pommern 1934/35 (Quellen)*, pp. 322-6.
14. Ibid., pp. 324-5.
15. Ibid., pp. 326-9; WAP Szczecin, RS/240, ff. 19-59: police reports concerning conflicts between the SA and the NSDFB during the first half of 1934.
16. For accounts of the incident, see BA, Sammlung Schumacher/402: newspaper clipping from an unnamed newspaper, dated 25 June 1934; *VB*, 26 June 1934, pp. 1-2; *Stettiner Abendpost*, 26 June 1934, p. 3; Thévoz/Branig/Lowenthal-Hensel, *Pommern 1934/35 (Darstellung)*, pp. 83-5.
17. *VB*, 26 June 1934, p. 2.
18. See Bracher/Sauer/Schulz, *Die nationalsozialistische Machtergreifung*, pp. 880-96; Broszat, *Der Staat Hitlers*, pp. 256-63.
19. BA, Sammlung Schumacher/406: The *Chef des Stabes*, 'Wahrung der Disziplin', Munich, 25 Feb. 1933. See also above, p. 114.
20. BA, R 43 II/1195, f. 61.
21. OT Gliwice, Landratsamt Gleiwitz/G63, f. 147; *VB*, 14 Mar. 1933, p. 2; Uhlig, *Die Warenhäuser im Dritten Reich*, p. 196; Genschel, *Die Verdrängung der Juden*, pp. 45-6; Mason, *Sozialpolitik im Dritten Reich*, pp. 84-5.
22. BA, R 43 II/1195, f. 210: 'Anordnung der politischen Zentralkommission der NSDAP', 7 Apr. 1933. See also Pätzold, *Faschismus Rassenwahn Judenverfolgung*, p. 76.
23. BA, R 43 II/1203, f. 2: The *Reichsminister des Innern* to the *Staatssekretär in der Reichskanzlei*, Berlin, 27 Apr. 1933.
24. WAP Wrocław, RO I/1797, ff. 39-40, and StAG, Rep. 10/30, f. 288: The *Pr. Minister des Innern* to all *Regierungspräsidenten*, Berlin, 15 Feb. 1933.
25. BA, NS 23/1: The *Chef des Stabes*, 'Scheringer-Staffeln', Munich, 10 Mar. 1933.
26. BA, Sammlung Schumacher/407: The *Chef des Stabes*, 'Aufnahme in die SA', Munich, 20 Mar. 1933.
27. *VWS*, 2 Feb. 1933, p. 1.
28. See *Weißbuch über die Erschießungen am 30. Juni 1934* (Paris, 1935), p. 47. Another target for left-wing infiltration was the NSBO, especially in Silesia. See GStA, Rep. 77/16: *Treuhänder der Arbeit* to the *Reichsarbeitsminister*, Breslau, 7 Aug. 1933.
29. StAG, Rep. 240/C.61.a: *Ortsgruppenleiter* Lange, 'Zur Geschichte der Ortsgruppe Upalten', Grunau, 4 Mar. 1942.
30. For example, WAP Poznań, OPS/177, f. 62: The *Landrat* to the *Regierungspräsident*, Schlochau, 10 Apr. 1933.
31. WAP Wrocław, RO I/1797, ff. 63-5: NSDAP *Untergauleitung Oberschlesien* to the *Preußisches Innenministerium*, Oppeln, 5 May 1933; ibid., ff. 67-8: The *komm. Polizeidirektor, Staatspolizeistelle*, to the *Regierungspräsident*, Oppeln, 31 May 1933.
32. Bullock, *Hitler*, pp. 281-2.
33. BA, R 43 II/1263, ff. 91-2: The *Reichsminister des Innern* to the *Reichsstatthalter* and *sämtliche Landesregierungen*, Berlin, 10 July 1933.
34. BA, NS 6/215: The *Stellvertreter des Führers*, 'Verfügung', Munich, 24 July 1933.
35. BA, Sammlung Schumacher/403: The *Chef des Stabes*, 'Disziplin', Munich, 31 July 1933.
36. WAP Katowice, SA-Brigade Gleiwitz/1: *Sturmbannführer* Mannchen to *Standarte 156* in Beuthen, Gleiwitz, 11 July 1933.
37. WAP Opole, SA-*Untergruppe Oberschlesien*: The *Führer der Brigade Oberschlesien*, 'Untergruppenbefehl 33/33', Oppeln, 20 July 1933; ibid.: The *Führer der Brigade Oberschlesien*, 'Untergruppenbefehl Nr. 36/33'. Oppeln, 26 July 1933. Nevertheless, the violence continued, and in late October Ramshorn felt compelled to issue another sharp warning about insufficient discipline within the SA. See WAP Katowice, SA-*Brigade* Gleiwitz/1: The *Führer der Brigade 17*, 'Brigadebefehl 52/33', Gleiwitz, 30 Oct. 1933.
38. BA, R 43 II/395, ff. 2-3: The *Reichsminister des Innern* to the *Reichsstatthalter* and the

Landesregierungen, Berlin, 6 Oct. 1933.

39. Jamin, 'Zur Rolle der SA', pp. 330-1, 341-2; Fischer, *Stormtroopers*, pp. 82-109. Unfortunately, records of how the storm troopers fared on the job market during 1933 and 1934 could not be found for the eastern Prussian provinces.

40. *Schlesischer N.S. Beobachter*, 27 May 1933, p. 6; ibid., 3 June 1933, p. 11; ibid., 10 June 1933, p. 9; ibid., 24 June 1933, p. 5; ibid., 7 Oct. 1933, p. 1.

41. *Der SA-Mann*, 10 June 1933, p. 3.

42. WAP Szczecin, RS/32, ff. 59-61: The *Regierungspräsident*, Stettin, 14 June 1933.

43. WAP Szczecin, RS/22, ff. 457-8: The *Landrat des Kreises* Randow, 'Schiesserei in Frauendorf', Stettin, 26 June 1933.

44. StAG, Rep. 240/B.17.e.: NSBO *Ortsgruppenbetriebswart*, 'Stimmungsbericht Juli 1933', Königsberg, 14 July 1933.

45. WAP Poznań, OPS/169, ff. 213-14: Hermann Kanthak to the *Landrat* in Schlochau, Quaks bei Penkuhl, 14 Aug. 1933.

46. WAP Wrocław, RO I/1797, ff. 675-7: *Staatspolizeistelle*, 'Ereignismeldung', Oppeln, 7 Nov. 1933.

47. Charges eventually were brought against some SA men for their part in the affair.

48. WAP Wrocław, RO I/1797, ff. 565-9: Walter Redlich to NSDAP *Kreisleiter* Hörmann, Neisse, 19 Dec. 1933; ibid., ff. 577-8: The *Oberbürgermeister*, Neisse, 21 Dec. 1933.

49. The two SA men eventually were disciplined by the regional SA leadership. See ibid., f. 581: NSDAP *Kreisleiter* Hörmann to *Polizeioberinspekteur* Heinze, Neisse, 23 Dec. 1933; ibid., f. 595: *Brigadeführer* Ramshorn to the *Staatspolizeistelle für die Regierungsbezirk* Oppeln, Gleiwitz, 5 Apr. 1934.

50. Ibid., ff. 483-4: The *Amtsvorsteher* to the *Landrat* in Oppeln, Dombrovka a.d. Oder, 20 Jan. 1934.

51. For an account of similar difficulties caused by the SA in Wuppertal, see Ulrich Klein, 'SA-Terror und Bevölkerung in Wuppertal 1933/34', in Peukert and Reulecke (eds.), *Die Reihen fast geschlossen*, pp. 45-61.

52. WAP Wrocław, RO I/1797, ff. 361-3: The *Führer der Standarte 21*, 'Standartenbefehl Nr. 1/33', Neustadt OS (undated, from early December 1933).

53. See, for example, R 43 II/1202, ff. 195-8: *Inspekteur der Geheimen Staatspolizei* to *Staatssekretär* Lammers, Berlin, 17 Feb. 1934; Diels, *Lucifer ante Portas*, pp. 275-6.

54. BDC, SA-Akte, Arwed Theuermann: Dr Bartels to the *komm. Führer der Brigade 10*, Greifswald, 7 Aug. 1934.

55. BDC, SA-Akte, Max Heydebreck, f. 21: 'Einige Ausschnitte seines bisher gewohnten Auftretens', Rummelsburg, 22 July 1934; WAP Szczecin, RS/25, ff. 147-8: *Gendarmerieposten* Penkun to the *Landrat des Kreises* Randow, Penkun, 24 June 1934; ibid., f. 151: The *Beauftragte des Chefs des Ausbildungswesens der* SA to the *Regierungspräsident*, Stettin, 2 Aug. 1934.

56. WAP Poznań, OPS/153, ff. 310-13: The *Landrat* to the *Regierungspräsident*, Züllichau, 8 May 1934.

57. Ibid., f. 314: The *Regierungspräsident* to the *Landrat des Kreises* Bomst, Schneidemühl, 31 May 1934.

58. This has been asserted by Dietrich Orlow, *The History of the Nazi Party 1933-1945* (Pittsburgh, 1973), pp. 106-7.

59. For example, Mau, 'Die "Zweite Revolution"'; Bloch, *Die SA und die Krise des NS-Regimes*.

60. Karl Martin Graß has observed that the 'second revolution' was a slogan used not by the SA but by its conservative opponents. See Graß, 'Edgar Jung', p. 181.

61. StAG, Rep. 10/30, f. 322: The *Führer der Obergruppe I*, 'Disziplin in der SA', Königsberg, 22 Feb. 1934.

Notes to Chapter IX

1. For accounts of the purge, see Mau, 'Die "Zweite Revolution"'; Krausnick, 'Der 30. Juni 1934'; Bracher/Sauer/Schulz, *Die nationalsozialistische Machtergreifung*, pp. 934-66; *Weißbuch über die Erschießungen am 30. Juni 1934*; Heinrich Bennecke, *Die Reichswehr*

und der 'Röhm-Putsch' (Munich and Vienna, 1964); Klaus-Jürgen Müller, *Das Heer und Hitler. Armee und nationalsozialistisches Regime 1933-1940* (Stuttgart, 1969), pp. 88-141; Bloch, *Die SA und die Krise des NS-Regimes*; Gossweiler, 'Die Rolle des Monopolkapitals'; Graß, 'Edgar Jung', pp. 171-98, 246-85.

2. See Bennecke, *Die Reichswehr*, p. 37; Jamin, 'Zur Rolle der SA', pp. 340-3; BDC, Führer-Akte, Peter Vogt: *Deutsche Arbeitsfront, Abteilung Abwehr*, 9 June 1934.
3. Bennecke, *Die Reichswehr*, p. 43; Müller, *Das Heer und Hitler*, p. 100.
4. *Stettiner Abendpost*, 26/27 May 1934, pp. 1-3; ibid., 28 May 1934, p. 3.
5. See Thévoz/Branig/Lowenthal-Hensel, *Pommern 1934/35 (Darstellung)*, p. 40. Afterwards it was alleged that during the tour Röhm had plotted with Pomeranian SA leaders, a number of whom suffered because they had had contact with him at this time (for example, Erich von Neindorff, leader of the SA-*Brigade* in Schivelbein, who was arrested on 30 June). See Thévoz/Branig/Lowenthal-Hensel, *Pommern 1934/35 (Quellen)*, pp. 299-307.
6. Quoted in Bennecke, *Die Reichswehr*, pp. 43-44.
7. BDC, SA-Akte, Max Heydebreck, ff. 11-12: report dated Rummelsburg, 24 July 1934.
8. BDC, SA-Akte, Arwed Theuermann: *Frhr.* von Forstner, Stettin, 22 July 1934.
9. WAP Szczecin, RS/32, ff. 149-52: *Staatspolizeistelle* to the *Regierungspräsident*, Stettin, 25 July 1934. Precisely where the phrase 'night of the long knives' originated is impossible to say.
10. More generally, see Müller, *Das Heer und Hitler*, pp. 112-16; Graß, 'Edgar Jung', pp. 185-93.
11. BDC, AOPG, Erich von Neindorff, ff. 125-8: *Gaugericht,* 'Beschluß', Stettin, 7 Aug. 1936.
12. Thévoz/Branig/Lowenthal-Hensel, *Pommern 1934/35 (Quellen)*, pp. 286-7.
13. BDC, SA-Akte, Max Heydebreck, f. 17: report of evidence given Reichswehr soldier Kurt Hoffmann, dated Rummelsburg, 24 July 1934.
14. BA/MA, RW 6/67: The *Oberstaatsanwalt* to the *Reichswehrministerium*, the *Reichsjustizminister* and the *Preußischer Justizminister*, Breslau, 2 Aug. 1934.
15. WAP Wrocław, RO I/1797, ff. 607-9: *Kommandatur* Oppeln to the *2. Kavallerie-Division* in Breslau, Oppeln, 29 June 1934; ibid., ff. 615-17: The *Regierungspräsident* to *Gruppenführer* Ramshorn, Oppeln, 30 June 1934; ibid., f. 619: The *Regierungspräsident* to *Standartenführer* Metz, Oppeln, [?] June 1934.
16. See von Kleist's affidavit presented to the International Military Tribunal at Nürnberg in 1946, printed in Bennecke, *Die Reichswehr*, p. 85. See also Mau, 'Die "Zweite Revolution"', p. 131; Krausnick, 'Der 30. Juni 1934', p. 321; Bracher/Sauer/Schulz, *Die nationalsozialistische Machtergreifung*, pp. 957-8; Robert J. O'Neill, *The German Army and the Nazi Party, 1933-1939* (London, 1966), p. 47; Müller, *Das Heer und Hitler*, p. 115.
17. Similarly, in Schweidnitz SA-*Brigadeführer* Wilhelm von Grolmann gave a written declaration of loyalty to the Reichswehr commandant in the city. See Mau, 'Die "Zweite Revolution"', p. 132.
18. Von Kleist's affidavit in Bennecke, *Die Reichswehr*, p. 85. See also Müller, *Das Heer und Hitler*, p. 117.
19. Krausnick, 'Der 30. Juni 1934', p. 321.
20. Ibid., p. 321; 'Urteil des Schwurgerichts beim Landgericht Osnabrück vom 2. August 1957 in der Strafsache gegen Udo von Woyrsch und Ernst Müller', p. 17; Bracher/Sauer/Schulz, *Die nationalsozialistische Machtergreifung*, pp. 955-6; Graß, 'Edgar Jung', p. 255.
21. For further discussion of the help given by the Reichswehr to the Gestapo and SS, see Müller, *Das Heer und Hitler*, pp. 120-2.
22. 'Urteil gegen Udo von Woyrsch', p. 18. See also BDC, Mordsache Kamphausen, ff. 37-9-84: SS-*Gericht*, 'Vernehmungsschrift', Munich, 23 Mar. 1936.
23. IfZ, MA 198/2, microfilm of ZStAM, Rep. 77, tit. 4093, Nr. 483: The *Oberpräsident*, 'Verhaftung verschiedener Persönlichkeiten in Bunzlau durch SS', Breslau, 29 Aug. 1934.
24. 'Urteil gegen Udo von Woyrsch', p. 19. Records of preparations for the purge in the other eastern regions unfortunately are not available. It would appear, however, that preparations in Silesia were the most extensive.
25. After Heines was executed his homosexuality was reported openly in the press. See, for example, *Oberschlesische Tageszeitung*, 2 July 1934, p. 2.
26. According to one account, Heydebreck had come to Bavaria merely to discuss outstanding

financial problems of his SA group. See *Weißbuch über die Erschießungen am 30. Juni 1934*, p. 95.

27. Bennecke, *Die Reichswehr*, p. 61.
28. 'Urteil gegen Udo von Woyrsch', pp. 21-3; Graß, 'Edgar Jung', pp. 280-1.
29. 'Urteil gegen Udo von Woyrsch', pp. 24-9; Graß, 'Edgar Jung', pp. 281-2.
30. BA, Sammlung Schumacher/402: The *Pr. Ministerpräsident*, 'Befehl an die L.P.J. Südost', Berlin, 30 June 1934.
31. 'Urteil gegen Udo von Woyrsch', pp. 29-38.
32.ʺ Ibid., pp. 38-9.
33. Ibid., pp. 40-4.
34. For background to the relations between Sembach and von Woyrsch, see BDC, Mordsache Kamphausen, ff. 2-4: The *Oberpräsident* to Major Buch, Breslau, 17 Feb. 1934; ibid., ff. 9-12: 'Denkschrift des schlesischen Gauleiters und Oberpräsidenten' (written in late 1934).
35. 'Urteil gegen Udo von Woyrsch', pp. 53-4; Graß, 'Edgar Jung', pp. 283-4.
36. BDC, Mordsache Kamphausen, ff. 256-9: list of people arrested by the SS, Munich, 30 Aug. 1934; ibid., f. 286: W. Pohl to the *Treuhänder der Arbeit* in Görlitz Dr Zinnemann, Bad Elster, 9 July 1934; ibid., ff. 314-17: 'Bericht über die Verhaftung des Rittmeisters a.D. Karl von Eggeling vom 1.7. bis 4.7.34', Giessmannsdorf, 16 July 1934; ibid., ff. 320a-1: *Frhr.* von Wrangel to Hermann Göring, Rothlach, 31 July 1934; IfZ, MA 198/2, microfilm of ZStAM, Rep. 77, tit. 4043, Nr. 483: The *Oberpräsident*, 'Verhaftung verschiedener Persönlichkeiten in Bunzlau durch SS', Breslau,29 Aug. 1934.
37. 'Urteil gegen Udo von Woyrsch', pp. 54-6.
38. Ibid., pp. 55-6.
39. Ibid., pp. 52-3; BDC, Mordsache Kamphausen, ff. 106-10: letter to the *Reichsführer* SS, Berlin, 9 Jan. 1935. The men involved in the killing were convicted and sentenced to prison terms, as their motives were deemed personal. However, von Woyrsch intervened to secure pardons. See ibid., f. 123: The *Führer des SS-Oberabschnitts Südost* to the *Reichsführer* SS, Brieg, 28 Nov. 1934.
40. BA, Sammlung Schumacher/402: The *Pr. Ministerpräsident*, 'Befehl an die L.P.J. Südost', Berlin, 30 June 1934.
41. 'Urteil gegen Udo von Woyrsch', pp. 12-13.
42. WAP Wrocław, RO I/1799, ff. 3-4: 'Zur Nachweisung der von Revierpolizei, Gemeindepolizei und Gendarmerie im Regierungsbezirk Oppeln beschlagnahmten Waffen einschl. P.O. Waffen', Oppeln, 5 July 1934.
43. Ibid., ff. 40-2: report of materials seized from the SA in Groß Strehlitz (from August 1934).
44. 'Urteil gegen Udo von Woyrsch', pp. 44-8; WAP Wrocław, RO I/1930, ff. 197-201: The *Landrat* to the *Staatspolizeistelle*, Leobschütz, 2 July 1934; BDC, SA-Akte, Alois Bittmann, ff. 13-14: The *Führer der Gruppe Schlesien* to the *Oberste SA-Führung*, Breslau, 11 Nov. 1935.
45. For example, PAP Bytom, Gemeinde-Verwaltung Miechowitz/G.M. 123: The *Führer der SAR I Brigade Schlesien* to the 'Führer und Männer der schlesischen SA-Reserve I', Breslau, 1 July 1934.
46. Thévoz/Branig/Lowenthal-Hensel, *Pommern 1934/35 (Darstellung)*, pp. 287, 292, 301. For a list of victims killed on the weekend of 30 June-1 July, see BA, NS 23/474, ff. 103458-64, copied in Bennecke, *Die Reichswehr*, pp. 87-8.
47. WAP Szczecin, RS/120, f. 7: *Landespolizei-Inspektion Nord*, Stettin, 30 June 1934; ibid., ff. 65-7: The *Regierungspräsident* to the *Oberpräsident*, Stettin, 1 July 1934. The text of the report is copied in Drewniak, *Początki ruchu hitlerowski*, pp. 274-5, and in Thévoz/Branig/Lowenthal-Hensel, *Pommern 1934/35 (Darstellung)*, pp. 40-1.
48. WAP Szczecin, RS/120, f. 7; Drewniak, *Początki ruchu hitlerowski*, p. 199.
49. Ibid., p. 203; Thévoz/Branig/Lowenthal-Hensel, *Pommern 1934/35 (Darstellung)*, p. 42.
50. WAP Szczecin, RS/120, ff. 65-7.
51. WAP Szczecin, RS/122, f. 1: *Landespolizei-Inspektion Nord*, 'Lagebericht', Stettin, 30 June 1934; WAP Szczecin, RS/120, ff. 87-8: The *Polizeipräsident*, 'Lagemeldung Nr. 1', Stettin, 1 July 1934; ibid. ff. 89-90: The *Polizeipräsident*, 'Lagemeldung Nr. 2', Stettin, 2 July 1934; Drewniak, *Początki ruchu hitlerowski*, pp. 207-8.

52. WAP Szczecin, RS/120, ff. 91-2; ibid., f. 93: 'Namentliches Verzeichnis der am 2.7.1934 — 19.55 Uhr — von Stettin nach Berlin mittels Kraftwagen überführten festgenommenen Personen'; ibid., ff. 129-30: The *Regierungspräsident* to the *Pr. Minister des Innern*, Stettin, 3 July 1934.

53. For a list of the people in the *Regierungsbezirk* Stettin who had been arrested by the morning of 1 July, as well as of the buildings occupied and weapons seized, see WAP Szczecin, RS/120, ff. 31-6: The *Regierungspräsident*, 'Lagebericht', Stettin, 1 July 1934.

54. For details, see author's thesis, 'The S.A. in the Eastern Regions of Germany', pp. 322-3.

55. BDC, SA-Akte, Arwed Theuermann: The *Führer der* SS-*Reserve* Rügen, 'Lagebericht', Greifswald, 2 July 1934; WAP Szczecin, RS/18, ff. 213–15: The *Landrat* to the *Regierungspräsident*, Greifswald, 14 July 1934.

56. WAP Szczecin, RS/121, ff. 13-14: *Landespolizei-Inspektion Nord*, 'Sonderbefehl für die Entwaffnung der SA', Stettin, 1 July 1934; ibid., f. 17: *Landespolizei-Inspektion Nord*, 'Entwaffnung der SA', Stettin, 2 July 1934.

57. WAP Szczecin, RS/120, f. 37: The *Kommandeur der L.P.J. Nord*, Stettin, 1 July 1934.

58. *PT*, 2 July 1934, p. 1.

59. BA, Sammlung Schumacher/402: The *Oberster* SA-*Führer*, 'Verfügung', Berlin, 2 July 1934.

60. 'Urteil gegen Udo von Woyrsch', p. 56.

61. *Deutsche Ostfront*, 4 July 1934, p. 1. According to Peter Hüttenberger, Brückner was arrested in connection with the purge (Hüttenberger, *Die Gauleiter*, p. 200). This remains unsubstantiated, however, and appears doubtful.

62. BA, NS 23/1: The *Oberster* SA-*Führer*, Berlin, 4 July 1934; *Deutsche Ostfront*, 6 July 1934, p. 1.

63. Ibid., 7 July 1934, p. 1.

64. *PT*, 2 July 1934, p. 1; WAP Szczecin, RS/120, f. 53: The *Kommandeur der L.P.J. Nord*, 'Sonderbefehl Nr. 8', Stettin, 2 July 1934; *Stettiner Abendpost*, 16 July 1934, p. 3.

65. WAP Szczecin, RS/122, f. 1; *Stettiner Abendpost*, 2 July 1934, p. 5; *PT*, 3 July 1934, p. 1; Thévoz/Branig/Lowenthal-Hensel, *Pommern 1934/35 (Darstellung)*, pp. 42-3.

66. *Stettiner Abendpost*, 23 July 1934, p. 2.

67. Thévoz/Branig/Lowenthal-Hensel, *Pommern 1934/35 (Darstellung)*, pp. 44-5.

68. *Oberschlesische Tageszeitung*, 2 July 1934, p. 6.

69. See Engelbrechten, *Eine braune Armee entsteht*, p. 293.

70. BA, Sammlung Schumacher/403: The *Chef des Stabes*, 'Säuberungsaktion innerhalb des SA Führerkorps, Untersuchungsausschüsse bei den Gruppen', Munich, 9 Aug. 1934.

71. Jamin, 'Zur Rolle der SA', p. 353.

72. Thévoz/Branig/Lowenthal-Hensel, *Pommern 1934/35 (Quellen)*, pp. 288-9.

73. Ibid., pp. 288-9.

74. BDC, SA-Akte, Wilhelm Leuschner, ff. 58-9: Wilhelm Leuschner to the *Oberste* SA-*Führung*, Steinseiffen Rsgb., 4 Mar. 1935.

75. Ibid., ff. 3-4: 'Bericht der Untersuchungsausschusses der SA-Gruppe Pommern in Sachen des beurlaubten Standartenführers Leuschner z.Zt. in Haft', Stettin, 16 Aug. 1934; ibid., ff. 14-15: 'Zusammenfassender Bericht über die Beschuldigungen gegen den ehem. SA-Standartenführer Wilhelm Leuschner'.

76. Ibid., f. 37: 'Abschluss-Bericht des Untersuchungsausschusses der SA-Gruppe Pommern in Sachen des Standartenführers Leuschner', Stettin, 1 Sept. 1934.

77. BDC, SA-Akte, Arwed Theuermann: 'Bericht des Untersuchungsausschusses der SA-Gruppe Pommern in Sachen des Oberführers Theuermann z.Zt. in Berlin in Haft', Stettin, 22 Aug. 1934; ibid.: *Obersturmführer* Rudolf Holland, 'Bericht über Oberführer Theuermann und die Verhältnisse bei der SA-Brigade 10 in Greifswald'.

78. Ibid.: 'Bericht des SA-Truppführers Koschinsky, Wolgast'; ibid.: Dr Bartels to the *komm. Führer der Brigade 10*, Greifswald, 7 Aug. 1934.

79. BDC, SA-Akte, Max Heydebreck: The *Führer der Gruppe Pommern*, Stettin, 27 July 1934; BDC, AOPG, Max Heydebreck: statements of SS-*Untersturmführer* Paul Braasch and Max Heydebreck before the Pomeranian *Gaugericht*, Stettin, 18 Feb. 1935.

80. Heydebreck insisted he had become a member only to defend the nationalist point of view. See BDC, SA-Akte, Max Heydebreck: statement by Heydebreck, dated Stettin, 11 Sept. 1934.

81. Ibid.: statement by Otto Schulz, dated Rummelsburg, 24 July 1934; ibid.: SS-*Sturmführer* Braasch to the 39. SS-*R Standarte*, Rummelsburg, 3 July 1934.
82. BA, NS 23/210: 'Zusammenstellung betr. Pommern-Fälle', 21 Dec. 1934.
83. Ibid.; BDC, SA-Akte, Hans Gotthard von Arnim: The *Führer der Gruppe Pommern*, Stettin, 27 July 1934.
84. BA, Sammlung Schumacher/403: The *Chef des Stabes*, 'Säuberungsaktion innerhalb des SA Führerkorps, Untersuchungsausschüsse bei den Gruppen', Munich, 9 Aug. 1934. On the structure and functions of SA disciplinary courts, see Jamin, 'Zur Rolle der SA', pp. 344-5.
85. Thévoz/Branig/Lowenthal-Hensel, *Pommern 1934/35 (Quellen)*, p. 32; Ian Kershaw, 'The Führer Image and Political Integration: The Popular Conception of Hitler in Bavaria during the Third Reich', in Hirschfeld and Kettenacker (eds.), *Der 'Führerstaat'*, p. 144.
86. BA, Sammlung Schumacher/402: The *Führer der Gruppe Schlesien* to the *Oberste SA-Führung*, Breslau, 26 July 1934.
87. See also Jamin, 'Zur Rolle der SA', pp. 347-53.
88. WAP Szczecin, RS/120, ff. 65-7.
89. Ibid., ff. 131-2.
90. Text of Hitler's speech in Erhard Klöss (ed.), *Reden des Führers. Politik und Propaganda Adolf Hitlers* (Munich, 1967), p. 137.
91. Thévoz/Branig/Lowenthal-Hensel, *Pommern 1934/35 (Quellen)*, pp. 31-4.
92. WAP Szczecin, RS/9, ff. 339-45: 'Lagebericht Monat Juli 1934', signed by *Kreisbauernführer* Mildebrath, Kahlen, 19 July 1934. For evidence of similar sentiments in East Prussia, see BA, R 18/5643, ff. 83-5: The *Landrat* to the *Staatspolizeistelle* in Königsberg, Pr. Eylau, 12 July 1934. More generally, see *Deutschland-Berichte der Sozialdemokratischen Partei Deutschlands (Sopade) 1934-1940* (Salzhausen and Frankfurt/Main, 1980), Vol. I (1934), pp. 197-202 (including reports from Pomerania and Silesia).
93. BA/MA, RW 6/69: *Abwehrstelle Schlesien*, 'Stimmen aus dem Volke zur innenpolitischen Lage Deutschlands', Breslau, 3 Aug. 1934.
94. Kershaw, *Der Hitler-Mythos*, p. 81.
95. See Hertz-Eichenrode, *Politik und Landwirtschaft in Ostpreußen*, pp. 264-5; Görlitz, *Die Junker*, pp. 394-5; Władysław Bartoszewski, *Erich von dem Bach* (Poznań, 1961), pp. 8, 13.
96. StAG, Rep. 240/B.31.c.: The *Kreisleiter*, Heiligenbeil, 17 Oct. 1941; StAG, Rep. 10/34, f. 122: The *Oberpräsident*, Königsberg, 20 July 1934; ibid., f. 137: The *Oberpräsident*, Königsberg, 19 July 1934; BA, NS 23/210: *Obergruppenführer* Schoene to the *Oberster SA-Führer* (undated, from early August 1934).
97. See Horst Gies, 'Die Rolle des Reichsnährstandes im nationalsozialistischen Herrschaftssystem', in Hirschfeld and Kettenacker (eds.), *Der 'Führerstaat'*, pp. 294-5.
98. *RGBl*, 1934, I, p. 529.
99. For a survey of the more prominent victims, see Bracher/Sauer/Schulz, *Die nationalsozialistische Machtergreifung*, p. 961.
100. IfZ, Fa 107, f. 135: The *Chef des Stabes*, 'Auflösung von Ämtern der Obersten SA-Führung', Berlin, 14 July 1934; Graß, 'Edgar Jung', p. 131.
101. BA, Sammlung Schumacher/402: 'Bericht', Stettin, 21 Aug. 1935.
102. On another occasion Lutze had described one of the dead Silesian SA leaders, von Wechmar, as 'completely innocent'. See BDC, Mordsache Kamphausen, f. 8: The *Chef des Stabes* to Walther Darré, Berlin, 12 Nov. 1934.
103. BDC, AOPG, Helmuth Brückner: Brückner to Darré, 'Denkschrift des schlesischen Gauleiters und Oberpräsidenten', Breslau, 10 Oct. 1934. Another copy of Brückner's memorandum may be found in BDC, Mordsache Kamphausen, ff. 9-12.
104. Thus Orlow, *The History of the Nazi Party 1933-1945*, pp. 106-11.

Notes to the Epilogue

1. The best discussion of the position of the SA in the power structures of the 'Third Reich' is to be found in Jamin, 'Zur Rolle der SA'.
2. WAP Wrocław, RO I/1930, f. 225: *Staatspolizeistelle*, 'Tagesbericht zum Erlaß vom 24. Mai

1934', Oppeln, 3 Dec. 1934. Similar problems arose in Bavaria. See Ian Kershaw, *Popular Opinion and Political Dissent in the Third Reich: Bavaria 1933-1945* (Oxford, 1983), pp. 129-30.

3. Thévoz/Branig/Lowenthal-Hensel, *Pommern 1934/35 (Quellen)*, pp. 59-62, 86-95.
4. BA, Sammlung Schumacher/409: The *Polizeipräsident* to the *Regierungspräsident*, Breslau, 9 July 1935.
5. For a fine analysis of the public reaction to the program, see William Sheridan Allen, 'Die deutsche Öffentlichkeit und die "Reichskyrstallnacht" — Konflikte zwischen Werthier-archie und Propaganda im Dritten Reich', in Peukert and Reulecke (eds.), *Die Reihen fast geschlossen,* pp. 397/411.
6. See Genschel, *Die Verdrängung der Juden*, pp. 177-80.
7. Thévoz/Branig/Lowenthal-Hensel, *Pommern 1934/35 (Quellen)*, p. 62.
8. Ibid., p. 94. For details of the effects of conscription upon the SA membership, see Fischer, *Stormtroopers*, pp. 90-1.
9. For a discussion of the introduction of the compulsory 'labour service', see Fritz Petrick, *Zur sozialen Lage der Arbeiterjugend in Deutschland 1933-1939* (Berlin, 1974), pp. 14-21.
10. WAP Poznań, OPS/148, ff. 387-413: The *Landrat* to the *Regierungspräsident*, Züllichau, 27 Sept. 1934; BA, NS 23/68: The *Führer der* SA *Gruppe Niedersachsen* to the *Oberste* SA-*Führung*, Hannover, 12 Feb. 1938.
11. Jamin, 'Zur Rolle der SA', p. 356.
12. Ibid., pp. 354-5.
13. Reports of SA strength in August and September 1934 in BA, Sammlung Schumacher/ 415.
14. BA, NS 23/68: The *Chef des Führungsamts* to the *Reichskassenverwalter der* SA, Munich, 23 Oct. 1937.
15. BA, Sammlung Schumacher/415: The *Chef des Dienststelle Schriftum* to the *Pressestelle des Stabschefs*, Munich, 16 Apr. 1943; Jamin, 'Zur Rolle der SA', pp. 357-8.

Notes to the Conclusion

1. For a recent discussion of Fascist violence, see Adrian Lyttelton, 'Fascism and Violence in Post-War Italy: Political Strategy and Social Conflict', in Wolfgang J. Mommsen and Gerhard Hirschfeld (eds.), *Social Protest, Violence and Terror in Nineteenth- and Twentieth-century Europe* (London, 1982), pp. 257-74.
2. Martin Broszat, 'Die Struktur der NS-Massenbewegung', *Vierteljahrshefte für Zeitge-schichte*, xxxi (1983), p. 72.
3. See, for example, the occupations listed of the Nazi movement's 'martyrs' to August 1932 in *Halbmast. Ein Heldenbuch der SA und SS.*
4. See Bessel, 'The Rise of the NSDAP'.
5. See, for example, the comments in Allen, *The Nazi Seizure of Power*, p. 25.
6. See above, pp. 83–5.
7. See Bessel, 'Militarismus im innenpolitischen Leben'.
8. Natalie Z. Davis, *Society and Culture in Early Modern France* (London, 1975), p. 186, quoted by Adrian Lyttelton in 'Fascism and Violence in Post-War Italy', p. 272.
9. This has been suggested by Peter Merkl in his article, 'Approaches to Political Violence: the Stormtroopers, 1925-33', in Mommsen and Hirschfeld (eds.), *Social Protest, Violence and Terror*, p. 380.

Bibliography

A. UNPUBLISHED SOURCES

1. Bundesarchiv (Koblenz)
   R 18   Reichsministerium des Innern
   R 43 I and II   Reichskanzlei
   NS 1   Reichsschatzmeister der NSDAP
   NS 6   Stellvertreter des Führers
   NS 22   Reichsorganisationsleiter der NSDAP
   NS 23   SA
   NS 26   NSDAP Hauptarchiv
   Sammlung Schumacher
   Kleine Erwerbungen 569   Heinrich Bennecke
2. Bundesarchiv/Militärarchiv (Freiburg i. Br.)
   RW 6   Allgemeines Wehrmachtsamt
3. Berlin Document Center
   SA Sammelliste 49
   Mordsache Kamphausen in Waldenburg
   NSDAP Personal Files
4. Geheimes Staatsarchiv preußischer Kulturbesitz (Berlin-Dahlem)
   Repositur 77   Preußisches Ministerium des Innern
   Repositur 84a   Preußisches Justizministerium
5. Institut für Zeitgeschichte (Munich)
   Fa 107   Akten der Obersten SA-Führung
   Sammlung Carl Paeschke
   MA 198   (Microfilm of ZStAM, Repositur 77, Preußisches Ministerium des Innern)
6. National Archives Microfilm Collection
   T 253
7. Staatliches Archivlager Göttingen (Note: Since these materials were consulted, they have been transferred to the Geheimes Staatsarchiv preußischer Kulturbesitz in Berlin-Dahlem.)
   Repositur 10   Regierung Königsberg

Repositur 14   Regierung Allenstein
Repositur 240   Gauarchiv NSDAP Ostpreußen
8. Powiatowe archiwum państwowe w Bytomiu
   Gemeinde-Verwaltung Miechowitz
9. Wojewódzkie archiwum państwowe w Katowicach
   SA Bryg. Gliwice (SA-Brigade Gleiwitz)
10. Wojewódzkie archiwum państwowe w Katowicach, Oddzial terenowy
    w Gliwicach
    Landrat Gleiwitz
11. Wojewódzkie archiwum państwowe w Olsztynie
    Landratsamt Braunsberg
    Landratsamt Lötzen
    Magistrat Johannisburg
    Magistrat Wartenburg
12. Wojewódzkie archiwum państwowe w Opolu
    Oberpräsidium der Provinz Oberschlesien zu Oppeln
    SA der NSDAP
13. Archiwum państwowe miasta Poznania i województwa Poznanskiego
    Oberpräsidium Schneidemühl
    Rejencja w Pile (Regierung Grenzmark Posen-Westpreußen in
    Schneidemühl)
14. Wojewódzkie archiwum państwowe w Szczecinie
    Regierung Stettin — Präsidial Abteilung Polizei
15. Wojewódzkie archiwum państwowe w Wrocławiu
    SA der NSDAP Neumarkt
    SA Gruppe Schlesien
    Rejencja Opolska (Regierung Oppeln)
16. 'Urteil des Schwurgerichts beim Landgericht Osnabrück vom 2. August
    1957 in der Strafsache gegen Udo von Woyrsch und Ernst Müller'.
17. Sabatzky, Kurt, 'Meine Erinnerungen an den Nationalsozialismus'. MS
    in the Wiener Library, London.
18. Tausk, Walter, 'Tagebücher'. MS in the University Library, Wrocław
    (Ako. 1949 KN 1351).

B. PUBLISHED SOURCES

1. Primary Sources

a. The Press

Arbeiter-Zeitung (Breslau, KPD), 1930-1933.
Breslauer Neueste Nachrichten, 1931-1933.
Breslauer 8 Uhr-Abendblatt, 1931-1933.
Deutsche Ostfront (Gleiwitz, NSDAP), 1932-1934.
Illustrierter Beobachter (NSDAP), 1928-1934.

Königsberger Tageblatt, 1931-1934.

Königsberger Volkszeitung (SPD), 1932-1933.

National-Sozialistische Schlesische Tageszeitung (Breslau, NSDAP, until 31 June 1931 *Schlesische Tageszeitung*), 1930-1933.

Oberschlesische Tageszeitung (Oppeln), 1934.

Oberschlesische Volksbote (Oppeln, SPD), 1931-1932.

Oberschlesische Volksstimme (Gleiwitz, Zentrum), 1929-1933.

Oppelner Kurier (Zentrum), 1933-1934.

Pommersche Tagespost (Stettin, DNVP), 1930-1934.

Pommersche Zeitung (Stettin, NSDAP), 1932-1933.

Preußische Zeitung (Königsberg, NSDAP), 1931.

Der SA-Mann (NSDAP), 1932-1934.

Schlesische Bergwacht (Waldenburg, SPD), 1929-1933.

Schlesische Tagespost (Breslau, DNVP), 1930-1934.

Schlesische Zeitung (Breslau), 1928-1934.

Schlesischer N.S. Beobachter (Breslau, NSDAP, until 11 July 1931 *Schlesischer Beobachter*), 1931, 1933.

Stettiner Abendpost, 1929-1934.

Völkischer Beobachter (NSDAP), 1925-1934.

Volks-Bote (Stettin, SPD), 1931-1933.

Volkswacht (Breslau, SPD), 1923, 1929-1933.

Volkswacht (Stettin, KPD), 1930-1931, 1933.

b. Statistical and Documentary Material

Anpassung oder Widerstand? Aus den Akten des Parteivorstandes der der deutschen Sozialdemokratie, ed. Hagen Schulze (Bonn-Bad Godesberg, 1975).

Bayern in der NS-Zeit. Soziale Lage und politisches Verhalten der Bevölkerung im Spiegel vertraulicher Berichte, ed. Martin Broszat, Elke Fröhlich and Falk Wiesemann (Munich and Vienna, 1977).

Beier, Gerhard, *Das Lehrstück vom 1. und 2. Mai 1933* (Frankfurt/Main and Cologne, 1975).

Das Deutsche Reich von 1918 bis heute, ed. Cuno Horkenbach (Berlin, 1930).

Deutschland-Berichte der Sozialdemokratischen Partei Deutschlands (Sopade) 1934-1940 (Salzhausen and Frankfurt/Main, 1980). Vol. i (1934).

Dittmann, Wilhelm, *Das politische Deutschland vor Hitler* (Zürich and New York, 1945).

Milatz, Alfred, *Wähler und Wahlen in der Weimarer Republik* (Bonn, 1965).

Der Nationalsozialismus. Dokumente 1933-1945, ed. Walther Hofer (Frankfurt/Main, 1957).

Nationalsozialismus und Revolution. Ursprung und Geschichte der

NSDAP in Hamburg 1922-33. Dokumente, ed. Werner Jochmann (Frankfurt/Main, 1963).

Partei-Statistik. Stand 1. Januar 1935, ed. Reichsorganisationsleiter der NSDAP.

Pommern 1934/35 im Spiegel von Gestapo-Lageberichten und Sachakten (Quellen), ed. Robert Thévoz, Hans Branig and Cécile Lowenthal-Hensel (Cologne and Berlin, 1974).

Reichsgesetzblatt, 1930-1934.

Reichstags-Handbuch. IX. Wahlperiode 1933 (Berlin, 1933).

Schlag Nach! Wissenswerten Tatsachen aus allen Gebieten (Leipzig, 1939).

Schmerbach, Günther, 'Dokumente zum faschistischen Terror gegen die Arbeiterbewegung (1933 und 1934)', in *Zeitschrift für Geschichtswissenschaft*, iii (1955).

Staat und NSDAP 1930-1932. Quellen zur Ära Brüning, ed. Ilse Mauer and Udo Wengst (Düsseldorf, 1977).

Statistik des Deutschen Reiches.
    Vol. 403 (Berlin, 1929).
    Vol. 434 (Berlin, 1935).
    Vol. 451 (Berlin, 1936).
    Vol. 454 (Berlin, 1936).

Statistisches Handbuch für die Provinz Ostpreußen 1938, ed. Statistisches Amt der Provinz Ostpreußen (Schloßberg and Leipzig, 1938).

Statistisches Jahrbuch für das Deutsche Reich, 1928-1932.

Trial of the Major War Criminals before the International Military Tribunal. Vol. xxi (Nuremberg, 1947).

Tyrell, Albrecht, *Führer befiehl . . . Selbstzeugnisse aus der 'Kampfzeit' der NSDAP* (Düsseldorf, 1969).

Vogelsang, Thilo, 'Neue Dokumente zur Geschichte der Reichswehr 1930-1933', in *Vierteljahrshefte für Zeitgeschichte*, ii (1954).

Vogelsang, Thilo, 'Hitlers Brief an Reichenau vom 4. Dezember 1932', in *Vierteljahrshefte für Zeitgeschichte*, vii (1959).

c. Memoirs, Speeches, etc.

Bade, Wilfred, *Die SA erobert Berlin. Ein Tatsachenbericht* (Munich, 1934).

Bayer, Ernst, *Die SA. Geschichte, Zweck und Organisation der Sturmabteilungen des Führers und der Obersten SA-Führung* (Berlin, 1938).

Bergerhof, Karl, *Die Schwarze Schar in O/S. Ein historischer Abschnitt aus Oberschlesiens Schreckenstagen* (Gleiwitz, 1932).

Braun, Otto, *Von Weimar zu Hitler* (2nd edn., New York, 1940).

Braunbuch über Reichstagsbrand und Hitlerterror (Basel, 1933).

Diels, Rudolf, *Lucifer ante Portas. Zwischen Severing und Heydrich* (Zürich, 1950).

Duesterberg, Theodor, *Der Stahlhelm und Hitler* (Hannover, 1948).

Engelbrechten, Julek Karl von, *Eine braune Armee entsteht. Die Geschichte der Berlin-Brandenburger SA* (Munich, 1937).

Gaede, Herbert, *Pommern* (Berlin, 1940).

Goebbels, Joseph, *Kampf um Berlin* (9th edn., Munich, 1936).

Goebbels, Joseph, *Vom Kaiserhof zur Reichskanzlei* (Munich, 1934).

Grzesinski, Albert, *Inside Germany* (New York, 1939).

Gundelach, Klaus, *Vom Kampf und Sieg der schlesischen SA* (Breslau, 1934).

Halbmast. Ein Heldenbuch der SA und SS (Munich, 1932).

Hitler, Adolf, *Mein Kampf* (213/217th edn., Munich, 1936).

Hoeser, Karl, *Oberschlesien in der Aufstandszeit 1918-1921. Erinnerungen und Dokumente* (Berlin, 1938).

Jakubaschk, Paul-Willi, *Helmuth Brückner. Sein Kampf und Sieg in Schlesien* (Hirschberg, 1933).

Krebs, Albert, *Tendenzen und Gestalten der NSDAP. Erinnerungen an die Frühzeit der Partei* (Stuttgart, 1959).

Löbe, Paul, *Erinnerungen eines Reichstagspräsidenten* (Berlin, 1949).

Die Not der preußischen Ostprovinzen, ed. Landeshauptleute der Provinzen Ostpreußen, Grenzmark Posen-Westpreußen, Pommern, Brandenburg, Niederschlesien und Oberschlesien (Königsberg, 1930).

Oppelner Heimat Kalender für Stadt und Land 1934, ed. Fr. Stumpe (Oppeln, 1934).

Paschke, Hans, *Chronik der Stadt Hindenburg in Oberschlesien* (Berlin, 1941).

Potempa. Die Ermordung des Arbeiters Pietczuch (Berlin, n.d.).

Reden des Führers. Politik und Propaganda Adolf Hitlers, ed. Erhard Klöss (Munich, 1967).

Röhm, Ernst, *Die Geschichte eines Hochverräters* (7th edn., Munich, 1934).

Rossbach, Gerhard, *Mein Weg durch die Zeit. Erinnerungen und Bekenntnisse* (Weilburg-Lahn, 1950).

Das Schwarzbuch. Tatsachen und Dokumente. Die Lage der Juden in Deutschland 1933, ed. Comité des Délégations Juives (Paris, 1934).

Severing, Carl, *Mein Lebensweg* (Cologne, 1950).

Tausk, Walter, *Breslauer Tagebuch 1933-1940* (Berlin, 1975).

Trotsky, Leon, *The Struggle against Fascism in Germany* (Harmondsworth, 1975).

Volz, Hans, *Die Geschichte der SA* (Berlin, 1934).

Weißbuch über die Erschießungen am 30. Juni 1934 (3rd edn., Paris, 1935).

Zehn Jahre Provinz Oberschlesien, ed. Presse-, Statistisches und Verkehrsamt der Provinzverwaltung von Oberschlesien (Ratibor, 1929).

2. Secondary Sources

Abel, Theodore, *The Nazi Movement. Why Hitler Came to Power* (New York, 1966).

Adam, Uwe Dietrich, *Judenpolitik im Dritten Reich* (Düsseldorf, 1972).

Allen, William Sheridan, *The Nazi Seizure of Power. The Experience of a Single German Town 1930-1935* (Chicago, 1965).

Allen, William Sheridan, 'Die deutsche Öffentlichkeit und die "Reichskrystallnacht" — Konflikte zwischen Werthierarchie und Propaganda im Dritten Reich', in Detlev Peukert and Jürgen Reulecke (eds.), *Die Reihen fast geschlossen. Beiträge zur Geschichte des Alltags unterm Nationalsozialismus* (Wuppertal, 1981).

Aretz, Jürgen, *Katholische Arbeiterbewegung und Nationalsozialismus. Der Verband katholischer Arbeiter- und Knappenvereine Westdeutschlands 1923-1945* (Mainz, 1978).

Baier, Roland, *Der deutsche Osten als soziale Frage. Eine Studie zur preußischen und deutschen Siedlungs- und Polenpolitik in den Ostprovinzen während des Kaiserreichs und der Weimarer Republik* (Cologne and Vienna, 1980).

Bartoszewski, Władysław, *Erich von dem Bach* (Poznań, 1961).

Bednara, Ernst, *Geschichte Schlesiens* (Aschaffenburg, 1953).

Bennecke, Heinrich, *Hitler und die SA* (Munich and Vienna, 1962).

Bennecke, Heinrich, *Die Reichswehr und der 'Röhm-Putsch'* (Munich and Vienna, 1962).

Bennett, Edward W., *German Rearmament and the West, 1932-1933* (Princeton, 1979).

Berghahn, Volker R., *Der Stahlhelm Bund der Frontsoldaten* (Düsseldorf, 1966).

Bessel, Richard, 'Eastern Germany as a Structural Problem in the Weimar Republic', in *Social History*, iii (1978).

Bessel, Richard, 'Militarismus im innenpolitischen Leben der Weimarer Republik. Von den Freikorps zur SA', in Klaus-Jürgen Müller and Eckardt Opitz (eds.), *Militär und Militarismus in der Weimarer Republik* (Düsseldorf, 1978).

Bessel, Richard, 'The Potempa Murder', in *Central European History*, x (1977).

Bessel, Richard, 'The Rise of the NSDAP and the Myth of Nazi Propaganda', in *The Wiener Library Bulletin*, xxxiii, nos. 51/52 (1980).

Bessel, Richard, and Feuchtwanger, E.J. (eds.), *Social Change and Political Development in Weimar Germany* (London, 1981).

Bessel, Richard, and Jamin, Mathilde, 'Nazis, Workers and the Uses of Quantitative Evidence', in *Social History*, iv (1979).

Bloch, Charles, *Die SA und die Krise des NS-Regimes 1934* (Frankfurt/Main, 1970).

Böhnke, Wilfried, *Die NSDAP im Ruhrgebiet 1920-1933* (Bonn-Bad Godesberg, 1974).

Bor, Peter, *Gespräche mit Halder* (Wiesbaden, 1950).

Borchardt, Knut, 'The Industrial Revolution in Germany 1700-1914', in Carlo M. Cipolla (ed.), *The Fontana Economic History of Europe. The Emergence of Industrial Societies — 1* (Glasgow, 1973).

Bracher, Karl Dietrich, *Die Auflösung der Weimarer Republik. Eine Studie zum Problem des Machtverfalls in der Demokratie* (4th edn., Villingen, 1964).

Bracher, Karl Dietrich, *The German Dictatorship. The Origins, Structure and Consequences of National Socialism* (Harmondsworth, 1973).

Bracher, Karl Dietrich, Sauer, Wolfgang, and Schulz, Gerhard, *Die nationalsozialistische Machtergreifung. Studien zur Errichtung des totalitären Herrschaftssystems in Deutschland 1933/34* (2nd edn., Cologne and Opladen, 1962).

Braunthal, Gerard, *Socialist Labor and Politics in Weimar Germany. The General Federation of German Trade Unions* (Hamden, Conn., 1978).

Broszat, Martin, 'Die Anfänge der Berliner NSDAP 1926/27', in *Vierteljahrshefte für Zeitgeschichte*, viii (1960).

Broszat, Martin, *Der Staat Hitlers* (Munich, 1969).

Broszat, Martin, 'Die Struktur der NS-Massenbewegung', in *Vierteljahrshefte für Zeitgeschichte*, xxxi (1983).

Buchta, Bruno, *Die Junker und die Weimarer Republik. Charakter und Bedeutung der Osthilfe in den Jahren 1928-1931* (Berlin, 1959).

Bullock, Alan, *Hitler. A Study in Tyranny* (Harmondsworth, 1962).

Caplan, Jane, 'Civil Service Support for National Socialism: An Evaluation', in Gerhard Hirschfeld and Lothar Kettenacker (eds.), *Der 'Führerstaat': Mythos und Realität* (Stuttgart, 1981).

Carsten, Francis L., *The Reichswehr and Politics 1918-1933* (Oxford, 1966).

Castellan, Georges, *Le réarmament clandestin du Reich 1930-1935 vue par le 2ᵉ Bureau de l'État-Major Français* (Paris, 1954).

Childers, Thomas, 'The Social Bases of the National Socialist Vote', in *Journal of Contemporary History*, xi (1976).

Conze, Werner, and Raupach, Hans (eds.), *Die Staats- und Wirtschaftskrise des Deutschen Reiches 1929/33* (Stuttgart, 1967).

Corner, Paul, *Fascism in Ferrara 1915-1925* (London, 1975).

Cygański, Mirosław, *Hitlerowskie organizacje dywersyjne w województwie śląskim 1931-1936* (Katowice, 1971).

Cygański, Mirosław, 'SS w pruskich prowincjach Śląska w latach 1929-1935', *Studia Śląskie*, xxv (1974).

Czarnik, Andrzej, *Ruch hitlerowski na Pomorzu Zachodnim 1933-1939* (Poznań, 1969).

Die deutschen Ostgebiete zur Zeit der Weimarer Republik (Cologne and Graz, 1966).

Diehl, James M., *Paramilitary Politics in Weimar Germany* (Bloomington and London, 1977).

Drage, Charles, *The Amiable Prussian* (London, 1958).

Drewniak, Bogusław, *Początki ruchu hitlerowskiego na Pomorzu Zachodnim 1923-1934* (Poznań, 1962).

Ehni, Hans-Peter, *Bollwerk Preußen? Preußen-Regierung, Reich-Länder-Problem und Sozialdemokratie 1928-1932* (Bonn-Bad Godesberg, 1975).

Erfurth, Waldemar, *Die Geschichte des deutschen Generalstabes 1918-1945* (Göttingen, 1957).

Farquharson, J.E., *The Plough and the Swastika. The NSDAP and Agriculture in Germany 1928-1945* (London and Beverly Hills, 1976).

Fiedor, Karol, *Antypolskie organizacje w Niemczech 1918-1933* (Wrocław, 1973).

Fiedor, Karol, 'The Character of State Assistance to the German Eastern Provinces in the Years 1919-1933', in *Polish Western Affairs*, xii (1971).

Fiedor, Karol, 'Obóz koncentracyjny we Wrocławiu w 1933 r', in *Śląski Kwartalnik Historyczny Sobótka* (1967).

Finker, Kurt, 'Die militaristischen Wehrverbände in der Weimarer Republik. Ein Beitrag zur Strategie und Taktik der deutschen Großbourgeoisie', in *Zeitschrift für Geschichtswissenschaft*, xiv (1966).

Fischer, Conan, 'The Occupational Background of the SA's Rank and File Membership during the Depression Years, 1929 to mid-1934', in Peter D. Stachura (ed.), *The Shaping of the Nazi State* (London, 1978).

Fischer, Conan, *Stormtroopers. A Social, Economic and Ideological Analysis, 1929-35* (London, 1983).

Fischer, Conan, and Hicks, Carolyn, 'Statistics and the Historian: the Occupational Profile of the SA of the NSDAP', in *Social History*, v (1980).

Gallo, Max, *The Night of the Long Knives* (Glasgow, 1974).

Gause, Fritz, *Die Geschichte der Stadt Königsberg in Preussen*, iii *(Vom ersten Weltkrieg bis zum Untergang Königsbergs)*, (Cologne, 1971).

Geiger, Theodor, *Die soziale Schichtung des deutschen Volkes* (Stuttgart, 1932).

Genschel, Helmut, *Die Verdrängung der Juden aus der Wirtschaft in Dritten Reich* (Göttingen, 1966).

Gerschenkron, Alexander, *Bread and Democracy in Germany* (Berkeley and Los Angeles, 1943).

Gessner, Dieter, *Agrarverbände in der Weimarer Republik. Wirtschaftliche und soziale Voraussetzungen agrarkonservativer Politik vor 1933* (Düsseldorf, 1976).

Geyer, Michael, *Aufrüstung oder Sicherheit. Die Reichswehr in der Krise der Machtpolitik 1924-1936* (Wiesbaden, 1980).

Geyer, Michael, 'Professionals and Junkers: German Rearmament and Politics in the Weimar Republic', in Richard Bessel and E.J. Feuchtwanger (eds.), *Social Change and Political Development in Weimar Germany* (London, 1981).

Gies, Horst, 'NSDAP und landwirtschaftliche Organisationen in der Endphase der Weimarer Republik', in *Vierteljahrshefte für Zeitgeschichte*, xv (1967).

Gies, Horst, 'Die nationalsozialistische Machtergreifung auf dem agrarpolitischen Sektor', in *Zeitschrift für Agrargeschichte und Agrarsoziologie*, xvi (1968).

Gies, Horst, 'Die Rolle des Reichsnährstandes im nationalsozialistischen Herrschaftssystem', in Gerhard Hirschfeld and Lothar Kettenacker (eds.), *Die 'Führerstaat': Mythos und Realität* (Stuttgart, 1981).

Gleitze, Bruno, *Ostdeutsche Wirtschaft* (Berlin, 1956).

Göppinger, Horst, *Die Verfolgung der Juristen jüdischer Abstammung durch den Nationalsozialismus* (Villingen, 1963).

Görlitz, Walter, *Die Junker. Adel und Bauer im deutschen Osten* (Glücksburg, 1956).

Gumbel, Emil Julius, *Vier Jahre politischer Mord* (Berlin, 1922).

Gurr, Ted Robert, *Why Men Rebel* (Princeton, 1970).

Hambrecht, Rainer, *Der Aufstieg der NSDAP in Mittel- und Oberfranken (1925-1933)* (Nuremberg, 1976).

Hamilton, Richard F., *Who Voted for Hitler?* (Princeton, 1982).

Hannover, Heinrich, and Hannover-Drück, Elisabeth, *Politische Justiz 1918-1933* (Frankfurt/Main, 1966).

Heberle, Rudolf, *Landbevölkerung und Nationalsozialismus. Eine soziologische Untersuchung der politischen Willensbildung in Schleswig-Holstein 1918 bis 1932* (Stuttgart, 1963).

Heiden, Konrad, *Geburt des Dritten Reiches. Die Geschichte des Nationalsozialismus bis Herbst 1933* (Zürich, 1934).

Heiden, Konrad, *Der Fuehrer. Hitler's Rise to Power* (London, 1944).

Hennig, Eike, *Bürgerliche Gesellschaft und Faschismus in Deutschland. Ein Forschungsbericht* (Frankfurt/Main, 1977).

Hentschel, Volker, *Weimars letzte Monate. Hitler und der Untergang der Republik* (Düsseldorf, 1978).

Hermens, Ferdinand A., and Schieder, Theodor (eds.), *Staat, Wirtschaft und Politik in der Weimarer Republik. Festschrift für Heinrich Brüning* (Berlin, 1967).

Hertz-Eichenrode, Dieter, *Politik und Landwirtschaft in Ostpreußen 1919-1930. Untersuchung eines Strukturproblems in der Weimarer Republik* (Cologne and Opladen, 1969).

Heuß, Theodor, *Hitlers Weg. Eine historisch-politische Studie über den Nationalsozialismus* (Stuttgart, 1932).

Hirschfeld, Gerhard, and Kettenacker, Lothar (eds.), *Der 'Führerstaat: Mythos und Realität* (Stuttgart, 1981).

Horn, Wolfgang, *Führerideologie und Parteiorganisation in der NSDAP*

(1919-1933) (Düsseldorf, 1972).

Hornung, Klaus, *Der Jungdeutscher Orden* (Düsseldorf, 1958).

Hüttenberger, Peter, *Die Gauleiter. Studie zum Wandel des Machtgefüges in der NSDAP* (Stuttgart, 1969).

Jamin, Mathilde, 'Methodische Konzeptionen einer quantitativen Analyse zur sozialen Zusammensetzung der SA', in Reinhard Mann (ed.), *Die Nationalsozialisten. Analysen faschistischer Bewegungen* (Stuttgart, 1980).

Jamin, Mathilde, 'Zur Rolle der SA im nationalsozialistischen Herrschaftssystem', in Gerhard Hirschfeld and Lothar Kettenacker (eds.), *Der 'Führerstaat': Mythos und Realität* (Stuttgart, 1981).

Jasper, Gotthard, *Der Schutz der Republik. Studien zur staatlichen Sicherung der Demokratie in der Weimarer Republik 1922-1930* (Tübingen, 1963).

Jasper, Gotthard (ed.), *Von Weimar zu Hitler 1930-1933* (Cologne and Berlin, 1968).

Jonca, Karol, *Polityka narodowościowa Treciej Rzeszy na Śląsku Opolskim (1933-1940). Studium polityczno-prawne* (Katowice, 1970).

Kater, Michael H., 'Ansätze zu einer Soziologie der SA bis zur Röhm-Krise', in Ulrich Engelherdt, Volker Sellin and Horst Stuke (eds.), *Soziale Bewegung und politische Verfassung* (Stuttgart, 1976).

Kater, Michael, H., 'Zum gegenseitigen Verhältnis von SA und SS in der Sozialgeschichte des Nationalsozialismus von 1925 bis 1939', in *Vierteljahrsschrift für Sozial- und Wirtschaftsgeschichte*, lxii (1975).

Kater, Michael H., 'Zur Soziographie der Frühen NSDAP', in *Vierteljahrshefte für Zeitgeschichte*, xix (1971).

Kele, Max, *Nazis and Workers. National Socialist Appeals to German Labor 1919-1933* (Chapel Hill, 1972).

Kershaw, Ian, *Der Hitler-Mythos. Volksmeinung und Propaganda im Dritten Reich* (Stuttgart, 1980).

Kershaw, Ian, 'The Führer Image and Political Integration: The Popular Conception of Hitler in Bavaria during the Third Reich', in Gerhard Hirschfeld and Lothar Kettenacker (eds.), *Der 'Führerstaat': Mythos und Realität* (Stuttgart, 1981).

Kershaw, Ian, *Popular Opinion and Political Dissent in the Third Reich: Bavaria 1933-1945* (Oxford, 1983).

Kinder, Christian, *Neue Beiträge zur Geschichte der evangelischen Kirche in Schleswig-Holstein und im Reich 1924-1945* (Flensburg, 1966).

Klein, Ulrich, 'SA-Terror und Bevölkerung in Wuppertal 1933/34', in Detlev Peukert and Jürgen Reulecke (eds.), *Die Reihen fast geschlossen. Beiträge zur Geschichte des Alltags unterm Nationalsozialismus* (Wuppertal, 1981).

Kluke, Paul, 'Der Fall Potempa', in *Vierteljahrshefte für Zeitgeschichte*, v (1957).

Koch, H.W., *The Hitler Youth. Origins and Development, 1922-45* (London, 1975).

Koshar, Rudy, '"Two Nazisms": the Social Context of Nazi Mobilization in Marburg and Tübingen', in *Social History,* vii (1982).

Koszyk, Kurt, 'Die Presse der schlesischen Sozialdemokratie', in *Jahrbuch der schlesischen Friedrich-Wilhelms-Universität zu Breslau*, v (1960).

Krausnick, Helmut, 'Der 30. Juni 1934. Bedeutung — Hintergründe — Verlauf', in *Aus Politik und Zeitgeschichte. Beilage zur Wochenzeitung Das Parlament* (1954).

Krausnick, Helmut, Buchheim, Hans, Broszat, Martin, and Jacobsen, Hans-Adolf, *Anatomy of the SS State* (London, 1968).

Kühnl, Reinhard, *Die nationalsozialistische Linke 1925-1930* (Meisenheim/Glan, 1966).

Levine, Herbert S., *Hitler's Free City. A History of the Nazi Party in Danzig, 1925-1939* (Chicago, 1973).

Linck, Hugo, *Der Kirchenkampf in Ostpreußen 1933-1945* (Munich, 1968).

Loomis, Charles P., and Beegle, J. Allan, 'The Spread of German Nazism in Rural Areas', in *American Sociological Review*, xi (1946).

Lyttelton, Adrian, *The Seizure of Power. Fascism in Italy 1919-1929* (London, 1973).

Lyttelton, Adrian, 'Fascism and Violence in Post-War Italy: Political Strategy and Social Conflict', in Wolfgang J. Mommsen and Gerhard Hirschfeld (eds.), *Social Protest, Violence and Terror in Nineteenth- and Twentieth-Century Europe* (London, 1982).

Maciejewski, Marek, 'Śląskie oddziały szturmowe narodowych socjalistów w sporach o władze polityczna (1932-1934)', in *Studia Śląskie*, xxv (1974).

Maciejewski, Marek, 'Uwagi o genezie partii narodowych socjalistów i jej ideologii na Śląsku Opolskim (1925-1932)', in *Studia Śląskie*, xxiv (1973).

Mann, Reinhard (ed.), *Die Nationalsozialisten. Analysen faschistischer Bewegung* (Stuttgart, 1980).

Maser, Werner, *Die Frühgeschichte der NSDAP. Hitlers Weg bis 1924* (Frankfurt/Main and Bonn, 1965).

Mason, Timothy W., *Sozialpolitik im Dritten Reich. Arbeiterklasse und Volksgemeinschaft* (Opladen, 1977).

Mason, Timothy W., 'Intention and Explanation: A Current Controversy about the Interpretation of National Socialism', in Gerhard Hirschfeld and Lothar Kettenacker (eds.), *Der 'Führerstaat': Mythos und Realität* (Stuttgart, 1981).

Mason, Timothy W., 'Die Bändigung der Abeiterklasse im nationalsozialistischen Deutschland', in Carola Sachse, Tilla Siegel, Hasso Spode and Wolfgang Spohn, *Angst, Belohnung, Zucht und Ordnung. Herrschaftsmechanismen im Nationalsozialismus* (Opladen, 1982).

Matthias, Erich, and Morsey, Rudolf (eds.), *Das Ende der Parteien 1933*

(Düsseldorf, 1960).

Matull, Wilhelm, *Ostdeutschlands Arbeiterbewegung. Abriß ihrer Geschichte, Leistung und Opfer* (Würzburg, 1973).

Matull, Wilhelm, *Ostpreußens Arbeiterbewegung. Geschichte und Leistung im Überblick* (Würzburg, 1970).

Mau, Hermann, 'Die "Zweite Revolution" — Der 30. Juni 1934', in *Vierteljahrshefte für Zeitgeschichte*, i (1953).

Mazerath, Horst, *Nationalsozialismus und kommunale Selbstverwaltung* (Stuttgart, 1970).

Mazerath, Horst, and Turner, Henry A., 'Die Selbstfinanzierung der NSDAP 1930-1933', in *Geschichte und Gesellschaft*, iii (1977).

Mendel, Edward, *Stosunki spoleczne i polityczne w Opolu w latach 1919-1933* (Warsaw and Wrocław, 1975).

Merkl, Peter H., *Political Violence under the Swastika. 581 Early Nazis* (Princeton, 1975).

Merkl, Peter H., *The Making of a Stormtrooper* (Princeton, 1980).

Merkl, Peter H., 'Approaches to Political Violence: the Stormtroopers, 1925-33', in Wolfgang J. Mommsen and Gerhard Hirschfeld (eds.), *Social Protest, Violence and Terror in Nineteenth- and Twentieth-Century Europe* (London, 1982).

Migdal, Stefan, *Opolszczyzna przeciw faszyzmowi w przededniu dojścia Hitlera do władzy* (Katowice, 1960).

Minczakiewicz, Tadeusz, *Stosunki spoleczne na Śląsku Opolskim w latach 1922-1933* (Wrocław, 1976).

Mommsen, Wolfgang J., and Hirschfeld, Gerhard (eds.), *Social Protest, Violence and Terror in Nineteenth- and Twentieth-Century Europe* (London, 1982).

Moore, Barrington Jr., *Injustice. The Social Bases of Obedience and Revolt* (London, 1978).

Mühlberger, Detlev, 'The Sociology of the NSDAP: The Question of Working-Class Membership', in *Journal of Contemporary History*, xv (1980).

Müller, Klaus-Jürgen, *Das Heer und Hitler. Armee und nationalsozialistisches Regime 1933-1940* (Stuttgart, 1969).

Müller, Klaus-Jürgen, and Opitz, Eckardt (eds.), *Militär und Militarismus in der Weimarer Republik* (Düsseldorf, 1978).

Neumann, Franz, *Behemoth. The Structure and Practice of National Socialism* (New York and Princeton, 1966).

Niethammer, Lutz, 'Male Fantasies: an Argument for and with an important new Study in History and Psychoanalysis', in *History Workshop. A Journal of Socialist Historians*, no. 7 (1980).

Noakes, Jeremy, *The Nazi Party in Lower Saxony 1921-1933* (London, 1971).

Nolte, Ernst, *Three Faces of Fascism* (London, 1965).

Nyomarkay, Joseph, *Charisma and Factionalism in the Nazi Party* (Minneapolis, 1967).

Olszewski, Bogusław, *'Osthilfe' interwencjonizm państwowy w rolnictwie śląskim w latach 1919-1939* (Wrocław, 1974).

O'Neill, Robert J., *The German Army and the Nazi Party, 1933-1939* (London, 1966).

Orlow, Dietrich, *The History of the Nazi Party 1919-1933* (Pittsburgh, 1969).

Orlow, Dietrich, *The History of the Nazi Party 1933-1945* (Pittsburgh, 1973).

Pätzold, Kurt, *Faschismus Rassenwahn Judenverfolgung. Eine Studie zur politischen Strategie und Taktik des faschistischen deutschen Imperialismus (1933-1945)* (Berlin, 1975).

Pätzold, Kurt, and Weißbecker, Manfred, *Geschichte der NSDAP 1920-1945* (Cologne, 1981).

Peterson, Edward N., *The Limits of Hitler's Power* (Princeton, 1969).

Petrick, Fritz, *Zur sozialen Lage der Arbeiterjugend in Deutschland 1933 bis 1939* (Berlin, 1974).

Petzina, Dieter, 'Hauptprobleme der deutschen Wirtschaftsgeschichte 1932/33', in *Vierteljahrshefte für Zeitgeschichte*, xv (1967).

Peukert, Detlev, *Die KPD im Widerstand. Verfolgung und Untergrundarbeit an Rhein und Ruhr 1933 bis 1945* (Wuppertal, 1980).

Peukert, Detlev, and Reulecke, Jürgen (eds.), *Die Reihen fast geschlossen. Beiträge zur Geschichte des Alltags unterm Nationalsozialismus* (Wuppertal, 1981).

Post, Gaines, *The Civil-Military Fabric of Weimar Foreign Policy* (Princeton, 1973).

Preller, Ludwig, *Sozialpolitik in der Weimarer Republik* (Stuttgart, 1949).

Pridham, Geoffrey, *Hitler's Rise to Power. The Nazi Movement in Bavaria, 1923-1933* (London, 1973).

Raupach, Hans, 'Der interregionale Wohlfahrtsausgleich als Problem der Politik des Deutschen Reiches', in Werner Conze and Hans Raupach (eds.), *Die Staats- und Wirtschaftskrise des Deutschen Reiches 1929/33* (Stuttgart, 1967).

Reiche, Eric G., 'From "Spontaneous" to Legal Terror: SA, Police and the Judiciary in Nürnberg, 1933-34', in *European Studies Review*, ix (1979).

Reifferscheid, Gerhard, *Das Bistum Ermland und das Dritte Reich* (Cologne and Vienna, 1975).

Rhode, Gotthold, *Die Ostgebiete des Deutschen Reiches* (Würzburg, 1956).

Rogmann, Heinz, *Die Bevölkerungsentwicklung im preußischen Osten in den letzten hundert Jahren* (Berlin, 1937).

Rogmann, Heinz, *Ostdeutschlands große Not. Zahlen und Tatsachen* (Berlin, 1930).

Rohe, Karl, *Das Reichsbanner Schwarz-Rot-Gold. Ein Beitrag zur Ge-*

schichte und Struktur der politischen Kampfverbände zur Zeit der Weimarer Republik (Düsseldorf, 1966).

Roloff, Ernst-August, *Bürgertum und Nationalsozialismus 1930-1933. Braunschweigs Weg ins Dritte Reich* (Hannover, 1961).

Rosenberg, Arthur, *Geschichte der Weimarer Republik* (Frankfurt/Main, 1961).

Rosenhaft, Eve, 'Gewalt in der Politik: Zum Problem des "Sozialen Militarismus"', in Klaus-Jürgen Müller and Eckardt Opitz (eds.), *Militär und Militarismus in der Weimarer Republik* (Düsseldorf, 1978).

Rosenhaft, Eve, 'Working-Class Life and Working-Class Politics: Communists, Nazis and the State in the Battle for the Streets, Berlin 1928-1932', in Richard Bessel and E.J. Feuchtwanger (eds.), *Social Change and Political Development in Weimar Germany* (London, 1981).

Rosenhaft, Eve, *Beating the Fascists? The German Communists and Political Violence 1929-1933* (Cambridge, 1983).

Schäfer, Wolfgang, *NSDAP. Entwicklung und Struktur der Staatspartei des Dritten Reiches* (Hannover, 1956).

Schleunes, Karl, *The Twisted Road to Auschwitz. Nazi Policy toward German Jews 1933-39* (London, 1972).

Schmidt, Christoph, 'Zu den Motiven "alter Kämpfer" in der NSDAP', in Detlev Peukert and Jürgen Reulecke (eds.), *Die Reihen fast geschlossen. Beiträge zur Geschichte des Alltags unterm Nationalsozialismus* (Wuppertal, 1981).

Schön, Eberhart, *Die Entstehung des Nationalsozialismus in Hessen* (Meisenheim/Glan, 1972).

Schoenbaum, David, *Hitler's Social Revolution: Class and Status in Nazi Germany 1933-39* (Garden City, N.Y., 1966).

Schüddekopf, Otto-Ernst, *Das Heer und die Republik. Quellen zur Politik der Reichswehrführung 1918 bis 1933* (Hannover and Frankfurt/Main, 1955).

Schüddekopf, Otto-Ernst, *Linke Leute von Rechts. Die Nationalrevolutionären Minderheiten und der Kommunismus in der Weimarer Republik* (Stuttgart, 1960).

Schützle, Kurt, *Reichswehr wider die Nation. Zur Rolle der Reichswehr bei der Vorbereitung und Errichtung der faschistischen Diktatur in Deutschland (1929-1933)* (Berlin, 1963).

Schulz, Gerhard, *Die deutschen Ostgebiete. Zu ihrer historisch-politischen Lage* (Pfullingen, 1967).

Schulz, Gerhard, *Aufstieg des Nationalsozialismus. Krise und Revolution in Deutschland* (Frankfurt/Main, Berlin and Vienna, 1975).

Schulze, Hagen, *Freikorps und Republik 1918-1920* (Boppard am Rhein, 1969).

Schumann, Hans-Gerd, *Nationalsozialismus und Gewerkschaftsbewegung* (Hannover and Frankfurt/Main, 1958).

Schuster, Kurt, *Der Rote Frontkämpferbund 1924-1929* (Düsseldorf, 1975).

Schwarzwälder, Herbert, *Die Machtergreifung der NSDAP in Bremen 1933* (Bremen, 1966).

Stachura, Peter D., *Nazi Youth in the Weimar Republic* (Santa Barbara and Oxford, 1975).

Stachura, Peter D. (ed.), *The Shaping of the Nazi State* (London, 1978).

Stachura, Peter D., 'Who Were the Nazis? A Socio-Political Analysis of the National Socialist *Machtübernahme*', in *European Studies Review*, xi (1981).

Stokes, Lawrence D., 'The Social Composition of the Nazi Party in Eutin, 1925-32', in *International Review of Social History*, xxiii (1978).

Tasca, Angelo, *Naissance du fascisme. L'Italie de l'armistice à la marche sur Rome* (Paris, 1967).

Thévoz, Robert, Branig, Hans, and Lowenthal-Hensel, Cécile, *Pommern 1934/35 im Spiegel von Gestapo-Lageberichten und Sachakten (Darstellung)* (Cologne and Berlin, 1974).

Theweleit, Klaus, *Männerphantasien 1. Frauen, Fluten, Körper, Geschichte* (Frankfurt/Main, 1977).

Theweleit, Klaus, *Männerphantasien 2. Männerkörper. Zur Psychoanalyse des weißen Terrors* (Frankfurt/Main, 1978).

Uhlig, Heinrich, *Die Warenhäuser im Dritten Reich* (Cologne and Opladen, 1956).

von Unruh, Friedrich Franz, *Nationalsozialismus* (Frankfurt/Main, 1931).

Vogelsang, Thilo, *Reichswehr, Staat und NSDAP. Beiträge zur deutschen Geschichte 1930-1932* (Stuttgart, 1962).

Waite, Robert G.L., *Vanguard of Nazism. The Free Corps Movement in Postwar Germany 1918-1933* (Cambridge, Mass., 1952).

Ward, James J., '"Smash the Fascists . . ." German Communist Efforts to Counter the Nazis', in *Central European History*, xiv (1981).

Weber, Hermann, *Die Wandlung des deutschen Kommunismus. Die Stalinisierung der KPD in der Weimarer Republik* (Frankfurt/Main, 1969).

Webersinn, Gerhard, 'Prälat Karl Ulitzka', in *Jahrbuch der schlesischen Friedrich-Wilhelms-Universität zu Breslau*, xv (1960).

Wiesemann, Falk, *Die Vorgeschichte der nationalsozialistischen Machtübernahme in Bayern 1932/33* (Berlin, 1975).

Wiesemann, Falk, 'Juden auf dem Lande: die wirtschaftliche Ausgrenzung der jüdischen Viehhändler in Bayern', in Detlev Peukert and Jürgen Reulecke (eds.), *Die Reihen fast geschlossen. Beiträge zur Geschichte des Alltags unterm Nationalsozialismus* (Wuppertal, 1981).

Winkler, Heinrich August, *Mittelstand Demokratie und Nationalsozialismus. Die politische Entwicklung von Handwerk und Kleinhandel in der Weimarer Republik* (Cologne, 1972).

Wohlfeil, Rainer, and von Matuschka, Edgar, *Reichswehr und Republik (1918-1933)* (Frankfurt/Main, 1970).

Woytinski, Wladimir, *The Social Consequences of Economic Depression* (London and Geneva, 1936).

Zeman, Z.A.B., Nazi Propaganda (Oxford, 1964).

Zimmermann, Michael, '"Ein schwer zu bearbeitendes Pflaster": der Bergarbeiterort Hochlarmark unter dem Nationalsozialismus', in Detlev Peukert and Jürgen Reulecke (eds.), *Die Reihen fast geschlossen. Beiträge zur Geschichte des Alltags unterm Nationalsozialismus* (Wuppertal, 1981).

Zofka, Zdenek, *Die Ausbreitung des Nationalsozialismus auf dem Lande. Eine regionale Fallstudie zur politischen Einstellung der Landbevölkerung in der Zeit des Aufstiegs und der Machtergreifung der NSDAP 1928-1936* (Munich, 1979).

C. UNPUBLISHED THESES

Bessel, Richard, 'The S.A. in the Eastern Regions of Germany, 1925-1934' (Univ. Oxford D. Phil. thesis 1980).

Elliott, Christopher James, 'Ex-Servicemen's Organisations and the Weimar Republic' (Univ. London Ph.D. thesis 1971).

Finker, Kurt, 'Die militaristischen Wehrverbände in der Weimarer Republik und ihre Rolle bei der Unterdrückung der Arbeiterklasse und bei der Vorbereitung eines neuen imperialistischen Krieges (1924-1929)' (Pädagogische Hochschule Potsdam Phil. Habil. 1964).

Frank, Robert Henry, 'Hitler and the National Socialist Coalition: 1924-1932' (Johns Hopkins Univ. Ph.D. thesis 1969).

Gladosch, Hans, 'Untersuchungen über die Notwendigkeit, Maßnahmen und Ergebnisse der Osthilfe in Oberschlesien' (Univ. Heidelberg Phil. Diss. 1933).

Gossweiler, Kurt, 'Die Rolle des Monopolkapitals bei der Herbeiführung der Röhm-Affäre' (Humbolt Univ. Berlin Phil. Diss. 1963).

Graß, Karl Martin, 'Edgar Jung, Papenkreis und Röhmkrise 1933/34' (Univ. Heidelberg Phil. Diss. 1966).

Grill, Johnpeter Horst, 'The Nazi Party in Baden, 1920-1945' (Univ. Michigan Ph.D. thesis 1975).

Jahnke, Karl-Heinz, 'Die Geschichte der revolutionären Arbeiterbewegung in Stralsund von ihren Anfängen bis zur Gründung der SED (1891-1946)' (Univ. Greifswald Phil. Diss. 1960).

Jamin, Mathilde, 'Zwischen den Klassen. Eine quantitative Untersuchung zur Sozialstruktur der SA-Führerschaft' (Ruhr-Univ. Bochum Phil. Diss. 1982).

Klotzbücher, Alois, 'Der politische Weg des Stahlhelms, Bund der Frontsoldaten, in der Weimarer Republik. Ein Beitrag zur Geschichte der Nationalen Opposition 1918-1933' (Univ. Erlangen Phil. Diss. 1964).

Koshar, Rudy John, 'Organisational Life and Nazism: A Study of Mobilization in Marburg an der Lahn, 1918-1935' (Univ. Michigan Ph.D. thesis 1979).

Lamprecht, Werner, 'Der Kampf der Stettiner Parteiorganisation der KPD gegen die faschistische Diktatur (1933-1945)' (Univ. Greifswald Phil. Diss. 1965).

Mitchell, Otis C., 'An Institutional History of the National Socialist SA: A Study of the SA as a Functioning Organisation within the Party Structure (1931-1934)' (Univ. Kansas Ph.D. thesis 1964).

Reiche, Eric G., 'The Development of the SA in Nuremberg, 1922 to 1934' (Univ. Delaware Ph.D. thesis 1972).

Schmerbach, Günther, 'Der Kampf der Kommunistischen Partei Deutschlands gegen Faschismus und Kriegsgefahr im Bezirk Oberschlesien 1932/33' (Univ. Jena Phil. Diss. 1957).

Werner, Andreas, 'SA der NSDAP. SA: "Wehrverband", "Parteitruppe" oder "Revolutionsarmee"? Studien zur Geschichte der SA und der NSDAP 1920 bis 1933' (Univ. Erlangen Phil. Diss. 1964).

Wernette, Dee Richard, 'Political Violence and German Elections: 1930 and July 1932' (Univ. Michigan Ph.D. thesis 1974).

INDEX